Takehisa Yumeji

# Takehisa Yumeji

Nozomi Naoi

Sabine Schenk

Maureen de Vries

Hotei Publishing

Nihon no hanga

Nihon no hanga - Amsterdam

# Colophon

**Publisher**

**Hotei Publishing**

P.O. Box 9000

2300 PA Leiden

The Netherlands

http://www.brill.com/hotei

**Editing**

Amy Reigle Newland, Adelaide, Australia

**Design**

Robert Schaap, Bergeijk, The Netherlands

**Production**

High Trade bv, Zwolle, The Netherlands

Printed in Slovakia

ISBN 9789004279827



**On the cover**

*Dutch lantern*

From the series *Yumeji's masterpieces*

(see fig. 1.5, p. 15)

# Contents

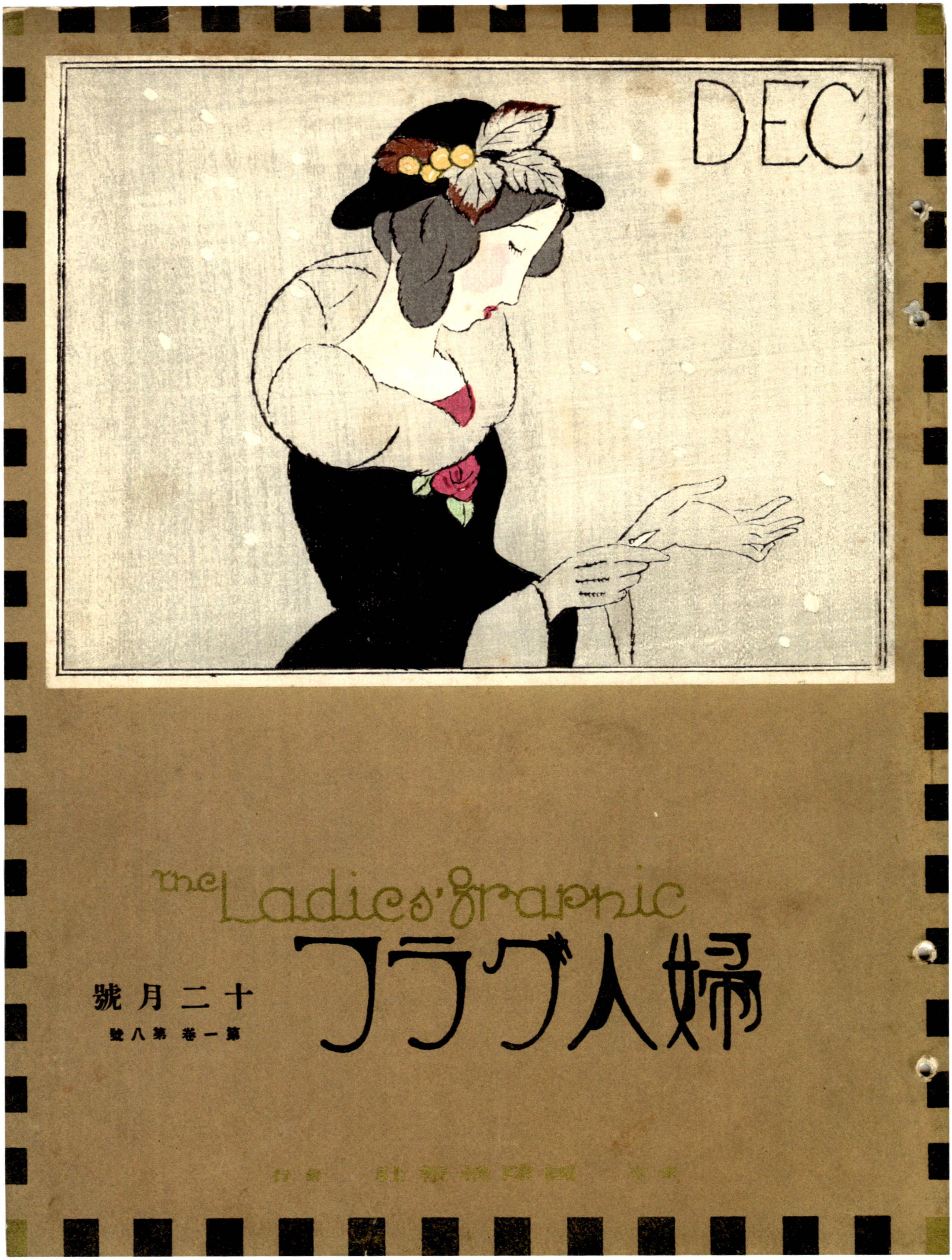
DEC
The Ladies' Graphic
婦人グラフ
十二月號
第一巻第八號
東京 國際情報社 發行

# Foreword

*Previous page*
*Snowy wind*
From *The ladies' graphic*
(see cat. 47, p. 118)

It gives me great pleasure to present the first catalogue in a Western language on the Japanese artist Takehisa Yumeji (1884–1934). When we began collecting almost twenty-five years ago, we were immediately drawn to the twentieth century, in particular, to the prints of artists such as Torii Kotondo, Hashiguchi Goyō and Itō Shinsui. For us, the portrayal of the female form by these masters was the quintessence of Japanese prints of this era. Somewhat later, we were introduced to the adherents of the *sōsaku hanga* ('Creative print') movement and were equally enthusiastic about the expressive strength conveyed in their oeuvre.

In Japan, there is almost no escaping the art created by Takehisa Yumeji during the Taishō and early Shōwa eras. Even today his distinctive imagery pops up on phone cards, stationery, handkerchiefs, door curtains (*noren*) and T-shirts. The ubiquity of his work inspired us to visit the many Yumeji museums around Japan—six in all—that outnumber the institutions dedicated to the internationally celebrated artists Katsushika Hokusai and Utagawa Hiroshige. The more we saw of Yumeji's art, the more we wished to acquire pieces for the Nihon no Hanga collection: it currently holds over 400 Yumeji items. To our surprise we also realised that the enormous interest in Yumeji was limited to Japan. Eager to learn more about him, but not versed in Japanese, we discovered that there was little information on him in Western languages. I was resolved to set the record straight—this publication is the result of that effort.

I was fortunate enough to meet Nozomi Naoi and Sabine Schenk, who both have undertaken extensive research on Yumeji. They were willing to publish aspects of their findings in the essays in this volume, and I would like to extend my heartfelt thanks to them for their participation and cooperation with Nihon no Hanga on this project. Maureen de Vries, assistant curator at Nihon no Hanga, contributed descriptions of the pieces selected from the collection, and curator Chris Uhlenbeck wrote a short historical introduction. Robert Schaap's elegant sense of design has added to the book's visual appeal. A difficult task rested on the shoulders of Amy Reigle Newland, who was required to shape the individual efforts into a uniform publication, and I am grateful for her dedication and excellent work.

It is my hope that this publication will introduce Western audiences to an artist who, while praised in his native Japan, has been neglected far too long on the international stage.

*Elise Wessels*
*Director*
*Nihon no Hanga, Amsterdam*

# Notes to readers

Japanese names and terms have been transliterated in accordance with the modified Hepburn system of romanisation. The order of Japanese names is generally given in the native form, with surname preceding first name, unless otherwise known in the West. Personal names, place and era designations appear in their original accented form, except when they have entered into common English usage (e.g. Tokyo not Tōkyō).

Titles of individual artworks and series titles of prints, books and journals are supplied in both English translation and in the original (transliterated) Japanese, wherever possible. There are a number of works discussed in this publication, which were not given titles by the artists, so where possible, we have attempted to provide descriptive titles. In the main texts, the titles of artworks, journals, as well as the names of organisations and institutions, are usually cited in English translation followed by the original (transliterated) Japanese, except if the work is otherwise better recognised by its original language title such as the Minatoya (not 'Harbour Shop'). For reasons of readability '*Yumeji gashū*' is employed after the first mention in each of the sections, rather than the more cumbersome *The Yumeji collection of work.*

Dates given on artworks are indicated as such; when undated, an approximate date has been supplied, wherever possible. Dates of artists, writers and so forth are generally provided at first mention and only when known. Yumeji's age is listed using the Western calendar, but according to the Japanese system his age would have been calculated based on the traditional system of 'inclusive counting' (*kazoe-doshi*), in which a child was in 'year 1' at birth. In the Yumeji accounts included in this volume we have retained his age based on this system and the Western equivalent then follows in square brackets. Signatures and seals are given when documented. An abbreviated bibliographical form is used in the endnotes, with full citations included in the Bibliography. Sizes are given in centimetres, height before width; unless indicated, all works are woodblock printed (this does not apply to drawings and sketches).

Contributors to the catalogue section are indicated as such:

| | |
|---|---|
| NN | Nozomi Naoi |
| SS | Sabine Schenk |
| MdV | Maureen de Vries |

# Takehisa Yumeji and his times

Chris Uhlenbeck

The life and career of Takehisa Yumeji (1884–1934) bridged distinctly different eras. He came of age in the later Meiji (1868–1912), and was at the height of his artistry during the comparatively liberal Taishō (1912–1926) and the early Shōwa (1926–1989) when Japan's political landscape was undergoing tremendous change.

Unprecedented social, cultural and economic transformation characterised the Meiji era as Japan sought to develop as a modern nation state and evolve a sense of national identity. The country's victory in the Sino-Japanese (1894–1895) and Russo-Japanese (1904–1905) Wars inspired patriotic fervour in many quarters and resulted in a growing recognition of the country as a world power on the geo-political stage. For Prime Minister and founder of Waseda University, Okuma Shigenobu (1838–1922), Japan was 'no longer a Japan for Japan, but a Japan for the world', reflecting a newly found national confidence and a reversal of the inward-looking attitude prevalent during the previous Edo period (1615–1868).[1] However, Japan's treatment by other Western powers following the Sino-Japanese and Russo-Japanese conflicts, and even the First World War, whereby it was awarded neither the spoils of war nor acknowledged on equal footing with Western powers, caused deep resentment within the government and the populace.[2] Such turns of events helped spawn strong nationalist sentiment, particularly among the military and in certain official sectors.

Both the Sino-Japanese and the Russo-Japanese Wars greatly impacted daily life. The demand of the war efforts resulted in intensive industrial production and incidents unfolding abroad contributed to expanded coverage in printed media. During the Sino-Japanese War the technology of woodblock-printed broadsheets (and imagery) was still in use, but the explosion of mass-media reporting led to the increased adoption of mechanical printing technologies to meet this boom. By 1911, and at the dawn of the Taishō era, the number of newspapers tripled to 236 titles, with the circulation of the seven biggest dailies reaching one hundred thousand copies.[3] The manufacture of books also appears to have reached new heights, aided by metal typesetting and the development of alternatives for woodblock printing as a means of illustration—lithography, photography and collotype—that relegated woodblock-printed images and texts to the realm of 'art'. Magazines, too, appeared in ever-greater numbers, catering to all tastes and readerships. This burgeoning of the publishing industry went hand in hand with a growing literate population: school enrolment levels were almost one hundred percent and information could now be widely distributed. And it was not only the printed media that witnessed advancement: radio, cinema and gramophones were likewise being integrated into the country's cultural fabric.

## *Women as consumers*

Societal changes at the end of the Meiji and the beginning of Taishō also extended to the position of women. Women became a cog in the Japanese capitalist machine as the industrial revolution demanded a larger labour force for mass production, even though economically and legally their status lagged far behind their male counterparts. However, the evolution of the media and the rise of women as consumers led to a flourishing of women's magazines. While many were short lived, their influence cannot be underestimated: some were principally practical how-to magazines acquainting Japanese women with modern domestic gadgets or imported Western styles, including fashions, all of which were significant in creating a space for women's independent identity. Such magazines can be considered among the first items of mass consumerism and the more successful titles had editions of several hundred thousand. Women bought them, read them and participated in them, sending in contributions that offered commentary, posed questions and requested advice. Another aspect of Yumeji's work comprised illustrations for these women's magazines as well as other types of journals and newspapers (see cat. 37–65).

### *A society in ferment*

The rise of socialism in Japan paralleled developments in Europe and resulted from the widening gaps in wealth due to the rapidly growing capitalist system of production. Between 1900 and 1917 alone, the number of factory workers tripled and social discord surfaced as the country was repeatedly rocked by strikes and riots. The government reacted by enacting a policy aimed at suppressing socialism, with the potential of the mass media a worrying trend, '. . . recipes for omelets and pork cutlets to which the government did not greatly object', but 'pornography and socialism, to which it did, found increasingly wider audiences'.[4] It banned socialist parties and touted propagandistic stances that centred on 'traditional' Japanese values stressing harmony and cooperation, familial unity and a respect for ancestral customs. The trade unions aligned themselves with the leftist political parties (Socialist, Communist and Marxist), limiting their influence on a central government dominated by centre right and right-wing parties and ideologies.

### *A changing art scene*

From the later 1800s, foreign magazines and art publications channelled the information and imagery arriving from the West, and they served as catalysts for artistic change. By the early twentieth century, when Yumeji was embarking on his own career, Western-style painting had been subsumed into the curriculum of recently established art schools. It offered a parallel visual mode to traditional Japanese art. During this period, too, Japanese artists sought training abroad in Europe or the United States. Upon their return to Japan they introduced new sets of values, not just relating to social issues, but also to art practice. It was a period of intense discussion and interaction among those inhabiting the cultural landscape. Artists (and writers) were torn between their Japanese roots and incoming Western values, between the increasingly apparent social inequalities and governmental propaganda that argued for national unity and the exclusion of individualism. Art associations formed and disbanded, and the discourse surrounding art and its creation sowed the seeds for experiments in all fields of artistic endeavour. Despite the fact that Taishō society was on one level a society in ferment, on another it was a crucible for vibrancy and innovation in the arts and literature, often equated with *la belle époque* in Europe: a world of clubs, beer and dance halls, coffee shops, department stores and images of the self-assured 'modern girls' (*modan gaaru* or *moga*) strolling along the avenues of fashionable Tokyo districts like Ginza. This era's cultural milieu is often described as one representing what some Japanese scholars label as 'Taishō Romanticism' (*Taishō roman*). While at times a problematic term, 'Taishō Romanticism' reflects the emphasis on a romantic vision of the world in which women's independence was paramount, and the emergence of the female consumer explains in part the success of Yumeji's mass-produced designs with this audience. European fashion took Japan by storm and the affluence resulting from the booming economy during the First World War allowed many of the nouveau riche to partake of the offerings of modernity.

## *The repression of freedom of thought and expression*

Another term frequently associated with this era—'Taishō democracy' (*Taishō demokurashii*)—has been coined to reflect an age perceived as possessing relative liberalism, an age wedged between the more hierarchical Meiji era and the growing militarism typifying the later 1920s and the 1930s. Political participation increased markedly with the elimination of tax qualification for voters and with men receiving full voting rights in 1925 (women much later in 1945). But the practice of censorship and the control over ideas was firmly entrenched in Japanese history, and in the early twentieth century the dramatic societal changes led to repressive laws as a means to deal with protests, strikes and violence.[5] The most celebrated of these was the 'High Treason Incident' of 1910 when a socialist-anarchist plot to assassinate the Meiji Emperor was foiled. Twenty-six left-wing activists were arrested on questionable charges and twelve were executed in January 1911.

Even within the seeming liberality of Taishō, measures of control targeted trade unions and official trade unions were banned until after the First World War. Established in 1911 in the aftermath of the 'High Treason Incident' and in an effort to monitor the development of Marxism and socialism, as well as the activities of political groups and individuals, the 'Special Higher Police' or 'Thought Police' further extended its long arm following the passage of the Peace Preservation Law in 1925. This gave the government the opportunity and excuse to eradicate the Communist party, and the raids that followed were soon widened to include the hunt for any person with 'deviant' ideas (i.e. liberals and radicals). With the mounting holding power of an increasingly nationalist and imperialist Japanese government in the 1930s, repression became more commonplace, and severely restricted the freedom of thought and speech. The government also expected artists to take an augmented nationalistic expression in their choice of subject matter and to lend moral support to the war effort, particularly from 1931 with the commencement of the 'Fifteen Years War'. Artists were sent abroad to oil the propaganda machine with the depiction of victorious Japanese troops or to teach in the occupied territories. The majority complied, some grudgingly and others more enthusiastically, with the rules and restrictions because they provided one method of gaining access to the tools and materials required for their artistic production. The general attitude of the artists seems to have been one grounded in practicality, aimed at survival and not necessarily imbued with strong political feeling.

As the essays in this publication demonstrate, the historical, social and cultural events of the later Meiji and Taishō profoundly impacted the course of Yumeji's art: the arrival of Japan on the world stage, the emergence of a middle class, the creation of a multi-faceted cultural scene, the move towards the emancipation of women and the build-up of a totalitarian state were all aspects that contributed to Yumeji's artistic vision.

## *Notes*

**1.** Duus, ed., *The twentieth century*, 654.

**2.** After the Sino-Japanese War, Russia, France and Germany intervened to force Japan's return of the Liaodong peninsula and Port Arthur to China, even though Russia then immediately occupied Liaodong, and the Germans and English moved into parts of China. Japan was outmanoeuvred following the Russo-Japanese War by the Russians and never received reparation payments from the defeated. These events, coupled with the hardships endured by the Japanese for the war effort, led to public outcry and riots (e.g. the 1905 Hibiya riots). Following the First World War and despite its alliance with the Allies against Germany, Japan was not seen as coequal with other nations.

**3.** Gluck, *Japan's modern myths*, 171.

**4.** Ibid., 174.

**5.** For example, the censorship of the content of prints was well established in the Edo period. From the early eighteenth century, the portrayal of contemporary events, erotic imagery and political ideas were banned in woodblock prints.

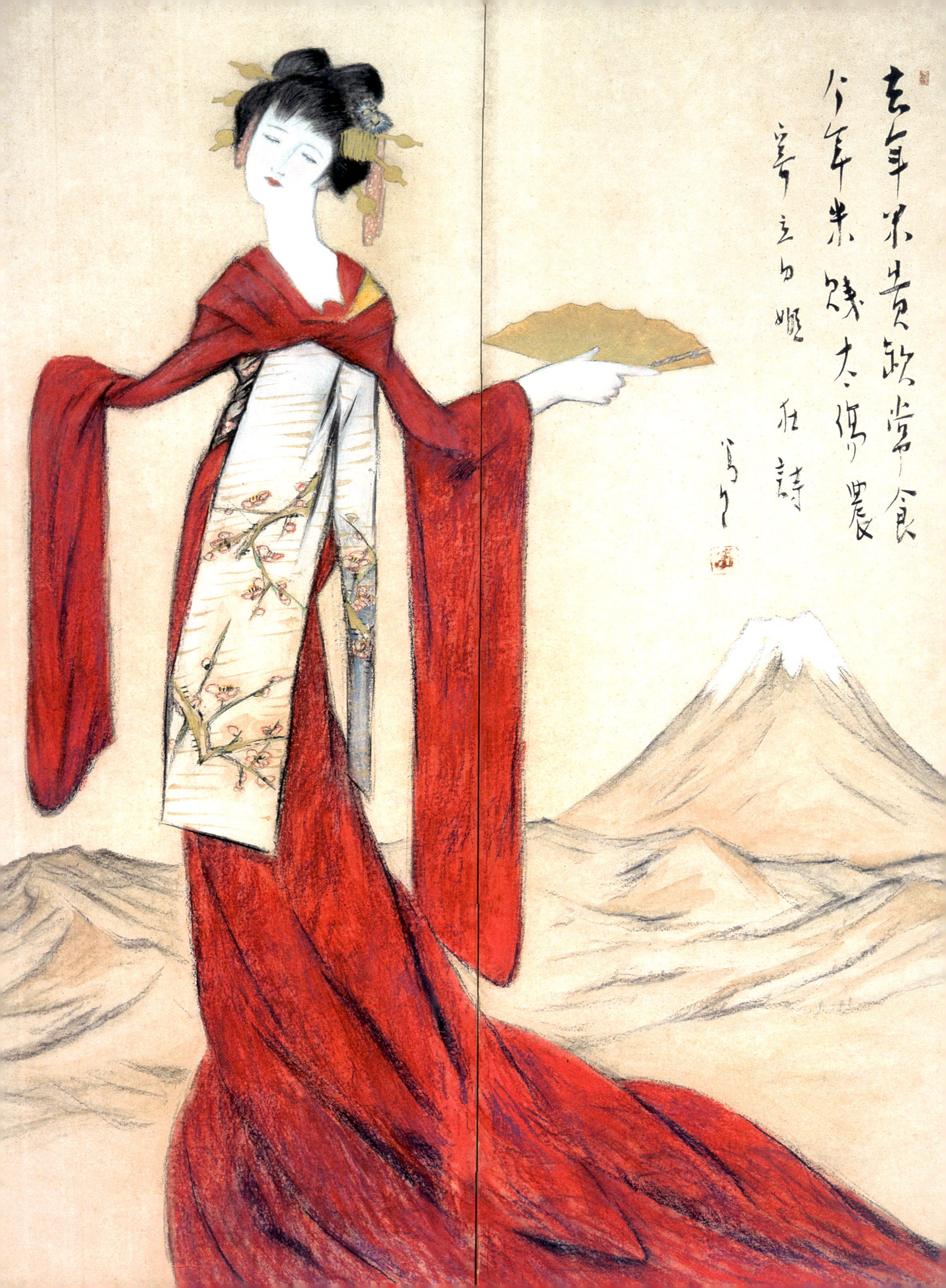

# Finding an aesthetic language: the early years, 1884–1911

Nozomi Naoi

The year 2014 marked the 130th anniversary of the birth of Takehisa Yumeji (1884–1934). Commemorative events and shows, including a travelling exhibition held at Takashimaya department stores in Kyoto, Okayama, Tokyo and Yokohama, testified to the enduring popularity and relevance of this iconic early twentieth-century Japanese artist.[1] Today six museums and one gallery in Japan are dedicated to his work, an astonishing number when compared to other artists of his generation.[2]

Yumeji is particularly celebrated for his work in the genre of 'beautiful women' (*bijinga*). His signature 'Yumeji-style beauty' (*Yumeji-shiki bijin*) appealed to a broad audience, ranging from young girls and boys, established artists and authors, amateur art collectors, avant-garde artists to socialists and anarchists. The popularity of his imagery was such that it not only had a lasting imprint on contemporaneous cultural trends, but also exercised a tremendous influence on the field of Meiji- and Taishō-era modern art.[3] Yumeji's artistic evolution and the career path that he would ultimately take were shaped by his early experiences in his native Okayama, Kobe and then Tokyo, and this formative period is the subject of this essay.

## *Yumeji's childhood in Okayama*

*Princess Tatsuta*
(*Tatsutahime*, 立田姫)
Painting on paper,
121.2 x 97.5 cm
Date: 1931
Signature/seal: *Mushō* with square seal
Yumeji Art Museum, Okayama
Princess Tatsuta is the Shinto goddess of autumn and the harvest. The inscription to the right was inspired by a Chinese poem by Du Fu (712–770): 'Last year rice was expensive and daily food is scarce; this year rice will be cheap and the peasantry will be badly off'. Yumeji was fond of this painting and is recorded to have said: 'She's the crowning woman of my life. She's Miss Nippon!'[2]

1. Yūjōbō, ed. *Taiyō 20*, 86. The original Chinese poem is entitled *Sui yan xing*.
2. Quoted on the British Museum website.

Takehisa Yumeji was born Takehisa Mojirō on 16 September 1884 in the small village of Honjō in the Oku district in southeastern Okayama prefecture. His father Kikuzō was thirty-two at the time of his birth, his mother Yasuno twenty-eight, and his elder sister Matsuka just seven. His elder brother died the previous year, which meant that Yumeji was in effect an only son. His younger sister was born in 1890. The Takehisa family became wealthy landowning merchants in Honjō, but by 1884 his father was engaged principally as a *sake* distributor. Kikuzō also served as a member on its village council.

Honjō was a post-town situated between the temple, Saiji, in Nara, and Ushimado harbour on the Seto Island Sea, the latter connecting the maritime routes between mainland Japan and the islands of Shikoku and Kyushu. It was a bustling port area, attracting people from all walks of life—travelling performance troops, jōruri puppeteers, Buddhist monks and others. Such an environment must have intrigued the young Yumeji, and the harbour scenes of boats and distant mountains in a number of his later prints may have been based upon these childhood memories (fig. 1.1). Other landscapes, such as *Day in, day out at a bay* (fig. 1.2) and *Hometown* (fig. 1.3), are similarly reminiscent of his native Okayama.

Yumeji's childhood home was nestled at the foot of a small hill overlooking the main road leading to Ushimado port. Today the original house is part of the Yumeji Art Museum (Yumeji Kyōdo Bijutsukan) in Okayama, where visitors are invited to share in the same landscape vista of mountains and water that the young Yumeji would have seen from his own room. A camellia plant grew near the Takehisa home—one is planted there even today—and this flower was a common decorative motif in his compositions of women (fig. 1.4).

From an early age Yumeji was exposed to the world of colour and design because his mother's family were traditional fabric dyers. He frequented their dye house, where he would have become familiar with stencil patterns and various dyestuffs, and this experience would have undoubtedly nurtured Yumeji's sensibility for

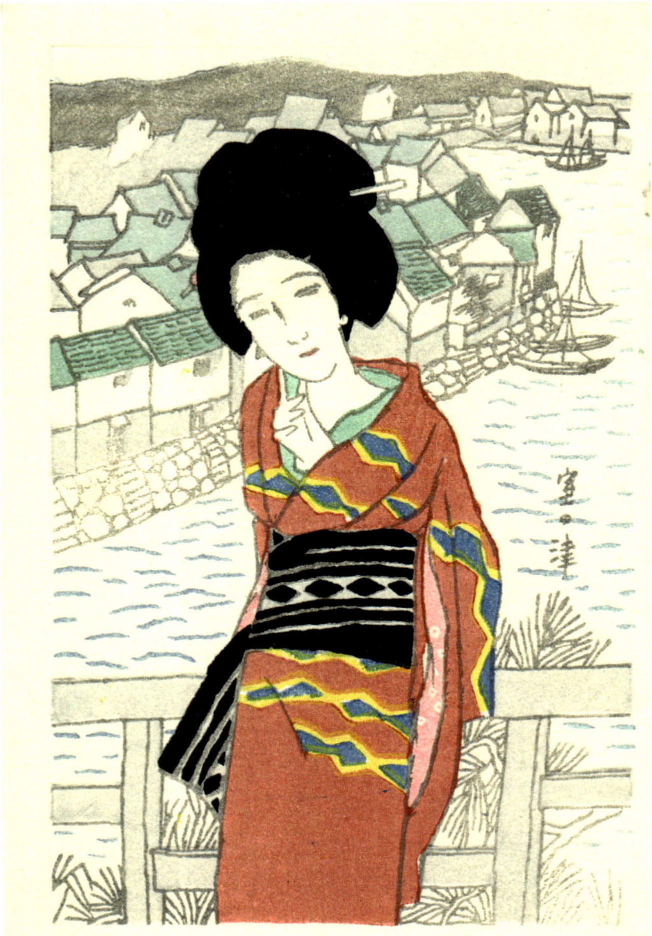


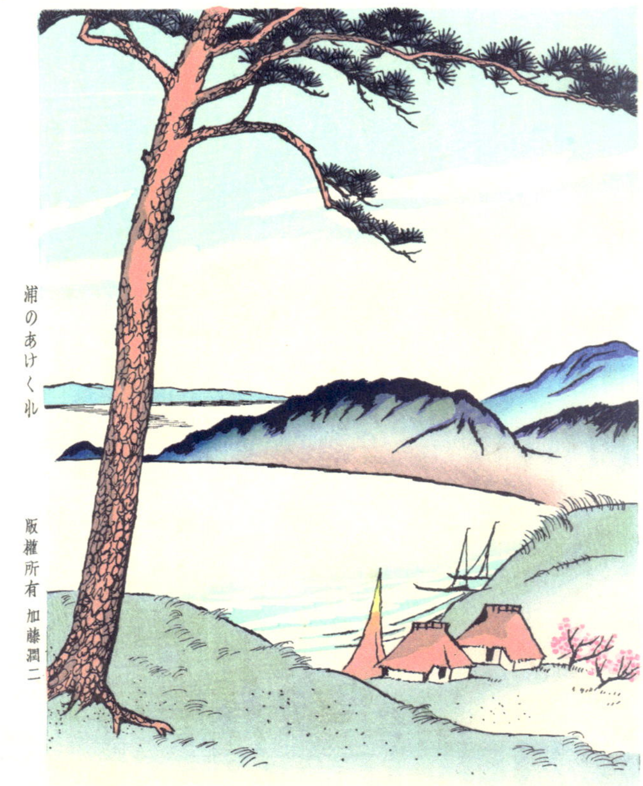


Fig. 1.1. *Muro harbour* (*Muro no tsu,* 室の津)
From the series *A collection of prints by Yumeji* (*Yumeji hangashū,* 夢二版画集)
15.0 x 10.2 cm

In 1917, Yumeji visited Muro in Hyōgo prefecture with his second son Fujihiko. The town's bustling harbour featured in the work of many authors and artists. The area was also celebrated for its courtesans, perhaps explaining why Yumeji chose this beauty, who poses against the setting of a bay and its settlement. For another image from this set, see fig. 1.13.

Fig. 1.2. *Day in, day out at a bay* (*Ura no akekure,* 浦のあけくれ)
From the series *Yumeji's masterpieces* (*Yumeji meisakushū,* 夢二名作集)
33.8 x 24.8 cm
Date: 1938–1939
Publisher: Katō Hanga Kenkyūjo

The prints in *Yumeji masterpieces* highlight Yumeji's skilful treatment of the landscape genre. Tranquil, bucolic scenes such as this illustrating a hamlet nestled along a bay were a frequent theme in Yumeji's art, and it could be conjectured that it conveyed a sense of nostalgia for his native Okayama or the port city of Kobe where he briefly spent time during his childhood (see also fig. 1.3). For other images from this set, see figs. 1.5, 1.12, 3.11, 4.6, 4.14; cat. 68–72.

Fig. 1.3. *Hometown* (*Furusato, ふるさと*)
From the series *A collection of poetry and prints by Yumeji* (*Yumeji shigashū, 夢二詩画集*)
13.3 x 20.8 cm
Date: 1941
Seal: *Yume*
Publisher: Katō Hanga Kenkyūjo

The *Yume* seal on this example is seen on the artist's work from the early Taishō era. For other images from this set, see figs. 2.3a, 3.12; cat. 73–79.

[MdV]

*Bottom left*
Fig. 1.4. *Camellia* (*Tsubaki no hana, 椿の花*)
From the series *A collection of poetry and prints by Yumeji* (*Yumeji shigashū, 夢二詩画集*)
19.9 x 13.2 cm
Date: 1941
Publisher: Katō Hanga Kenkyūjo

In this work a girl fashions a garland from red camellia blossoms. The strung flowers almost envelop her figure, while the camellia tree frames her upper torso.

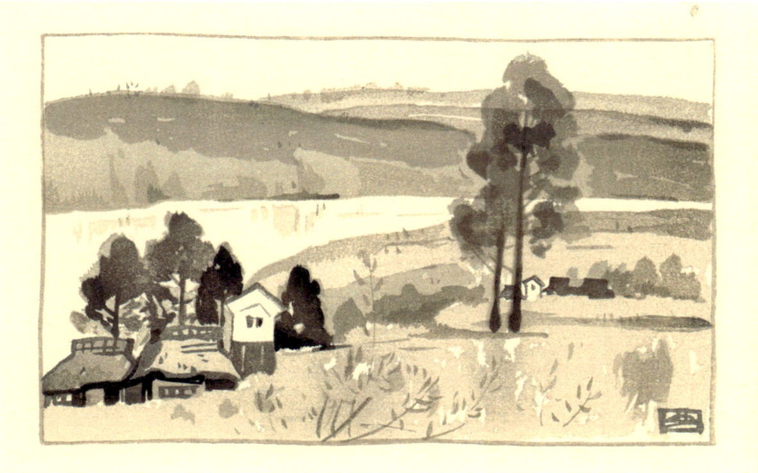

Fig. 1.5. *Dutch lantern* (*Rantō, 蘭燈*)
From the series *Yumeji's masterpieces* (*Yumeji meisakushū, 夢二名作集*)
33.9 x 24.8 cm
Date: 1938–1939
Seal: artist's comma-shaped (*tomoe*) seal
Publisher: Katō Hanga Kenkyūjo

This woodblock print exemplifies Yumeji's lifelong interest in the exotic and foreign, as manifest in the recurring imagery of port cities. Here, a woman dressed in a vivid red kimono with *shibori*-dyed patterns and floral motifs casually plays a *shamisen*. A large paper lantern hangs behind her, with a view of the bay in the distance. For other images from this set, see figs. 1.2, 1.12, 3.11, 4.6, 4.14; cat. 68–72.

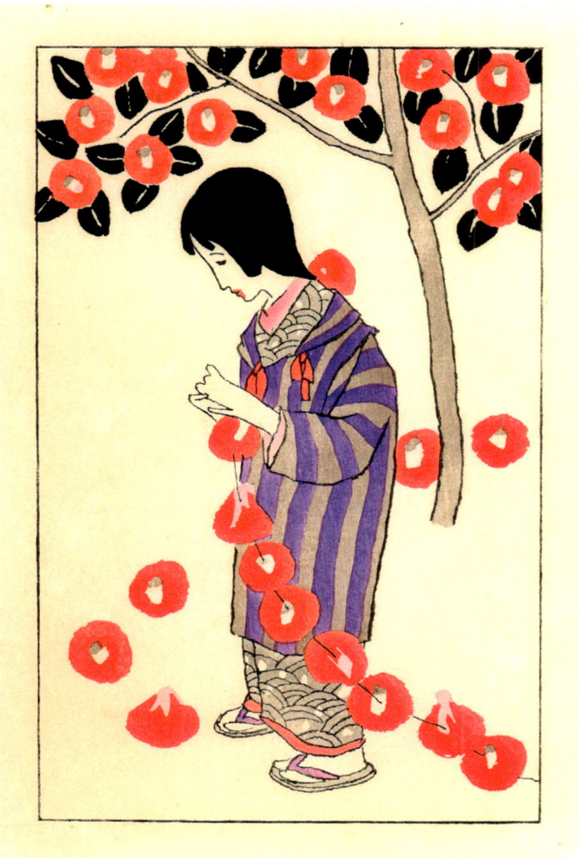

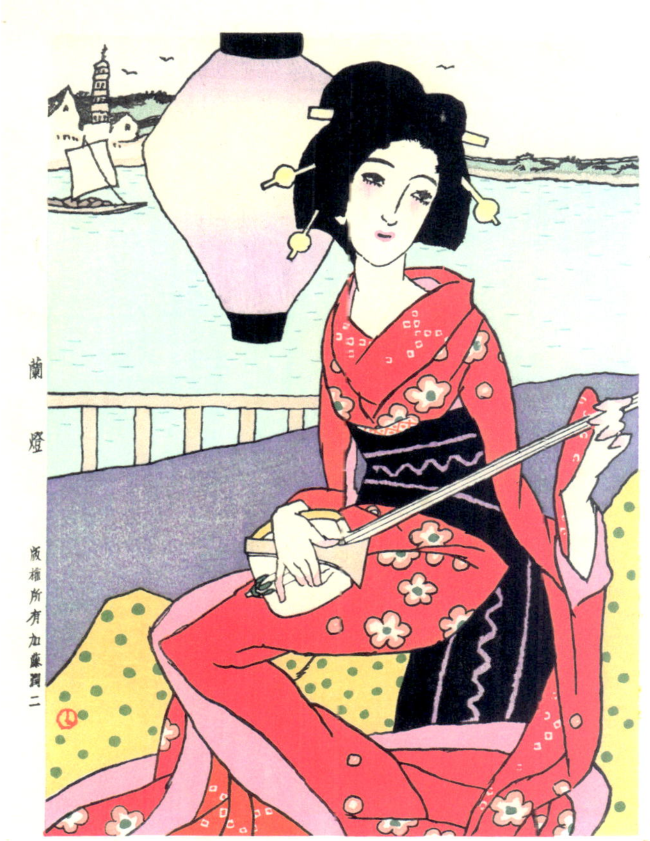

bold designs. When Yumeji entered elementary school, his dabbling in sketching found a supportive figure in his maternal grandfather, who encouraged the young boy's artistic interests and talents.

In 1891, the seven-year-old Yumeji entered the Meitoku Elementary School in Honjō. Four years later, Yumeji attended the Oku County Higher Elementary School, where he was fortunate to have a liberal-minded art teacher named Hattori Mokusaburō. Hattori's approach broke with the strict adherence to textbooks and conventional methods of grading and critiquing. He instilled in his pupils a love of creating art, and he encouraged freer methods in pencil sketching and drawing such as the direct observation from nature. Hattori would have an enormous impact on Yumeji, who later recounted that Hattori was his first and last art instructor. Yumeji dedicated his book *Quick sketches* (*Sōga*, 1914) to him and in the preface the artist fondly reminisces about his tutelage under Hattori:

> *Mr. Hattori would always set the textbooks aside and permit his students to go outside and freely sketch things such as the Japanese sago palm plants in our schoolyard, crab-apple flowers, our shoes, or shrine gates* (torii)*. He never said a word about how to frame our drawings or how to add shading. He would simply stare at us with his somewhat frightening bearded face, which possessed a kind of severity but also conveyed a sense of fondness, as we fumbled with our childish hands. He always gave me a full mark on my drawings, but he never once told me how good my drawing skills were or why my pictures were well done.*

Hattori's less fettered pedagogical approach was extremely unusual for art teachers at this time. Yet it fostered Yumeji's creative spirit and gave him the confidence to pursue an artistic career. Yumeji concludes in *Quick sketches* that he believed that Hattori intuited that he would become an artist. Yumeji's future path as a self-trained artist, one who did not study at an official art institution, was most likely the result of Hattori's liberal views towards art training. The influence of his teacher is also evident in Yumeji's comments in the preface of his earlier 1910 *Winter* (*Fuyu no maki*) regarding the making of art:

> *. . . a picture is not an explanation, it is a song . . . I do not care for skills that will make me draw better or for the techniques needed to produce bust portraits of scholars or beauties; above anything else, I desire the richness [gleaned] from delicate sensual pleasures and feelings full of amazement.*

### *Yumeji in Kobe and Fukuoka*

In the spring of 1899, the fifteen-year-old Yumeji entered a new phase when he moved to Kobe to live with his uncle and where he entered the Kobe Middle School. His brief sojourn in Kobe—a mere eight months—would spawn eclectic interests that he visualised throughout his career. It was also at this time that Yumeji developed a desire to travel abroad, inspired by his exposure to the Western-influenced urban atmosphere of the international port of Kobe with its foreign-style architecture such as the 'American Pier' (Meriken Hatoba). A government building erected in 1868 in Hyōgo Bay, the American Pier derived its name from its location near the American consulate and the foreign settlement. As a teenager with newfound freedom from family and village life, Kobe would have been an exciting adventure for Yumeji, who would have taken in the sights of docked foreign ships and the casual encounters with Westerners. Recurring compositions of foreigners and port cities in his work such as in *Dutch lantern* (fig. 1.5) certainly reflects his time here.

The Kobe Middle School held Bible classes with a foreign female instructor, with whom Yumeji met and discussed various aspects of Western culture and Christianity. Yumeji became intrigued with Christian imagery as well as forms of Japanese art such as the seventeenth- and eighteenth-century *nanban* ('southern barbarian') paintings that were influenced by contact with Portuguese and Dutch traders and missionaries. These interests were manifest in Yumeji's later series of scenes from Nagasaki, a city that had deep historical ties with foreigners. Although the main focus is on the female figure, both *Megane Bridge* and *Deshima* show elaborate scenes enhanced by exotic Western-style elements in the background (figs. 1.6 & 1.7). Other works, such as *Nine connected rings*, underscore the foreign atmosphere near a pier by depicting a Japanese beauty with a European missionary (fig. 1.8). Yumeji would continue his fascination with the Bible and Christianity for the remainder of his life. When he left Kobe in his late teens, Yumeji established close ties with pastors in Tokyo, and it is reported that he even travelled with a copy of the Bible.[4]

Eight months into his stay, Yumeji's father was forced to shut down his *sake* business in Okayama and he moved the family to take up a position at a steelworks factory in Fukuoka on the southern island of Kyushu. Yumeji briefly worked at the factory to help support the family. He also helped draw up blueprints and designs, and it could be conjectured that this training impacted his later forays into industrial design.

### *Yumeji in Tokyo: his artistic debut*

Yumeji found employment at the factory unbearable and a far cry from his creative aspirations. In 1901, after eighteen months at the factory, he left for Tokyo where he initially stayed with the family of a distant relative, Kondō Yahachi. It was Yumeji's intention to pursue his art, but to appease his father he entered the Waseda Business School (Waseda Jitsugyō Gakkō) in 1902.[5] The financial assistance from his father was insufficient to pay his bills, pushing Yumeji to find work delivering newspapers and pulling a rickshaw. Some of his later cover designs, such as that of the Waseda baseball team, provide a glimpse of his student days (fig. 1.9).

A rather poetic message written on the back of a photographic postcard from 1904 not only expresses Yumeji's excitement and hopes for the future, but also reveals a young artist grappling with the insecurities and doubts regarding his artistic direction. The 'elder sister' is the oldest daughter of the Kotake family, who also hosted Yumeji when he first arrived in Tokyo:

> *Dear 'Elder sister',*
> *Though a mere nineteen* [*twenty*] *years since I was born, it seems like a long time and yet, too, a very short time. Unable to stay at shore, there are moments when I am sinking to the bottom or I am floating on the open sea like a drifting boat of leaves. If the wind blows, I go east; if it doesn't, I go south. Oh, violent wind, blow from the south and to the west. Oh, tornado, whirl the skies for a thousand miles. If my life is only worth the potatoes that I survive on, then I can soar through the heavens. I may be young, but without wife or children, there is only the grave if I fail.*
> *From* Boku *(Me)*[6]

At this time, Yumeji formed close ties with his Waseda cohort, leading to his interest in socialist thought and empathy for the common people. In 1904, Yumeji rented modest lodgings in Zōshigaya with his classmates, including the future socialist, Oka Eijirō. This era coincided with a rise in the Japanese socialist movement: for example, in November 1903 the socialist publisher Heiminsha launched its newspaper, *The weekly commoner's news* (*Shūkan heimin shinbun*).[7] It was a tumultuous time for the nation, particularly with its entry into the Russo-Japanese War of 1904–1905.

It was through Oka that Yumeji became acquainted with the socialist ideology for which he felt a special affinity as a struggling student. He writes that Oka was 'the one who taught me Marx and Engels. He was also the one who taught me the hardships of poverty'.[8] Oka introduced Yumeji to the socialist Arahata Kanson

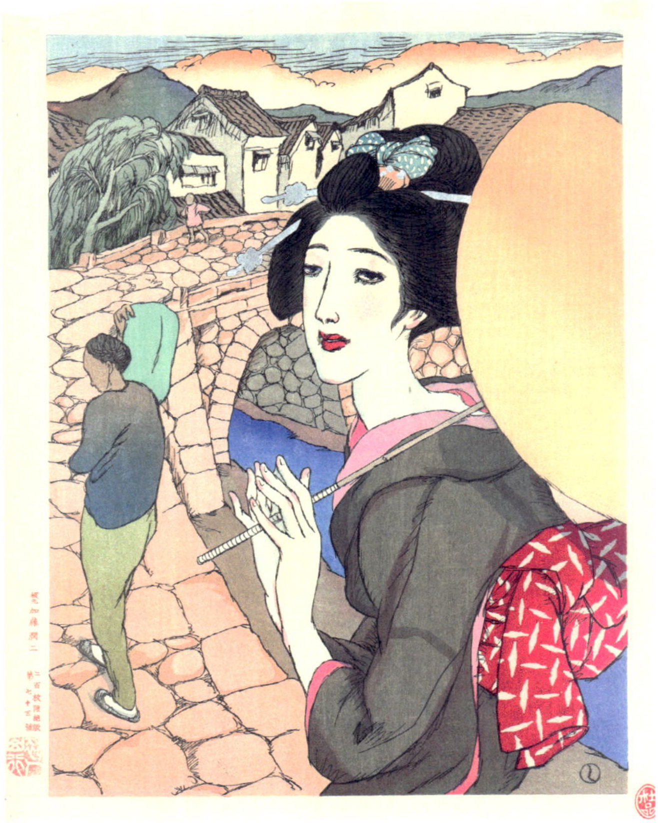

Fig. 1.6. *Megane Bridge* (*Meganebashi*, めがね橋)
From the series *Six views of Nagasaki by Takehisa Yumeji* (*Nagasaki rokkei Takehisa Yumeji*, 長崎六景 竹久夢二)
40.5 x 30.5 cm
Date: 1941
Seals: artist's comma-shaped (*tomoe*) and *Shūjin sankō* seals, collector's seal (James Tobin)
Publisher: Katō Hanga Kenkyūjo

The figure of a beauty with a large parasol wearing a diaphanous kimono is set against an elaborate scene accented by exotic Western-style elements. The cobblestone path, the double-arched Megane ('Eyeglass') Bridge and the elderly Chinese woman add a 'foreign' flavour, and the rendition of the woman's long, slender fingers also draws the viewer's attention. Yumeji's artist's seal *Shūjin sankō* (愁人山行)—literally 'Sorrowful man walking in the mountains'—might be a personal reference to himself as a lonely soul. For other images from this set, see fig. 1.7 & cat. 82.

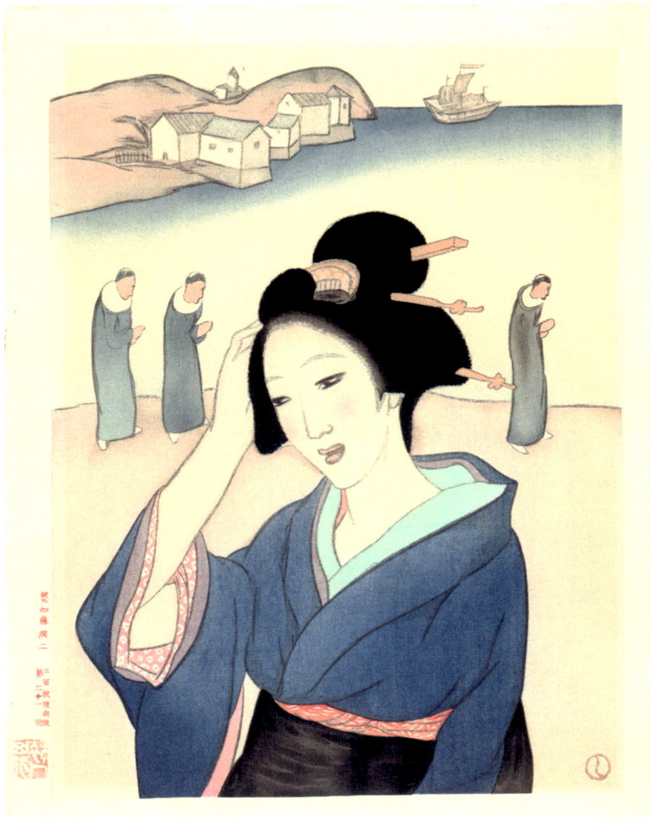

Fig. 1.7. *Deshima* (*Deshima*, 出島)
From the series *Six views of Nagasaki by Takehisa Yumeji* (*Nagasaki rokkei Takehisa Yumeji*, 長崎六景 竹久夢二)
40.3 x 30.5 cm
Date: 1938
Seals: artist's comma-shaped (*tomoe*) and *Shūjin sankō* seals
Publisher: Katō Hanga Kenkyūjo

Yumeji's fascination with Christianity is evident in this print. In the far distance and lining the bay at Deshima are a church and monastery buildings. Behind the woman are three monks in prayer. The woman holds one hand to her head as if she is deep in thought, inviting the viewer to ponder on the link between her and the overtly Christian imagery.

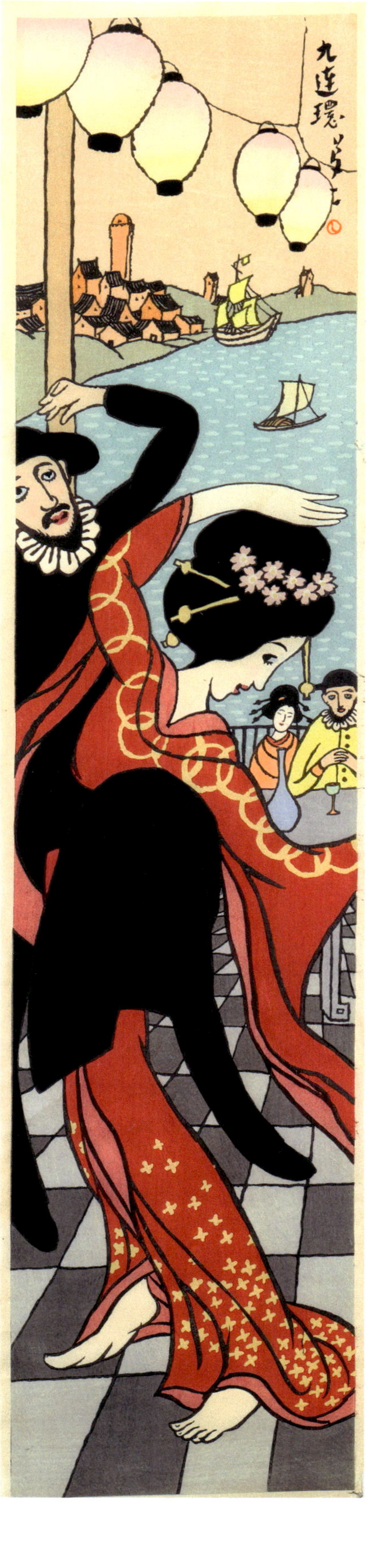


Fig. 1.8. *Nine connected rings* (*Kyurenkan* 九連環) 95.7 x 22.2 cm
Date: 1940–1943
Signature/seal: *Yumeji* with artist's comma-shaped (*tomoe*) seal
Publisher: Katō Hanga Kenkyūjo

The title of this unusually formatted work, *Kyurenkan*, refers to the hugely popular Chinese folk toy that has nine connected metal rings. The rings are fastened to a horizontal bar or frame and the aim is to link up all of the rings or to release them. Designs of the connected rings decorate the shoulders of the woman's kimono as she twists her body in what appears to be a kind of dance.

Fig. 1.9. Preparatory drawing for a music score by Nakayama Shinpei: *Waseda baseball* (*Waseda Daigaku yakyū ōenka,* 早稲田大学野球鷹援歌)
23.2 x 15.5 cm

This drawing was for a cover design for a cheer song of the Waseda University baseball team. Despite his financial difficulties and eventual withdrawal from Waseda Business School, diary entries and other commentaries suggest that Yumeji enjoyed his time as a student, frequenting Waseda baseball games and participating in other activities.

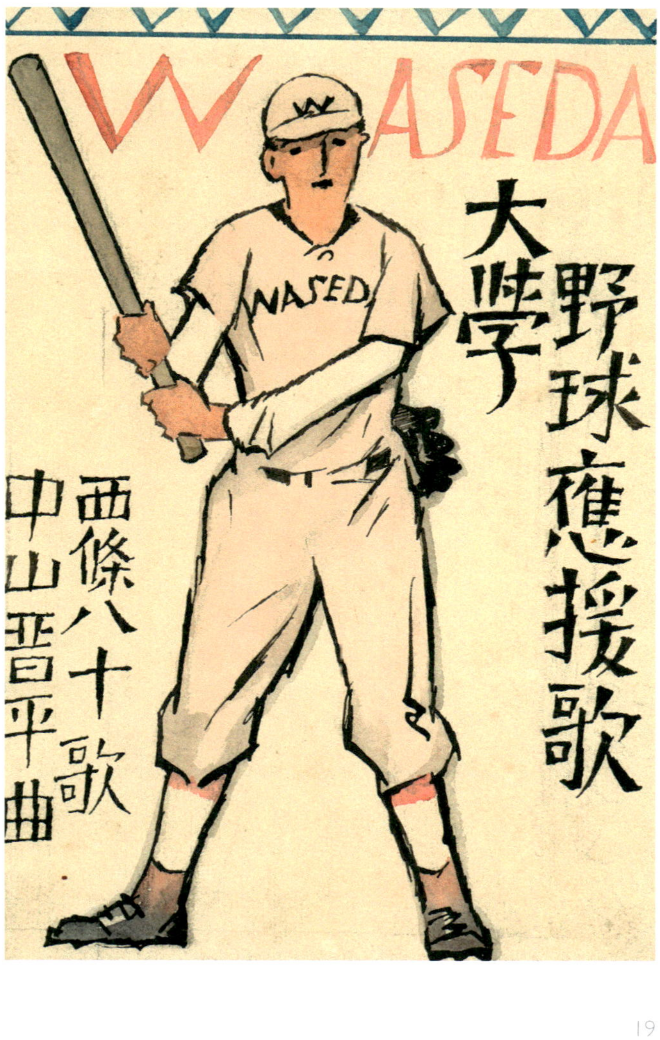

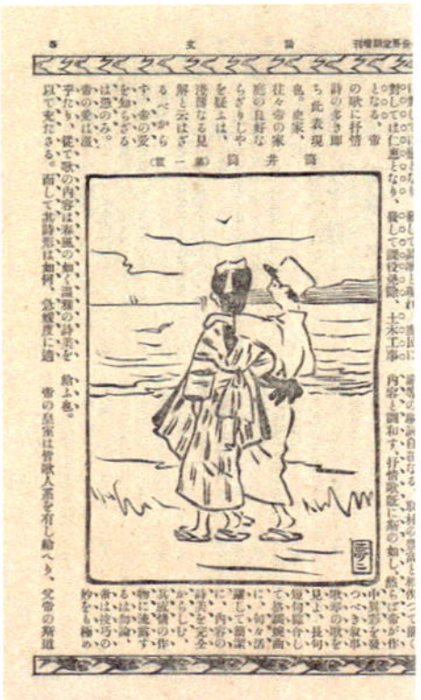

Fig. 1.10. *The well curb* (*Tsutsui-zutsu,* 筒井筒)
From the magazine *Junior world* (*Chūgaku sekai,* 中学世界)
Originally woodblock printed (mechanically reproduced for publication)
Date: Summer issue, 1905
Yumeji Art Museum, Okayama

This work demonstrates Yumeji's literary sensibilities. It references chapter 23, *The well curb* (*Tsutsui-zutsu*), from the Heian period (794–1185) literary classic, *Tales of Ise* (*Ise monogatari*), in which two childhood friends who had played around a water well would later marry.

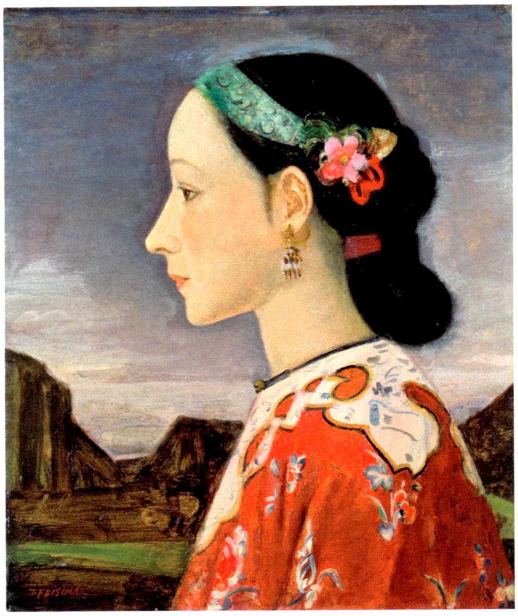

Fig. 1.11. Fujishima Takeji (1867–1943)
*Profile view of a woman* (*Onna no yokogao,* 女の横顔 )
Oil painting on panel, 45.8 x 37.4 cm
Date: 1926–1927
Pola Museum of Art, Hakone

This painting is one of many by Fujishima that drew inspiration from Italian Renaissance portraits, as evidenced by the profile view and background landscape rendered with a low horizon line. Fujishima was also known for his paintings of women attired in exotic Chinese dress. The model for this work, Sasaki Kaneyo (Oyō, 1904–1980), would later become Yumeji's model and lover.[1]

1. Fujishima famously complained that there were no Japanese models with beautiful facial profiles, although he seems to have been satisfied with the model Oyō. While Yumeji had little personal contact with Fujishima, their connection through Oyō is intriguing. See Kaizuka, ed., *Chinese-style dresses*, 32–33.

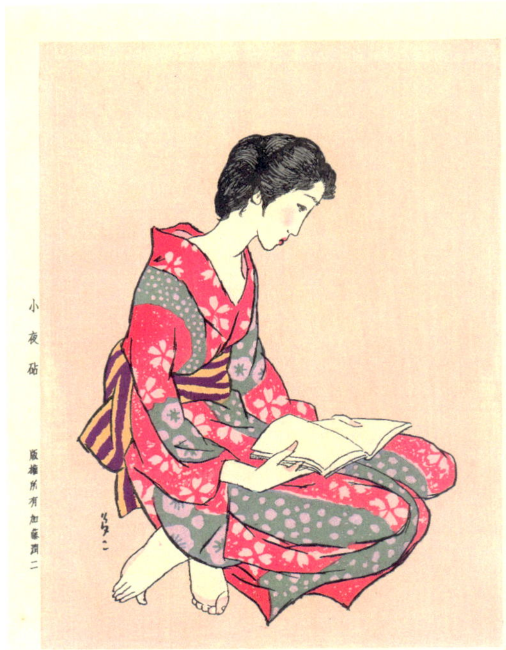

Fig. 1.12. *Sayo ginuta* (小夜砧)
From the series *Yumeji's masterpieces* (*Yumeji meisakushū,* 夢二名作集)
33.8 x 25.5 cm
Date: 1938–1939
Signature: *Yumeji*
Publisher: Katō Hanga Kenkyūjo

The title of this piece, *Sayo ginuta*, calls forth associations of a woman labouring late into the night (*sayo*)—perhaps during the colder seasons of autumn or winter—as she pounds cloth on a wooden or stone block (*kinuta*). Yumeji does not actually depict the woman at work or make reference to a cooler season, instead he clothes her in a kimono with an elaborate pattern of cherry blossoms, a striped *obi* and shows her seated reading a book. For other images from this set, see figs. 1.2, 1.5, 3.11, 4.6, 4.14; cat. 68–72.

(1887–1981), who lived briefly at the Zōshigaya residence. Kanson later recounts that the experience was one in which the 'three of us didn't mind spending our days eating just bread and water. We indulged in idle fantasies about realising a utopian socialism and freely engaged in heated discussions'.[9] Kanson would have a tremendous impact on Yumeji, not only because of his political views but also because of his support of Yumeji's artistic pursuits. Kanson describes Yumeji's efforts during these days:

> *Takehisa had initially been interested in Western-style painting. While he kept his official affiliation with the Waseda Business School because of his father, he visited the White Horse Society (Hakubakai) Western-style painting studio almost daily. This resulted in him failing his exams and losing his allowance from home. He was quite overwhelmed and seemed like he was at his wit's end, and it was then that he thought of designing the hand-drawn postcards that were fashionable at this time. He bought postcard-sized paper and painted them in watercolours. He dropped them off at postcard shops near the Tsurumaki-chō and Mejiro area. The next day he would go around collecting money from the sales and would use that for his living expenses.*[10]

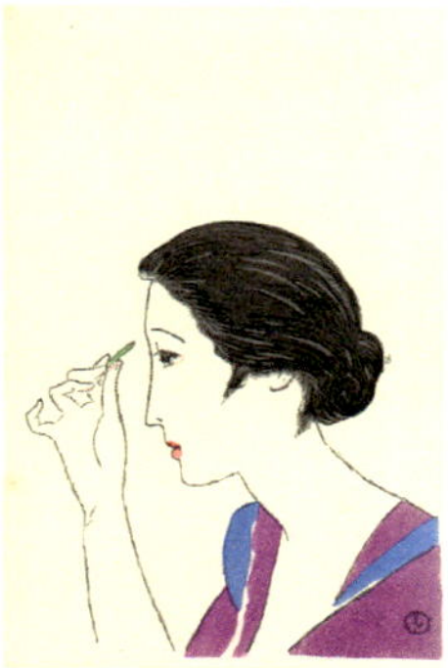

Fig. 1.13. *Applying make-up*
From the series *A collection of prints by Yumeji* (*Yumeji hangashū*, 夢二版画集),
15.0 x 10.2 x cm
Seal: artist's comma-shaped (*tomoe*) seal
This composition captures an intimate moment, just as a woman is about to apply her make-up. The effect imbues us with a sense of quiet anticipation as we are drawn into her world. For another image from this set, see fig. 1.1 and for an identical design, see cat. 32a & 61.

Life as a poor student would have made it difficult for Yumeji to devote himself entirely to an artistic career, however, he devised original ways to earn money while creating art. He was able to satisfy both needs with the production of newspaper illustrations and other graphic media. They constituted Yumeji's first platform for visual expression and Kanson encouraged Yumeji's involvement in these fields.

Impressed by Yumeji's drawings, in 1905 Kanson introduced the twenty-one-year-old artist to the members of the Heiminsha. The members and leading writers of Heiminsha were principally united by their anti-war pacifist ideology, which was in response to the increasingly militaristic policies of the Japanese government following the Russo-Japanese War. Kanson's intervention resulted in Yumeji's first published illustration (and mass-media debut) in the 18 June issue of the Heiminsha's bulletin *Plain speaking* (*Chokugen*). In keeping with the generally socialist message in *Plain speaking*, Yumeji adopts a simple, yet strikingly bold, visual language to render a woeful looking, disheartened young woman whose lover has fallen in war.

Just two days later, on 20 June, Yumeji was awarded first prize for the illustration *The well curb* in the magazine *Junior world* (*Chūgaku sekai*) (fig. 1.10). This was the earliest piece to use the artist's name 'Yumeji', which he formulated in homage to the first name, 'Takeji', of the celebrated *yōga* ('Western painting') artist, Fujishima Takeji (1867–1943). Yumeji greatly admired Fujishima, who was known for his romantic portraits of beautiful women (fig. 1.11) and whose work resonated with a sentiment that appealed to the younger artist. Fujishima was, writes Yumeji, 'the one in Japan who could truly depict *bijinga*'.[11] The first prize money, three yen, would have been a generous sum (Yumeji's monthly rent was about four *yen*). Perhaps his debut as an illustrator, and the added bonus of the prize money, gave Yumeji the conviction and confidence to persevere with his art, since that year he withdrew from the Waseda Business School.

Yumeji continued to contribute illustrations to numerous newspapers and magazines during his first year working as an independent artist. The manner in which Yumeji captured moments in everyday life and his focus on ordinary people was an especially good fit for socialist publications. He made two, three, or sometimes even four, illustrations a week for the Heiminsha. His ability to express the commonplace details of daily life simply and sympathetically is evidenced in his female imagery of this period, such as *Sayo ginuta* and *Applying make-up* (figs. 1.12 & 1.13).

*Marriage and first achievements*

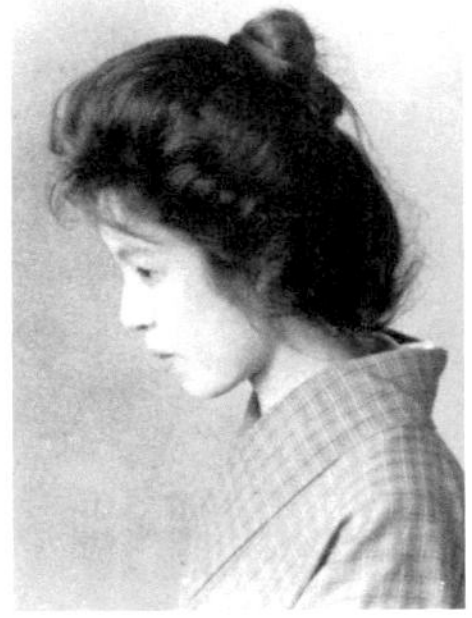

Fig. 1.14. Kishi Tamaki (1882–1945)

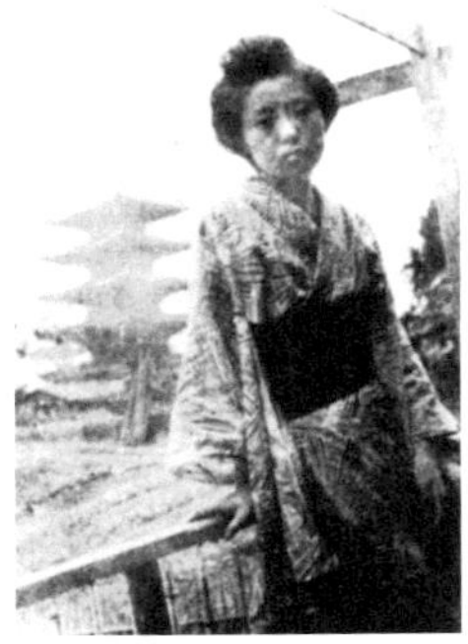

Fig. 1.15. Kasai Hikono (1896–1920)

Accounts of Yumeji's personal life often revolve around his relationships with three women: Kishi Tamaki, Kasai Hikono and Sasaki Kaneyo (Oyō) (figs. 1.14–1.16). The year 1907 was a watershed in Yumeji's private life when he married Tamaki, a slightly older widow with two children. She was the proprietor of the shop near Waseda where Yumeji sold his postcards. On 24 January, the *The weekly commoner's news* announced their marriage, reporting that Yumeji 'will be married to a most beautiful woman with large eyes'. The focus on Tamaki's eyes is significant, and the article explains further that the reason why the eyes of Yumeji's beauties became even more exaggerated following his marriage is because they were modelled after Tamaki.[12] Yumeji's output of illustrations for various magazines and newspapers, especially those targeting a young female readership, was also quite prodigious around this time.

Tamaki gave birth to Yumeji's first son Kōnosuke on 27 February 1908, but the couple's marriage was troubled even at this early stage. They agreed to divorce in 1909 but they remained close and would live together at different times in the years that followed. They also had more children, with a second son, Fujihiko, born on 1 May 1911 and a third son, Sōichi, born in late February 1916. Yumeji was extremely fond of his sons, especially Fujihiko, who lived with the artist for several years and who accompanied him on long trips throughout Japan. Many drawings of boys survive from his sketchbooks and they are most likely of his sons (fig. 1.17).

The year 1909 might have been a challenging time for Yumeji personally, but it coincided with a turning point in his artistic career. Concurrent with his production of illustrations for socialist publications, Yumeji's increasingly popular 'Yumeji-style beauties' resulted in the release of his first volume of illustrations and short poems, *Spring* (*Haru no maki*), in *The Yumeji collection of work* (*Yumeji gashū*). *Spring* was a compilation of the artist's magazines and newspaper illustrations, for which he collected the woodblocks of previously issued prints from publishers and reused them. This approach was unusual and particularly so since woodblocks for 'fast-cycle' publications were often discarded or reused after their initial carving. *Spring* was an immediate hit

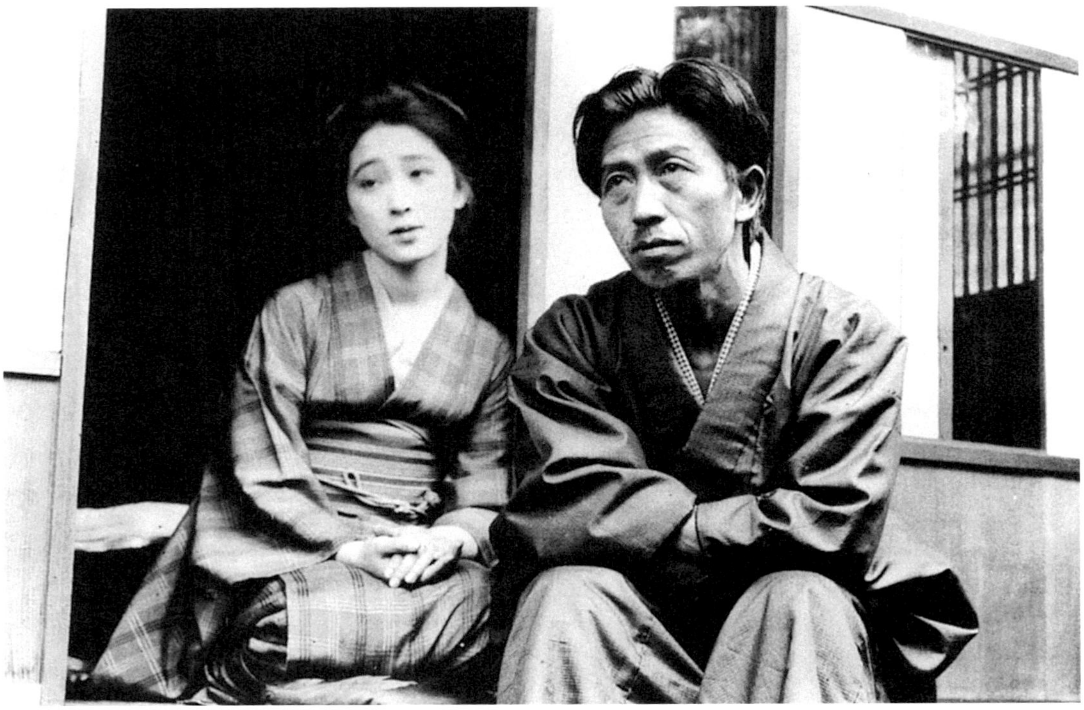

Fig. 1.16. Yumeji and Sasaki Kaneyo (Oyō, 1904–1980) in front of their house in Udagawa, Shibuya ward
Date: c. 1922

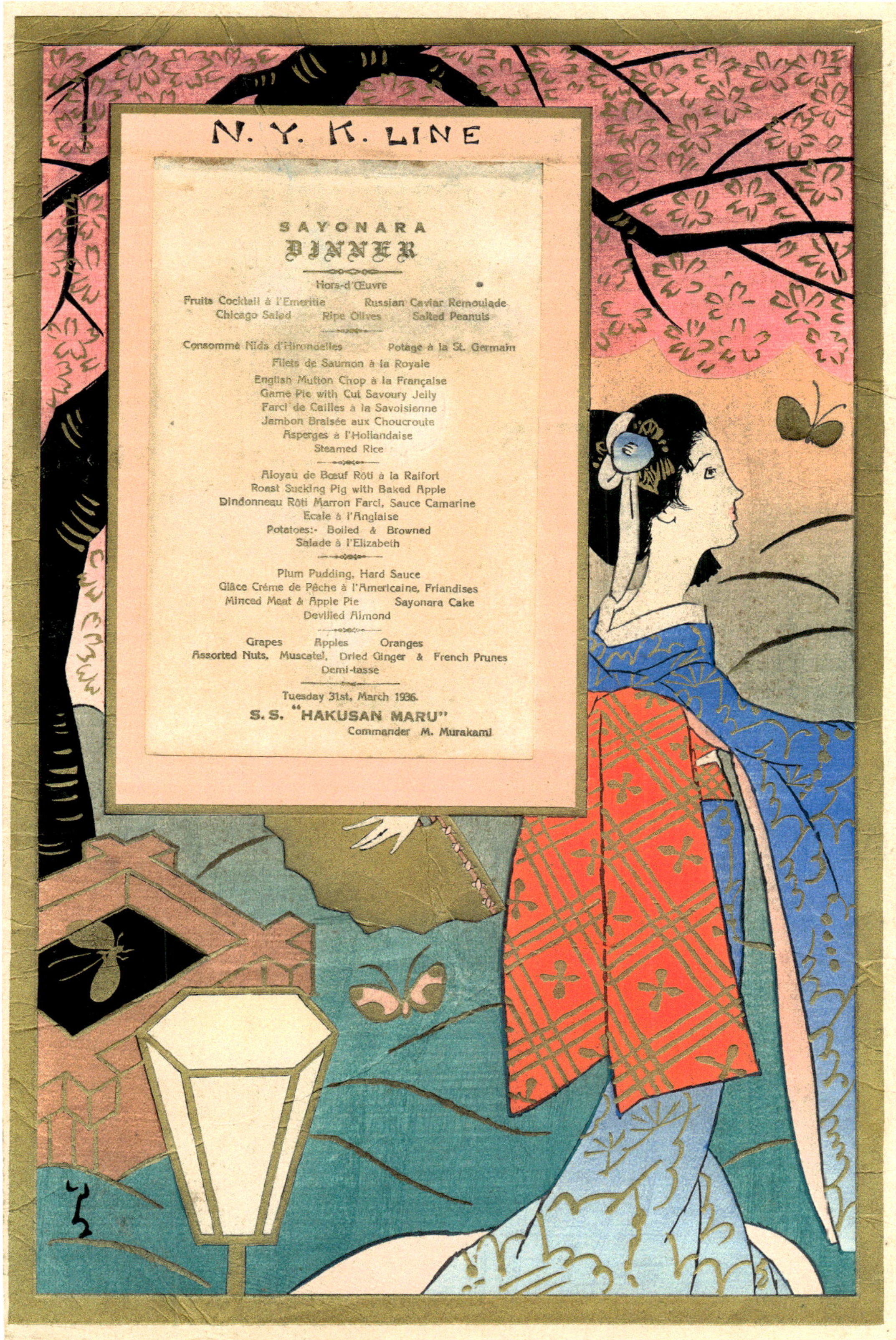


'Sayonara' dinner menu for the S.S. *Hakusan Maru*
36.7 x 23.8 cm
Date: 1936
Signature: *Yume*
Publisher: NYK Line

This woodblock-printed menu exemplifies Yumeji's commercial graphic work. A similar design for the shipping company NYK (Nippon Yūsen Kaisha) Line dating to 1929 is in the collection of the British Museum, and it is known that Yumeji was closely involved in its production.[1] This piece has been printed on thick, luxurious paper to withstand constant handling and is embellished with gold accents. Inset into the central cartouche, the menu on this example dates from Tuesday 21 March 1936, two years after Yumeji's death. It may have been part of a series of menus he made for the NYK Line before or around 1929.

[MdV]

1. Smith, *Modern Japanese prints 1912–1989*, pl. 53, 51. The British Museum example can be viewed online, museum number: 1981,1023,0.1.

and a year later, on 10 January 1910, Yumeji notes in his diary: '*Yumeji gashū* one thousand copies sold out'.[13] It was so popular that by the time it went through nine printings, it is estimated that approximately 9,000 copies of *Spring* had been sold.[14] The success of this collection led to the publication of further volumes in 1910: *Summer* (*Natsu no maki*), *Flower* (*Hana no maki*), *Travel* (*Tabi no maki*), *Autumn* (*Aki no maki*) and *Winter* (*Fuyu no maki*). The volumes of *Yumeji gashū* established Yumeji's reputation as an artist; he even became something of a celebrity. His 'Yumeji-style beauties' possessed an allure that extended beyond their existence as artworks, becoming in effect a social phenomenon inspiring women to seek out a 'Yumeji-style' look, be it in demeanour, fashion or by consuming goods designed by the artist.

This period witnessed a shift in Yumeji's involvement with socialist publications. Although this was due in part to the success of his female imagery, the year 1911 was also a dramatic moment for the Japanese socialist movement. On 24/25 January, the government indicted a group of socialists in Tokyo for plotting the assassination of the Meiji emperor. Twenty-six individuals were arrested and twenty-four received the death penalty. Twelve members, including the high-profile figure Kōtoku Shūsui (1871–1911), were executed that year as a result of what is known as the 'High Treason Incident'.[15] This chain of events shocked many Japanese. Yumeji had been close to a number of those implicated or condemned, and he held a wake, burning candles and incense to commemorate the executed.[16] It remains unclear whether Yumeji wholeheartedly believed in the socialist agenda or whether it was only its concern with the welfare of the common people that struck a personal chord. The dramatic political developments of 1911 may have proved too much for the young artist, as suggested by a short poem that he contributed to the magazine *Collection of socialist poetry* (*Shakaishugi shishū*): 'My arms are far too feeble to destroy my paintbrush and hold [Maxim] Gorky's hands'.[17] He subsequently distanced himself from the socialist movement and his production of socialist-related illustrations ceased.

Yumeji's artistic path after 1911 reveals a different trajectory, but Yumeji's upbringing and his beginnings as a struggling student, illustrator and supporter of socialist thought coalesced to shape his future artistic career. What is most significant when discussing Yumeji's early period is that the socialist platform directed his focus on the lives of common people and offered him a springboard for the development of his visual expression. Moreover, mass-media publications provided Yumeji with an outlet through which he achieved public recognition as an artist.

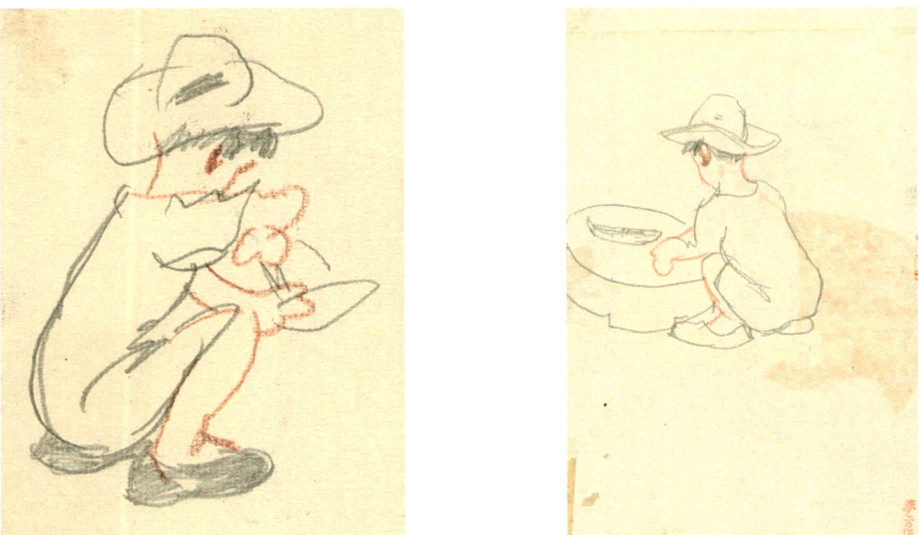

Fig. 1.17. *Squatting child* (recto)
*Squatting child over a tub* (verso)
18.3 x 11.0 cm
Date: c. 1915(?)
Seal (stamp): *Yumeji no saku (work by Yumeji)* (verso)

## Notes

**1.** The Takehisa Yumeji Art Museum, Yumeji Art Museum and Kanazawa Yuwaku Yumeji Museum organised special exhibitions commemorating the 130th anniversary of Yumeji's birth. The travelling exhibition at the Takashimaya department stores, *Seitan 130nen Takehisa Yumeji ten: beru epokku o ikita Yumeji to Lotorekku* (see under Okabe Masayuki in Bibliography), finished in October 2014. The title of this event was inspired by the award to the Yumeji Art Museum of a Michelin guide star in 2007, in which Yumeji was described as the 'Lautrec of Japan'. As part of the celebrations, Yumeji's art was also chosen to adorn public transport: Okayama's oldest streetcar (in operation since 1953), the *Kuro*, showcased designs of Yumeji's work as conceptualised by the famous industrial designer, Mitooka Eiji. Three sightseeing buses were also decorated with Yumeji's art.

**2.** These include the Takehisa Yumeji Art Museum (Takehisa Yumeji Bijutsukan) in Tokyo; Yumeji Art Museum (Yumeji Kyōdo Bijutsukan) in Okayama; Takehisa Yumeji Ikaho Memorial [Museum] (Takehisa Yumeji Ikaho Kinenkan) in Ikaho, Gunma prefecture; Kanazawa Yuwaku Yumeji Museum (Kanazawa Yuwaku Yumeji-kan) in Kanazawa, Ishikawa prefecture; Sakata City Takehisa Yumeji Art Museum (Sakata Takehisa Yumeji Bijutsukan) in Sakata, Yamagata prefecture; and Nikkō Takehisa Yumeji Museum (Nikkō Takehisa Yumeji Bijutsukan). In 2011, Yumeji's granddaughter, Takehisa Minami, also opened the Gallery Yumeji (Gyararii Yumeji) in the Zōshigaya area in Tokyo where the artist lived.

**3.** The biographical details of Yumeji's life in this essay have been drawn from Kawano, ed., *Yumeji 1884–1934*; Kanazawa Cultural Promotion Foundation, ed., *Takehisa Yumeji*; Ogawa, *Motto shiritai Takehisa Yumeji*; Yamamoto, *Oshiminaki seishun*; and Ogura Tadao, 'Yumeji no shōgai: gaka toshite no shuppatsu' ('Yumeji's life and his artistic beginnings'), in Yūjōbō, ed., *Taiyō 20*, 21–27. Unless otherwise indicated, all translations are by the author.

**4.** Ogura, 'Yumeji no shōgai', in Yūjōbō, ed., *Taiyō 20*, 24.

**5.** The present-day Waseda Jitsugyō Gakkō runs only to the high school level, but during Yumeji's time it had a two- to three-year vocational school component; Yumeji was enrolled in this program.

**6.** This note was jotted down on the back of a portrait of Yumeji taken at the Kudō Photography Studio (Kudō Shashinkan) in Nishiki-chō, Kanda; the postcard is now housed in the Kanazawa Yuwaku Yumeji Museum. See Kanazawa Cultural Promotion Foundation, ed., *Takehisa Yumeji* and Nagata Mikio, 'Shafu, shosei, Heiminsha no koro' ('Rickshaw man, student and the Heiminsha'), in Yūjōbō, ed., *Taiyō 20*, 28–32.

**7.** *The daily commoner's news* eventually ceased circulation on 29 January 1905 and the company would later launch the daily, *The commoner's news* (*Nikkan heimin shinbun*), which was in circulation from January to April 1907.

**8.** Kawano, ed., *Yumeji 1884–1934*, 356. From Takehisa Yumeji, 'My first debt' ('Watashi no saisho no shakkin'), n.p; quoted in ibid., *Yumeji 1884–1934*, 356.

**9.** Iino, 'Dokuro no jidai; Takehisa Yumeji ni okeru hankō no genki' ('The age of skulls: Takehisa Yumeji and the origin of his resistance'), in Kawano, ed., *Yumeji 1884–1934*, 306. From Arahata Kanson's autobiography, *Kanson jiden*.

**10.** Kawano, ed., Yumeji 1884–1934, 356. From Arahata Kanson's autobiography, *Kanson jiden*.

**11.** This is excerpted from Yumeji's response to the first Bunten (Monbushō Bijutsu Tenrankai) or Ministry of Education Art Exhibition in 1907. See Kawano, ed., *Yumeji 1884–1934*, 359. From Takehisa Yumeji, 'The path I have taken' ('Watashi ga aruite kita michi'), *The middle-school student* (*Chūgakusei*), vol. 1 no. 8 (January 1923). Reproduced in Takehisa Yumeji, *Sunagaki*, 21. On Fujishima Takeji and his contributions to Western-style painting, see Winther-Tamaki, *Maximum embodiment*, 104–7.

**12.** From *The weekly commoner's news*, 24 January 1907. They were wed in Ushigome in Tokyo; the article demonstrates that events in Yumeji's life and his art are interwoven. See Ogura, 'Yumeji no shōgai', in Yūjōbō, ed., *Taiyō 20*, 26.

**13.** Quoted in Ogawa, *Takehisa Yumeji ten*, 133, and Nagata, *Yumeji nikki*.

**14.** Ogawa, *Takehisa Yumeji ten*, 133.

**15.** In an attempt to suppress the increasing popularity of the socialist movement among workers and the common people at this time, the government used this incident as an example of the potential risks of conducting anti-government activities. For more details, see Kanzaki, *Taigyaku jiken*.

**16.** Kawano, ed., *Yumeji 1884–1934*, 363–64.

**17.** Nagata Mikio, 'Yumeji no shōgai: gaka toshite no shuppatsu' ('Yumeji's life and his artistic beginnings'), in Yūjōbō, ed., *Taiyō 20*, 26

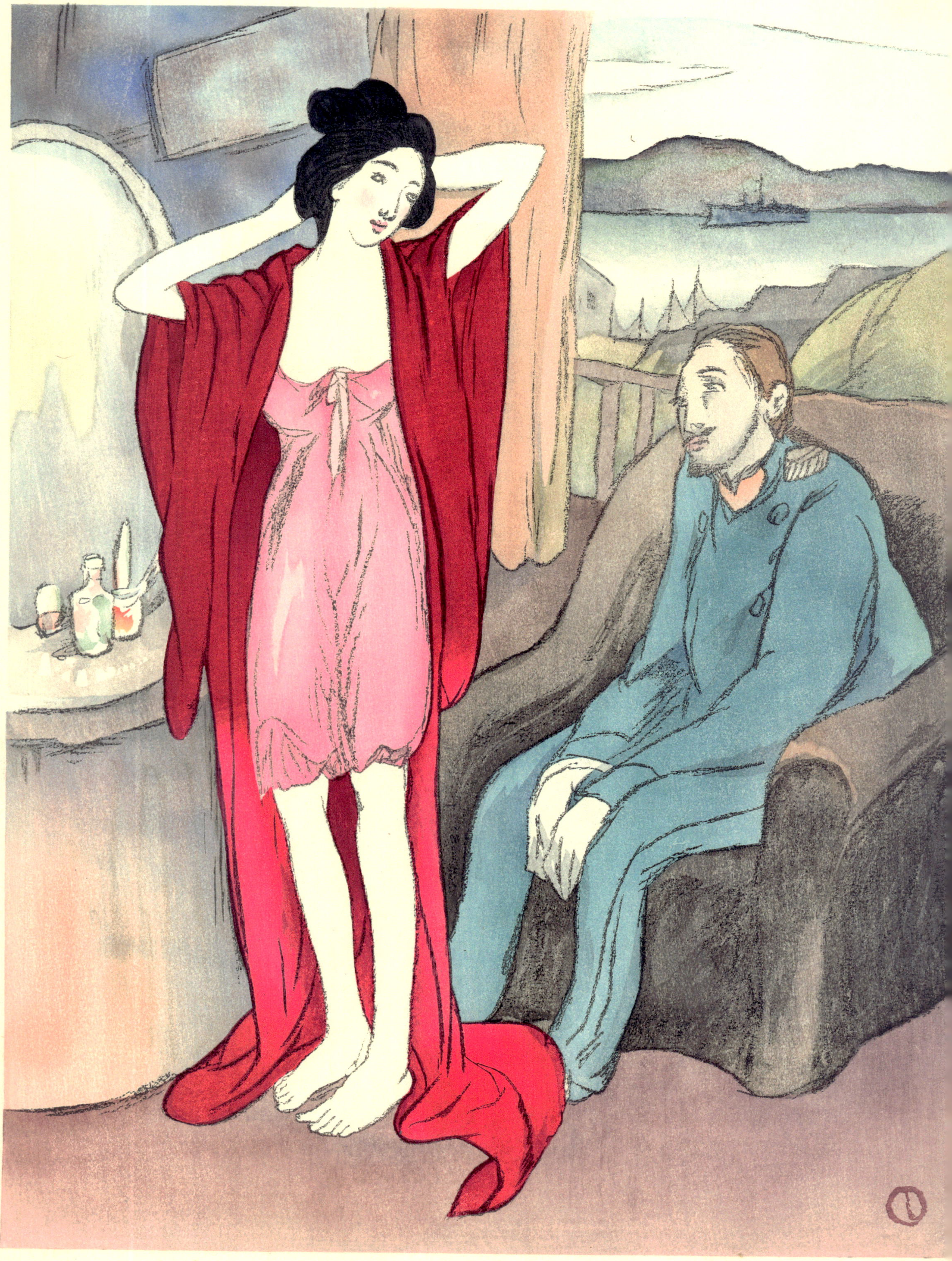

# An independent artist in an era of change: the later years, 1912–1934

**Sabine Schenk**

Takehisa Yumeji's art has frequently been interpreted as representative of the lyrical, sentimental style associated with 'Taishō Romanticism' (*Taishō roman*).[1] Though the relevance of this term is still much debated, the popular perception of 'Taishō Romanticism' continues today in Japan with the production of related imagery, films and cafes following Taishō- and early Shōwa-era styles.[2] The focus of Yumeji's paintings and graphic work on the portrayal of 'fragile' female figures and the theme of romantic love also help underscore the perception of his art as emblematic of the aesthetic of 'Taishō Romanticism' . The period from the 1910s to the mid-1920s likewise witnessed a thriving popular culture and coincided with the emergence of modern graphic design. All these elements coalesced to nurture an urban lifestyle and media environment that were crucial to the rise of artists and illustrators like Yumeji.[3]

Early in his career Yumeji formed a reputation for his illustrations in socialist publications, but even at this time he had already begun experimenting with different styles and genres to fashion a varied, compelling corpus of work that found broad reception among his contemporaries. This essay will examine Yumeji's creative activity after 1912, the year corresponding to his first solo exhibition of paintings and his growing artistic independence. It will also touch upon the impact of the Great Kantō Earthquake of 1 September 1923 on his art practice, and his travels to the United States and Europe from 1931 to 1933.[4]

## *Yumeji as an emerging artist and poet*

Several events in 1912 contribute to Yumeji's establishment as an artist and poet. Significant among these was the release of his most famous poem 'Yoimachigusa' (Evening primrose), which was released that year in the magazine *Maiden* (*Shōjo*). The verse speaks of a man's emotional loss when his lover marries another: '*yoimachigusa*' refers to the nocturnal blossoming primrose, but the words *yoi* (evening) and *machi* (from the verb *matsu*, to wait) carry the additional meaning as an expression of the man's feelings of abandonment. In actuality, the text alludes to Yumeji's separation from his ex-wife Kishi Tamaki (1882–1945) and his unrequited love for Hasegawa Kata (1890–1967).[5] The better-known three-line version was first published in Yumeji's celebrated poem (*kouta*) anthology *Sunday* (*Dontaku*) in 1913:

*matedo kurasedo konu hito o / yoimachigusa no yarusenasa / koyohi wa tsuki mo denu sō na*

*I waited a long time for the one who will not return;*
*the sorrow of the evening primrose—*
*it seems that the moon will not appear tonight.*[6]

Yumeji composed the poems and was responsible for the frontispiece (*kuchi-e*) and the illustrations. The artist Onchi Kōshirō (1891–1955), a member of Yumeji's circle of followers, designed the cover to the 1913 edition.

The melancholic tone of 'Yoimachigusa' typifies Yumeji's verse but its sentiment is equally manifest in his

Previous page
*The dressing table*
From the series
*Twelve views of Nagasaki*
(see fig. 2.5, p. 31)

visual art. Yumeji writes earlier in the 1909 *Spring* (*Haru no maki*) volume of his *The Yumeji collection of work* (*Yumeji gashū*), that he aimed to convey lyrical emotions in his paintings. This self-promotion as a poet-painter emphasises the interconnectedness between text and image in Yumeji's art practice. His focus on a visual artistic expression was driven in large part by economic necessity; nonetheless, there are a sizable number of literary works within his oeuvre. These range from short prose texts, illustrated books, contributions to women and children's magazines as well as essays on art history. Imagery plays an important role in many of his literary pieces, and in these text and image coalesce to form a unified whole. When Yumeji's friend, the composer Ōno Tadasuke (1895–1929), set 'Yoimachigusa' to music in 1918, it was enormously popular. It remains so today, and in 1966 the poem was selected as the inscription for a memorial stone to Yumeji in the park, Kōrakuen, in Okayama.

In 1912, Yumeji had another career breakthrough with his first solo exhibition. By this time, Yumeji had been in Tokyo for over a decade and his path to becoming an artist had not been without its challenges. From 1904, he had enrolled in painting lessons with the art group White Horse Society (Hakubakai) as he pondered whether he should pursue further art training. In his 1923 essay 'The path I have taken' ('Watashi no aruite kita michi'), Yumeji describes his introduction to Okada Saburōsuke (1869–1939).[7] Okada was an influential *yōga* ('Western painting') artist and professor of Western art at the Tokyo School of Fine Arts (Tōkyō Bijutsu Gakkō). Yumeji showed him a watercolour and inquired whether he would recommend his formal study of *yōga*, to which Okada responded that self-study was perhaps a better option.[8] Scholarly interpretations of this anecdote vary. Some maintain that Okada's advice should be seen as proof that he did not consider Yumeji's efforts worthy of merit. Others speculate that Okada might have recognised Yumeji's natural talent, believing that institutionalised education would spoil it. We cannot know for certainty whether Okada actually approved of Yumeji's artistic endeavours, even though Okada appears to have supported Yumeji in his later efforts. However, both interpretations do point to an increasingly formalised system of art education emerging in Japan during the late nineteenth to early twentieth centuries, one that was modelled on the European and North American traditions of art academies and salons. Such a system may not have been a good fit with a self-taught individual like Yumeji. Ultimately, Okada's advice resulted in Yumeji's distancing himself from the Japanese fine-art establishment.

Seen against this backdrop it is not surprising that, with the exception of his commercial illustrations, Yumeji's more artistic endeavours were not well known by his contemporaries. In addition to his illustrated volumes, such as his 1912 *Spring dawn* (*Haru no kawatare*) from *Island of blossoming cherries* (*Sakura saku shima*) (fig. 2.1), Yumeji was actively turning out watercolour, oil and *nihonga* paintings. He eventually amassed enough work to stage his first solo exhibition, which ran from 23 November to 2 December 1912 at the Kyoto Prefectural Library (fig. 2.2). The exhibition did much to raise awareness of Yumeji's art beyond his commercial designs. The *nihonga* ('Japanese painting') artist Nakazawa Reisen commented on the show's success in this regard and in passing compares it with the annual government sponsored Ministry of Education Art Exhibition (Monbushō Bijutsu Tenrankai, or Bunten) held nearby:

> *At the same time that Yumeji released the* [*volumes of*] Yumeji gashū *he was also producing lyrical illustrations for daily newspapers and, of course, for many magazines. This corresponded to the height of his popularity, but there was only a handful of people who actually knew what he created outside his illustrations—the over one hundred oil paintings* (abura-e), nihonga, *watercolours, pen drawings arranged at the venue were viewed with geniality and admiration. It* [*the exhibition*] *was crowded everyday with visitors, and not to put too fine a point on it, it was rumoured that there were considerably more visitors here than at the Bunten exhibition.*[9]

One painting in the exhibition, *Green fruit* (*Aoi konomi*), would later reappear as a print by Katō Junji (1885–1961) (fig. 2.3b).[10]

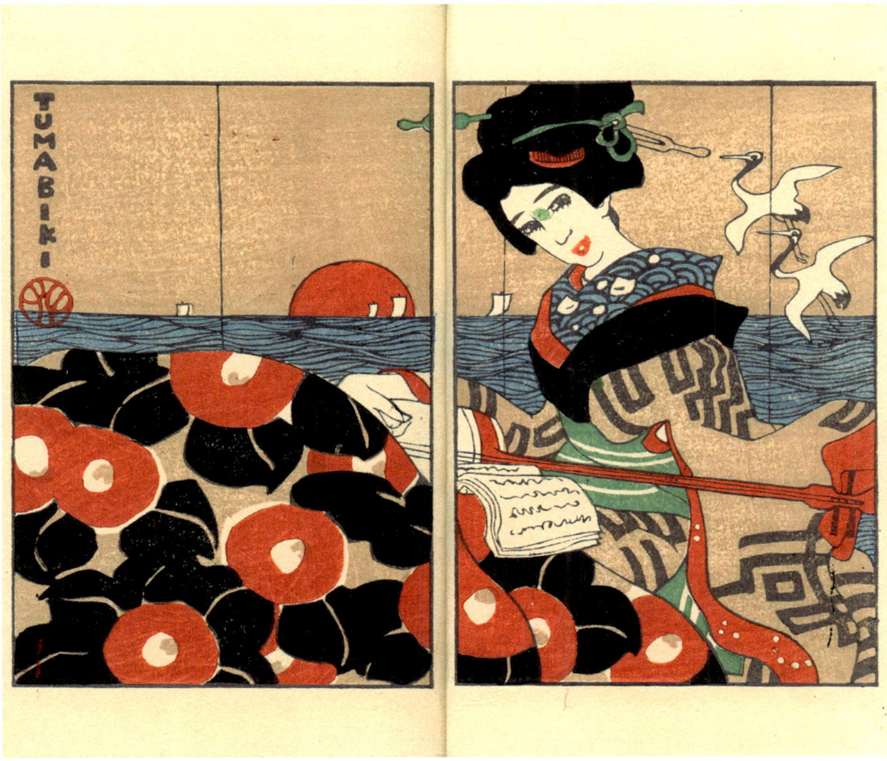


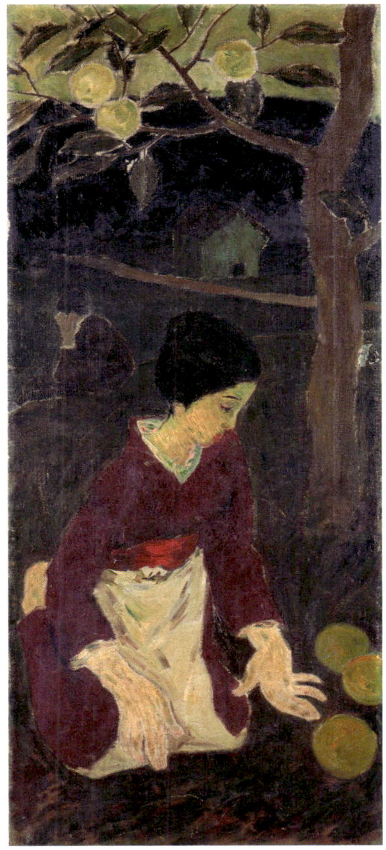

Fig. 2.1. *Strumming the strings* (*Tumabiki*) (frontispiece)
From *Spring dawn* (*Haru no kawatare*, 春のかはたれ)
Vol. 1 of *Island of blossoming cherries* (*Sakura saku shima*, 桜さく島)
18.0 x 21.2 cm
Date: 1912
Seal: artist's 'grass' (*kusa*) seal
Publisher: Rakuyōdō

Of the two known volumes of *Island of blossoming cherries*, *Spring dawn* was released first in February 1912, followed by *Unknown world* (*Mishiranu sekai*) in April (see fig. 3.9a–b). Both have undecorated covers and are bound in the traditional *fukuro-toji* format. The last page of both books announce three further volumes: *Memorandum of shamisen* (*Shamisen no memo*), *Japanese girl* (*Nihon no musume*) and *Farewell on the beach* (*Hama no wakare*). Yumeji produced the poetry, the colour frontispieces (*kuchi-e*) and fourteen black-and-white woodblock-printed illustrations for *Spring dawn*. The double-paged frontispiece shows a woman in a beautifully patterned kimono playing the *shamisen*, a songbook resting on her knees. A *kotatsu* cover with a bold camellia design fills the lower left. The figure is set against an ocean vista defined by stylised wave patterns, sailing boats, a setting red sun and cranes in flight. This background view is divided into vertical panels, suggesting that it is not an actual scene, rather a folding screen composition.

The title of the frontispiece, *Tumabiki* (*tsumabiki*, 爪弾き, 'strumming the strings'), appears in romanised script in the upper left, followed by the artist's circular red seal with the character 'grass' (*kusa*, 艸). Yumeji employs the character *kusa* (borrowed from the cursive 'grass' mode of calligraphic script, or *sōsho* 艸[草]書) in one of his art seals, perhaps as a reference to the immediate, sketchy and cursive nature underlying his work.

Fig. 2.2. *First love* (*Hatsukoi*, 初恋)
Oil on canvas, 91.0 x 39.5 cm
Date: 1912
Yumeji Art Museum, Okayama

This painting was featured in Yumeji's first art exhibition at the Kyoto Prefectural Library in late 1912. It is based on the 1897 poem 'First love' (*Hatsukoi*) by Shimazaki Tōson (1872–1943):

*When I saw you under the apple tree*
*with your hair swept up for the first time*
*I thought you were the flower*
*in the flower comb you wore in front*

*when you gently extended your soft white hand*
*and gave me an apple*
*it was the very first time I loved someone*
*with the pale red of the autumn fruit*

*when my sigh unknowingly*
*passed through the threads of your hair*
*I drank of your passion*
*From the cup of my tender love*

*the narrow, natural path*
*under the trees in the apple grove*
*who first trod this path?*
*whose steps left the first traces?*
*you asked, how lovely, I thought.*[1]

1. Translation from Rimer and Gessel, eds., *The Columbia anthology of modern Japanese literature*, 25–26.

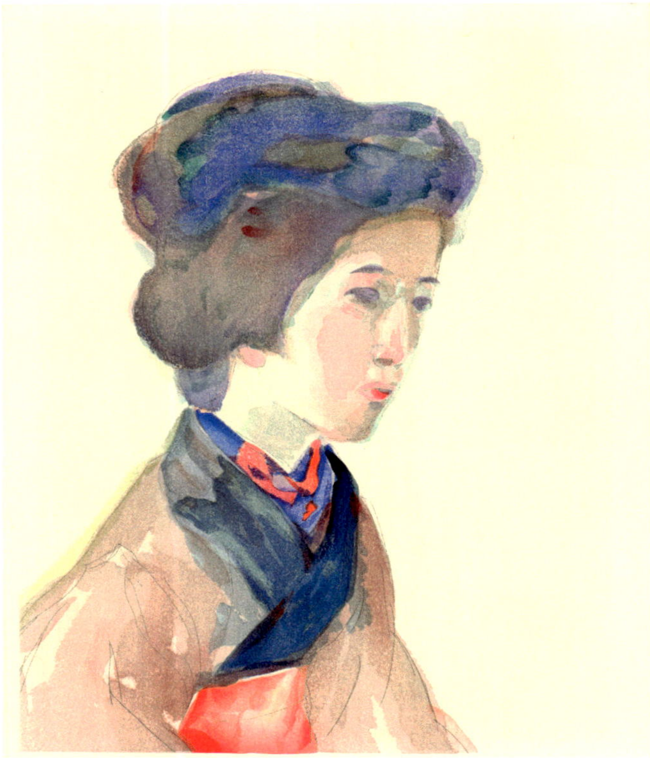

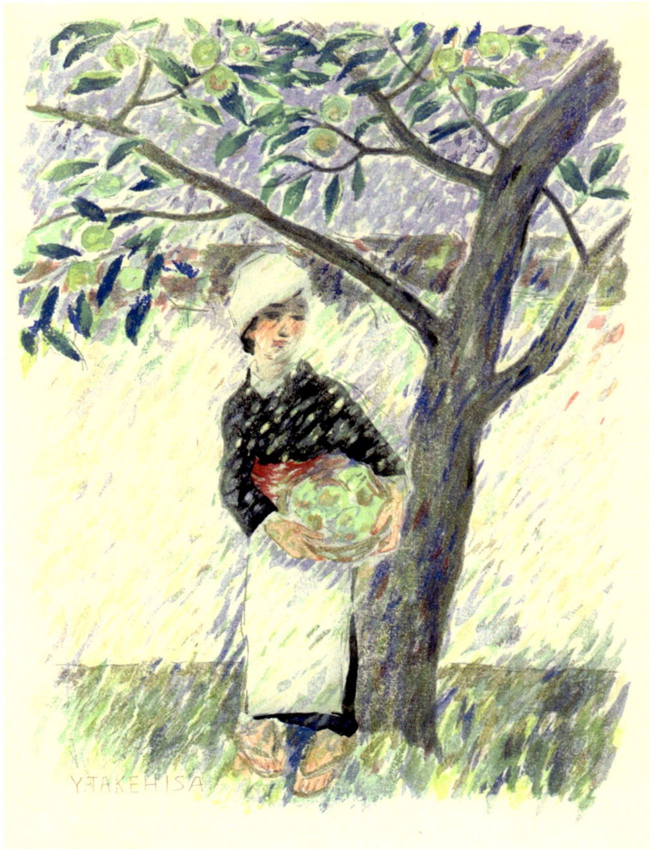


Fig. 2.3a. *Young woman* (*Shōjo*, 少女)
From *A collection of poetry and prints by Yumeji* (*Yumeji shigashū*, 夢二詩画集)
31.3 x 25.8 cm
Date: 1941
Publisher: Katō Hanga Kenkyūjo

Fig. 2.3b. *Spring sunlight* (*Haru no hizashi*, 春の陽ざし)
From *A collection of poetry and prints by Yumeji* (*Yumeji shigashū*, 夢二詩画集)
36.7 x 28.6 cm
Date: 1941
Signature: *Y. Takehisa*
Publisher: Katō Hanga Kenkyūjo

*Young woman* is characteristic of Yumeji's later portrayals of women in its subtle visualisation of an aloof female figure. It is a woodblock-printed reproduction of a watercolour that he painted in 1930 entitled *Daughter* (*Musume*). *Spring sunlight* is based on a painting—originally entitled *Green fruit* (*Aoi konomi*)—that was displayed at Yumeji's first exhibition held in Kyoto in 1912 (see also fig. 2.2). By this time, Yumeji was well known for his illustrations, but the Kyoto show introduced his hitherto unappreciated paintings to a broader audience. This composition illustrates a figure with head cloth and apron holding a basket with green fruit, perhaps just picked from the adjacent tree; the background wall suggests a private garden.

*Spring sunlight* is representative of the artist's earlier responses to Western-style painting (*yōga*): the scene, rendered in an almost 'Pointillist' painting mode, is caste in shimmering light. For other images from this set, see figs. 1.3, 3.12; cat. 73–79.

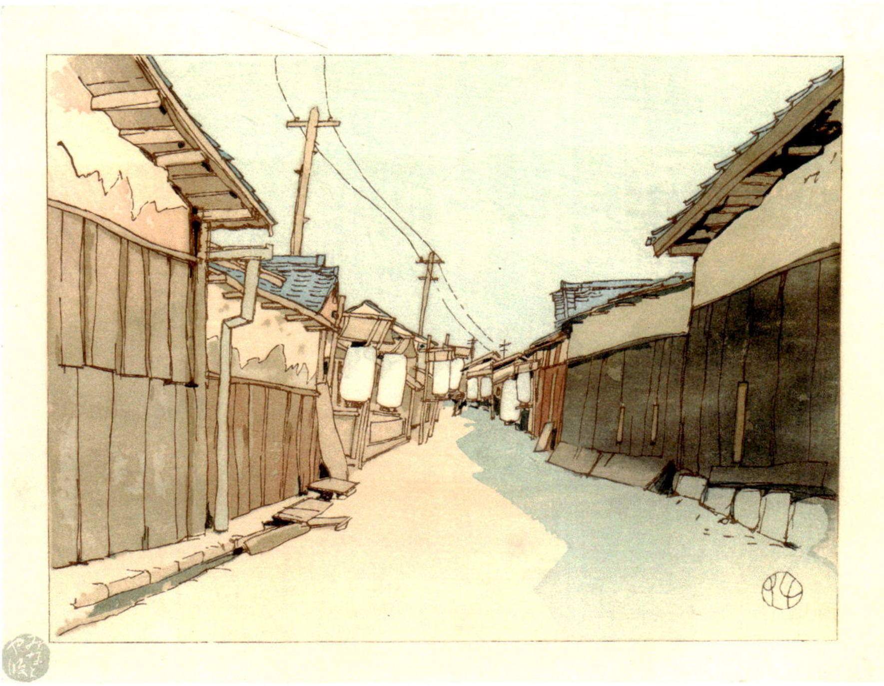

Fig. 2.4. *Paper lanterns* (*Chōchin*, ちょうちん)
25.4 x 32.0 cm
Date: 1914
Seals: artist's 'grass' (*kusa*) seal, Minatoya publisher's trademark
Publisher: Minatoya

Paper lanterns are visible in the middle ground of this deserted street scene. The verticality of the telephone poles contrasts the horizontal lines of the wires and the street. Such landscape views devoid of figures are rare in Yumeji's oeuvre. The unusually realistic style of this print also points to the reciprocal influence between Yumeji and his followers, including Fujimori Shizuo.

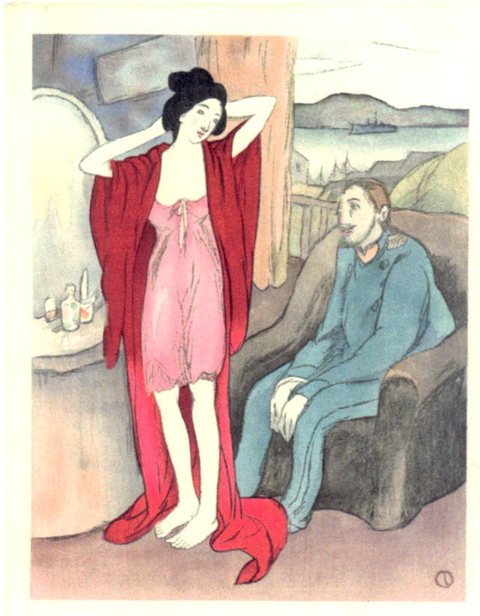

Fig. 2.5. *The dressing table* (*Keshō*, 化粧台)
From the series *Twelve views of Nagasaki* (*Nagasaki jūnikei*, 長崎十二景)
39.9 x 30.5 cm
Date: 1941
Seal: artist's comma-shaped (*tomoe*) seal (as seen on original painting)
Publisher: Katō Hanga Kenkyūjo

In this scene a prostitute clad in Western-style lingerie and an under-kimono stands before a blond-haired officer seated in an armchair in what is presumably a brothel catering to a foreign clientele. The view behind them opens onto Nagasaki bay, an anchored ship visible in the distance. The sensuality underlying this scene is indicative of 'erotic, grotesque, nonsense' (*ero guro nansensu*)—a term describing the Japanese equivalent of the 'flapper age'—of the late 1910s and the 1920s.[1] For another image from this set, see cat. 81.

1. See Merritt and Yamada, 'Yumeji's Twelve views of Nagasaki', and Jackson, 'Fashioning the "Greater Taishō" era', 110.

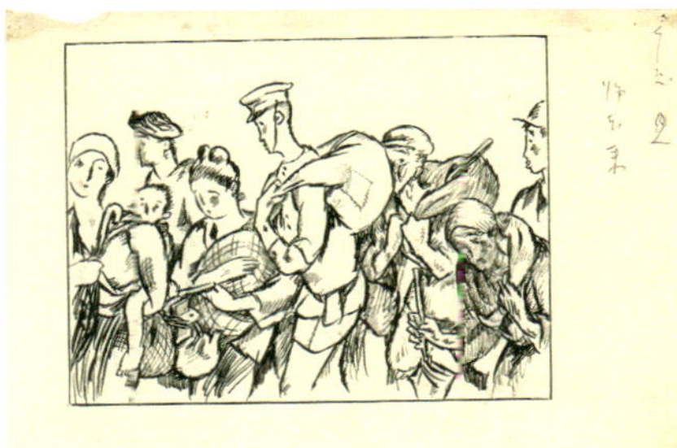

Fig. 2.6. *Returning home* (*Kikyorai* 帰去来)
Preparatory drawing for *True pictures of the Tokyo calamity* (*Tōkyō sainan gashin*, 東京災難画信)
19.0 x 28.1 cm
Date: 1923
Inscription: (partially legible) *Kikyorai*

After the catastrophic Great Kantō Earthquake of 1 September 1923, Yumeji wandered through Tokyo and made sketches of the ruins he saw around him. The newspaper, *Miyako shinbun*, published several as *True pictures of the Tokyo calamity*, and this drawing is very similar to print no. 19 in the series. Here, the composition shows a group of displaced residents escaping the devastation of Tokyo to return to their hometowns.

In 1914, together with his ex-wife Tamaki, Yumeji founded the Minatoya (Harbour Shop) Bookstore (Minatoya Ezōshi-ten) in order to generate income for Tamaki and their children. Located in Gofuku-chō in Tokyo's Nihonbashi district, the Minatoya sold graphic pieces such as single-sheet woodblock prints, stationery as well as everyday items designed and produced by Yumeji. The Minatoya was, however, not simply a shop. From the outset, it was a popular gathering point for admirers, writers and young artists, most notably, the members of the group Tsukuhae (Moon Glow) established by Onchi and his fellow students Tanaka Kyōkichi (1892–1915) and Fujimori Shizuo (1891–1943). Their journal, *Moon glow* (*Tsukuhae*), promoted modern graphics and poetry.[11] They and other young *sōsaku hanga* ('Creative print') artists formed a small 'salon' and the Minatoya served as an exhibition venue. Onchi, who had known Yumeji since 1909, was particularly influenced by his work. The Minatoya also represented a publisher's 'brand name', as demonstrated on a 1914 woodblock print that includes a title cartouche reading *Minatoya Ezōshi-ten* (Minatoya Bookstore).[12] The Minatoya seal comprised a circular cartouche, with *Minatoya han* (printed by Minatoya) inscribed in *hiragana* script. Despite its lofty beginnings, the shop was not an economic success and was forced to close after only two years. Nevertheless, the single-sheet prints done for the Minatoya, such as *Paper lanterns* (fig. 2.4), are much coveted today, especially since to date only nine such Minatoya designs have been documented.[13]

At the Minatoya, Yumeji met the art student Kasai Hikono (1896–1920), who is generally acknowledged to have been the artist's great love.[14] In 1916, Yumeji moved to Kyoto to live with Hikono and the following year, they travelled to the hot-spring resort Yuwaku near Kanazawa, today the location of the Kanazawa Yuwaku Yumeji Museum (Kanazawa Yuwaku Yumeji-kan) dedicated to the artist's work and part of the Kanazawa Cultural Promotion Foundation (Kanazawa Bunka Shinkō Zaidan). In 1918, Hikono became ill with tuberculosis en route to Kyushu where she was to meet Yumeji in Beppu (he was himself delayed when his son Fujihiko suddenly became sick in Nagasaki). Hikono's health worsened, forcing her return to Tokyo. Yumeji was subsequently barred from seeing her, and she would die just two years later, in 1920.

From 1914 onwards, Yumeji was designing illustrations for magazines, such as *The children's companion* (*Kodomo no tomo*). During this time, he also created illustrations for sheet-music covers for the *Senow music scores* released by music publisher Senō Kōyō (1891–1961) (see figs. 2.7, 4.5, 4.7, 4.8, 4.10. 4.11, 4.13; cat. 16–32). Moreover, he mounted work in several exhibitions, including the 1919 show at the Mitsukoshi department store in Nihonbashi that featured paintings of women and children.[15] While in Nagasaki in 1918 and awaiting his son's recovery, Yumeji stayed with the art collector Nagami Tokutarō. Once back in Tokyo, Yumeji produced two sets of watercolours for Nagami as a gift: *Twelve views of Nagasaki* (*Nagasaki jūnikei*, 1920) and *Ten subjects of women* (*Onna jūdai*, 1921) (see fig. 2.5; cat. 81; fig. 3.6; cat. 66–67, respectively). The international feel of Nagasaki permeates these examples, as seen as the eleventh painting (and later print) in the Nagasaki suite, *The dressing table* (fig. 2.5). Yumeji forwarded the first three paintings to Nagami shortly after his stay, however, both series were not completed before 1920.[16] Katō Junji later issued both sets as prints, in 1941 and 1937–1938, respectively.

During Hikono's hospitalisation in 1918, Yumeji met Sasaki Kaneyo (Oyō, 1904–1980), who like Tamaki and Hikono before her, became an important model for Yumeji and greatly impacted his style of the 1920s (for photographs of these women, see p. 22).[17] A professional studio model, Oyō worked at the Tokyo School of Fine Arts for artists including Fujishima Takeji (1867–1943). She also posed for the illustrator and poster designer Itō Seiu (1882–1961) who was renowned for his sadomasochistic compositions.[18] Yumeji's and Oyō's house in Tokyo's Shibuya ward was destroyed in the Great Kantō Earthquake, and today a stele marks its location. The couple's relationship ended in 1925 following Yumeji's scandalous affair with the female author Yamada Junko, who the press of the time labelled as the 'Nora of the Taishō era'.[19]

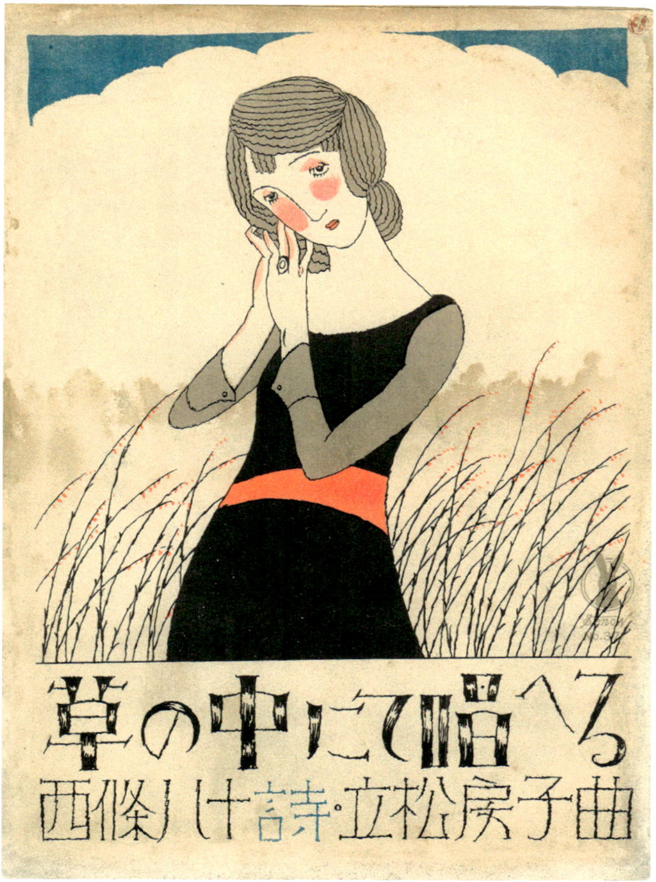


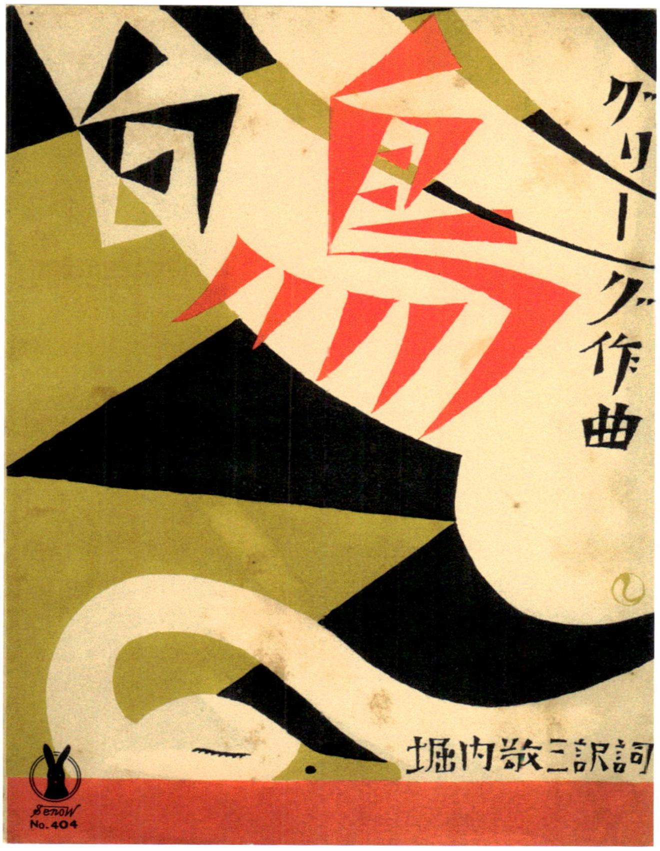


Fig. 2.7. *Singing in the meadow* (*Kusa no naka nite utaeru*, 草の中にて唱へる),
From *Senow music scores* (*Senow gakufu*, セノオ楽譜), no. 371
31.0 x 22.6 cm
Date: 1924
Publisher: Senow Ongaku Shuppansha
Composer: Tatematsu Fusako (1891–1992)
Verse: Saijō Yaso (1892–1970)

This illustrated music score is for a vocal solo. The poet and songwriter Saijō Yaso wrote the lyrics, which were performed by the soprano and this piece's composer Tatematsu Fusako (1891–1992). The composition shows a woman in modern dress standing in a field of flowering grasses; she tilts her head downwards as if deep in thought. Although the woman's clothing and hairstyle hint at a less nostalgic and less romanticised portrayal of the type frequently encountered in Yumeji's work following the Great Kantō Earthquake of 1 September 1923, it nonetheless showcases the sweet melancholic sentiment characteristic of his earlier 'Yumeji-style beauties'.

Fig. 2.8. *A swan* (*Shiratori*, 白鳥)
From *Senow music scores* (*Senow gakufu*, セノオ楽譜), no. 404
30.3 x 22.7 cm
Date: 1926
Seal: artist's comma-shaped (*tomoe*) seal
Publisher: Senow Ongaku Shuppansha
Composer: Edvard Grieg (1843–1907)
Translator: Horiuchi Keizō (1897–1983)

The song for this score is based on a poem by Henrik Ibsen (1828–1906); it was set to music by Edvard Grieg under the title *Ein Schwan*. Particularly in his later work Yumeji experiments with abstract Cubist forms: here the characters of the Japanese title (*Shiratori*) are highly stylised and this accords with the overall representation in which the form of the swan seems to dissolve into geometrical shapes.

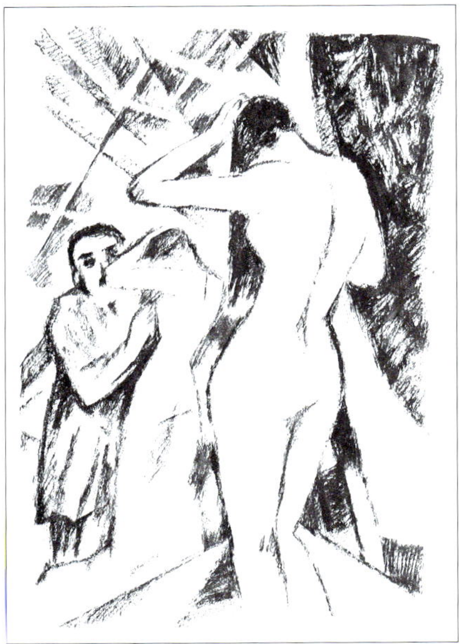

Fig. 2.9. *Departure* (*Shuppan*, 出帆)
26.5 x 19.0 cm
Date: 1972
Publisher: Ryūseikaku

This image is included in a posthumous hardback edition of Yumeji's semi-autobiographical illustrated novel. It is bound in cloth and shows a stylised embossed image of a sailing ship on the cover; the case for the book is decorated with a wave design. Four colour plates depicting Yumeji's *bijinga* paintings, a biography and an epilogue by the editor Sawada Ishirō have been added to the images and texts, which were originally published as a serialised contribution to the newspaper *Miyako shinbun*. This illustration belongs to episode 57 and portrays an artist sketching a nude model in his studio. The perspective is rendered in such a way that allows the viewer to see the model, the artist at work and his canvas, thus constructing a layered 'image in image' effect. The background space softens into diagonal and triangular shapes. The protagonist of the story is the artist Yamaoka Santarō, whose lover Ohana is fashioned after Yumeji's paramour Oyō. The text and date of the original text suggest that the intended subject(s) of this illustration are Ohana/Oyō.

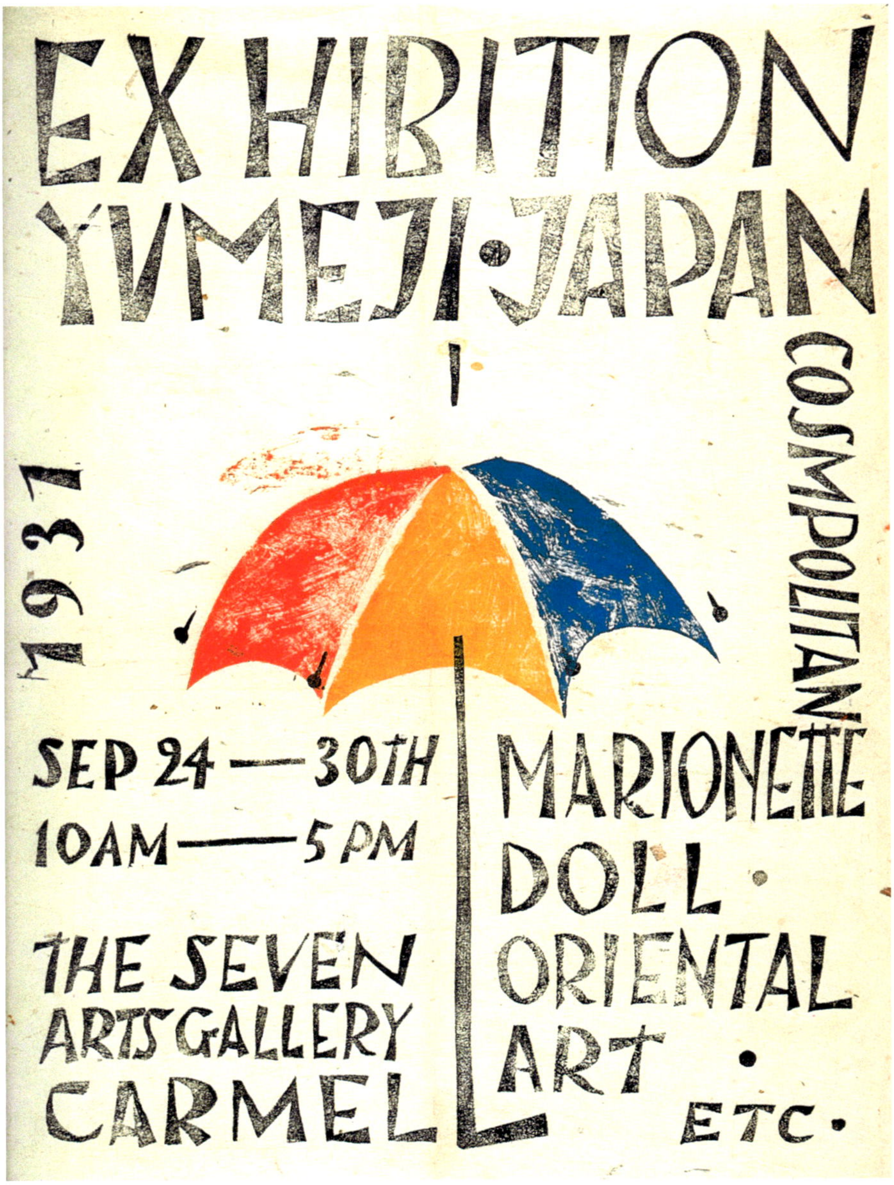


Fig. 2.10. Exhibition poster
41.9 x 29.6 cm
Date: 1931

This poster advertises the *Exhibition: Yumeji · Japan* (*Cosmopolitan Marionette Doll Oriental Art · Etc*), which ran from 24 to 30 September 1931 at the Seven Arts Gallery in Carmel, California. This show was organised during Yumeji's stay in California and it marked the first such event held outside the Japanese community in that state. While some of the twenty works on display were made in California, the majority were pieces Yumeji brought from Japan. As the poster indicates, the exhibition also included handmade dolls and marionettes. Yumeji began crafting dolls in Japan and continued to produce these while in California (see cat. 2.11).[1]

1. Sodei, *Yumeji ikoku e no tabi*, 64–67.

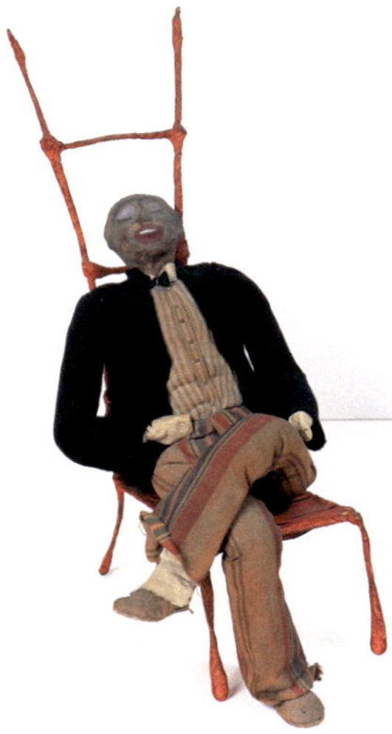

Fig. 2.11. *Male doll*
Paper, cloth and wire, 32 cm (h)
Date: early Shōwa era
Yumeji Art Museum, Okayama

Yumeji also created three-dimensional objects, including handmade dolls for which he used antique fabrics.[1] He worked with the Sunday Society (Dontakusha), a group of artisans who wielded influence in the world of early Shōwa-era doll craftsmanship. His first public doll display was with them in 1930. At this time, Yumeji was probably searching for new forms of artistic expression in the face of his declining popularity. During his stay in the United States in 1931, Yumeji continued to make and exhibit dolls and marionettes.

1. Yamada Tokubei, 'Yumeji ningyō no hanashi' ('A discussion of Yumeji's dolls'), in Yūjōbō, ed., *Taiyō 20*, 88–89.

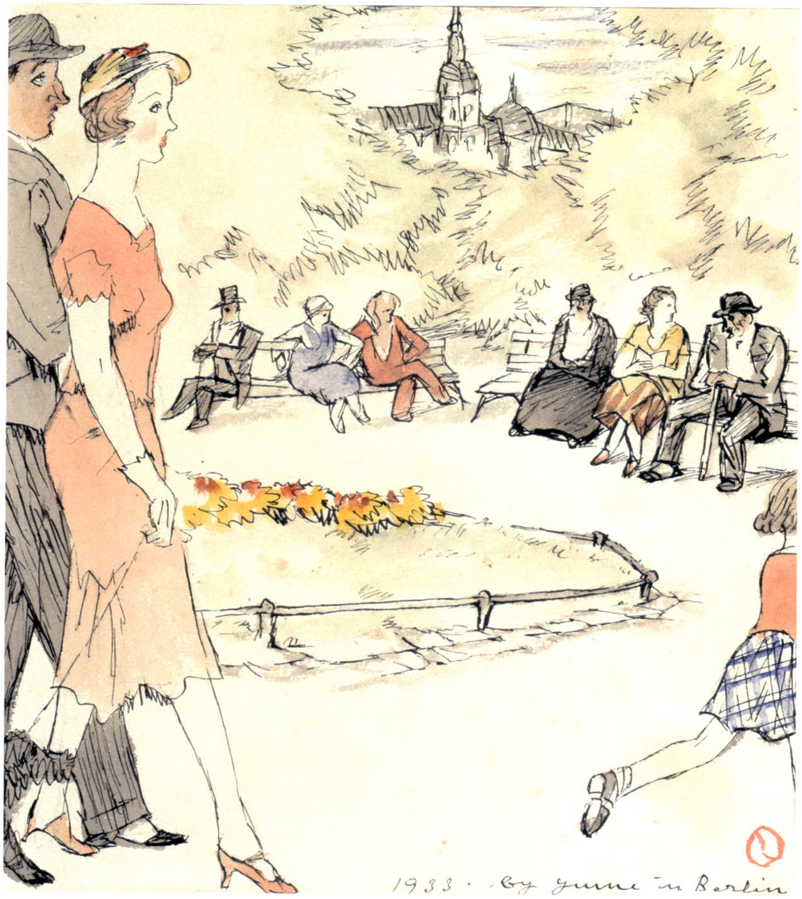


Fig. 2.12. *Park in Berlin*
(*Berurin no kōen*, ベルリンの公園)
27.0 x 24.0 cm
Date: 1933
Signature/seal: *1933 · by Yume in Berlin* with artist's comma-shaped (*tomoe*) seal
Yumeji Art Museum, Okayama

This delicately rendered ink and watercolour drawing illustrates a park scene in Berlin during Yumeji's stay there in 1933. In the middle ground people seated on benches are enjoying the day; the grove behind them opens onto a city view behind. The figures in the foreground—a couple with a dog and a young child—are cropped on either side of the composition. This drawing captures the atmosphere of a day out in Berlin. It is an outstanding example of the types of sketches and drawings Yumeji made during his travels in the United States and Europe in the early 1930s.

### *The Great Kantō Earthquake and changing aesthetics*

On around on midday 1 September 1923, an earthquake struck Tokyo, Yokohama and surrounding areas; the 7.9 quake and the subsequent tsunami and conflagration resulted in a death toll estimated at 140,000.[20] The Great Kantō Earthquake was a watershed event, the enormity of the quake's devastation proving a catalyst for significant shifts in Japanese politics, society and culture. This included a further decline in the demand for 'romantic' imagery, an aesthetic embodied in the 'Yumeji-style beauty' (*Yumeji-shiki bijin*). For Yumeji, who continued to produce work in this signature style, the changing tastes after the earthquake had serious repercussions on his artistic career.

Even before the earthquake his relationship with his earlier follower Onchi, whose art came to represent a more 'modern' and less romantic trend, may have cooled at this time. Despite this and Yumeji's changing fortunes during this era, the two men continued their plans to form the company, Sunday Design Publisher (Dontaku Zuansha). It was their hope to publish the magazine *Design and print* (*Zuan to insatsu*) and they announced their plans publicly on 1 May 1923. Yumeji actively promoted the project and even though his popularity was waning at this time his involvement was nonetheless intended to serve as a sort of name branding. The printmaker Fujimori Shizuo recalls the launch of the magazine and the apparent support by established masters such as Okada Saburōsuke and Fujishima Takeji:

> *I went several times with Yumeji and Onchi to the fairly large printer K. in Honjo Midorimachi. It was arranged to collaborate with this printer and to have* Design and print *appear monthly. Before the launch of the publication, a celebration of the announcement of this event was held in May 1913* [*sic*; *1923*] *at the Imperial Hotel. . . On the very day* [*of the celebration*], *we drove to the Imperial Hotel, while Onchi, Okada-sensei and I picked up Fujishima-sensei by car. It was a very successful event. Several well-known proprietors of printing shops were present.*[21]

Fujimori's recollections suggest that preparations were in place for the journal's launch, but sadly the destruction of the printing shop during the Great Kantō Earthquake prevented its realisation.

The earthquake and its aftermath impacted the work of many artists, and Yumeji was no exception.[22] From 14 September—a mere two weeks after the earthquake—until 4 October 1923 he published a series of short illustrated articles in the newspaper, *Miyako shinbun*, which were based on rough sketches he did while walking through the ruined capital.[23] These *True pictures of the Tokyo calamity* are dramatic examples of Yumeji's first-hand observations and they, like the numerous sketches he made throughout his life, testify to his skill at capturing the pulse of life around him (fig. 2.6).[24]

After the earthquake Yumeji moved into a house and studio in Setagaya ward that he designed and that he named 'The Youth's Mountain Villa' (Shōnen Sanso). Today the building has been moved close to the family home near Okayama and is annexed to the Yumeji Art Museum (Yumeji Kyōdo Bijutsukan). He continued with illustrations for book covers and from 1924 onwards contributed to the then recently launched magazine *The ladies' graphic* (*Fujin gurafu*). He also pursued his collaboration with the music publisher Senō Kōyō and the *Senow music scores* (*Senow gakufu*) (fig. 2.7). None of these commissions, however, equalled his earlier success with the *Yumeji gashū*. As the art historian Kawakita Michiaki observes, Yumeji, 'whose style had dominated an entire generation', witnessed a significant decline in popularity in the post-earthquake period.[25] Kawakita also notes that the image of the romantic woman in traditional attire—the 'Yumeji-style beauty'—no longer mirrored contemporary tastes. Nevertheless, Yumeji continued to paint his 'signature' female types and at the same time experimented with new styles. In the memorial issue of *Study window* (*Shosō*) Arishima

Ikuma (1882–1974) writes that in the post-earthquake period Yumeji was ignored by the contemporary art world, dismissed as a 'sweet lyricist' (*amai jojōshijin*) and treated unsympathetically in the press.[26]

Although Yumeji's paintings, prints and illustrations clearly centred on the subject of beautiful women—seconded only by images of children—a number of his compositions also feature abstract designs. His art is stylistically diverse, including elements drawn from Art Nouveau, Art Deco, Cubism and Futurism (fig. 2.8). Onchi Kōshirō describes the evolution of Yumeji's work as one that initially comprised the 'naïve' imagery of women generally associated with the 'Yumeji-style beauties', the popularity of which placed continued pressure on him to reproduce similar pieces. This was followed by an increasingly 'mannerist' depiction of women and finally it encompassed a greater independence and distancing from the expectations of an audience that demanded his Yumeji brand (see fig. 2.3b).[27] Onchi elaborates further:

> *After completing work on the many [volumes of]* Yumeji gashū, *his illustration for magazines and his paintings became a repetitive form of work, but he couldn't stop [producing them] because they were his bread and butter. The sketches he made were for his own pleasure; these did not restrict him [artistically].*[28]

Onchi's implication is that Yumeji's sketches were not necessarily the same style seen in his illustrations and paintings, and that in actual fact Yumeji's interests were diverse. For example, even before the earthquake, Fumon Gyō (1896–1972), the earliest representative of the Futurist movement in Japan, introduced him to Russian Futurist art. Yumeji was particularly fascinated by the work of David Burluik (1882–1967) and Victor Palmov (1882–1929).[29] Stylistic borrowings from Futurist art are seen in his illustrations for the semi-autobiographical serialised novel, *Departure* (*Shuppan*), which was first published from May to September 1927 in the newspaper *Miyako shinbun* (fig. 2.9). *Departure* was described by Sawada Ishirō, the editor of the 2nd edition of the novel in book form, as an 'autobiographical collection of pieces', with the 134 episodes of the narrative roughly linked with Yumeji's life narrative from 1920 to 1925.[30] As an example of Yumeji's later oeuvre, *Departure* not only demonstrates his grasp of a post-earthquake zeitgeist—one marked by increased modernisation and the beginning of Japan's militaristic ambitions—but also showcases his broad artistic range. And it was Yumeji's declining popularity at home at this time that prompted his desire to travel abroad in search of new avenues of artistic expression.

### *Sojourn in the United States and Europe: fresh artistic inspiration?*

Yumeji's independent status and lack of institutional affiliations (and funding) meant that, unlike many of his contemporaries, he did not receive sponsorship to travel and study outside Japan. European cities like Paris and Munich were especially attractive to Japanese artists in the early twentieth century, as were American cities like Boston and Chicago. Yumeji formed an understanding of modern Western art from his contact with Japanese artists working in a Western mode and more directly from magazine illustrations. He frequently assimilated styles of late nineteenth- and early twentieth-century European art into his own work. His interest in Western art already surfaces in his diary entries from 1909 and 1910, in which he indicates that he would welcome a chance to go abroad.[31] Yumeji scholar Sodei Rinjirō notes that Yumeji stated quite openly that he would especially like to see Paris.[32]

On the occasion of his first exhibition in Kyoto in 1912 Yumeji met the American ethnologist and curator Stewart Culin (1858–1929), with whom he discussed his schedule to visit the United States. However, the travel plans Yumeji made together with a group of Japanese painters were suspended with the outbreak of the First World War in 1914.[33] After a farewell exhibition in Kyoto in 1918 Yumeji once again intended to go aboard, but this trip was cancelled because of Hikono's illness. His choice to travel initially to the United States, rather than to Europe as originally intended, was guided by his belief that he could fund his trip to Europe with earnings from exhibitions in the US. The perception that the US could deliver financial benefits to Japanese artists was due in part to the successes of Japanese emigrants to Hawai'i and to America's east coast in the early twentieth century.[34]

As his travel itinerary was finally taking shape in the late 1920s Yumeji was already hatching ambitious plans upon his return to Japan. In 1929, Yumeji rented a studio near the hot-spring resort Ikaho in Gunma prefecture, today the location of the Takehisa Yumeji Ikaho Memorial [Museum] (Takehisa Yumeji Ikaho Kinenkan), and in 1930 he announced his idea of founding an art institute that would focus on the Art Nouveau-inspired concept of incorporating art into daily life. Yumeji envisioned this Mount Haruna Art Institute (Haruna-san Bijutsu Kenkyūjō)—named after a nearby area of natural beauty—as a place that would promote new artistic approaches based on his studies of art and design abroad.[35]

Prior to his departure in May 1931 Yumeji mounted two farewell exhibitions in Tokyo in order to generate funds for his journey. He left from Yokohama and arrived in San Francisco after two weeks in Hawai'i. He spent the majority of his time in California, mostly in San Francisco and Los Angeles, but he also visited other locales in the state, including Clear Lake, Berkeley and Morro Bay.

During his stay in California he published a series of short illustrated essays entitled 'I came, I saw' (written in Latin alphabet) in the Japanese-language American newspaper *Nichibei*. He rarely painted, his time instead mostly consumed by sketching. He organised exhibitions, but these were unsuccessful, such as those in Carmel from 24 to 30 September 1931 (fig. 2.10), and at the Department of Fine Arts at the University of California, Los Angeles (UCLA) and at the Olympic Hotel in Los Angeles's Little Tokyo, in February and March 1932, respectively. Despite these setbacks, Yumeji continued to work and he even hung out a sign in front of his lodgings in LA's Boyle Heights that read 'Yume art studio'. He also crafted dolls during this period, an art form he had undertaken some years preceding his departure (fig. 2.11).

Yumeji's sojourn in California was beset by financial difficulties and his stay would probably have been impossible without the support of the local Japanese community who hosted him.[36] Although he had originally planned to go straight to London and Paris, he eventually decided on a different route. He left Los Angeles in September 1932, travelling through the Panama Canal and then made an ocean crossing to Hamburg. Yumeji carefully chronicled his journey with his sketches.

Once in Germany, Yumeji went to Berlin and from there to Prague, Vienna and Innsbruck before arriving in Paris on 7 November 1932. As noted above, visiting Paris had been very important for Yumeji, but the entry in his diary from 9 November 1932 reveals a weary, despondent traveller:

> *I had eggs with ham and a French loaf. What a horrible meal. I can't walk. As a whole, I am feeling dizzy . . . as if I had been drinking wine. Paris is too bright, big and crowded. The people seem to drink at every hour. The stories of men and woman drowning themselves in the Seine affect me a great deal.*[37]

Paris clearly did not measure up to Yumeji's expectations as an art centre and this diary excerpt also hints at health problems. Yumeji remained in Paris until 21 November and then returned to Berlin, via Lyon, Geneva, Lausanne, Zurich, Salzburg and Vienna.

Yumeji faced increased financial hurdles in Berlin, but he continued to sketch his experiences, as seen in his impressions of a park there from 1933, which is housed in the Yumeji Art Museum in Okayama (fig. 2.12). With support from the diplomatic attachés Alexander Nagai and Imai Shigerō he mounted several exhibitions in Berlin. He also taught Japanese painting at the Ittenschule, which was founded in 1926 by Johannes Itten (1888–1967) to promote his ideas regarding art and his own interests, including East Asian traditions.[38] Yumeji led classes there from February to June 1933, with Imai assisting him as translator and interpreter (Yumeji spoke neither German nor English). He mainly gave instruction in *nanga* (literati painting), which during the earlier Meiji era was viewed as somewhat anachronistic. However, when seen against the backdrop of modernism, literati painting was recognised as an expression of 'anti-modernism'. The paintings Yumeji produced during these lessons testify to his emphasis on not one, but several painting styles. At the Ittenschule Yumeji also composed short annotations about the use of line in Japanese painting in the piece 'About lines' ('Sen ni tsuite') and a longer essay 'The concept of Japanese painting' ('Nihonga ni tsuite no gainen').[39] 'About lines' has descriptions on lines types, various brushstroke techniques and the application of different styles in painting. In 'The concept of Japanese painting' Yumeji remarks that he did not wish to present a formal theory of art, rather to offer a collection of thoughts on the principles of Japanese painting that would not limit artistic freedom. For Yumeji, Japanese art did not adhere to strict rules and thus it would be inappropriate to set forth systematic written theories. Moreover, he draws comparisons between Western and Japanese art and incorporates general information on aspects of Japanese culture.[40]

During his stay in Berlin, Yumeji became an unwilling witness to the rise of Nazism and was deeply affected by what he saw. Many of the students at the Ittenschule were Jewish and Yumeji was directly confronted with the increased wave of anti-Semitism. He expresses the following reaction to the boycott of Jewish shops from 1 April 1933:

> *On the way to lunch at the Bohème* [*restaurant I saw*] *several strange papers affixed to the glass shop windows. A doctor's nameplate was inscribed with the word* Jude [*Jew*] *and* [*a Star of David*] *on the glass. All the fancy shops were like that. There were also similar red papers when I went to check the house of Tikotin* [the Jewish German collector Felix Tikotin, 1893–1986]. *Presumably, the exhibition will be cancelled. How will the public opinion shift? Is there no place where Jews can live in peace? I want to see the creation of a Jewish country. The people flocking into the streets are eerie. It is even more depressing than a funeral cortege.*[41]

Throughout his stay in Berlin Yumeji was eager to organise exhibitions whenever he could, since he used the proceeds from these towards his return passage to Japan. The 'exhibition' mentioned in his diary is most probably his solo show that opened on 21 June at Berlin's German-Japanese Club (Doitsu Nihon Kurabu).[42]

Yumeji left Berlin on 26 June 1933 and travelled via Munich to Napoli, and there on 19 August he boarded a ship for Japan. He stopped over in Taiwan, where he held an exhibition to raise money, returning sick and exhausted to Tokyo in November 1933. By this time, Yumeji had almost been totally forgotten in his native country, and in January 1934 he was hospitalised in a sanatorium in Nagano where he died from tuberculosis on 1 September 1934, just short of his fiftieth birthday. He was buried in the Zōshigaya public cemetery, the resting place of numerous celebrated early twentieth-century Japanese writers and artists. It was here in Zōshigaya that thirty years earlier Yumeji had lived as a young artist.

Yumeji's life and art underwent continual re-evaluation in the post-war period, and more recent discussions of the artist have moved away from a focus on his romantic 'Yumeji-style beauties' and his amorous liaisons to those regarding a figure deserving of serious art historical study. His oeuvre is richly diverse, and while he has often been pigeonholed as a commercial artist, Yumeji's work demonstrates his search for greater individual artistic expression. His illustrations, paintings and prints all convey an aesthetic sense that can only be fully understood and appreciated through a re-examination of his life. Beneath the at times overly stylised 'Yumeji image' was an artist whose life—one coloured by success and failure, love and rejection, vitality and infirmity—provided the source for his unique creative voice.

## Notes

1. For example, Ishikawa, *Taishō roman techo.*

2. Stegewerns, *Adjusting to the new world*, 43.

3. Sharon A. Minichiello, 'Greater Taishō Japan 1900–1930', in Brown and Minichiello et al., eds., *Taishō chic*, 9–15.

4. The biographical information in this article draws on the following publications: Kawano, ed., *Yumeji 1884–1934*, 351–92; Chiba City Museum of Art, Yumeji Art Museum and Wakayama Prefectural Museum of Modern Art, eds., *Takehisa Yumeji ten*, 261–66; and the chronology given in Yūjōbō, ed., *Taiyō 20.* This essay is also indebted to the research of Aoe Shunjirō, Araki Mizuko, Ogasawara Yōko and Sodei Rinjirō, and would not have been possible without the generosity of the Kanazawa Yuwaku Yumeji Museum and the Yumeji Art Museum in Okayama. Unless otherwise indicated, all translations are by the author.

5. Smith, *Modern Japanese prints 1912–1989*, 36.

6. For other English translations of this poem, see Ōoka, ed., *Taiyaku*, 111, and in Merritt, *Modern Japanese woodblock prints*, 27.

7. In the magazine *The middle-school student* (*Chūgakusei*) 1 vol. 8 (January 1923).

8. See also Okazaki, *Yumeji seiden*, 55–56, Ogasawara, *Yumeji*, 43, and Strong McDonald, 'Onchi Kōshirō', 74.

9. Quoted in Kimura, *Takehisa Yumeji*, 88–89. The reference to *nihonga* states '*nihonga ga hansetsu*' (*nihonga* in 'half size' [format]), a reference to a paper size measuring 130.0 x 30.0 cm.

10. For a detailed description of this show, *The first exhibition of Yumeji's work* (*Daiikkai Yumeji sakuhin tenrankai*), see Inoue Masako, '"Daiikkai Yumeji sakuhin tenrankai" no zengo ni tsuite' ('The context of The first exhibition of Yumeji's work'), in Chiba City Museum of Art, Yumeji Art Museum and Wakayama Prefectural Museum of Modern Art, eds., *Takehisa Yumeji ten*, 224–29.

11. See Swinton, *The graphic art of Onchi Kōshirō*, 20–21.

12. Merritt, *Modern Japanese woodblock prints*, 27.

13. Ibid., 30.

14. Hikono was a student at the *nihonga* department at Tokyo's Women's Art School (Joshi Bijutsu Gakkō, present-day Joshi Bijutsu Daigaku); see Ogura, *Yumeji no shōgai*, 77–84, 81.

15. For an overview of pieces displayed in this exhibition, see Chiba City Museum of Art, Yumeji Art Museum and Wakayama Prefectural Museum of Modern Art, eds., *Takehisa Yumeji ten*, 256–60.

16. On the *Twelve views of Nagasaki*, see Merritt and Yamada, 'Yumeji's Twelve views of Nagasaki'.

17. See also Unno, *Toshi fūkei no hakken*, 144.

18. Kritter, ed., *Japanische Buchillustration*, 129–30.

19. Yamada Junko left her husband and three children to live in Tokyo. She was the lover and protégé of the author Tokuda Shūsei (1872–1943), a main proponent of literary Naturalism and the 'I-novel' (*shishōsetsu*). The name 'Nora' is a reference to the character in Henrik Ibsen's play *A doll's house* (1879) and to her image as a 'new woman' (*atarashii onna*) who seeks independence and sexual liberation. See also Okazaki, *Yumeji seiden*, 207.

20. For further details on the Great Kantō Earthquake and a close examination of its representation, see Weisenfeld, *Imaging disaster*.

21. Fujimori Shizuo, 'Yumesan no omoide. Take to nanten' ('Reminiscences of Yumeji. Bamboo and nandina'), in Onchi, ed. *Shosō. Yumeji tsuioku tokushū*, 277–81, quotation 279. The 'printer K.' refers to the printer Kanetani; Honjo Midorimachi is in Tokyo's Sumida ward. See also Strong McDonald, 'Onchi Kōshirō', 80.

22. For example, the novelist and artist Arishima Ikuma painted a large-scale panorama that depicted the devastation of the earthquake; this can be viewed at the memorial to earthquake and war disasters in Yokoamichō park, Tokyo.

23. Reproduced in Takehisa, Kawamura and Yamamura, *Yumeji to Karyō*.

24. Weisenfeld, *Imaging disaster*, 109–11.

25. Kawakita, *Modern currents in Japanese art*, 12.

26. Arishima Ikuma, 'Omoide futatsu mitsu' ('Some memories'), in Onchi, ed., *Shosō. Yumeji tsuioku tokushū*, 296–97; quoted in Strong McDonald, 'Onchi Kōshirō', 82.

27. Strong McDonald, 'Onchi Kōshirō', 81.

28. Onchi, *Yumeji suketchi chōshō*, 167.

29. Fumon Gyō assisted in organising Burluik's exhibitions in Japan. See also Omuka, 'David Burluik and the Japanese avant-garde', 111–25.

30. Takehisa Yumeji, *Shuppan*; see also Kritter, ed., *Japanische Buchillustration*.

31. Tsurutani, *Yumeji no mita Amerika*, 7–8.

32. Sodei, *Yumeji ikoku e no tabi*, 2.

33. Ibid.

34. Tsurutani, *Yumeji no mita Amerika*, 95.

35. Kaneko, 'Berurin ni okeru Yuhanesu Itten', 1–10.

36. For a detailed account of Yumeji's stay in California and Europe, see also Sodei, *Yumeji ikoku e no tabi*.

37. Quoted in Ogasawara, *Yumeji*, 238.

38. For more on the Ittenschule, see Kaneko, 'Berurin ni okeru Yuhanesu Itten'.

39 Aoe, *Takehisa Yumeji*, 326. The articles were translated into German as 'Über die Linien' and 'Das Konzept der Japanischen Malerei', respectively. Both the essays and his work during the Ittenschule period were in the possession of the Itten family and in 2008 were donated to the National Museum of Modern Art, Kyoto. See Yamano Hidetsugu, 'Kawanishi Hide korekushon ni tsuite/On the Kawanishi Hide collection', in Yamano, Ikezawa and Nakao, eds., *Kawanishi Hide korekushon*, 22–39, 322–38.

40. Kaneko, 'Berurin ni okeru Yuhanesu Itten', 95.

41. Quoted in Kudō, *Takehisa Yumeji saikō*, 253; see also Strong McDonald, 'Onchi Kōshirō', 81.

42. Sodei, *Yumeji ikoku e no tabi*, 250–53, 304.

# 'Poetry without voice': Yumeji and the graphic medium

Nozomi Naoi

Takehisa Yumeji's extensive body of work testifies to his artistic diversity: postcards, illustrations for newspapers, magazines and books, cover designs, paintings, watercolours, prints, poetry, and dolls, as well as the clothing and stationery items sold at his store Minatoya.[1] Of these, it is Yumeji's contributions to newspapers and magazines that mark the beginning of his involvement with the graphic medium. These early examples profoundly influenced the course of his artistic development, both stylistically and in terms of subject matter. Yumeji continued to create printed imagery throughout the remainder of his career, and they fall roughly into three groups: illustrations made as woodblock-printed inserts for mass-produced commercial publications, single-sheet woodblock prints that were sold independently at bookstores, and cover and image designs for his illustrated books. These printed works were not intended simply as objects destined for artistic appreciation, they were also meant for popular consumption. They were items of the everyday and not representations of highbrow art that could only be seen within a museum or gallery setting. Yumeji's success in the graphic medium was also fostered by the emergence of a new media culture during the early twentieth century that was based on an increasingly rich ecology of reprographic media. Different from a dependence on the woodblock-print medium and the mainstream idiom of *ukiyo-e* ('pictures of the floating world') from the Edo period (1615–1868), 'modern' Japanese visual culture at this time was articulated in lithography, collotype, offset printing, copperplate etchings and woodcuts. Moreover, these new media were vehicles for the dissemination of imagery that not only engaged popular culture but also served as an alternative form of expression for avant-garde artists. The medium of print, and its capacity for wide distribution, facilitated the circulation of Yumeji's art to a broader visual sphere.

## *Minatoya and Yanagiya: print store, publisher and more*

The commercial demand for Yumeji's art was such that in October 1914 he decided to establish the Minatoya Bookstore (Minatoya Ezōshi-ten) in Gofuku-chō, a neighbourhood in Tokyo's Nihonbashi district. The naming of this shop—commonly known as Minatoya—reflects not only his fascination with the exotic and the foreign but also his interest in the *ukiyo-e* print tradition of the Edo period. Yumeji's own childhood experiences in the international port city of Kobe may well have guided his choice of the name 'Minatoya' (Harbour Shop). The word *minato* was perhaps meant as a reference to the ports and harbours that featured so prominently in Yumeji's early life, or an allusion to the ports where imported goods arriving on foreign ships entered Japan. Helen Merritt suggests that the term *ezōshi-ten* (bookstore) may have had associations with the Edo-period publisher Tsutaya Jūzaburō (1750–1797), who is today most acknowledged for his work with the celebrated *ukiyo-e* artists Kitagawa Utamaro (1753–1806) and Tōshūsai Sharaku (active 1794–1795).[2] Although such a link cannot be substantiated, it is undeniable that the earlier *ukiyo-e* tradition deeply influenced Yumeji's activity in the woodblock medium and his collaboration with professional block-cutters and printers.

The Minatoya sold a wide array of objects designed by Yumeji, which were conceived, made and sold at the shop that Yumeji ran with his ex-wife Kishi Tamaki (1882–1945) (see also p. 32 regarding the Minatoya). However, despite its popularity, the Minatoya closed in 1916 after only two years. While little has been recorded about why the Minatoya ceased trading, it was most likely the result of several factors including Yumeji's lack of business acumen, his growing disinterest in the venture and the final breakdown of his relationship with Tamaki in 1916.[3]

With the closure of the Minatoya, Miyoshi Yonekichi (1881–1943) of the Yanagiya Bookshop (Yanagiya Shoten) acquired the Minatoya woodblocks. Miyoshi opened the Yanagiya in 1910 in Osaka's Hirano-machi district. In 1921, it moved to the city's Tatamiya-machi district, was renamed Yanagiya Gallery (Yanagiya Garō) and continued operation until Miyoshi's death. Miyoshi regarded the Yanagiya not only as a commercial endeavour, but also a vehicle through which he could support his favourite artists.[4] His Yanagiya Gallery had an adjoining space that exhibited and sold works by established painters and designers such as Kitano Tsunetomi (1880–1947), Minami Kunzō (1883–1950), Tomimoto Kenkichi (1886–1963) and Hada Teruo (1887–1945).[5] The Yanagiya also had a range of objects designed by Yumeji: envelopes, decorated papers (*chiyogami*), woodblock prints, handkerchiefs and other products originally made for the Minatoya. And it released new editions of Yumeji's single-sheet prints using Minatoya woodblocks, removing the *Minatoya han* (printed by Minatoya) seal from the woodblocks and plugging it with the Yanagiya *shamisen* plectrum-shaped seal.[6] Like the Minatoya, the Yanagiya marketed items by Yumeji and released woodblock prints, thereby functioning as a kind of publishing house with its own seal. Moreover, the Yanagiya commissioned new designs from Yumeji and many of the woodblock prints made exclusively for the shop were done through Ōtsuki Sasabune (1874–1920), the owner of the Kyoto printing company Seibundō.

### *Yumeji's woodblock prints: tradition and modernity*

There was enormous interest in the culture of the Edo period during the later Meiji and Taishō eras when Yumeji was coming of age artistically. Yumeji, too, was intrigued by this era. He incorporated aspects from Edo-period popular theatre and printmaking traditions in his work, but at the same time he was also inspired by various Western artistic styles and trends then entering Japan. In an advertisement for one of his illustrated books, *Spring dawn* (*Haru no kawatare*), Yumeji describes his artistic development as a metaphorical journey of exploration from his childhood to his encounter with other cultures:

> *I listened to lullabies and weaving songs as I came of age. . . . After I realised the pathos of the journey, my path crossed 'Hiroshige's ocean' and I parted ways at 'Utamaro's women', wandering through unfamiliar mountains and rivers. . . . I wept deeply when I was shown a sun by Van Gogh that looked as if a follower of Fudō Myōō was performing a walking-on-fire ritual, dancers by Matisse appearing like a stained-glass window and square apples by Cezanne.*[7]

The above conveys Yumeji's desire and openness to formulate a new artistic language, drawing from various traditions, be they perceived notions of Japan's own past or foreign modes. Like many of his contemporaries, Yumeji's art was eclectic, marrying in his graphic work traditional woodblock techniques and subject matter with modern Western stylistic influences to exploit the expressivity of the woodblock medium. However, Yumeji's art practice was extremely syncretic, since it was not confined to the production of single-sheet prints but also extended to the design of widely circulated commercial items that inhabited the realm of popular culture. Some of these were made and sold early on at his Minatoya shop, and they can be seen as coalescing art and life.

Emerging contemporary print movements in Japan at this time—*shin hanga* ('New print') and *sōsaku hanga* ('Creative print')—were characterised by their relationship with or reaction to the conventional *ukiyo-e* printmaking process that involved publisher, block-cutter, printer and designer. Although he did occasionally cut and print his own pieces, Yumeji was willing to cooperate with professional craftsmen—he accepted both the autonomy and importance of the artist as well as the skill of the artisan. And he was reputed to have been very particular about print quality. The printer Hirai Kōichi states that he worked closely with Yumeji until he was satisfied, mentioning that the artist even 'brought in old swatches of fabric, requesting that Hirai make colours similar to their faded or subtle shades'.[8] This collaboration with professional craftsman differentiated artists active in the graphic medium from the then newly surfacing concept of 'the artist', a contrast that inevitably forced printmakers and illustrators to defend their rightful place within an early twentieth-century art historical context. Hirai's description makes clear that Yumeji had complete control over each step in the printing process, however, he was comfortable in employing craftsman to execute certain aspects of production.

Many of Yumeji's prints were cut by Igami Bonkotsu (1875–1933) and Ōkura Hanbei, and printed by Hirai.[9] Igami was active as a professional block-cutter during the Meiji and Taishō eras, and had carved colour blocks for the reproductions of *yōga* ('Western painting') in literary magazines such as *Morning star* (*Myōjō*) and *Gentle breeze* (*Kōfū*). While later reprographic technology enabled mechanical colour separation, it was a highly sought-after manual skill, especially during the later Meiji era (1868–1912).[10] In our discussion of Yumeji, Igami played a particularly influential role because of his assistance in the manufacture of the artist's early prints. Most notable among these are the examples sold at his Minatoya shop, perhaps even the Koharu and Jihei set touched upon below.

As noted above, Yumeji's interest in the woodblock medium was greatly influenced by the techniques of Edo-period *ukiyo-e*, but the aesthetics and subjects of this popular art form also inspired him. For instance, he appears to have been drawn to the tales of tragic love affairs and double suicides, subjects sensationalised in the stories by the playwright Chikamatsu Monzaemon (1653–1725) and visualised in woodblock prints by artists such as Kitagawa Utamaro. Chikamatsu was one of the most influential playwrights of puppet theatre (*bunraku*), which combines narrative chanting and the *shamisen* music of *jōruri* plays with the use of puppets. This traditional and extremely popular form of entertainment originated in Osaka around the turn of the eighteenth century. The over one hundred plays attributed to Chikamatsu are famous for their dramatic portrayal of lovers, the struggles of social class and poverty, self-sacrifice and suicide. Chikamatsu's plays were dramatic in their portrayal of passion and love: they also conveyed and confronted the tension between emotion and reason, and the struggles of individuality and freedom over societal honour and obligation. Yumeji borrowed and translated such universal human struggles to fit within the context of early twentieth-century popular media and culture, and one representative work is his portrayal of the lovers Koharu and Jihei.

Koharu and Jihei are protagonists in Chikamatsu's fateful love story, *Love suicides at Amijima* (*Shinjūten no Amijima*). First performed in 1721, it counted among the playwright's most successful plays and was later adapted to the kabuki theatre. Koharu, a courtesan at a brothel in Sonezaki, and Jihei, a poor paper merchant married with two children, are deeply in love. However, Jihei cannot afford to visit Koharu or to buy out her contract. Helpless and trapped, the two lovers make a pact to commit double suicide, but this attempt fails when Koharu backs out due to fear and interference by Jihei's wife and family. After a tragic turn of events, the couple decide to run away and die together. They travel to the island of Amijima, where Jihei stabs Koharu with his short sword and then hangs himself on a sluice gate in a nearby stream. His body is discovered in a fisherman's net the next morning and the play ends with the narrator's words: 'They who were caught in the net of Buddha's vow immediately gained salvation and deliverance, and all who hear the tale of the love suicides at Amijima are moved to tears'.[11]

The stories surrounding such 'love suicides' were often based on actual incidents. In turn, the influence of

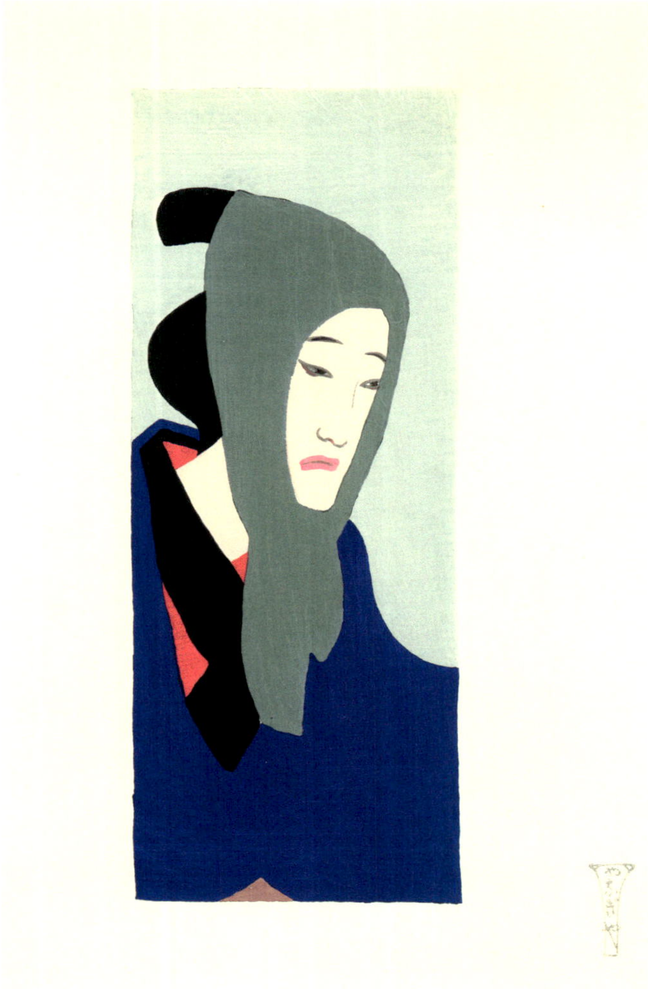

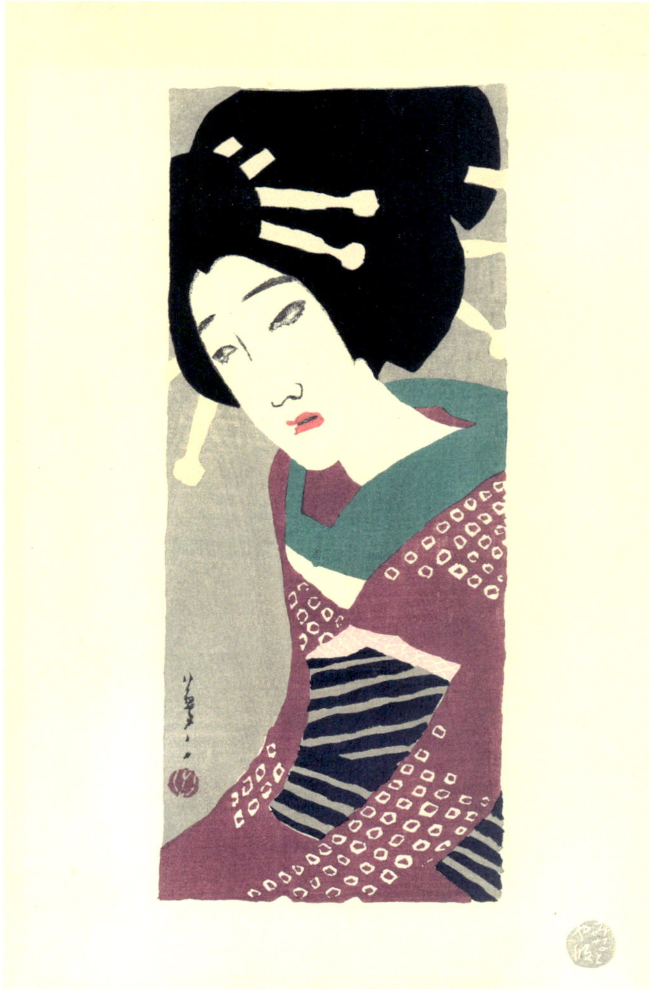

Fig. 3.1. *Jihei* (じへい)
43.2 x 28.3 cm
Date: 1914–1916
Seal: Yanagiya publisher's trademark
Publisher: Yanagiya

Fig. 3.2. *Koharu* (こはる)
37.4 x 23.8 cm
Date: 1914
Signature/seals: *Yumeji* with circular artist's seal, Minatoya publisher's trademark
Publisher: Minatoya

These two prints were designed and marketed as a set. They depict the two main protagonists of the celebrated puppet play, *Love suicides at Amijima* (*Shinjūten no Amijima*), written by the seventeenth-century playwright Chikamatsu Monzaemon. Koharu's hair accessories and elaborate red kimono with *shibori*-dyed patterns and a bright green collar convey the seemingly glamorous world of the courtesan and are a striking contrast to her emotionless expression. Jihei's face is partially concealed by a headscarf.

The original woodblocks for these works were produced for the Minatoya and *Koharu* bears the publisher's trademark reading *Minatoya han* (printed by Minatoya). When the Minatoya closed its doors in 1916, the woodblocks were sold to the Yanagiya in Osaka. The *Jihei* print here bears the easily recognisable Yanagiya *shamisen* plectrum-shaped seal, an indication that this was among the new editions marketed by the Yanagiya. The May 1915 issue of the magazine *Art and literature* (*Bijutsu to bungei*) advertises the Yanagiya set for the price of 40 *sen* (1 *sen* = 100th of a *yen*).[1]

Both *Koharu* and *Jihei* were printed employing flat planes of colour with no contour lines, which imbues them with a matte, almost 'lifeless' finish. This rendition could be a reference to their depiction as *bunraku* puppets, and not human actors.

1. Ogawa, *Motto shiritai Takehisa Yumeji*, 35.

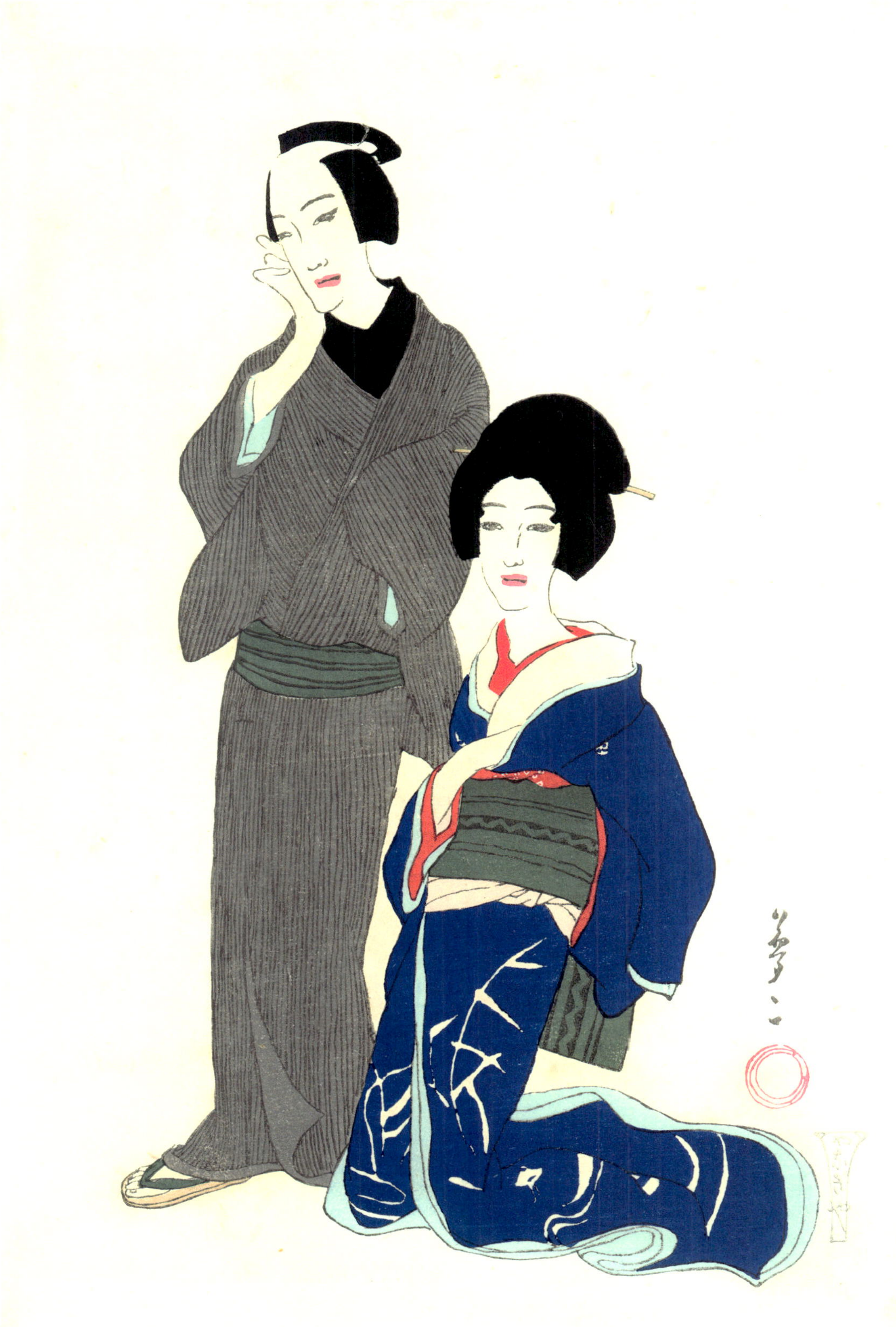

Fig. 3.3. *Umegawa and Chūbei* (*Umegawa Chūbei,* 梅川忠兵衛)
43.2 x 28.2 cm
Date: 1914
Signature/seals: *Takehisa Yumeji* with artist's circular seal, Yanagiya publisher's trademark
Publisher: Yanagiya

This print features two protagonists—the beautiful courtesan Umegawa and her lover Chūbei—in Chikamatsu Monzaemon's play *The courier for hell* (*Meido no hikyaku*). The withered plant motifs on Umegawa's deep blue kimono perhaps allude to the scene in a bleak snowy landscape where the two lovers meet their death. Chūbei pensively cradles his head in his right hand, while Umegawa is on bended knees, her stance accentuating the struggle and unhappiness of their fateful journey. Like *Koharu and Jihei* (figs. 3.1 & 3.2), the lifeless, awkward poses of the figures perhaps point to the two characters as representations of *bunraku* puppets.

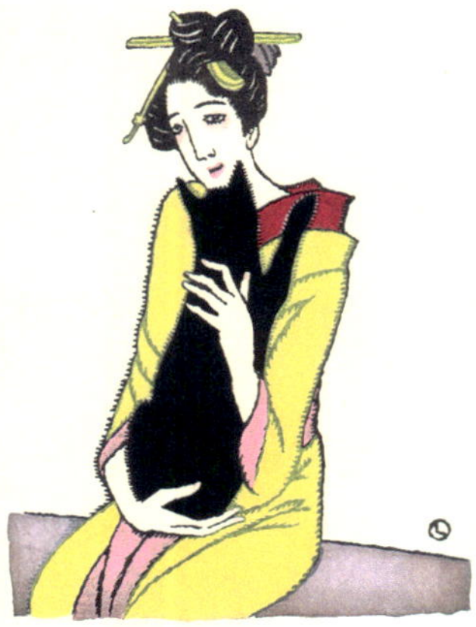

Fig. 3.4. *Woman holding a black cat* (*Kuroneko o daku onna*, 黒猫を抱く女)
36.8 x 26.3 cm
Date: 1920
Seal: artist's comma-shaped (*tomoe*) seal
Publisher: Yanagiya

This print depicts a seated woman holding a large black cat. The motif of the black cat with beauty was one of Yumeji's favourite subjects. It is seen in other works such as the print *Black cat* (see fig. 3.6) or the famous 1919 hanging scroll on silk, *The black ship shop* (*Kurofuneya*, 130.0 x 50.6 cm). The latter is today housed in the Takehisa Yumeji Ikaho Memorial [Museum] in Ikaho, Gunma prefecture.

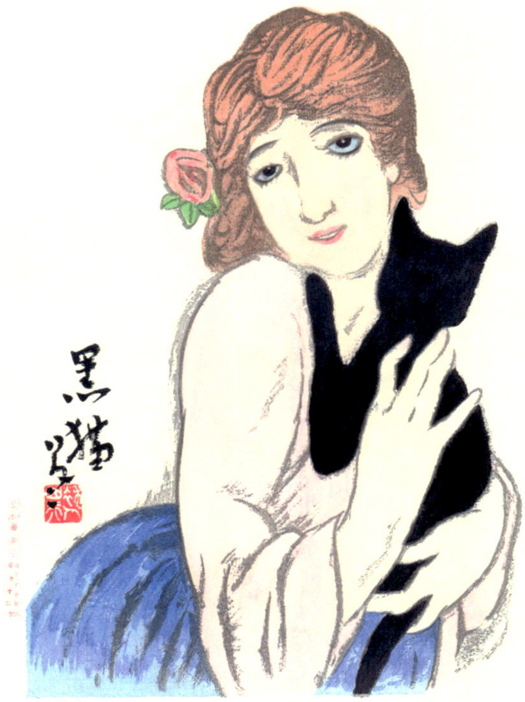


Fig. 3.6. *Black cat* (*Kuroneko*, 黒猫)
From the series *Ten subjects of women* (*Onna jūdai*, 女十題)
43.8 x 30.7 cm
Date: 1938
Signature/seal: *Yumeji* with artist's *Shūjin sankō* seal
Publisher: Katō Hanga Kenkyūjo

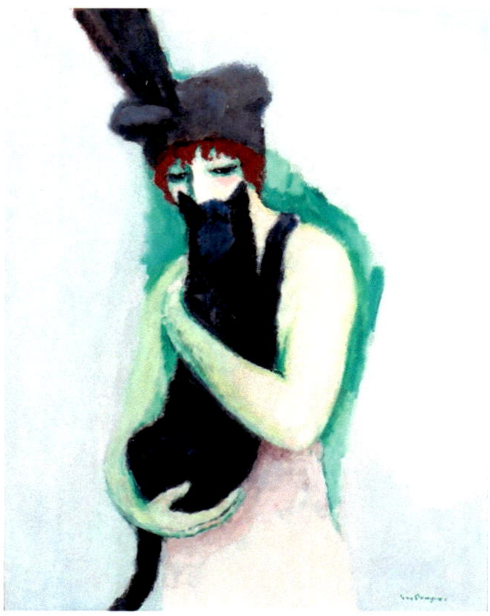

*Bottom left*
Fig. 3.5. Kees van Dongen (1877–1968)
*Woman with cat*, 1908
Oil on canvas, 91.76 x 73.66 cm



Born in the Netherlands, the French painter and printmaker Kees van Dongen was a leading Fauvist artist. He was known for his depictions of women in compositions characterised by a vivid, experimental use of colour as seen here in the juxtaposition of complementary shades in the woman's red hair and the green background. This intimate scene of a woman holding a black cat was first reproduced in Japan in the June 1919 issue of *Central arts* (*Chūō bijutsu*). Yumeji was obviously taken by the work, since a copy of it survives in his scrapbooks that are today housed in the Yumeji Art Museum in Okayama. Yumeji's adaptation of the subject testifies to the eclectic sources of inspiration encountered in his oeuvre.

*Next page*
Fig. 3.7. *Treasure boat* (*Takarabune*, 宝船)
58.2 x 40.3 cm
Date: 1920
Signature/seals: artist's *Yumeji* seal, Yanagiya publisher's trademark and official seal of the Sumiyoshi Shrine, Kyoto
Publisher: Yanagiya

Each year, the Yanagiya issued prints with the 'Treasure boat' theme for the *setsubun*, or Spring festival, that is celebrated on 3 February. While *setsubun* hails the beginning of spring in Japan, the motif of the 'Treasure boat' is actually associated with the lunar new year. The Yanagiya also produced 'Treasure boat' designs by other established artists of the period, including Nonagase Banka (1889–1964), Tomimoto Kenkichi and Yamamura Kōka. Yanagiya owner Miyoshi Yonekichi had long wanted to release a 'Treasure boat' print by Yumeji and he asked Ōtsuki Sasabune, who ran the Kyoto printing company Seibundō, to intercede and commission a work directly from the artist. Ōtsuki recalls that he visited Yumeji in January 1920 when he was a resident at the Kikufuji Hotel in Tokyo and that he had a difficult time convincing Yumeji that he should finish the piece.[1] He also records that it was printed with more than ten colour blocks.[2]

The seal in the right-hand corner appears on some impressions of this print, indicating that this particular example was ordered by the Sumiyoshi Shrine in Kyoto to be sold at its *setsubun* festival.

1. Kawano, ed., *Yumeji 1884–1934*, 330–31.
2. Ibid., 321. Although this print was issued in 1920, the year of Ōtsuki's death, it was commissioned earlier.

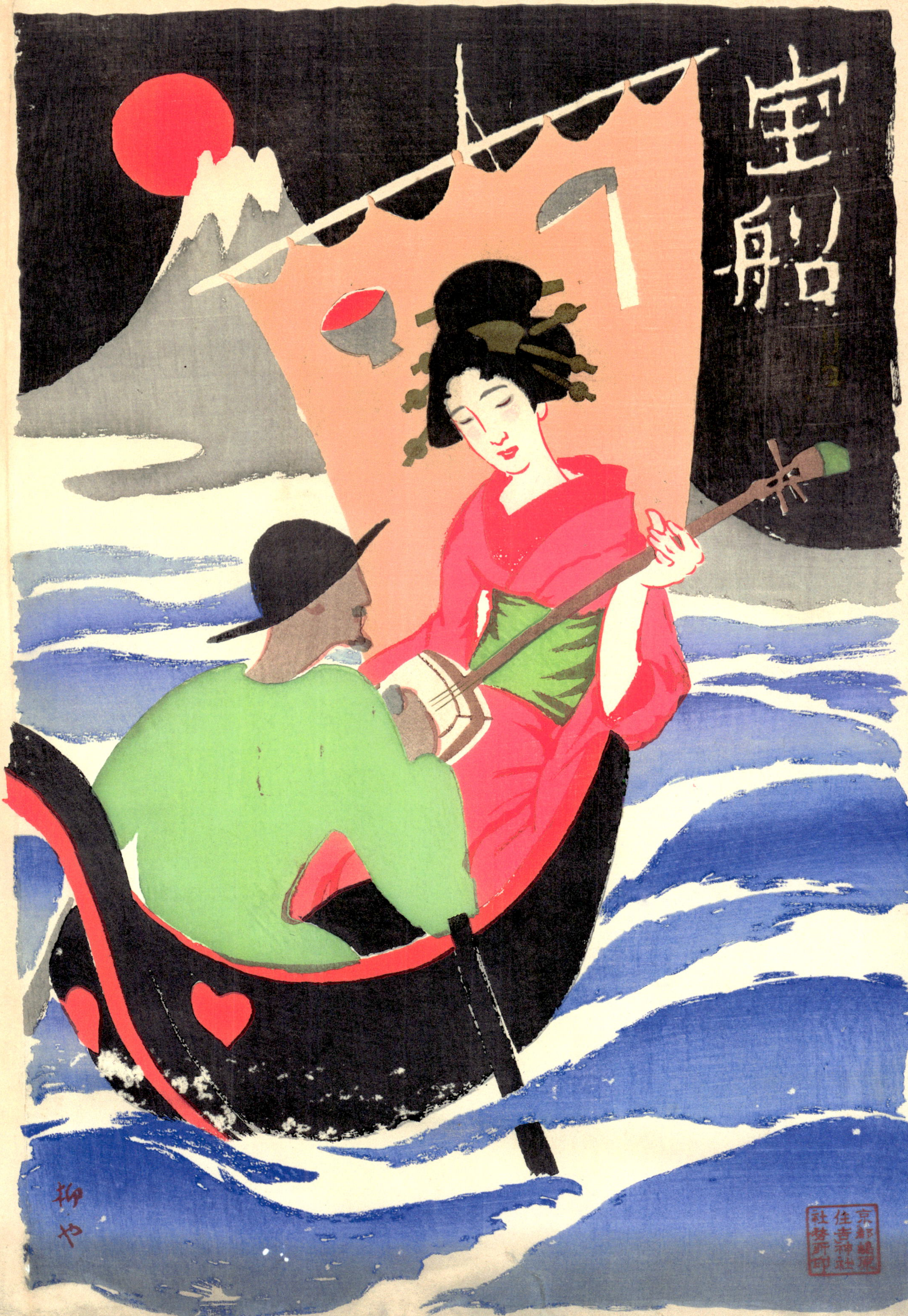
宝船
柳や

such plays also resulted in many couples attempting love suicides as an expression of their true love, or as an escape from their social and economic circumstances.[12] It was also believed that by committing double suicide lovers could be reborn together in the Buddhist Western Paradise.[13] The literary legacy of these tales, together with the fact that it stirred some in the public to desire a similar end, was such that these tales of star-crossed lovers appealed to Yumeji.[14]

Yumeji's *Koharu* and *Jihei* prints were conceived as a pair. The *Koharu* print exists in a Minatoya and Yanagiya version (figs. 3.1 & 3.2). Koharu's awkwardly tilted neck indicates that these characters would immediately have been associated with puppets, and not human actors. Other prints, such as *Bunraku dolls* (cat. 13) and *Umegawa and Chūbei* (fig. 3.3), equally showcase his fascination with the puppet theatre. The latter shows a couple whose sad plight is the subject of Chikamatsu's puppet play, *The courier for hell* (*Meido no hikyaku*), which originally appeared as the kabuki play *The broken seal* (*Fūingiri*). The storyline in both the puppet and kabuki plays was derived from a real incident that occurred in Osaka in late 1710. Though the specific details of the incident are today lost, at the time it was quite sensationalised. The plot is pure Chikamatsu: the popular courtesan, Umegawa, falls in love with the impoverished Chūbei, who works at a courier house. Chūbei has been secretly stealing money from his customers to fund his visits to Umegawa and for the down payment to buy out her contract. Chūbei falls into serious debt when he takes 800 gold coins from a samurai customer, thus forcing the couple to flee. The last act is a beautiful, yet doleful, scene as Umegawa and Chūbei escape into the snowy mountains. Eventually, alone and freezing, they die together.[15]

Yumeji's individualistic appropriation of both Japanese and Western artistic motifs is seen in the Yanagiya print, *Woman holding a black cat* from 1920 (fig. 3.4). The Seibundō had the woodblocks for this print cut using Yumeji's original drawing and sold the work at shops such as the Yanagiya. The composition demonstrates Yumeji's eclectic sources of inspiration and there is a direct correlation with materials he collected into scrapbooks. The positioning of the black cat and the woman's embrace are reminiscent of the 1908 *Woman with cat* by the Dutch painter Kees van Dongen (fig. 3.5). Yumeji's image depicts the woman in a boldly coloured, heavily layered yellow silk kimono, red collar and pink under-kimono; the elaborate coiffure also positions the figure as a distinctly Japanese beauty. Furthermore, the jagged outlines in the print are frequently interpreted as an influence of the contour lines of the *ukiyo-e* artist Isoda Koryūsai (1735–1790) as well as Western artists like the British artist and writer Aubrey Beardsley (1872–1898).[16] Scholars have also suggested that Yumeji's interest in the black cat motif may have associations with Japanese literature, such as *The black cat* (*Kuroneko*), a novel by Izumi Kyōka (1873–1939) that recounts the relationship between the female protagonist and her black feline.[17] Whatever the source, the theme of the black cat and beauty recurs in both his paintings and later prints. The beauty caressing the pet in *Black cat* (fig. 3.6), for example, is not kimono clad, and her Western clothing and brown hair conveying a more foreign feel.

The 1920 print *Treasure boat* is another example of how Yumeji marries a conventional Japanese subject with his own assimilation of foreign elements, here seen in the male figure and heart shapes (fig. 3.7). The 'Treasure boat' is a popular motif in Japanese folklore and appears at least as early as the Muromachi period (1392–1568). As a vessel that transports the Seven Gods of Good Fortune (*Shichifukujin*)—Hotei, Jurōjin, Fukurokuju, Bishamonten, Benzaiten, Daikokuten and Ebisu—the Treasure boat arrived at ports at the New Year replete with rice bushels and riches, symbols of wealth and abundance for the coming year. Moreover, it was thought that the placement of images of the Treasure boat under one's pillow on New Year's Eve would bring auspicious dreams. Yumeji's print contrasts this conventional interpretation by depicting a lonely scene of two figures in a black boat decorated with red hearts at one end. A woman dressed in a red kimono with a coiffure reminiscent of the Edo-period plays the *shamisen*, while a foreign man in a black hat and yellow shirt gently mans the oars. While felicitous New Year's motifs like Mount Fuji and a red sun are visible in the background, the coal-black sky sets an ominous tone and reminds the viewer of the uncertainty of the future.

### *Yumeji and illustrated books*

In addition to his prolific output of illustrations, covers, poetry and essays in more than 2,200 issues of magazines, journals and newspapers, Yumeji created over fifty artist's books (*chosakubon*), altogether an impressive accomplishment given his comparatively short life.[18] Yumeji wrote, designed and illustrated these books in their entirety, including their covers, as seen in the 1915 *Samisen* (*Shamisen*) *leaves* (fig. 3.8). For his illustrated books Yumeji often reprised many of the images from earlier magazine/newspaper illustrations and sketches. The act of republishing earlier compositions in a more permanent viewing format facilitated the appreciation of such pieces as individual artworks. It demonstrates Yumeji's stance on the artistic value and status of works made under the rubric of 'reproducible media'. He was likewise involved in book design for renowned authors of the period such as Tanizaki Jun'ichirō (1886–1965), Kume Masao (1891–1952) and Nagata Mikihiko (1887–1964) (see also p. 56).

Yumeji's interest in books (and thus texts) was a natural extension of his artistic expression, and he maintained that illustrations were a continuation of his writing and poetry, or 'poetry without voice' (*museishi*).[19] In the preface of his first compilation, the 1909 *Spring* (*Haru no maki*) volume of the *The Yumeji collection of work* (*Yumeji gashū*), he clearly regards his expression through text and image as tantamount:

> *I wanted to be a poet, however, my poetry was no substitute for earning a livelihood. Once, instead of using words, I expressed poetry in the form of an image. Unexpectedly, that image was published in a magazine and my timid heart was pleasantly surprised.*

Representative of this 'poetry without voice', and the close relationship between image and text in Yumeji's work, are examples such as *Unknown world* (*Mishiranu sekai*), the second volume of *Island of blossoming cherries* (*Sakura saku shima*) (fig. 3.9). *Unknown world* is a collection of seven illustrated short stories in which snippets of an 'unknown world' are translated through strange circumstances that are at once shocking, but also dreamy and sentimental. Most of the narratives are rather sombre in tone, touching upon death and uncertainty; they focus on the protagonist's various interactions with female characters, including girls, older sisters and mothers. They are evidence of Yumeji's curiosity about traditional Japanese folklore, such as the third and fourth tales 'Pilgrim's song of Awano strait' ('Awano naruto junrei uta') and 'Puppeteer' ('Kairaishi'). The illustrations for these stories also demonstrate his fascination with the puppet theatre, alongside the visual and textual expression of the female figure.

### *Reproducing Yumeji: the Katō Print Workshop*

Yumeji reused many of his own designs, however, the reprographic nature of his printed work was further re-invigorated through the efforts of the Katō Print Workshop (Katō Hanga Kenkyūjo). The publisher Katō Junji (1885–1961) established the Katō Print Workshop in 1934, motivated by a desire to provide greater exposure for art that he believed should be appreciated by a wider audience.[20] He reproduced the work of a number of celebrated artists with whom he was acquainted, including the *yōga* painters Kishida Ryūsei (1891–1929) and Umehara Ryūzaburō (1888–1986), and *shin hanga* artists Itō Shinsui (1898–1972) and Kawase Hasui (1883–1957).

The Katō Print Workshop reproduced prints after Yumeji's death drawing from the artist's body of

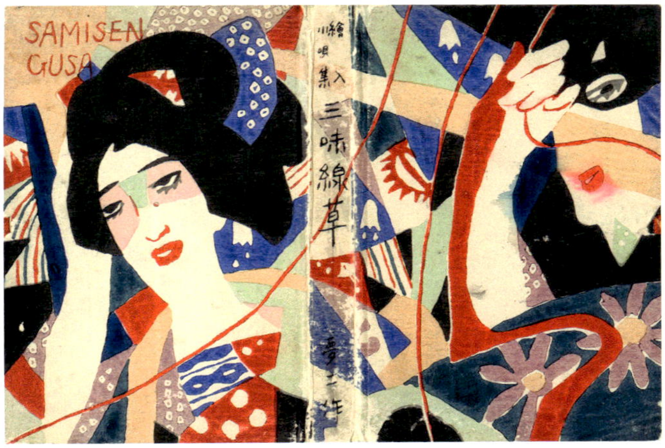


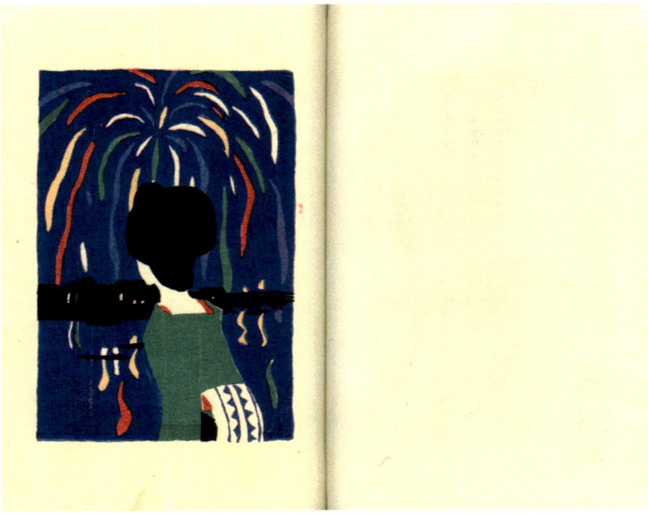

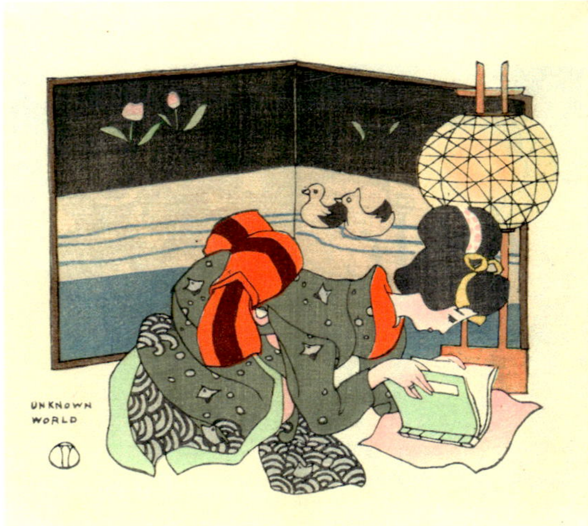


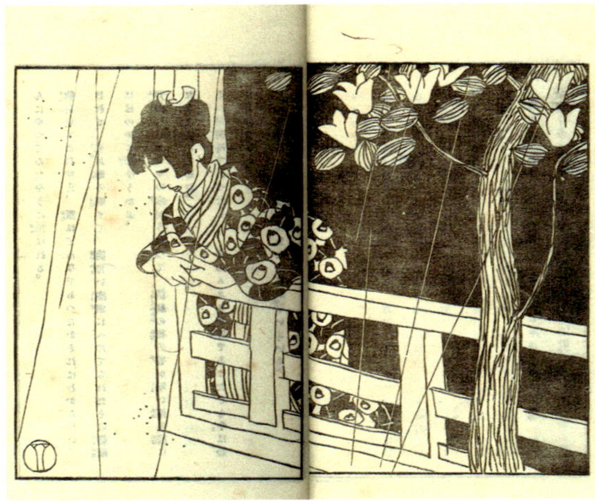

Fig. 3.8a–b. *A collection of illustrated songs (poems): Samisen (Shamisen) leaves (Eiri kouta shū: samisengusa,* 入小唄集 三味線草)
17.5 x 25.3 cm (cover open); 17.3 x 24.2 cm (book open, for *Fireworks*)
Date: 1915
Publisher: Shinchōsha

Yumeji reprised earlier work for use in this collection of illustrations and short poems. '*Shamisen* leaves' (*Shamisen* [*samisen*] *gusa*), more commonly known in English as 'shepherd's purse', is a common flowering plant in Japan. It acquired its name because of the resemblance between its triangularly shaped buds and a *shamisen* plectrum.

Yumeji's elaborate cover design (fig. 3.8a) is rendered through the dynamic, scattered arrangement of bright red, blue, yellow and purple areas to delineate a female figure in an abstracted style, but one nevertheless rooted in the Edo-period *ukiyo-e* tradition (a second less distinct figure is also depicted). A special feature of this book is the inclusion of six small woodblock-printed illustrations. One, *Fireworks* (*Hanabi*), highlights the contrast between the dark blue sky and water with the illumination of the fireworks (fig. 3.8b).

Fig. 3.9a–b. *Unknown world* (*Mishiranu sekai,* 見知らぬ世界)
Vol. 2 of *Island of blossoming cherries* (*Sakura saku shima,* 桜さく島)
18.4 x 22.1 cm (each image)
Seal: artist's seal 'grass' (*kusa*) seal
Date: 24 April 1912
Publisher: Rakuyōdō

*Unknown world* is the second volume of *Island of blossoming cherries* and is exemplary of Yumeji's many artist's books, for which he produced both text and image. The first volume, *Spring dawn* (*Haru no kawatare*) was published in February 1912 (fig. 2.1). The frontispiece of *Unknown world* shows a kimono-clad girl bent over an open book on the floor, her body poised as if to convey her eagerness to peep inside (fig. 3.9a). A large folding screen with simplified floral patterns and a paper lantern decorate the background. The composition likens the act of a reader opening a book with the girl in the illustration, creating a connection between the visual and textual experience of the reader.

In the sixth story, 'Young girl at the window' ('Mado no musume'), a young boy is smitten with a girl who he spies through a window. The boy asks his mother and older sister about her, but to no avail. He describes her as the girl who 'never lifted her head and continued looking down. She will forever cast a pale blue shadow in [his] memory like the silver rain showers on the grey oblivion'. A double-page spread portrays the girl, her eyes downcast as she leans over a handrail and gazes out at the rain (fig. 3.9b). Her kimono is ornamented with a camellia pattern and the tree on the right is perhaps a quince. The 'sweet' depiction of the young girl is in keeping with his 'Yumeji-style beauties' and the camellia is a recurring motif in his work.

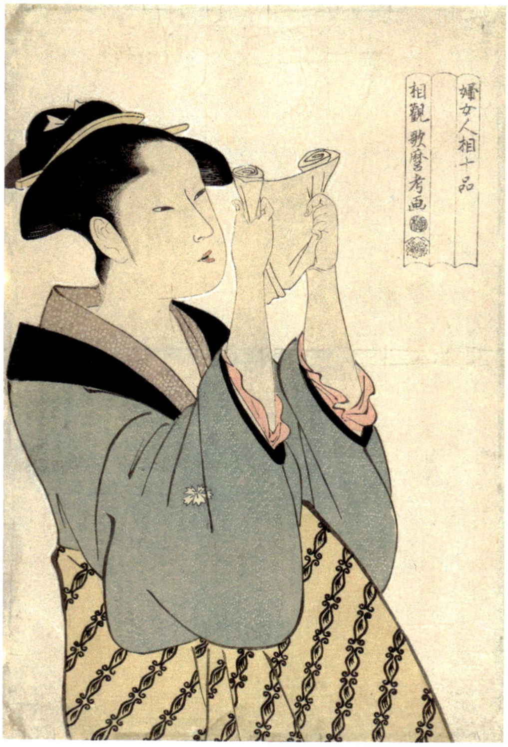


Fig. 3.10. Kitagawa Utamaro (1753–1806)
*Woman reading a letter* (*Fumi yomu onna*)
From the series *Ten classes of women's physiognomy* (*Fujo ninsō juppon*, 婦女人相十品)
Date: c. 1792–1793

Rijksmuseum, Amsterdam

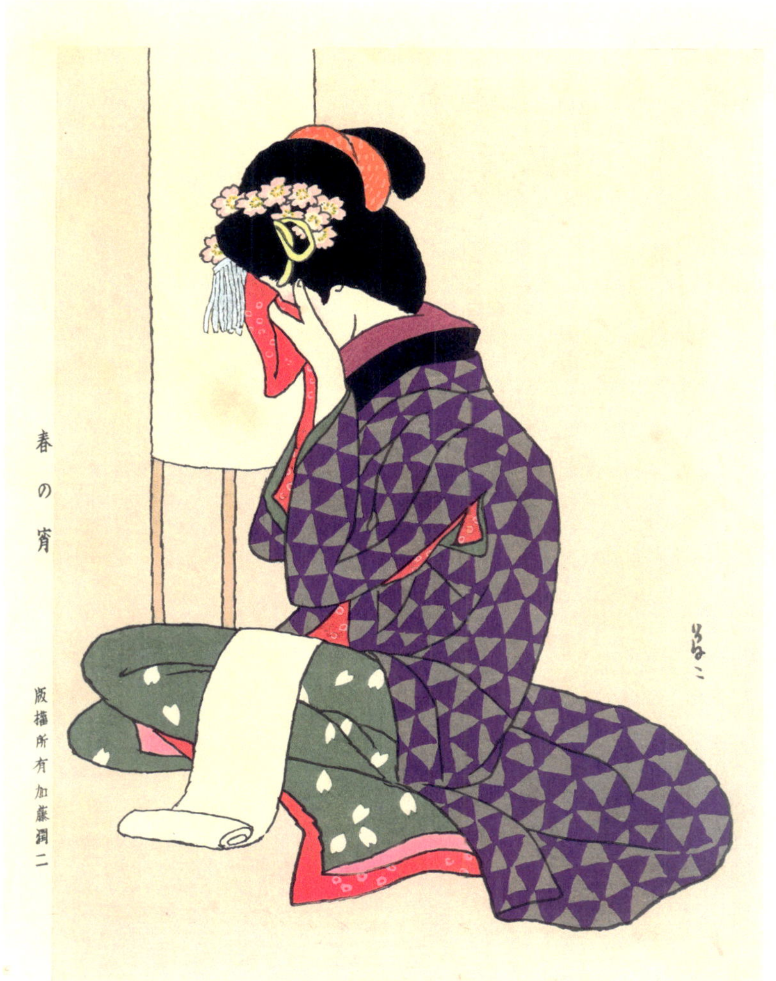


Fig. 3.11. *Spring evening* (*Haru no yoi*, 春のよい)
From the series *Yumeiji's masterpieces* (*Yumeji meisakushū*, 夢二名作集)
33.8 x 25.5 cm
Date: 1938–1939
Signature: *Yumeji*
Publisher: Katō Hanga Kenkyūjo

The portrayal of women caught in a moment of emotional unease is a common trope in Yumeji's work. The young woman in this print weeps into her red kimono sleeve—perhaps the contents of the letter beside her has distressed her. Though clearly unsettled emotionally, her perfectly coiffed hair, the beautifully envisioned hair ornaments, green kimono and overcoat with a striking triangular purple pattern nevertheless create a visually seductive image. For other images from this series, see figs. 1.2, 1.5, 1.12, 4.6, 4.14; cat. 68–72.

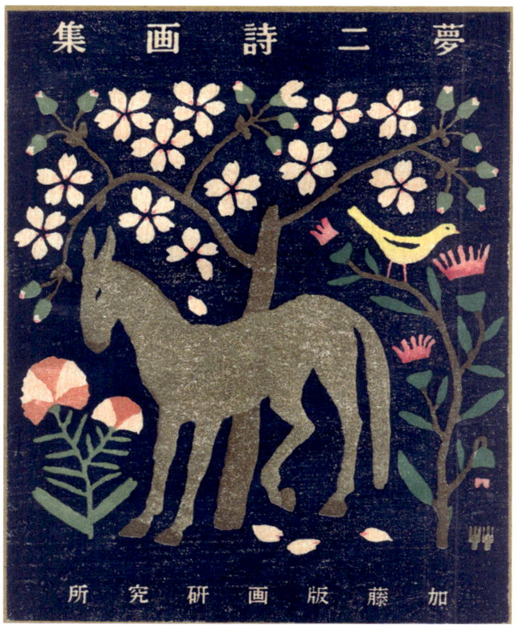


*Left*
Fig. 3.12. *Donkey* (*Roba*, 驢馬)
From the series *A collection of poetry and prints by Yumeji* (*Yumeji shigashū*, 夢二詩画集)
29.7 x 23.8 cm
Date: 1941
Seal: artist's 'grass' (*kusa*) seal
Publisher: Katō Hanga Kenkyūjo

The almost naïve folk-art treatment of this illustration of a donkey surrounded by flowers and a yellow bird adds to its decorative appea . For other images from this set, see figs. 1.3, 2.3a; cat. 73–79.

woodblock prints, illustrations and cover designs. These sets are principally images of beauties, perhaps reflecting what was popular during Yumeji's life and fuelling his reputation posthumously. They contributed to a rekindling of interest in Yumeji and have shaped our reception of his art. Katō also created new woodblocks based on Yumeji's paintings, such as the 1937–1938 series *Ten subjects of women* (*Onna jūdai*), which was derived from the 1921 set of ten watercolours of individual female figures Yumeji did for the wealthy Nagasaki collector Nagami Tokutarō (fig. 3.6 & cat. 66–67).

*Ten subjects of women* explored various types of women, with some clad in kimono, others in Western dress. While not a direct reference, the format of the ten-print series and the typology of the women portrayed could be seen as loosely connected with the sets of beautiful women such as Kitagawa Utamaro's *Ten classes of women's physiognomy*. Utamaro's series incorporated an aspect of psychological interiority that, although representing a broader type, contributed an inward dimension to his subjects. While in stylistic terms Yumeji's and Utamaro's beauties differ significantly, compositionally works such as Yumeji's *Rendezvous letter* and Utamaro's *Woman reading a letter* from the above set (fig. 3.10) share common ground in the conventional trope of women engrossed in reading love letters.

In addition to designs from earlier sets, the Katō Print Workshop also issued collections that Katō Junji compiled personally as a sampling of what he felt was necessary for the understanding of Yumeji's diverse corpus of work. For instance, *Yumeji's masterpieces* (*Yumeji meisakushū*) of 1938–1939 is a selection of thirty of the more than 270 cover images that Yumeji produced for the Senow Music Publishing Company (Senow Ongaku Shuppansha) (see figs. 2.7, 4,5, 4.7, 4.8, 4.10, 4.11, 413; cat. 16–32). This set included Yumeji's stock repertory of beautiful women in doleful states of 'romantic' expression such as *Spring evening* (fig. 3.11), or donning elaborately patterned Western-style dress as in *Our love is green* (cat. 70). Others channel Yumeji's interest in costume design for modern dance, such as *Dancing*, or in tranquil, bucolic views as in *Recollections of old songs* (cat. 71 & 72).

Another posthumous set, the 1941 *A collection of poetry and prints by Yumeji* (*Yumeji shigashū*), has thirteen prints with eleven poems, with the imagery drawn from a wide range of sources from magazine illustrations to watercolours. The charming cover design for the folder, *Donkey* (fig. 3.12), introduces the prints in this collection, which illustrate light-hearted scenes of girls gathering together such as *Playing cards* or women dressed in fashionable Western-style attire as in *Near the moat* (cat. 75 & 74).

The much later undated *Illustrated postcards by Yumeji* (*Yumeji ehagaki*) was Katō's brainchild; it was inspired by the numerous sets of postcards that Yumeji had designed and sold during his lifetime. The early twentieth century witnessed a boom in postcard production, and they became an extremely popular tool of communication between artists, authors and intellectuals. The Japanese postal service began in 1871 and the first postcards were issued in 1873 (one type was for mailing within Tokyo and another for other domestic addresses). However, the postcard boom did not occur until 1900 when the Japanese government introduced a flat rate for postcard postage; this allowed private companies and commercial venues to market their own postcards. Many bookstores subsequently carried diverse ranges and writing postcards emerged as a common, trendy means of communication.

*Illustrated postcards by Yumeji* comprises fifty postcard-sized prints taken from Yumeji's various designs for magazines and illustrated books. Yumeji did not originally conceive of these images as postcards, however, their reprinting in this format does reflect the types of postcards that he actually created, such as beauties inspired by an Edo-period style or scenes of love suicides. Some compositions convey his interest in modern kimono patterns, while others settle on an intimate moment, hinting at interiority and self-reflection (fig. 3.13). The majority of the works in this collection are figural; there are a few urban scenes and landscapes that call to mind his native Okayama (fig. 3.14).

Illustrations in magazines and newspapers, prints sold at bookstores, postcards and even collections of reproductions—the success of Yumeji's imagery and its enduring appeal lies in its ability to resonate with viewers and their everyday lives. Yumeji's close friend, the painter Arishima Ikuma (1882–1974), once wrote that:

> *It was impossible for Yumeji to observe, see, sketch, or reproduce anything without [drawing upon] his own individual style: whatever he saw or drew, all ended up in the so-called 'Yumeji style'* (Yumeji-shiki), *and the essence of this 'Yumeji style' courses through all of his work.*[21]

His style, characterised by the use of thin, curvilinear lines, was at once innovative and familiar. Yumeji wrote in the preface to his 1910 *Winter* (*Fuyu no maki*) that 'a picture is not an explanation, it is a song'. Text and image are an iteration of the Yumeji-style song, expressing snippets from the daily lives of contemporary Japanese through the lens of his own individualised visual and textual language.

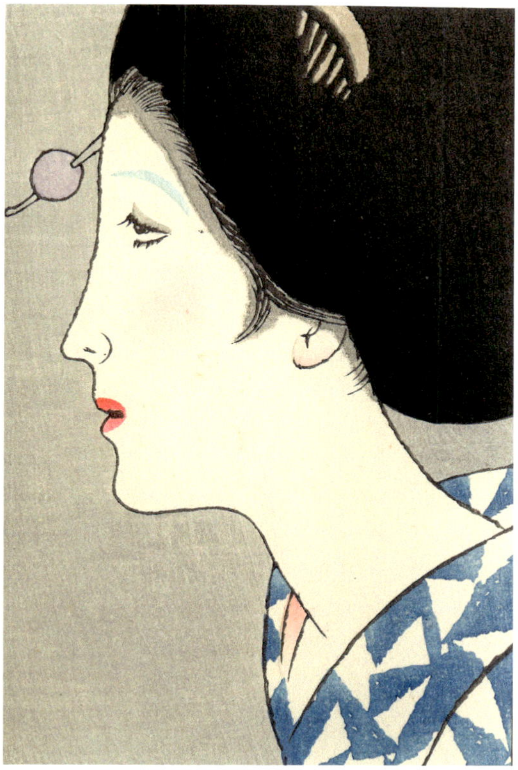

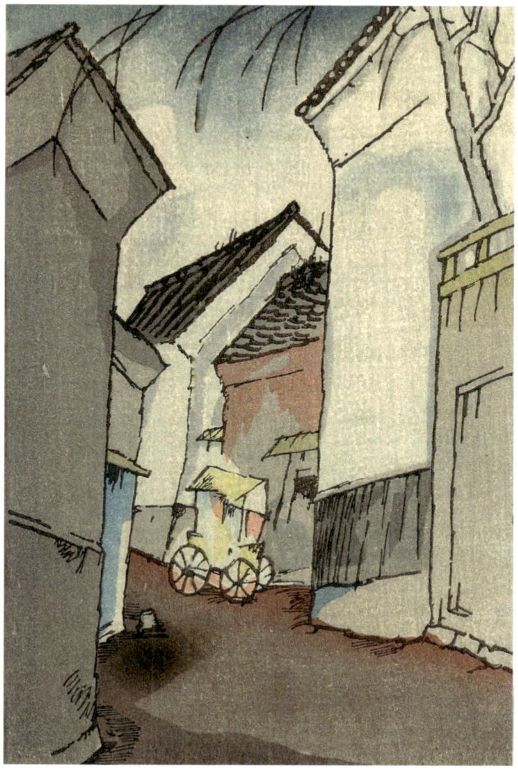

Fig. 3.13. *Profile of a beauty*
From the series *Illustrated postcards by Yumeji* (*Yumeji ehagaki,* 夢二絵葉書)
13.9 x 9.1 cm
Publisher: Katō Hanga Kenkyūjo

Fig. 3.14. *Street with cart*
From the series *Illustrated postcards by Yumeji* (*Yumeji ehagaki,* 夢二絵葉書)
13.9 x 9.1 cm
Publisher: Katō Hanga Kenkyūjo

During Yumeji's lifetime postcards became a popular means of communication and expression among artists. This posthumously produced collection references the many sets of postcards that Yumeji designed throughout his career. In fact, one of Yumeji's very first creative endeavours were the postcards he made and sold in 1905 to support himself when a student at Waseda Business School. *Profile of a beauty* represents Yumeji's signature image of a beauty, rendered in close-up to hint at an intimate moment of interiority and self-reflection. By contrast, prints such as *Street with cart* depict a city scene, indicating a shift from his usual figurative works. For other images from this set, see figs. 4.2; cat. 84–89.

## Notes

**1.** The biographical details of Yumeji's life in this essay have been drawn from Kawano, ed., *Yumeji 1884–1934*; Kanazawa Cultural Promotion Foundation, ed., *Takehisa Yumeji*; Ogawa, *Motto shiritai Takehisa Yumeji* and Shizuoka City Art Museum, ed., *Takehisa Yumeji to Shizuoka yukari no bijutsu*. Unless otherwise indicated, all translations are by the author.

**2.** Merritt, *Modern Japanese woodblock prints*, 27.

**3.** Ibid., 30.

**4.** Kanazawa Cultural Promotion Foundation, ed., *Takehisa Yumeji*, 151–53.

**5.** On the relationship between Yumeji and the Yanagiya store, see Kawano, ed., *Yumeji 1884–1934*, 326–35.

**6.** Ibid., 331.

**7.** Written for an advertisement published on 24 February 1912 for the *Spring dawn* (*Haru no kawatare*) volume of *Island of blossoming cherries* (*Sakura saku shima*). Quoted in (Japanese) in Kurita, ed., *Takehisa Yumeji—ai to shi no tabibito—*, 60.

**8.** Aiga, ed., *Hanga*, 178. See also Merritt, *Modern Japanese woodblock prints*, 30.

**9.** Kawano, ed., *Yumeji 1884–1934*, 321.

**10.** Tanaka, *Tsukuhae no gakatachi*, 69–72. For a general study, see also Iwakiri, *Meiji hangashi*.

**11.** Chikamatsu Monzaemon, 'The suicides at Amijima', in Simon, ed., *The Norton anthology of world literature*, 73.

**12.** Nosco, *Confucianism and Tokugawa culture*, 125.

**13.** Chikamatsu Monzaemon, 'The suicides at Amijima', in Simon, ed., *The Norton anthology of world literature*, 73.

**14.** The continual cultural relevance of Chikamatsu Monzaemon's plays in the Taishō era is seen, for instance, in a series of eighteen prints, *Supplements of the complete works of Chikamatsu* (*Dai Chikamatsu zenshū*), published from 1922 to 1926 as part the two hundredth anniversary of Chikamatsu's death in 1724. Celebrated artists, including Kitano Tsunetomi, Ishikawa Toraji (1875–1964), Yamamura Kōka (1885–1942), Kaburagi Kiyokata (1878–1972), Shima Seien (1892–1970) and Uemura Shōen (1875–1949), were involved in designing the prints. I would like to thank Chris Uhlenbeck for bringing this to my attention. For more on this series, see Stephens, ed., *The new wave*, and Hamanaka and Newland, *Onna-e / The female image*.

**15.** Haruo Shirane, 'Chikamatzu Monzaemon and puppet theater', in Shirane, ed., *Early modern Japanese literature*, 233–42.

**16.** Kawase, 'Kurofune o daku onna', 3.

**17.** Ibid.

**18.** Ishikawa, *Takehisa Yumeji 'zasshi no tanoshimi ten'*, 1.

**19.** Takehisa Yumeji, *Yumeji gashū: Natsu no maki*. Quoted in Kurita, ed., *Takehisa Yumeji*, 78.

**20.** Katō Junji was also known as Katō Junzō after around 1959. These artists' names were introduced in a notice about the workshop. See Katō Print Workshop, ed., *Katō Hanga Kenkyūjo annai*, 1937.

**21.** Takahashi, *Takehisa Yumeji*, 207.

# Expressions of popular culture: Yumeji and commercial illustration

Sabine Schenk

Takehisa Yumeji's unique artistic expression reveals numerous stylistic influences, from traditional Japanese art to the international avant-garde. While much of his work falls within the realm of commercial art, a closer inspection demonstrates that it also includes objects that can be appreciated for their high artistic merit. This navigation between the 'artistic' and the 'commercial' or 'popular' characterises the oeuvre of a number of early twentieth-century Japanese artists. As an individual operating outside and without the support of established academic institutions or artist coteries, Yumeji's economic success and the marketing of a 'Yumeji brand' were crucial in his self-promotion. In recent years, Yumeji has attracted increased scholarly attention and attempts to re-evaluate his oeuvre has positioned him alongside well-known artists of the period such as the *yōga* ('Western painting') artist Aoki Shigeru (1882–1911).[1] An examination of his commercial art—book and cover designs as well as mass-produced illustrations—is thus essential in understanding the Yumeji brand that continues to exercise its stylistic influence today.[2] This essay discusses these aspects of Yumeji's art and their role in early twentieth-century commercial art, using as examples his cover designs for literature, sheet-music scores and the mechanically woodblock-printed illustrations for the women's magazine *The ladies' graphic* (*Fujin gurafu*). These works also reflect the development of *bijinga* (pictures of beautiful women) from the 1910s to early 1930s.

## *Graphic design and consumerism: everyday objects and books*

Objects produced in *fin-de-siècle* Europe testify to the high artistic merit of commercial items: an important underlying concept in the then emergent Art Nouveau/Jugendstil on the European continent and the Arts and Crafts movement in the United Kingdom was the notion of incorporating decorative design into the manufacture of everyday items. By the early twentieth-century, this trend was also current in Japan, seen, for instance, in the images of artists and designers such as Fujishima Takeji (1867–1943) and Kamisaka Sekka (1866–1942). Furthermore, the tradition of illustration in Europe remained somewhat elitist until the invention of the lithographic process in the late eighteenth century, which enabled a higher production volume of printed imagery in colour. By contrast, in Japan a well-honed commercial woodblock industry in popular prints and books had already existed since the Edo period (1615–1868). In early twentieth-century Japan, the processes of lithography and woodblock printing existed side by side in a thriving culture of mass consumption in book art, illustrations and graphic design.[3]

It was within this milieu that Yumeji, while still a student in 1905, made his initial design objects that included the hand-painted postcards fashionable at this time. His production and sale of postcards provided an early source of income and Yumeji continued to design postcards even after he received praise with the release of *The Yumeji collection of work* (*Yumeji gashū*) beginning in 1909.[4] In the following years he continued to publish illustrated books and began to work as a designer. The period from 1914 to 1916, when he ran the Minatoya (Harbour Shop) with his ex-wife Kishi Tamaki (1882–1945), coincided with his manufacture of outstanding woodblock prints. It also witnessed his creation of a range of exceptional goods, such as decorated papers (*chiyogami*), textile patterns for *haneri* (detachable kimono collars), summer kimono (*yukata*) and wrapping cloths (*furoshiki*). All of these high-quality items were influenced by the tradition of Japanese craftsmanship and the art-into-life ideas of the Arts and Crafts movement and Art Nouveau/ Jugendstil. They testify to Yumeji's keen eye for colour and design, a talent he equally applied to other areas such as the illustration of book covers.[5] Together they consolidated his standing as designer.[6]

Book cover designs are well represented in Yumeji's corpus of work. The success of *Yumeji gashū* led to several books that feature his texts or poetry, illustrations and covers. For instance, in his 1919 collection of poetry *Illustrated love songs: the narrow road to the alleyways* (*Eiri jōka: roji no hosomichi*), Yumeji created the cover image and the overall look of the book jacket as well as the full-page woodblock-printed illustrations and the text. As a whole, they conjure up a nostalgic view of life in the city's narrow alleyways as may have existed (or was perceived to have existed) during the Edo period (figs. 4.1a–b & 4.2). Other examples, such as the cover for the compilation of romantic poetry *Into the mountains* (*Yama e yosuru*), display a more modern take and offer a glimpse of the literary coteries Yumeji was affiliated with (fig. 4.3). *Into the mountains* includes contributions by the female poets, writers and social reformers, Yanagiwara Byakuren (1885–1967), who was the first cousin to Emperor Taishō, Chino Masako (1880–1946) and Yosano Akiko (1878–1942). Yumeji also designed book covers, jackets and slipcases for literature by other celebrated writers, poets and playwrights of the day: Shimazaki Tōson (1872–1943), Tokuda Shūsei (1872–1943), Tanizaki Jun'ichirō (1886–1965), Osanai Kaoru (1881–1928) and Nagata Mikihiko (1887–1964).[7] From 1915 to 1916, Yumeji devised forty complete book covers for Nagata alone, an indication of his popularity as an artist working in this field.[8]

While Yumeji's book cover, jacket and slipcase designs include abstract and decorative elements, most are figurative. Some feature beautiful women, often dressed in colourful traditional kimono and on occasion referencing the Edo period, an era clearly viewed with nostalgia during the early twentieth century. Yumeji also meticulously harmonised his book covers with the publication's textual content. His 1916 illustration for the cover of *Oshichi Kichiza* portrays a modern, yet clearly romanticised, image of a beautiful young woman (fig. 4.4). Yumeji's ability to visualise the entire scheme of a book reflects his skill as a graphic designer and he would apply this talent in his creation of illustrated sheet-music covers.

### *Designs for illustrated sheet-music covers*

Yumeji also made a considerable number of covers for illustrated sheet music, which were popular from the late Meiji era until the 1930s when music making in the home was eventually superseded by playing musical recordings. After the adoption of a European system of musical notation in Japan from around 1870, the production of sheet music for the salon led to a demand for decorative covers, and this boosted the development of sheet-music covers as a graphic medium. Although forms of musical notation had previously existed in Japan for court music, the five-line musical notation introduced from the West had the advantage that it could be used to notate and reproduce any musical piece, regardless of cultural origin (e.g. Japanese and Western).[9] As a consequence, this system was used widely in Japan; it was also seen as a vehicle to promote Japanese music on the international stage. The music historian Rin Shukuki believes that the burgeoning of illustrated sheet-music publishing was closely connected to the consumer-oriented culture of the Taishō era, which was characterised by rapid urbanisation, the rise of a bourgeois society and a vibrant artistic milieu that spawned experimentation with avant-garde styles.[10]

In 1914, Yumeji embarked on a collaboration with one of the important sheet-music publishers operating in Taishō-era Tokyo, Senō (Senow) Kōyō (1891–1961). He founded his publishing business in 1910, and

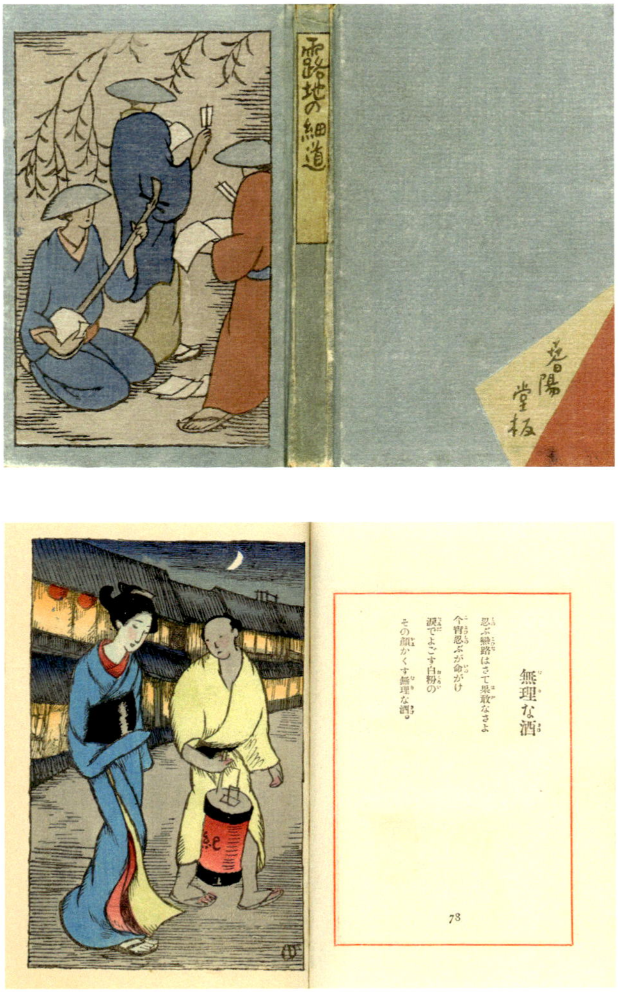


Fig. 4.1a–b. *Illustrated love songs: the narrow road to the alleyways* (*Eiri jōka: roji no hosomichi*, 繪入情歌 露地のほそみち)
17.3 x 10.5 x cm (cover closed, fig. 4.1a); 17.3 x 21.4 x cm (book open, fig. 4.1b)
Date: 1919
Seals: artist's comma-shaped (*tomoe*) and (in colophon) *Issōjin* seals
Publisher: Shunyōdō

This small book comprises 142 pages. The term '*roji*' in the title refers to the narrow alleys of older Japanese neighbourhoods and can perhaps be interpreted as an urban version of the *The narrow road to the interior* (*Oku no hosomichi*) by the celebrated poet Matsuo Bashō (1644–1694). The subjects of the seventeen woodblock-printed illustrations principally depict beautiful women engaged in different activities.

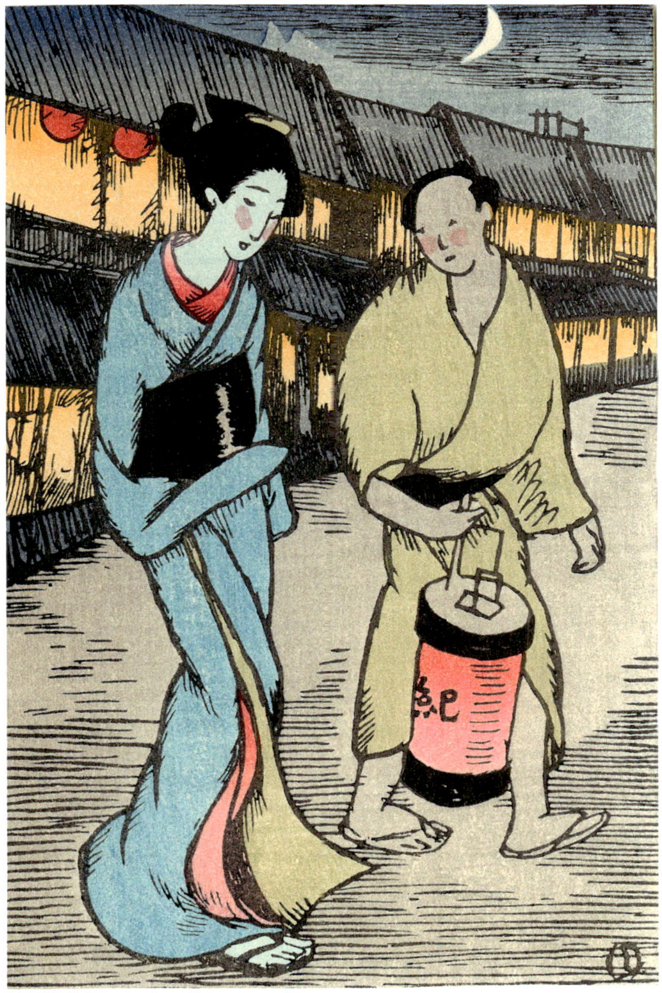

Fig. 4.2. *Woman accompanied by a man carrying a lantern*
From the series *Illustrated postcards by Yumeji* (*Yumeji ehagaki*, 夢二絵葉書)
13.9 x 9.1 cm
Seal: artist's comma-shaped (*tomoe*) seal (as on the original design)
Publisher: Katō Hanga Kenkyūjo

Five illustrations from Yumeji's 1919 *Illustrated love songs: the narrow road to the alleyways* (see fig. 4.1) were reprinted as postcards for this later set issued by the publisher Katō Junji. The reprinting of imagery in a new format reflects how Yumeji's designs were distributed and reinterpreted; they serve as an invaluable resource for his paintings, illustrations and designs that were initially not widely available. They also testify to the enduring charm of Yumeji's work, even when removed from their original context. For other images from this series see fig. 3.14; cat 84–89.

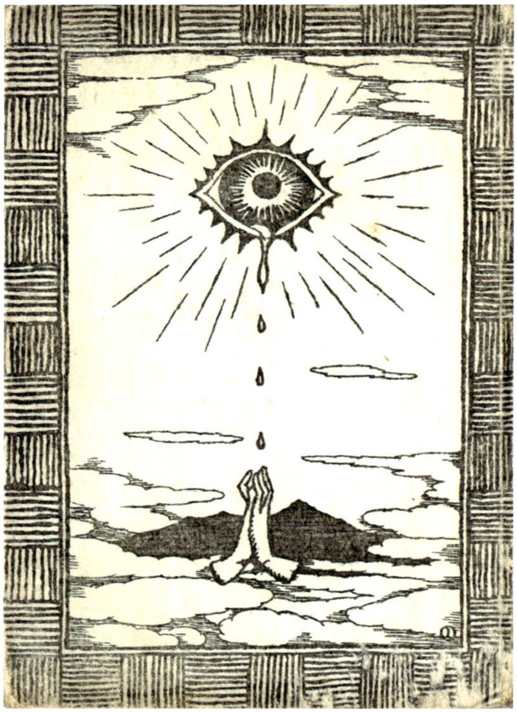

Fig. 4.3a–b. *Into the mountains* (*Yama e yosuru*, 山へよする)
15.8 x 11 cm (cover closed, fig. 4.3a); 15.8 x 22 cm (book open, fig. 4.3b)
Date: 1919
Seal: artist's *Issōjin* seal
Publisher: Shinchōsha

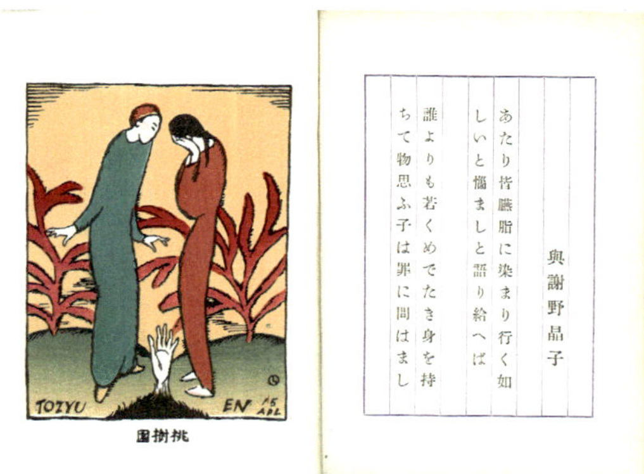


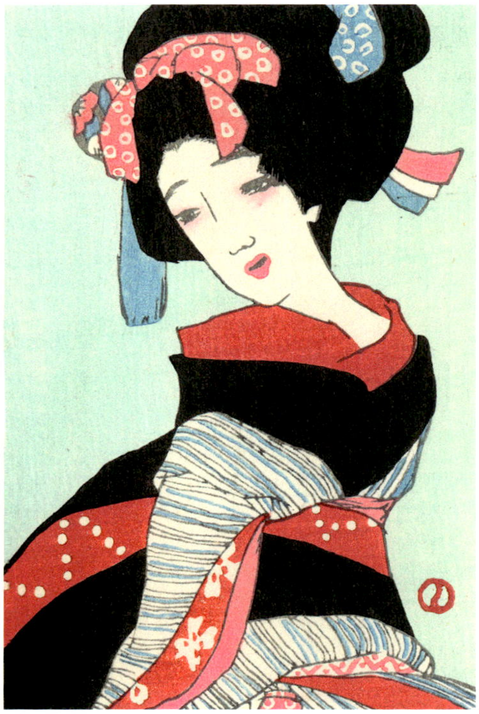

Fig. 4.4. *Oshichi* (*Oshichi*, お七)
From the series *Illustrated postcards by Yumeji* (*Yumeji ehagaki*, 夢二絵葉書)
13.9 x 9.1 cm
Seal: artist's comma-shaped (*tomoe*) seal (as on the original design)
Publisher: Katō Hanga Kenkyūjo

This postcard design is drawn from the cover of the ninth number of *A new collection of love stories* (*Jōwa shinshū*) by the feminist author Tamura Toshiko (1884–1945), which was published by the Shinchōsha in 1916. Tamura's work is an adaptation of the extremely popular tragic love story—and one frequently depicted earlier in *ukiyo-e* prints—between Oshichi, a greengrocer's daughter, and the temple page Kichiza.

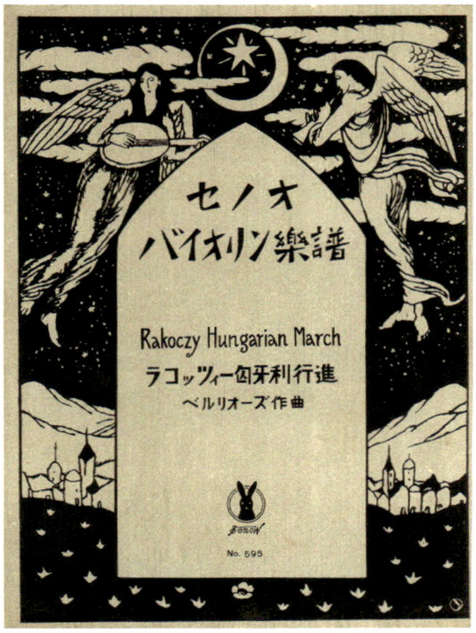


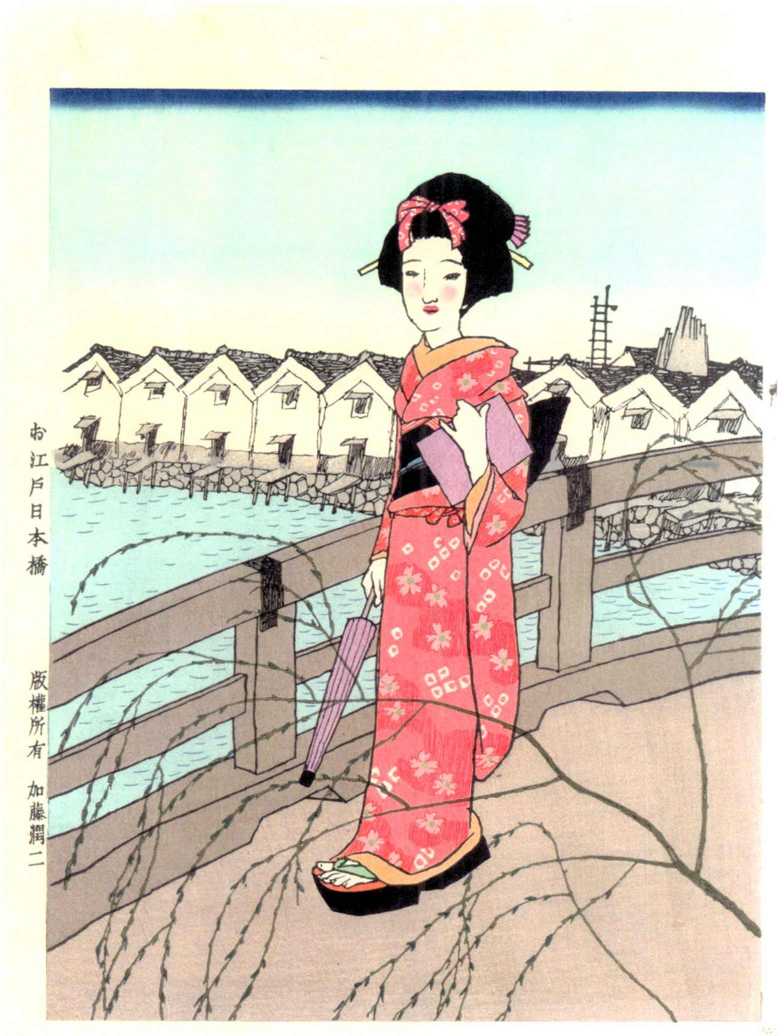


Fig. 4.5. *Rakoczy Hungarian march* (*Rakottsui hangari koshin*, ラコッツィー匈牙利行進)
From *Senow music scores for the violin* (*Senō baiorin gakufu*, セノオバイオリン楽譜), no. 595
31.0 x 22.5 cm
Date: 1924 (2nd edition)
Seals: artist's comma-shaped (*tomoe*) seal and Senow publisher's trademark
Publisher: Senō Ongaku Shuppansha
Composer: Louis Berlioz (1803–1869)

This cover was first published in 1923 and was part of a series within the *Senow music scores* that focused on violin music. The composition features a black-silhouetted motif of angels playing music set against a nocturnal landscape. A cartouche contains the series and image titles, the name of the composer and the Senow publisher's trademark. The overall cover design for each number in this set is the same and only distinguished by differing background colours.

Fig. 4.6. *Great Edo, Nihonbashi* (*Ōedo Nihonbashi*, お江戸日本橋)
From the series *Yumeji's masterpieces* (*Yumeji meisakushū*, 夢二名作集)
33.9 x 24.8 cm
Date: 1938–1939
Publisher: Katō Hanga Kenkyūjo

The publisher Katō Junji reprised this design from a composition Yumeji created in 1916 for *Senow music scores*. It illustrates a woman, dressed in a beautifully patterned red kimono and sporting a traditional hairstyle, as she crosses a wooden bridge; a willow branch fills the foreground. For other images from this series see figs. 1.2, 1.5, 1.12, 3.11, 4.14; cat. 68–72.

from 1915 it traded under the name Senō Music Publishing Company (Senō Ongaku Shuppansha) until it closed its doors after the Second World War.[11] Among its numerous musical publications are the one thousand illustrated sheet-music scores of the series *Senow music scores* (*Senow gakufu*) (see figs. 4.5, 4.7, 4.8, 4.10, 4.11, 4.13; cat. 16–32).

The covers for the *Senow music scores* are usually lithographs, although woodblock-printed editions in a smaller format are also known (see also p. 88). Illustrated music scores of the period by Senow and others customarily comprised a cover and four pages of music notation. The lithographic process for these works entailed the transfer of the original design or painting through methods such as brush transfer, transfer paper or monochrome photography. This contrasted the technique of traditional woodblock prints, whereby the preliminary drawings were often destroyed during the carving stage. Other new lithographic techniques such as chromolithography and offset lithography were also being employed at this time; they increased the possibilities of multi-coloured layouts because of the quick, low-cost processes of mass production.[12]

Senō was not only a successful publisher of music scores and a translator of lyrics—primarily from Italian and German into Japanese—but also a music critic. When a student at Keiō University, in 1912 he authored articles on Italian composers and classical opera. He was also engaged in the Western music section of the Tokyo Broadcasting Office (Tōkyō Hōsō Kyoku; today's NHK, the Japan Broadcasting Corporation) from its inception in 1925. Significant among Senō's work as a publisher was a wide range of celebrated pieces in musical genres from all periods and regions, including vocal solos, choruses or instrumental works for piano and violin that primarily targeted music-loving amateurs (fig. 4.5). Gramophones and records remained very expensive from the late Meiji to early Shōwa eras, and it was through illustrated sheet-music scores that Senō made a broad selection of music accessible to the general public.

The front covers of illustrated sheet-music scores such as *Senow music scores* usually have the title of the piece and an accompanying image. Typically the back covers are dedicated to song lyrics, translations, brief explanations and a colophon. An illustrated sheet-music score from the later 1910s to 1930s generally cost between 15 and 20 *sen* (1 *sen* = 100th of a *yen*), which was roughly equivalent to a cinema ticket or an issue of a popular woman's magazine such as *The world of women's learning* (*Jogaku sekai*) and *The ladies' graphic* (*Fujin gurafu*).

Illustrated sheet-music covers represented a significant part of Yumeji's graphic work: he made approximately 270 sheet-music covers for the *Senow music scores*, not including the two supplemental special series *Senow Yamada music scores* (*Senow Yamada gakufu*) and *Senow music scores: Fujiwara Yoshie* (*Senow gakufu: Fujiwara Yoshie*).[13] Although Yumeji appears to be Senō's most prodigious artist, a number of other illustrators and designers of the day, such as Sugiura Hisui (1876–1965) and Saitō Kazō (1887–1955), were also enlisted to create covers for the project.

Yumeji's first design for the *Senow music scores* was the cover for the well-known Japanese folk song 'Ōedo Nihonbashi' (1916) (see fig. 4.6). Collaboration on the *Senow music scores* initially helped boost Yumeji's popularity, but this diminished as his reputation waned following the Great Kantō Earthquake of 1 September 1923. Nevertheless, contemporaries referred to Yumeji's cover illustrations for the scores as 'Takehisa Yumeji images' (*Takehisa Yumeji ga*), an indication that they attracted an audience as enthusiastic about music as about his work.[14] They reflect Yumeji's skill at tapping into a broad stylistic and thematic range, from figural depictions featuring his acclaimed 'Yumeji-style beauties' (*Yumeji-shiki bijin*) to those adorned with traditional hairstyles and sumptuous *obi* inspired by Edo-period aesthetics, such as the illustration for *Dancing girl* (*Maihime*) (fig. 4.7).

Other pieces showcase styles that testify to the assimilation of modern Western stylistic elements. Yumeji had a special interest in Art Nouveau and, in particular, its German counterpart Jugendstil. There are several examples of his work in which he employed 'pictorial or visual quotations' (*Bildzitat*) linked with illustrations from the German magazine *Jugend*.[15] Ishikawa Keiko, curator of the Takehisa Yumeji Museum in Tokyo, points out that Yumeji's cover for Debussy's 'Beau soir' was clearly informed by a *Jugend* cover (figs. 4.8 & 4.9).[16]

The 'visual quotations' in Yumeji's independent graphic designs and illustrated books were also derived from his study of magazines and visits to art exhibitions, such as the show of European graphic art organised in 1911 by the members of the art and literary magazine *White birch* (*Shirakaba*).[17] Yumeji amassed scrapbooks of magazine covers, reproductions and illustrations, including those from *Jugend* (fig. 4.9).[18] The Yumeji scrapbooks housed in the Yumeji Art Museum in Okayama, for example, provide important clues about the types of magazines, artists and styles that impressed him. The materials collected into these scrapbooks indicate that Yumeji found inspiration in the work of Jugendstil and Art Nouveau artists, such as Heinrich Vogeler (1872–1942) and Aubrey Beardsley (1872–1898). The *sōsaku hanga* ('Creative print') artist Onchi Kōshirō (1891–1955) remembers Yumeji's fondness for the journal *Jugend* from a gathering at the Minatoya, where Yumeji had assembled a small salon of followers:

> *At Yumeji's place we sometimes spent half a day or even an entire day doing nothing. We didn't discuss art. Probably he [Yumeji] was lost in thought, thinking about and longing for someone who was absent. Yumeji was silent for the most part. He sat there, leafing through popular German art magazines such as* Jugend *that were readily available in Japan. We both did this. Particularly during that period young people who admired Yumeji joined us.*[19]

Some of Yumeji's covers for *Senow music scores* employ floral elements encountered in Jugendstil and Art Nouveau. But his cover designs also reflect modernist approaches. He was deeply impressed by the Russian Futurists and other more avant-garde art movements, and this influence is apparent in his cover images such as for Robert Schumann's 'Ich grolle nicht' (fig. 4.10).[20]

Yumeji harmonised the style and the genre of each score cover with the musical piece it advertised. He also paid careful attention to typography, which he synchronised with the mood of the score and the overall design concept. He freely used Japanese characters and syllabaries (*kanji*, *hiragana*, *katakana*) and the Latin alphabet to stress the significance of form, coloration and position of the script.[21] For instance, the title of the cover for the overture from Ambroise Thomas's opera *Mignon*, 'Connais-tu le pays?', shows an innovative arrangement of the typeface (fig. 4.11).

Several contemporary popular songs were already published in 1914 in a woodblock-printed special series for Senō and also later for the Senō Music Publishing Company entitled *New little songs* (*Shin kouta*). Yumeji's covers for these small-sized music sheets were delicately hand printed on Japanese paper.[22] The best-known examples are probably 'Katyusha's song' (*Kachūsha no uta*) and 'The song of the gondola' (*Gondora no uta*) written by Nakayama Shinpei (1887–1952), a noted composer of children's and popular songs (fig. 4.12). Also included within the corpus of illustrated sheet-music scores for Senow are twenty-four scores with Yumeji's own lyrics. His famous poem 'Evening primrose' ('Yoimachigusa') was set to music in 1918 by the composer Ōno Tadasuke (1895–1929) and included within the *Senow music scores* with a cover by Yumeji. Publisher Senō Kōyō describes the decision to release the work:

> *This* kouta *derives from [the chapter] Yumeji's 'Daughters of Japan' ('Nihon no musume') [and is] from Yumeji's* kouta *collection* Sunday (Dontaku). *Ōno was extremely happy to set it to music. When Yumeji heard about it, he was delighted. We mutually agreed to issue the publication in May 1918.*[23]

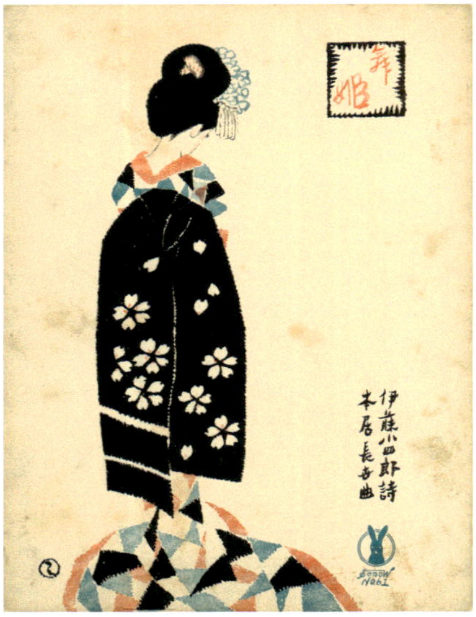


Fig. 4.7. *Dancing girl* (*Maihime*, 舞姫)
From *Senow music scores* (*Senow gakufu*, セノオ楽譜), no. 61
30.7 x 23.2 cm
Date: 1917
Seals: artist's comma-shaped (*tomoe*) seal, Senow publisher's trademark
Publisher: Senō Ongaku Shuppansha
Poem: Itō Koshirō (dates unknown)
Composer: Motoori Nagayo (1885–1945)

In this image Yumeji showcases the woman's luxurious *obi*, patterned kimono and ornately dressed hair. Her slender figure and downturned head typifies Yumeji's particular brand of female imagery.

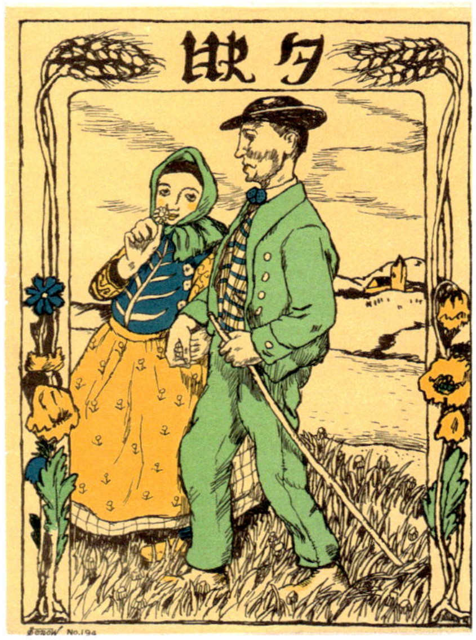


Fig. 4.8. *Beau Soir* (*Yūbae*, 夕映)
From *Senow music scores* (*Senow gakufu*, セノオ楽譜), no. 194
31.0 x 22.6 cm
Date: 1924 (4th edition)
Seal: Senow publisher's trademark
Publisher: Senō Ongaku Shuppansha

This cover reflects Yumeji abiding interest in Art Nouveau, including the German equivalent Jugendstil that emerged in the mid-1890s. The composition of a peasant couple in a rural landscape finds its stylistic roots in a cover from the Munich-based art journal *Jugend* from which Jugendstil derived its name (fig. 4.9). Even though Yumeji's much simplified design omits most of the allegories to peasant life seen in the original *Jugend* cover, the overall representation and the unusual foreground flowers provide hints at the source of inspiration.

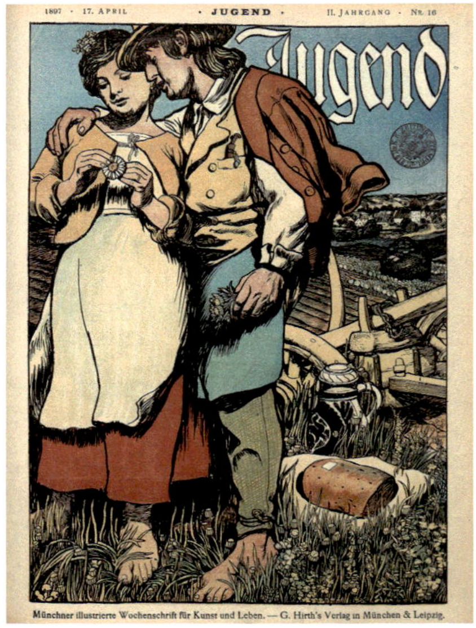


Fig. 4.9. *Cover of Jugend*
Date: vol. 2 no 16, 17 April 1897
Publisher: G. Hirth

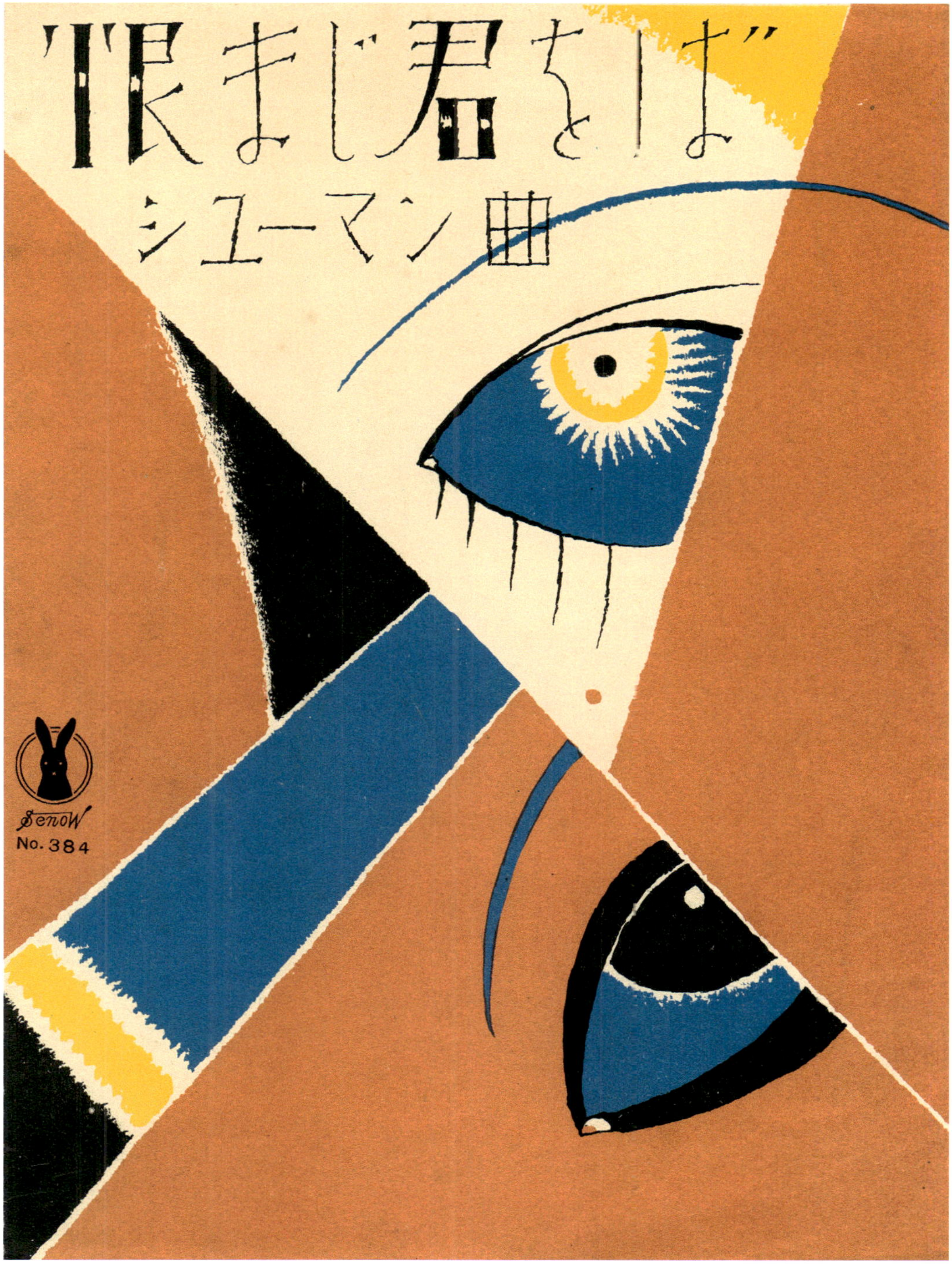


Fig. 4.10. *Ich grolle nicht* (*Uramaji kimi o ba*, 恨まじ君をば)
From *Senow music scores* (*Senow gakufu*, セノオ楽譜), no. 384
31.0 x 22.7 cm
Date: 1924
Seal: Senow publisher's trademark
Publisher: Senō Ongaku Shuppansha
Composer: Robert Schumann (1810–1856)
Translator: Horiuchi Keizō (1897–1983)

This cover illustrates triangular shapes and a distinctive eye motif, the latter frequently encountered in Yumeji's subsequent work. In contrast to the figural styles of most *Senow music scores*, this composition is extremely abstract and points to Yumeji's interest in Cubism.

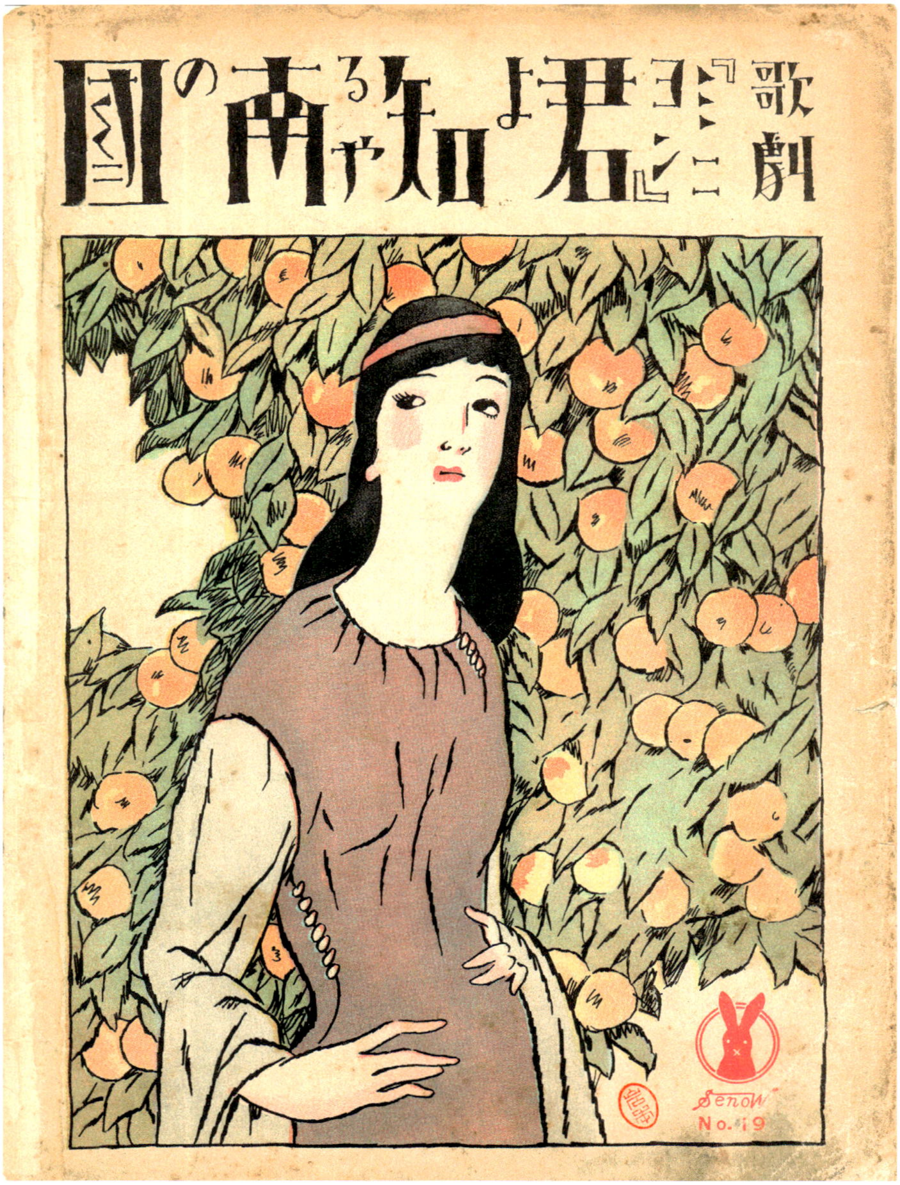


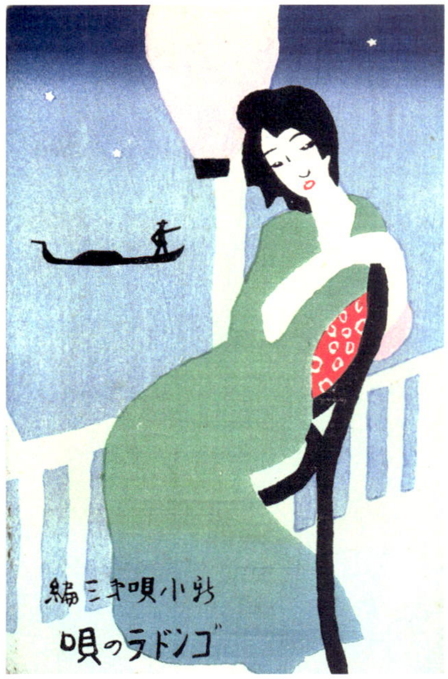


Fig. 4.11. *Mignon, 'Connais-tu les pays?'* (*Kimi yo shiru ya minami no kuni kageki* [*Minyon*], 君よ知るや南の国　歌劇「ミニョン」)
From *Senow music scores* (*Senow gakufu*, セノオ楽譜), no. 19
27.0 x 19.6 cm
Date: 1926 (13th edition)
Seals: Senow publisher's trademark, collector's seal
Publisher: Senō Ongaku Shuppansha
Composer: Ambroise Thomas (1811–1896)
Translator: Horiuchi Keizō (1897–1983)

The svelte figure of a woman dressed in a gown inspired by a 'medieval' European style stands before an orange tree. Her stance is relaxed, with her hands resting on her hips and her shoulders dropped in a form that is characteristically Yumeji. The equally ornate title font complements the decorative nature of the composition. This cover was originally published in 1916.

Fig. 4.12. *The song of the gondola* (*Gondora no uta*, ゴンドラの唄)
From the set *New little songs* (*Shin kouta*, 新小唄), no. 3
18.5 x 11.8 cm
Date: July 1916
Publisher: Senō Ongaku Shuppansha
Composer: Nakayama Shinpei (1887–1952)

The thirty-five contemporary songs in *New little songs* were published with small-sized woodblock-printed covers on Japanese paper. The term *kouta* in the title makes reference to the popular musical genre of the Meiji and Taishō eras known as *Edo kouta* (Edo 'little songs'), which had their roots in Edo-period love songs.

Yumeji designed the entire series, and each score contains the song's music and lyrics. The back covers have a colophon that includes a list of the songs that had been issued to date. This image, for example, lists a price of 15 *sen* (1 *sen* = 100th of a *yen*), which would have been about the price of a fashion magazine. The cover here depicts a woman in a green dress seated on a red upholstered chair on a veranda and under a lantern. The blue of the water and the starry evening sky has been rendered through the gradation of colour and offset by the silhouette of a Venetian gondola. Yumeji conceived the composition without the use of contour lines.

This initial cover design for 'Evening primrose' met with critical acclaim and was reissued four times. It was also updated with a completely new image for the 5th edition following the Great Kantō Earthquake of 1 September 1923 (fig. 4.13).[24] Moreover, the original 1918 composition was reprinted in 1938–1939 for *Yumeji's masterpieces* (*Yumeji meisakushū*), a compilation of noted works released by publisher Katō Junji (1885–1961) (fig. 4.14).

### *Yumeji and the genre of 'beautiful women'* (bijinga) *in his commercial illustration*

The visualisation of women is at the core of much of Yumeji's art practice, and the popularity of these compositions constitutes the basis for his artistic and commercial success. His *bijinga* also served to bridge the various media in which he worked, including graphic design and commercial illustration. Although the illustrations Yumeji produced early in his career and within the context of socialist activism had yet to foreshadow his future path, his *Yumeji gashū* is early testimony to his distinct approach in the representation of women. These were strongly influenced by the physical appearance of his first model (and briefly his wife) Tamaki.

Yumeji's portrayal of women evolved into an individualistic style in his paintings and graphic designs, which is believed to have been affected by his liaisons with three women: Tamaki, Kasai Hikono (1896–1920) and Sasaki Kaneyo (Oyō, 1904–1980) (for photographs of them, see p. 22).. The female image—the 'Yumeji-style beauty'—fashioned by Yumeji for his graphic work was also a marketing tool. However, Onchi Kōshirō maintained that Yumeji struggled with this aspect of his career, which may have met the expectations of his audience but did not satisfy his own artistic aspirations.[25]

Yumeji and others translated the *bijinga* genre into the pictorial language of the late Meiji and Taishō eras. An instrumental figure in the 'revival' of beautiful women prints, particularly during the Taishō, was the Tokyo publisher, proponent and driving force behind the *shin hanga* ('New print') movement, Watanabe Shōzaburō (1885–1962). At this time, and in keeping with then current Western academic notions, multiples such as prints were neither acknowledged nor accepted as representatives of 'fine art', but Watanabe sought to elevate the tradition of woodblock prints to objects worthy of appreciation as such. Watanabe played a significant role in promoting modern print art in Japan, although the works he commissioned initially targeted a predominantly foreign audience. In popular imagery, the portrayal of women in the Edo-period *ukiyo-e* tradition existed alongside the emerging image of the 'new woman' (*atarashii onna* or *shin fujin*) and the 'modern girl' (*modan gāru* or *moga*). While new magazines such as *The women's review* (*Fujin kōron*), published from 1916, and *The housewife's companion* (*Shufu no tomo*), launched the following year, were directed at this increasingly self-determined type of woman, the heroines of popular fiction and the subject of such magazines were still visualised in part as traditional 'beautiful women'. Illustrators of these publications therefore continued to be inspired by the earlier established *bijinga* ideal.[26] The result was a combination of the conventional visualisation of femininity—perpetuated in *bijinga* in *ukiyo-e*—with updated contemporary artistic and stylistic elements.[27] This more modern rendition of beautiful women can be observed in advertisements and promotional materials.[28] For instance, posters for department stores like Mitsukoshi were devised by respected artists and designers of the day, among them Sugiura Hisui, Okada Saburōsuke (1869–1939) and Hashiguchi Goyō (1881–1921).[29]

In the early twentieth century, the genre of *bijinga* in design and woodblock prints is closely aligned with the development of *nihonga* ('Japanese painting').[30] *Nihonga* artists like Kaburagi Kiyokata (1878–1972), Itō Shinsui (1898–1972) and Terashima Shimei (1892–1975) became influential representatives of *bijinga* and advocated its acceptance within academic circles of the day.[31] Kiyokata writes in 1931 that within this context

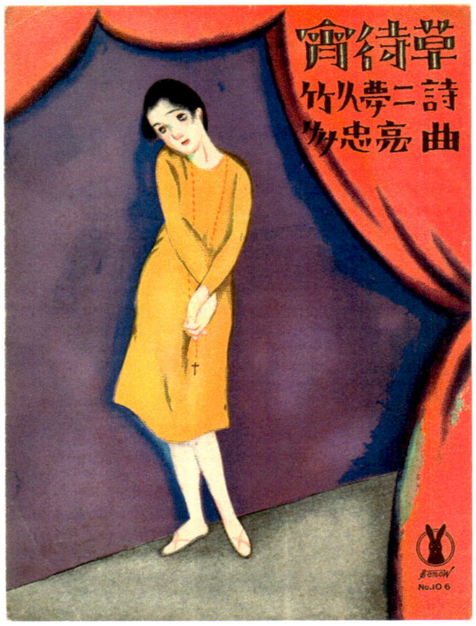


Fig. 4.13. *Evening primrose* (*Yoimachigusa*, 宵待草)
From *Senow music scores* (*Senow gakufu*, セノオ楽譜), no. 106
30.8 x 22.7 cm
Date: [20 May] 1924 (5th edition)
Seal: Senow publisher's trademark
Publisher: Senow Ongaku Shuppansha

As a display of solidarity following the devastating Great Kantō Earthquake of 1 September 1923, the publisher Senō Kōyō decided to publish a 5th edition of 'Yoimachigusa' with a new cover illustration by Yumeji. The publisher believed 'that the release of this song, especially in a city that again has been hit by an earthquake disaster, has special resonance, because this time too even the cover image has been changed'.[1] The subjects in both designs are women. In the earlier versions, the figure wears a kimono, but here the woman sports bobbed hair, Western dress and holds a rosary. She stands on what appears to be a curtained stage. Yumeji's interpretation conveys the shifting tastes before and after the earthquake (see also fig. 4.14).

1. Ishikawa, '"Senō gakufu" ni tsuite', 341.

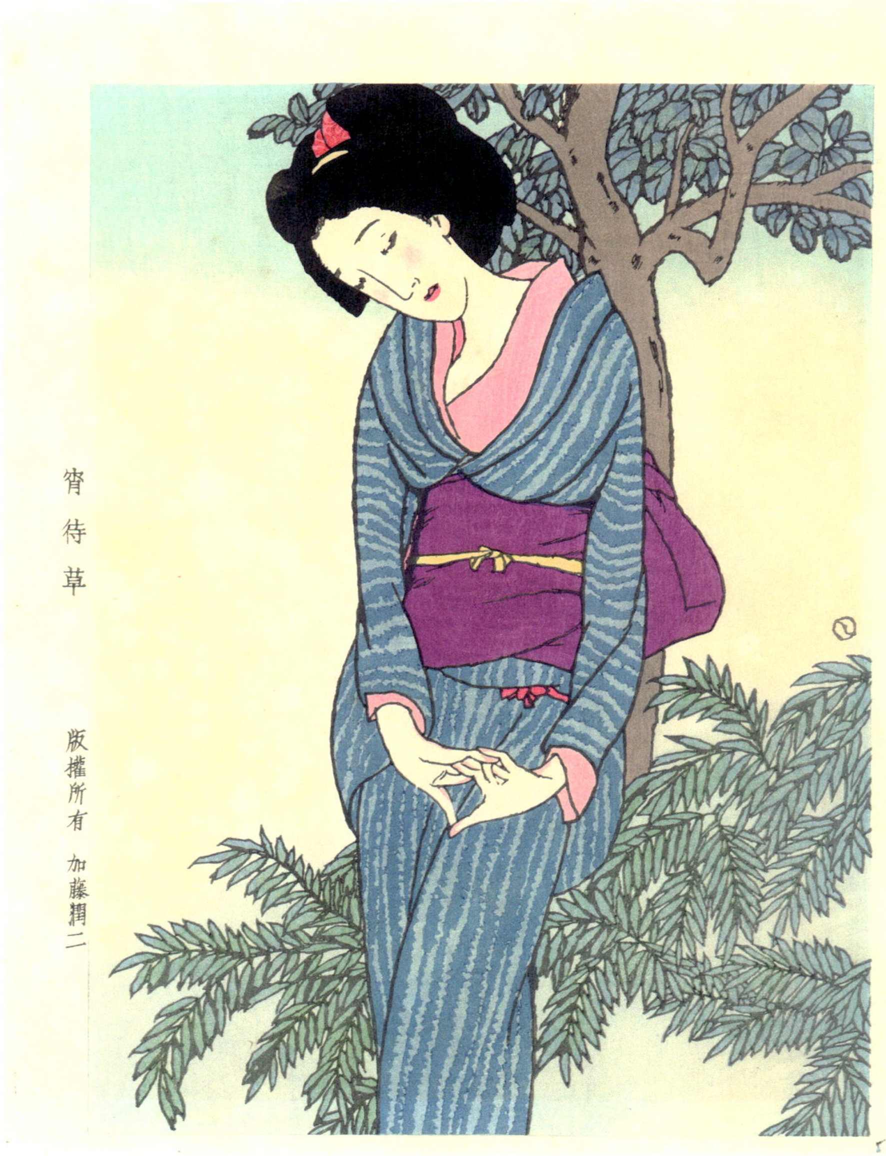


Fig. 4.14. *Evening primrose* (*Yoimachigusa*, 宵待草)
From the series *Yumeji's masterpieces* (*Yumeji meisakushū*, 夢二名作集)
34.3 x 25.5 cm
Date: 1938–1939
Seals: artist's comma-shaped (*tomoe*) (as on the original design), publisher's copyright seal
Publisher: Katō Hanga Kenkyūjo

Yumeji originally created this design in 1918 as the cover for the song sheet 'Evening primrose' in the *Senow music series*. This posthumously issued woodblock print is based on that edition. The publisher Katō Junji used the same design as on the sheet-music cover, however, he removed the title and the Senow publisher's trademark. He also altered the coloration: the woman wears a blue striped kimono with pink undergarments and an aubergine-coloured *obi*. She leans against a tree, her eyes downcast eyes and her fingers interlaced; the gradated coloration of the background sky is skilfully printed (see also fig. 4.13). For other images from this set, see figs. 1.2, 1.5, 1.12, 3.11, 4.6; cat. 68–72.

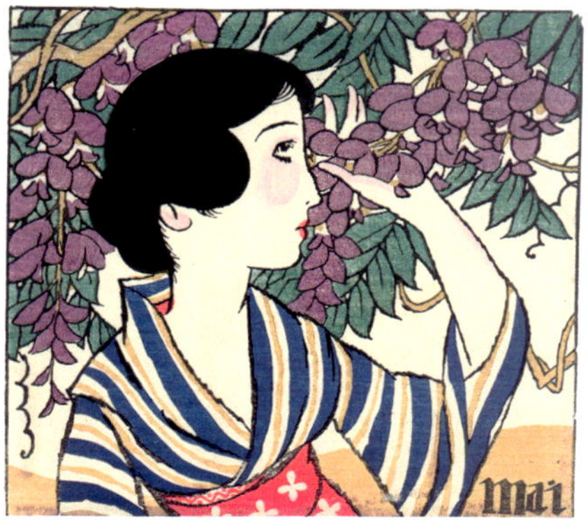


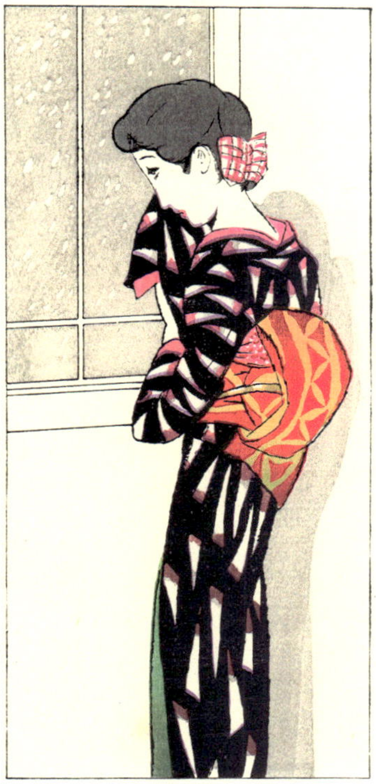

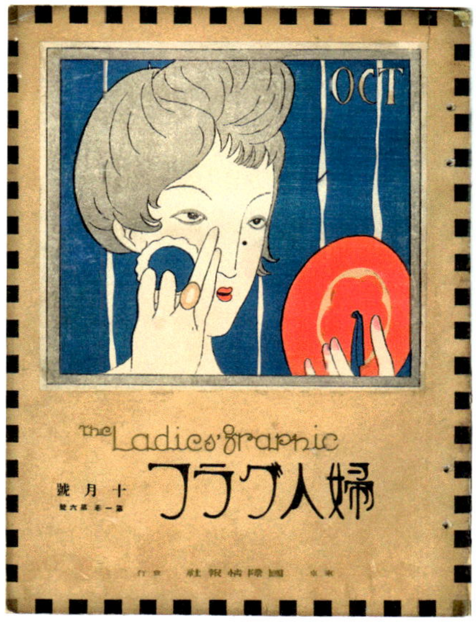


**Fig. 4.15.** *Mai* **(***May***) cover illustration**
**From** *The ladies' graphic* **(***Fujin gurafu*, **婦人グラフ)**
**19.5 x 17.9 cm**
**Date: vol. 3 no. 5, 1926**
**Publisher: Kokusai Jōhōsha**

This woodblock-printed cover illustration, inscribed with the French title *Mai*, shows a woman in a boldly striped kimono standing under a flowering wisteria. She cradles a cluster of blossoms in her left hand (see also cat. 57). For other images from this magazine, see figs. 4.16–4.18; cat. 37–65.

**Fig. 4.16.** *Nanbanji* **(***Nanbanji*, **南蛮寺)**
**From** *The ladies' graphic* **(***Fujin gurafu*, **婦人グラフ)**
**25.3 x 12.0 cm**
**Date: vol. 1 no. 8, December 1924**
**Publisher: Kokusai Jōhōsha**

This woodblock print was one illustration for the serialised literary work 'Women missionaries' (*Nyonin bateren*, 女人伴天連) by Kanbara Haruo (1900–1960), which was featured in *The ladies' graphic* from the first issue in May 1924. Kanbara's tale focuses on early Christianity in Japan, particularly in Nagasaki. This example is one of two prints that accompanied the seventh instalment of this story entitled 'Nanbanji' (the second print is a smaller and almost square, showing a dove clutching a banner). Prints like these served the function of attracting consumers with high-quality illustrations. This issue includes a cover design and three illustrations by Yumeji.

The name *Nanbanji* is a reference to an early Christian church in Kyoto and Yumeji illustrates the theme using his signature 'Yumeji-style beauty'. The woman here wears a colourful kimono and dries her eyes with a sleeve as she gazes out of the window at the snowy landscape.

**Fig. 4.17.** *Autumn make-up*
**(***Kesho no aki*, **化粧の秋)**
**Cover of** *The ladies' graphic*
**(***Fujin gurafu*, **婦人グラフ)**
**18.9 x 20.2 cm (image); 32.8 x 24.5 cm (cover)**
**Date: vol. 1 no. 6, October 1924**
**Publisher: Kokusai Jōhōsha**

A woman with a beauty mark below her left eye looks into a mirror as she applies make-up with a powder puff. The simplicity of the design, the stylised background and restricted palette contribute to the composition's overall formal feel. In style it approximates the cosmetic advertisements of the 1920s and exemplifies the influence of Art Deco on Yumeji's work.

An illustration of the short story entitled 'Spring glance' (*Haru no me*) from this issue is reproduced in cat. 44.

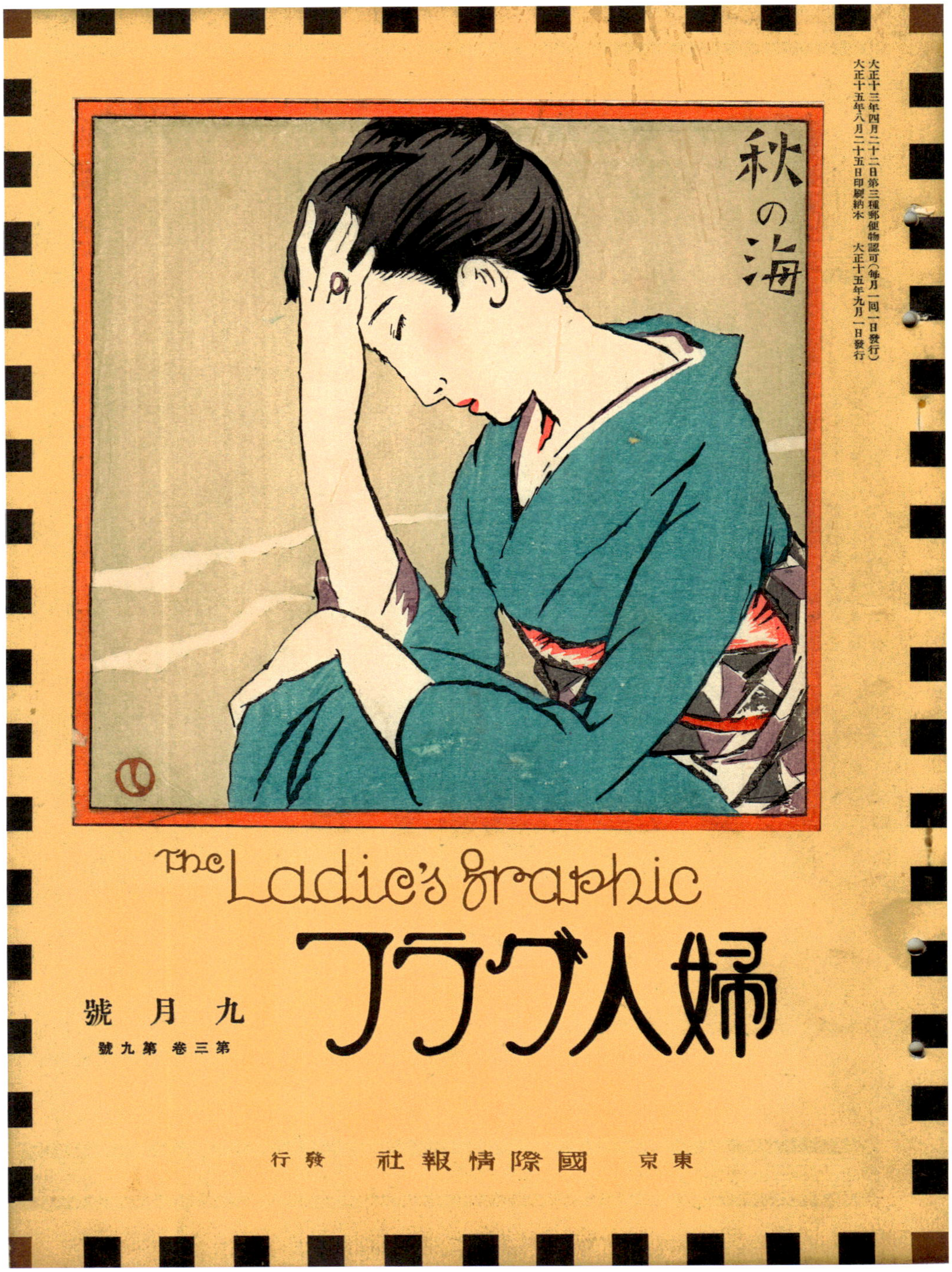


Fig. 4.18. *Autumn sea* (*Aki no umi*, 秋の海)
Cover of *The ladies' graphic* (*Fujin gurafu*, 婦人グラフ)
19.0 x 19.0 cm (image);
33.1 x 24.4 cm (cover)
Date: vol. 3 no. 9, September 1926
Seal: artist's comma-shaped (*tomoe*) seal
Publisher: Kokusai Jōhōsha

The melancholic expression of the woman in this example is typical of Yumeji's female imagery. Here, she cradles her forehead in one hand, her eyes shut, and her countenance seems to express a state of emotional turmoil. This pose is encountered in several of Yumeji's works, especially during his relationship in the 1920s with the model Oyō (Sasaki Kaneyo, 1904–1980). This issue of *The ladies' graphic* also contains illustrations by Tagaya Shino.

the genre evolved from one having highly charged sexual connotations—as he believed had been the case in *ukiyo-e*—to one that was a modern depiction of women that was accompanied by culturally imposed stereotypes such as purity, noblesse and compassion.[32] Bastions of academia, such as official art schools, and the jurors of government-sponsored exhibitions who banned paintings considered immoral from the official exhibitions, were the primary drivers of this trend.[33]

Yumeji's *bijinga* are similarly emblematic of the period. His decorative, romantic style evolved from influences by contemporary *bijinga* painters. While some of Yumeji's female images may appear to be erotically charged, albeit subliminally and especially when read against his own life experiences, they do not ooze eroticism. Many appear as slender girls in distinctly S-shaped poses: eyes downcast, head inclined and with sad, at times with partially concealed faces, they embody instead the typically melancholic flavour of the Yumeji style.

This characteristic expression—acknowledged during his lifetime as a 'Yumeji-style beauty' (*Yumeji-shiki bijin*)—was developed in the illustrations he made for a handful of magazines that catered to young women such as *The ladies' graphic*, *The world of women's learning* and *The women's literary world* (*Joshi bundan*).[34] Cover designs and illustrations, especially by artists like Yumeji who were extremely popular with girls and young women, were a vital means of advertisement for the publishers of these journals. His work for *The ladies' graphic*, for example, subsumes covers as well as illustrations; these underscore the full expressive potential of his female figures (figs. 4.15 & 4.16). They include stylised motifs alongside kimono-clad women or 'modern girls' in Western dress, thus reflecting the scope of his *bijinga* representation. The decorative composition of *Autumn make-up* could easily have been an Art Deco-styled advertisement for cosmetics (fig. 4.17), while the cover image for the September 1926 issue is more in keeping with the artist's archetypal portrayal of a doleful female figure (fig. 4.18).

The multi-coloured woodblock prints in *The ladies' graphic* are referred to as *kikai mokuhan* (machine-printed woodblock prints) and were produced by a printing shop run by Arashida Kokusui.[35] This mechanical process is rooted in traditional woodblock printing, in which an expert block-cutter prepares the woodblocks and a specialist printer transfers the colour onto the block and paper (if required, there were several printings for each colour). The block-cutter of machine-printed woodblock prints still prepared the woodblocks in a conventional manner, but the process differed since the printing was done with a printing press. This change in technology made it possible to up the volume of production. The vibrant coloration and finish of machine-printed woodblock prints is comparable to traditionally crafted prints. However, the small irregularities or adjustments necessary during the printing process could not be accommodated by this newer technique; ultimately it was the combination of a mass-production technology and the charm of the woodblock-print medium that proved the winning formula.

Following the initial success with *Yumeji gashū*, Yumeji's fan base grew quickly and fans awaited new volumes with great anticipation.[36] The effect of his work on his female audience, young adults and women was exceptional. It not only influenced the fashions of the day, but also contemporary artists, including Hikono who was herself an art student. Yumeji's association with and possible imprint on the *sōsaku hanga* movement has been much debated. From early in his career, *sōsaku hanga* proponent Onchi Kōshirō admired Yumeji and fellow *sōsaku hanga* artist Kawanishi Hide (1894–1965) collected Yumeji's art and was deeply impressed by his individuality.[37] The Hide collection, comprising around 350 pieces and since 2011 housed in the National Museum of Modern Art, Kyoto, perhaps offers another layer of meaning in our reception of Yumeji's art. Until recently, Yumeji's paintings, prints, illustrations and graphic design work have been kept in private holdings, museums devoted to Yumeji or as part of larger collections, but that this body of work entered a national art collection and has been the subject of a commemorative exhibition is significant.[38]

The impact of Yumeji's graphic art is enduring, and it has undergone numerous printings and reprinting. The publisher Katō Junji issued Yumeji's designs in the 1930s, and even today there are shops in Tokyo and Kyoto that have revived the concept of Yumeji's Minatoya. Among their inventory is a broad range of Yumeji-style items, including business card cases, stationery reproducing his original designs as well as prints and paintings by contemporary artists rendered in a Yumeji mode. The influence of his art also extends to modern kimono design. In 2006, a summer kimono collection by the fashion label Uniqlo indirectly referenced Yumeji's style with distinct Taishō-era patterns, while the upmarket Tokyo kimono shop Shara modelled its collection after the styles and motifs seen in the garments in Yumeji's paintings and illustrations.

The renewed interest in the art and culture of the Taishō era, together with acquisitions by institutions like the National Museum of Modern Art, Kyoto, have resulted in the scholarly re-evaluation of Yumeji's position within Japanese commercial graphic design from 1900 to 1930. Further research on the interrelationship between Yumeji's artistic aspirations and the commercial milieu in which he operated will shed further light on the life and work of this pioneering individual.

## *Notes*

1. See Ogura and Hashitomi, *Takehisa Yumeji. Aoki Shigeru*, 42. Unless otherwise indicated, all translations are by the author.

2. See also Naoi, 'Takehisa Yumeji and his modern beauty'.

3. Clark, *Modern Asian art*, 52.

4. Ogura, *Takehisa Yumeji*, 74, and Hosono, *Takehisa Yumeji*, 44–45.

5. See also Strong McDonald, 'Onchi Kōshirō', 74.

6. See also Merritt, *Modern Japanese woodblock prints*, 27.

7. Shimazaki Tōson and Tokuda Shūsei were known for their connection with Taishō-era literary naturalism; see Michael Bourdaghs, *The dawn that never comes, Shimazaki Tōson and Japanese nationalism* (New York: Columbia University Press, 2003) and Richard Torrance, *The fiction of Tokuda Shūsei and the emergence of Japan's new middle class* (Seattle: University of Washington Press, 1994). Yosano Akiko published her first poetry collection, *Tangled hair* (*Midaregami*), in 1901; on Yosano, see also Janine Beichman, *Embracing the firebird, Yosano Akiko and the birth of the female voice in modern Japanese poetry* (Honolulu: University of Hawai'i Press, 2002). On Yumeji and the writers of the White Birch Society (Shirakabaha), see Nagai Tatsuo, 'Yumeji to Shirakabaha' ('Yumeji and the Shirakaba school'), in Yūjōbō, ed., *Taiyō 20*, 6–7.

8. Hillier, *The art of the Japanese book*, vol. 2, 1001.

9. Rin, 'Gakufu no fūkei', 5.

10. Ibid., 10, and Nara, *Inexorable modernity*, 83.

11. For this section on *Senow music scores*, I have drawn from Ishikawa, '"Senō gakufu" ni tsuite', 336–42.

12. For printing details and techniques, see Iwakiri Shin'ichirō, 'Insatsu kara mita Yumeji sakuhin' ('The work of Yumeji seen from the perspective of printing'), in Kawano, ed., *Yumeji 1884–1934*, 318–25.

13. This number is confirmed in Ishikawa, '"Senō gakufu" ni tsuite', 336. These two supplemental sets feature the musical works of composer and conductor Yamada Kōsaku (1886–1965) and pieces by the Japanese tenor Fujiwara Yoshie (1898–1976), respectively.

14. Ishikawa, '"Senō gakufu" ni tsuite', 337–38.

15. This 'journal for art and life', *Jugend* (literally 'Youth') was published from 1896 to 1940; it marked a shift in applied graphics, maintaining that it would fill the gap in coping with the 'ideas and ambitions of our increasingly richer public life in an extremely free artistic manner' (quoted from *Jugend*'s editorial agenda by the publisher Georg Hirth and editorial journalist Fritz von Ostini, *Jugend*, no. 1, 1896, 2). *Jugend* focused on contemporary illustrations and ornaments; it included critiques on culture and literature.

16. Ishikawa, '"Senō gakufu" ni tsuite', 337–38.

17. See also Araki, *Yumeji no ikokushumi*; Kimata, 'Takehisa Yumeji *Dontaku*', 306–11, and Schamoni, 'Die Shirakaba-Gruppe', 57–85.

18. See also Takahashi, *Takehisa Yumeji*, 302–8.

19. From Onchi Kōshirō, 'Yumeji no geijutsu, sono hito' ('Yumeji's art and the person'), in Onchi, ed., *Shosō. Yumeji tsuioku tokushū*, 240, and translated in Strong McDonald, 'Onchi Kōshirō', 84.

20. For an investigation of Futurist approaches in Japan, see Omuka, 'David Burluik and the Japanese avant-garde', 111–25.

21. See Ishikawa, '"Senō gakufu" ni tsuite', 339.

22. Ibid., 342.

23. Ibid., 340.

24. Ibid.

25. Onchi, *Yumeji suketchi chōshō*, 167.

26. For a discussion of beautiful women in graphic art, see Ozaki Masato, 'Illustrationen der Taishō- und Shōwa-Zeit', in Kritter, ed., *Japanische Buchillustration*, 24.

27. Kendall H. Brown, 'Modernity and memory. Shin-hanga and Taishō

culture', in Brown and Goodall-Cristante, eds., *Shin-hanga*, 59.

**28.** Hamanaka Shinji, '*Bijinga*: the portrayal of beauties in modern Japan', in Hamanaka and Newland, *Onna-e / The female image*, 13.

**29.** Ibid. See also Brown, 'Modernity and memory', 60–61.

**30.** Brown, 'Modernity and memory', 60.

**31.** Hamanaka, *Bijinga*, 13.

**32.** From Kaburagi, ed., *Gendai sakka bijinga zenshū*, vol. 1, 2; noted in Merritt and Yamada, *Woodblock kuchi-e prints*, 126.

**33.** Merritt and Yamada, *Woodblock kuchi-e prints*, 127.

**34.** Honda, 'Takehisa Yumeji', in Rimer, ed., *Multiple meanings*, 49.

**35.** Iwakiri Shin'ichirō believes that a British printer calling himself Jonë Okada or Uchida, and in Arashida Kokusui's employ, introduced this technique. It is very likely that he printed (or at least supervised) the images for *The ladies' graphic*, since he left Arashida to open his own business in 1920. Further details about the life of this printer and why he assumed a Japanese name are unknown. On this and the *kikai mokuhan* process, see Iwakiri Shin'ichirō, 'Insatsu kara mita Yumeji sakuhin ('Yumeji's work seen from the standpoint of printing'), in Kawano, ed., *Yumeji 1884–1934*, 322.

**36.** See also Merritt, *Modern Japanese woodblock prints*, 25.

**37.** Yamano Hidetsugu, 'Kawanishi Hide korekushon' ni tsuite', in Yamano, Ikezawa and Nakao, eds., *Kawanishi Hide korekushon*, 322–38.

**38.** The exhibition, which ran from 11 November to 25 December 2011 at the National Museum of Modern Art, Kyoto, was entitled *Kawanishi Hide korekushon shūzō kinenten. Yumeji to tomo ni / Commemorate of acquisition: the Kawanishi Hide collection. Takehisa Yumeji in the memory.*

*Jihei* (じへい)
(see fig. 3.1, p. 44)

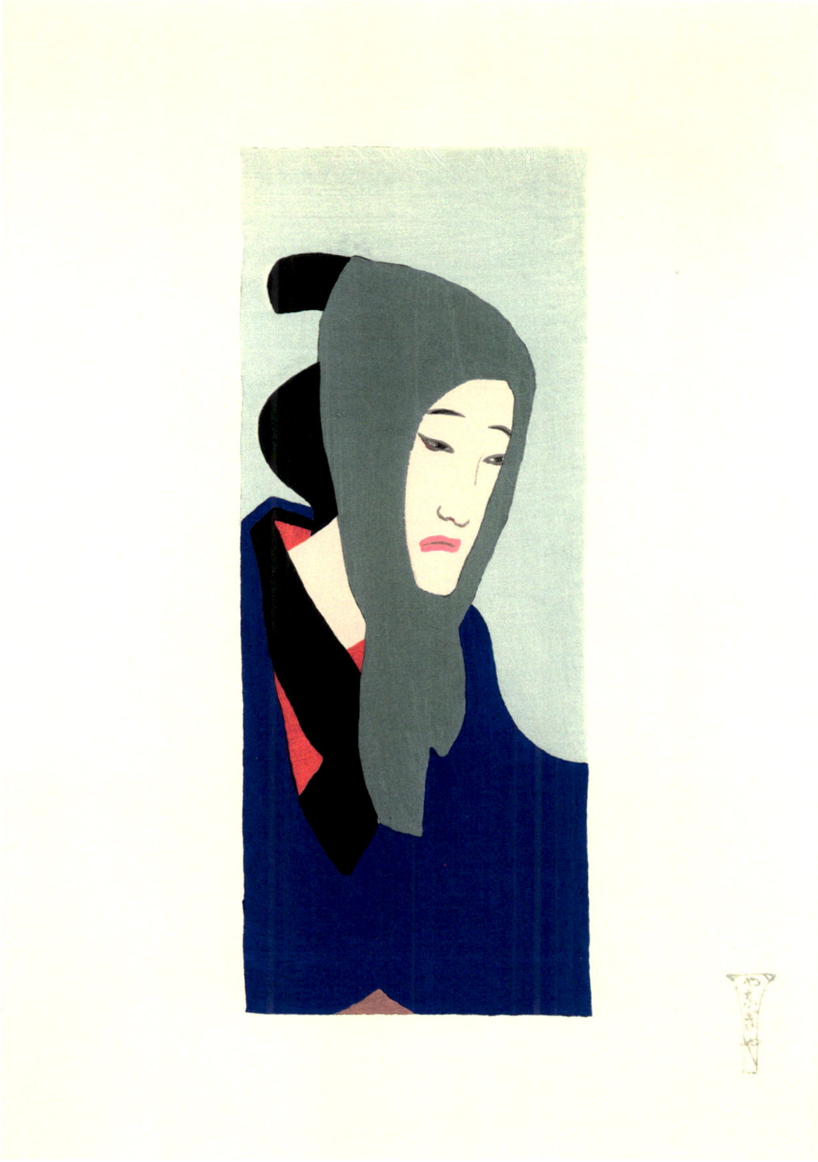

# Catalogue

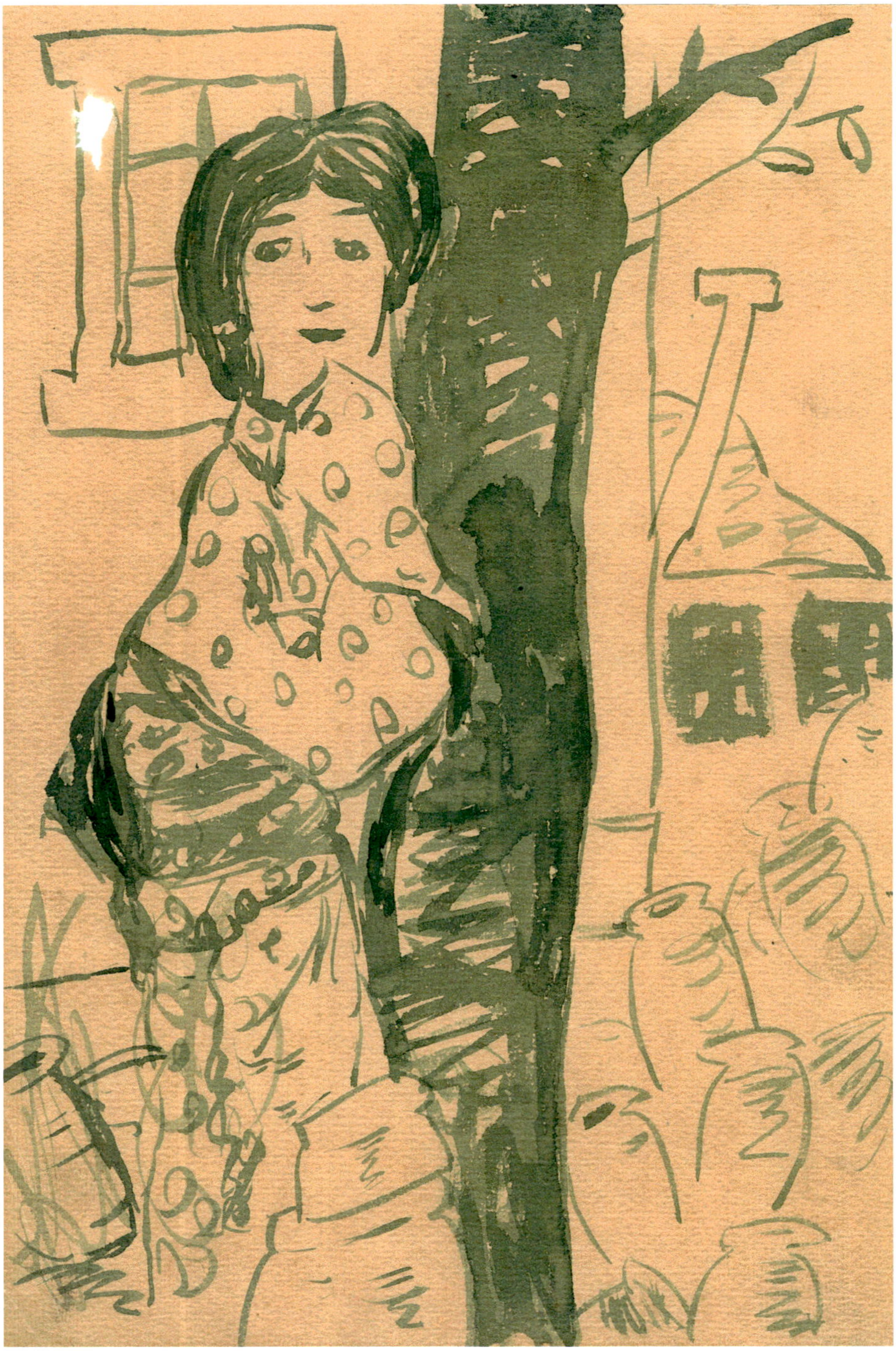

1. Preparatory drawing for *Behind a Chinese restaurant* (*Shina ryōriya no ura*, 支那料理屋の裏)
22.0 x 14.4 cm
Date: c. 1910

This drawing in green ink of a young woman standing near a tree and surrounded by empty pots is a preparatory drawing for Yumeji's 1910 *Winter* (*Fuyu no maki*) volume in *The Yumeji collection of work* (*Yumeji gashū*). There were five other volumes in *Yumeji gashū*: *Spring* (*Haru no maki*) of 1909 and from 1910, *Summer* (*Natsu no maki*), *Flower* (*Hana no maki*), *Travel* (*Tabi no maki*) and *Autumn* (*Aki no maki*). *Yumeji gashū* was the first publication to have Yumeji's short poems and illustrations.
[MdV]

1a. *Behind a Chinese restaurant* (*Shina ryōriya no ura*, 支那料理屋の裏)
From *The Yumeji collection of work: Winter* (*Yumeji gashū: Fuyu no maki*, 夢二画集 冬の巻)
Date: 1910
Publisher: Rakuyōdō
National Diet Library, Tokyo

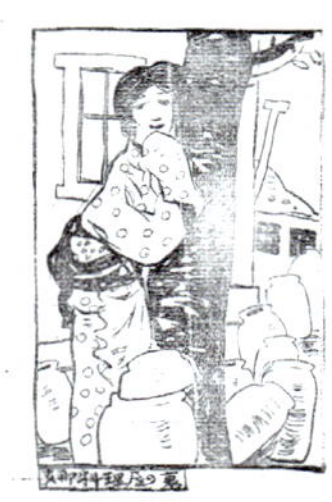

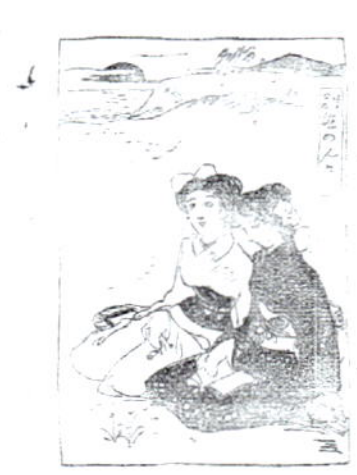

## Drawings and sketches
cat. 1–9

Yumeji was a keen observer and chronicler of the world around him, and he recorded his experiences in the numerous surviving sketchbooks he produced from his early twenties until his death in 1934. His friend, the print artist Onchi Kōshirō (1891–1955), remarked how Yumeji carried a sketchbook with him wherever he went and that 'sketching was like breathing for Yumeji'.[1] It is quite possible that Yumeji's practice of sketching developed early in life because of his elementary school art teacher, Hattori Mokusaburō, who encouraged him to create pencil sketches of things he saw in the world outside the classroom.[2]

Today many of Yumeji's sketchbooks are in museum and private collections. Nihon no hanga houses nineteen sheets with twenty-nine sketches and ink drawings as well as the portfolio, *Pictorial daily* (cat. 2), all of which are illustrated in this publication for the first time. Some sketches are easier to date based on their subject matter; others are more difficult to determine.

Yumeji's sketchbooks contain intimate studies of women and children, views of the aftermath of the Great Kantō Earthquake, and his travels in Japan and abroad. He visualises mundane, fleeting moments of daily life with a sense of beauty and design. Yumeji describes his sketches in the preface to the 1910 *Winter* (*Fuyu no maki*) from *The Yumeji collection of work* (*Yumeji gashū*): 'My sketchbook is filled with soft, round lines. Each line dances and sings with colour; That is how the small pictures are drawn'.

A number of his sketches were done in graphite pencil, while others employed coloured pencils and watercolours. Both his figural and landscape sketches served as sources of inspiration for his paintings and graphic work; they demonstrate that the emphasis on line was at the core of his art practice. His manner of sketching generally involved quick, abbreviated renditions, and this is evident in all aspects of his art, including his paintings. Yumeji was fond of drawing directly onto the canvas, the traces of the pencil and the outlines of the under-drawings often visible even after the application of pigment.

[NN]

1. Onchi Kōshirō, 'Yumeji no suketchi chō' ('Yumeji's sketchbooks'), in TakehisaYumeji, *Takehisa Yumeji suketchi chōshō*, 66–67; quoted in Takahashi, *Takehisa Yumeji*, 218.
2. Ogura Tadao, 'Yumeji no shōgai: gaka toshite no shuppatsu' ('Yumeji's life and his artistic beginnings'), in Yūjōbō, ed., *Taiyō* 20, 22.

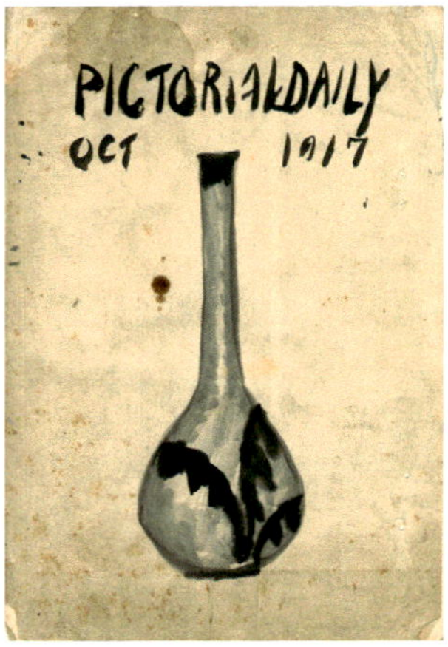


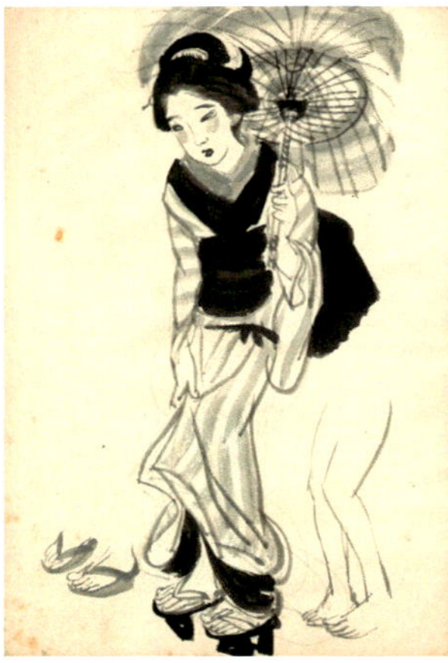

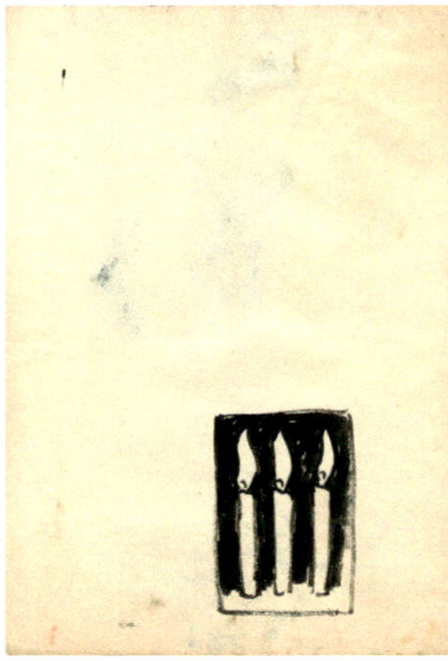

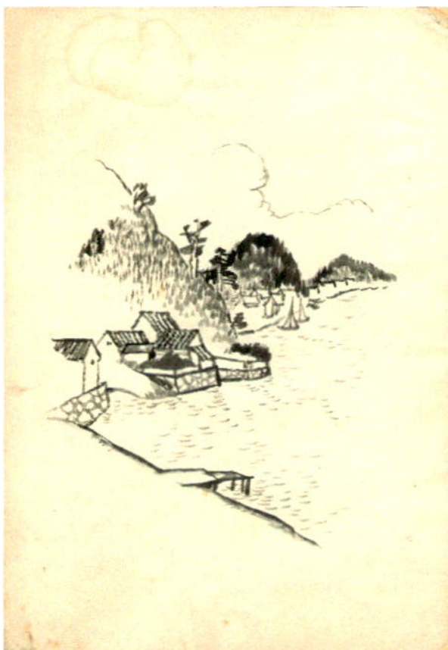

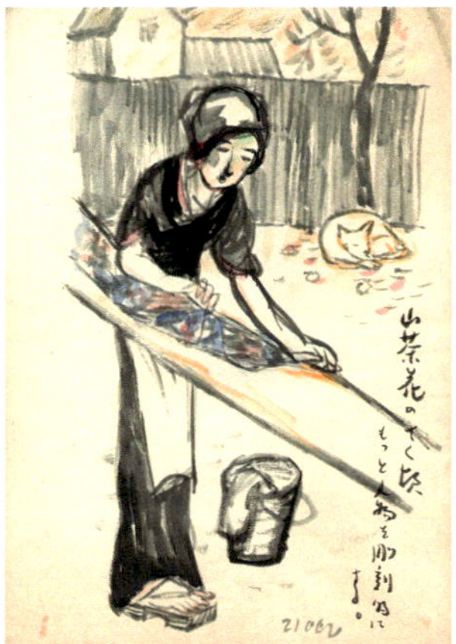

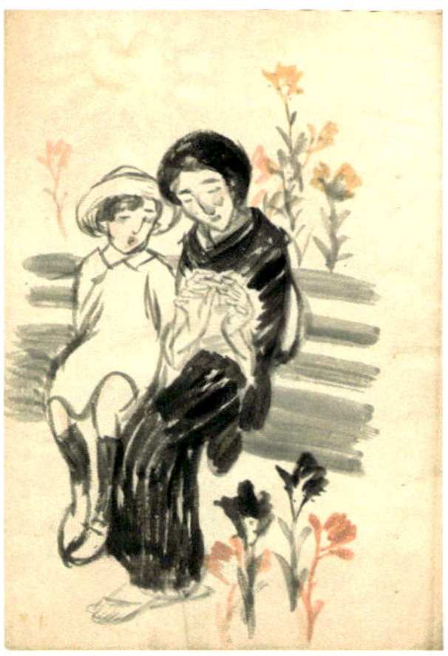

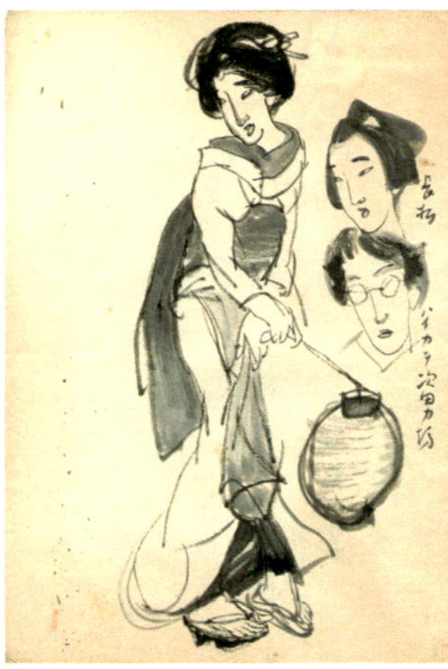

2. Six pages from the portfolio *Pictorial daily*
Date: 1917

2a. Cover.
2b. *Woman with umbrella* (recto)
2c. *Three candles* (verso)
38.2 x 26.3 cm

In the 1936 issue of the magazine *Study window* (*Shosō*) commemorating Yumeji, Onchi Kōshirō speculated that while numerous sketches by Yumeji were still extant, many more had probably been lost. The ink drawing in catalogue 2b shows a kimono-clad woman holding an umbrella; next to her are studies of legs and feet.

[MdV/SS]

2d. *Waterside village* (recto)
2e. *Woman placing cloth on a board to dry* (verso)
38.4 x 26 cm

2f. *Seated woman and child* (recto)
2g. *Woman with lantern, the heads of two men* (verso)
38.4 x 26.5 cm

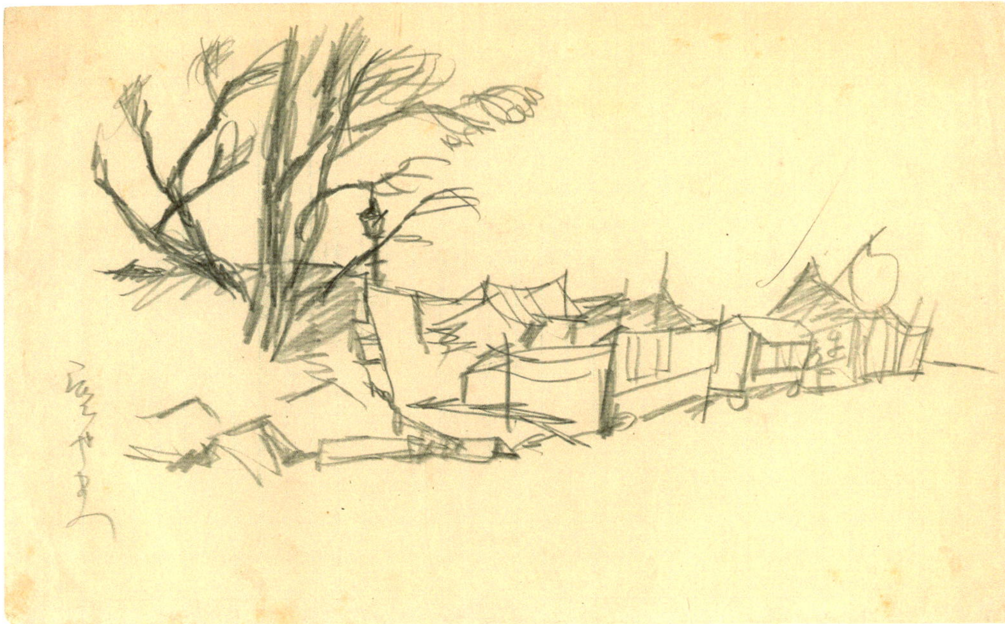

3. Group of pencil drawings
Date: 1923–1925

3a. *A row of houses and a shop*
19.0 x 28.1 cm

3b. *Woman holding a cup*
28.9 x 21.1 cm

3c. *Seated woman*
26.8 x 19.8 cm

3d. *Seated woman in striped kimono*
32.1 x 19.7 cm

3e. *Woman and a study of leaves*
24.0 x 28.5 cm

This group of sketches includes studies of women and a landscape; select examples are done on Western blue-lined paper.

[MdV]

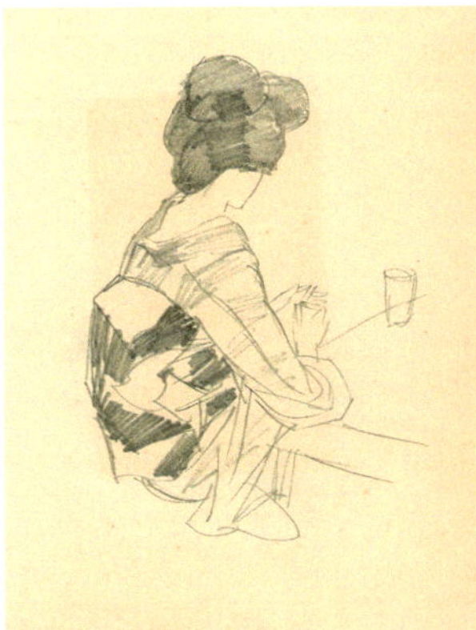

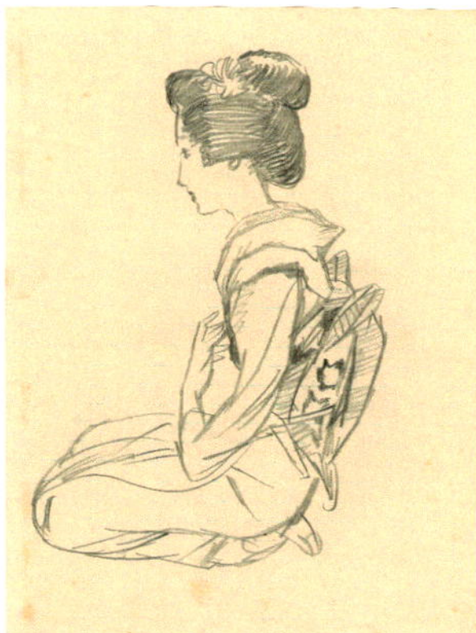

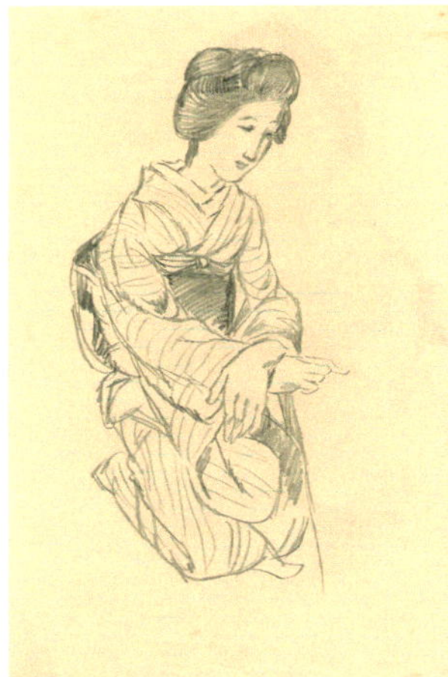

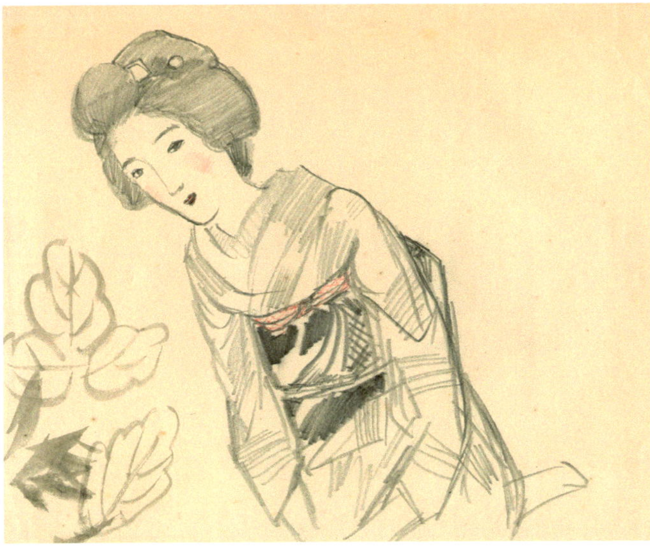

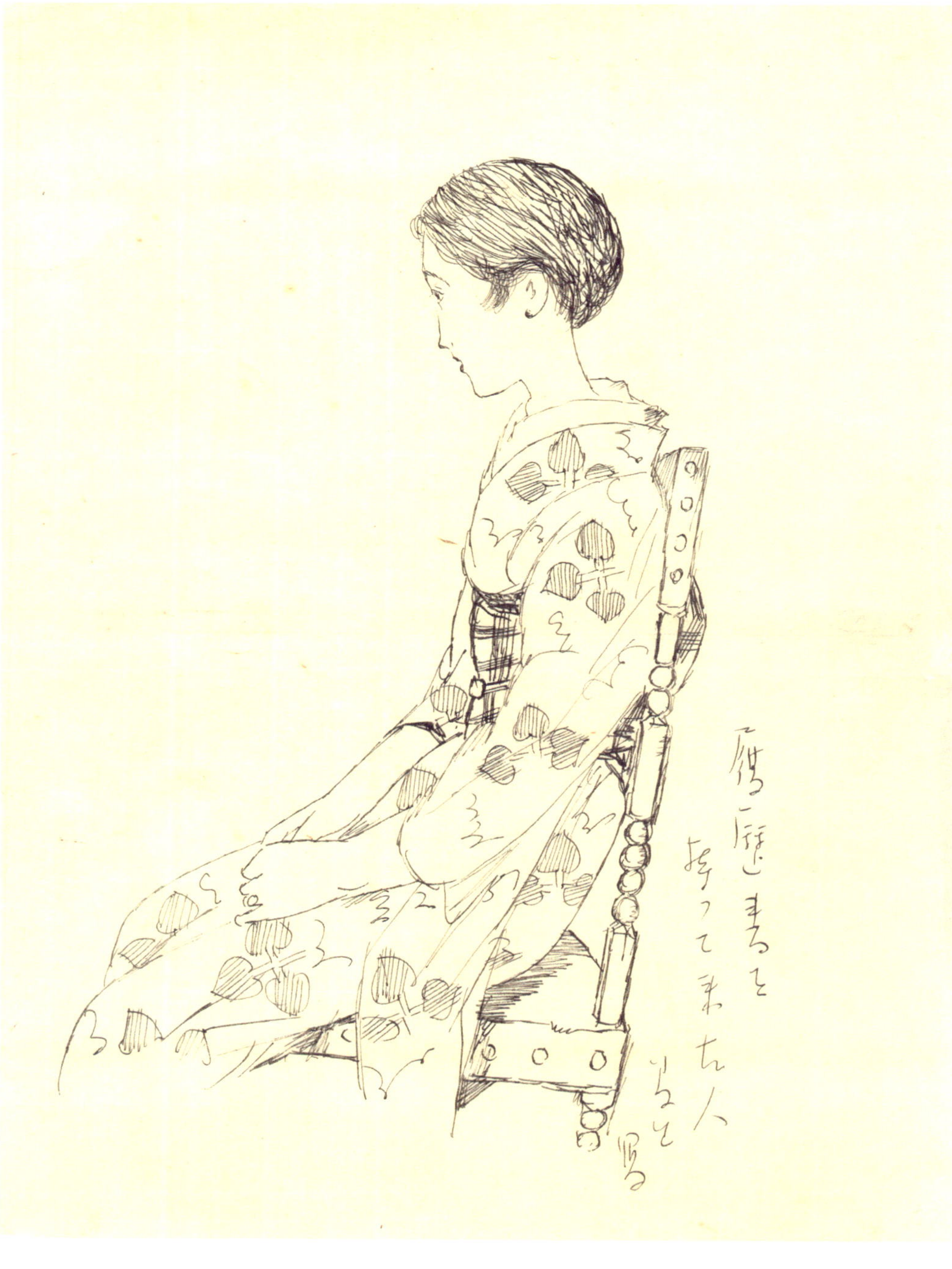

**4.** ***Seated woman***
**36.1 x 27.1 cm**
**Signature:** ***Mushō sha***

A young woman sits on a Western-style chair. She sports a bobbed haircut in the style of a 'modern girl' (*modan gaaru* or *moga*); her kimono is decorated with a clover design.

[MdV]

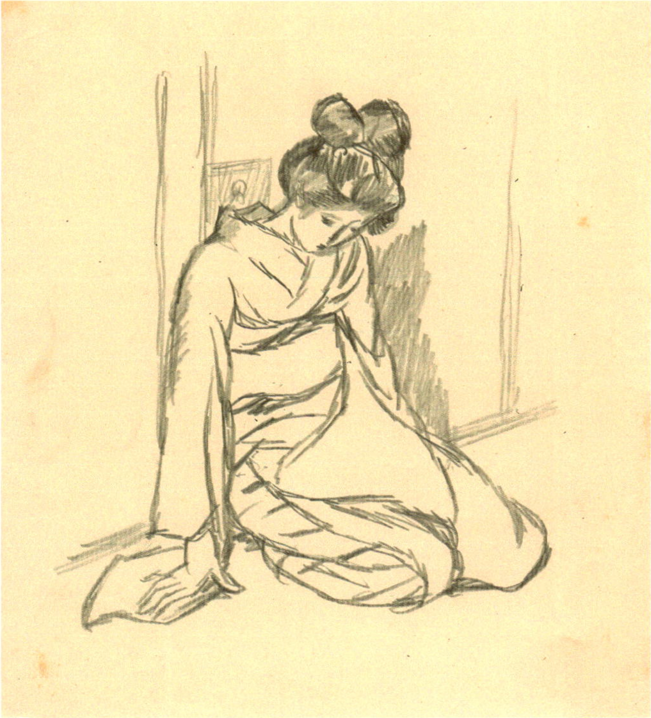

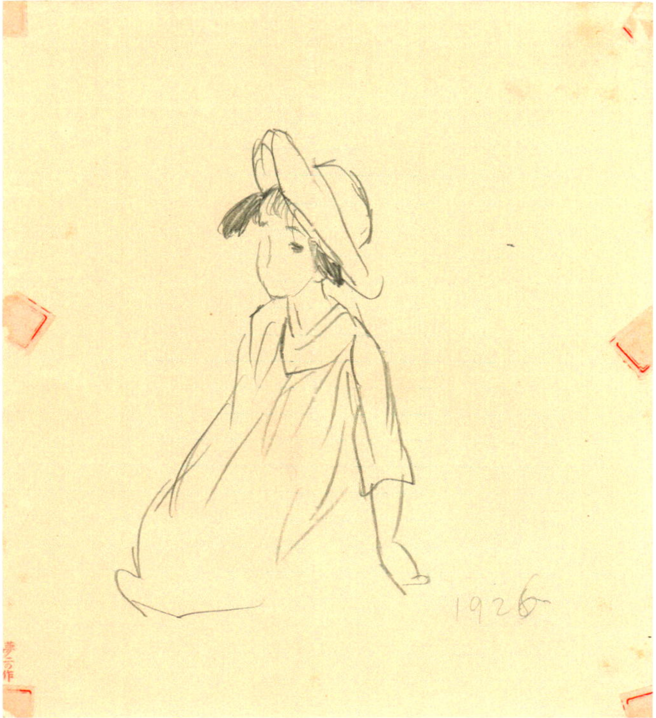


5. *Seated woman* (recto)
*Girl wearing a hat* (verso)
22.1 x 19.1 cm
Date (verso in pencil): '1926'
Seal (stamp): *Yumeji no saku* (*work by Yumeji*) (verso)

The subject in this drawing is slumped against a sliding door—her pose seems to convey an emotional weightiness. The darker lines, shading and the re-drawing of areas on the woman's kimono indicate that Yumeji took more time to render this scene than many of his impromptu sketches. The reverse side has a quickly drawn outline of a girl's dress. The slight tilt of the hat brim and the posture of the left arm as it hangs casually backwards captures a moment of repose in what is perhaps an otherwise lively scene of a young girl at play. The date '1926' is inscribed on the back, but it is not clear whether this was added at the time of creation or later.

[NN]

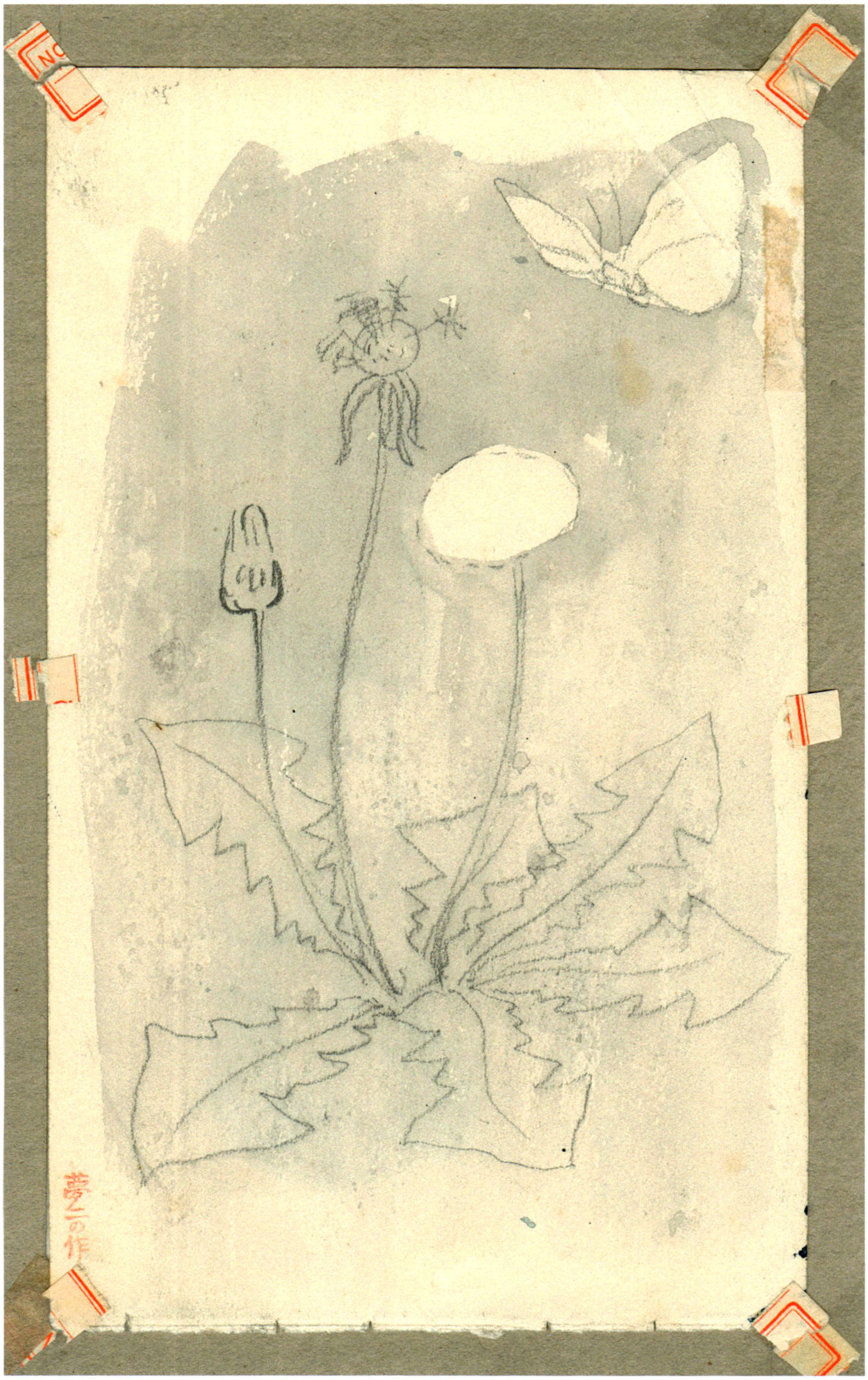

**6.** ***Dandelion and butterfly***
**18.0 x 10.1 cm (image)**
**Seal (stamp):** ***Yumeji no saku (work by Yumeji)***

This carefully executed drawing of a dandelion and a small butterfly represents another side of Yumeji's work—the portrayal of the natural world. Similar details of small flowers and insects are seen in the artist's other sketchbooks, such as his drawings from his trek up Mount Fuji in 1909 that are today housed in the Kanazawa Yuwaku Yumeji Museum.

[NN]

**7. *Woman washing her hands***
**18.3 x 10.9 cm (image)**
**Seal (stamp): *Yumeji no saku***
**(*work by Yumeji*)**

Many of Yumeji's drawings concentrate on the form and positioning of an individual figure. This particular composition of a woman washing her hands, however, focuses not only on her figure but also pays close attention to the depiction of the surrounding scene. Sketches like this example offer us a glimpse into the everyday scenes that Yumeji would have witnessed first-hand in his neighbourhood or during his travels.

[NN]

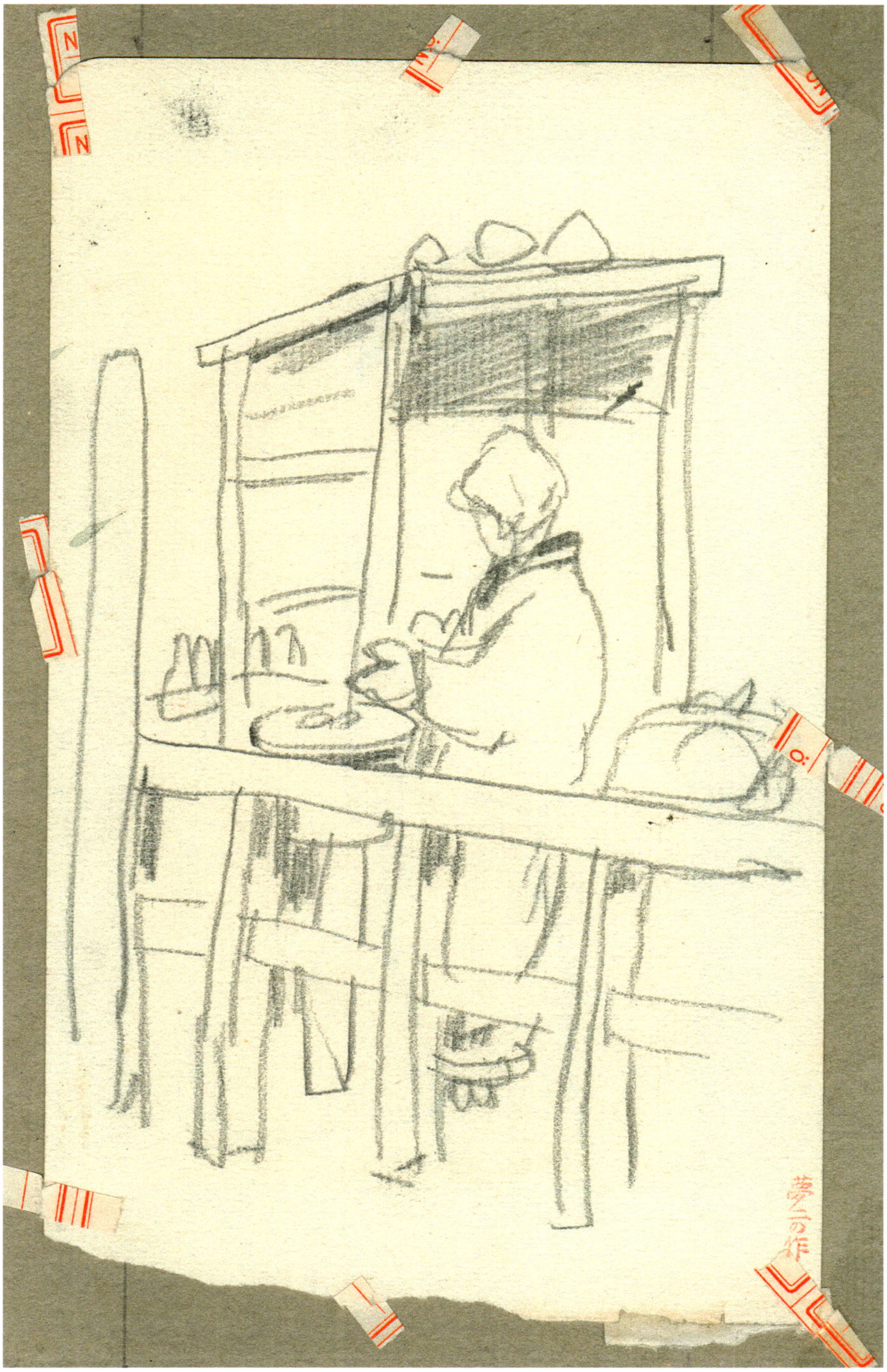

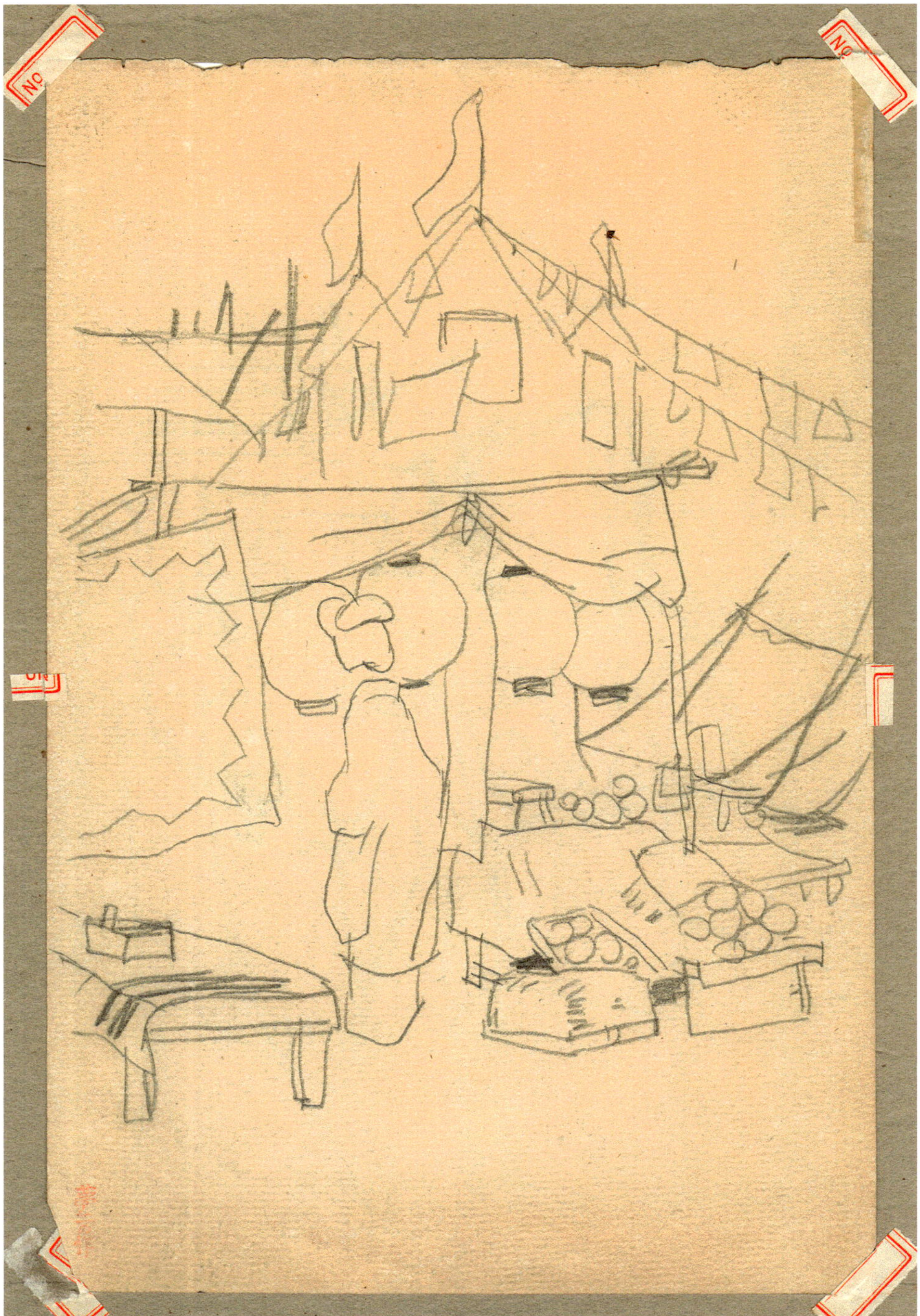

8. *Woman near market stalls*
22.4 x 14.1 cm (image);
35.4 x 25.9 cm (mount)
Seal (stamp): *Yumeji no saku*
(*work by Yumeji*)

**9.** ***A man and a young woman under a tree***
**35.4 x 23.8 cm (image);**
**40 x 27.7 cm (mount)**

The silhouettes of a capped man and a young girl with pigtails standing under a tree recalls a design Yumeji produced for the new waltz tune 'Swanee river moon' from the *Senow music scores* (cat. 21).

[MdV]

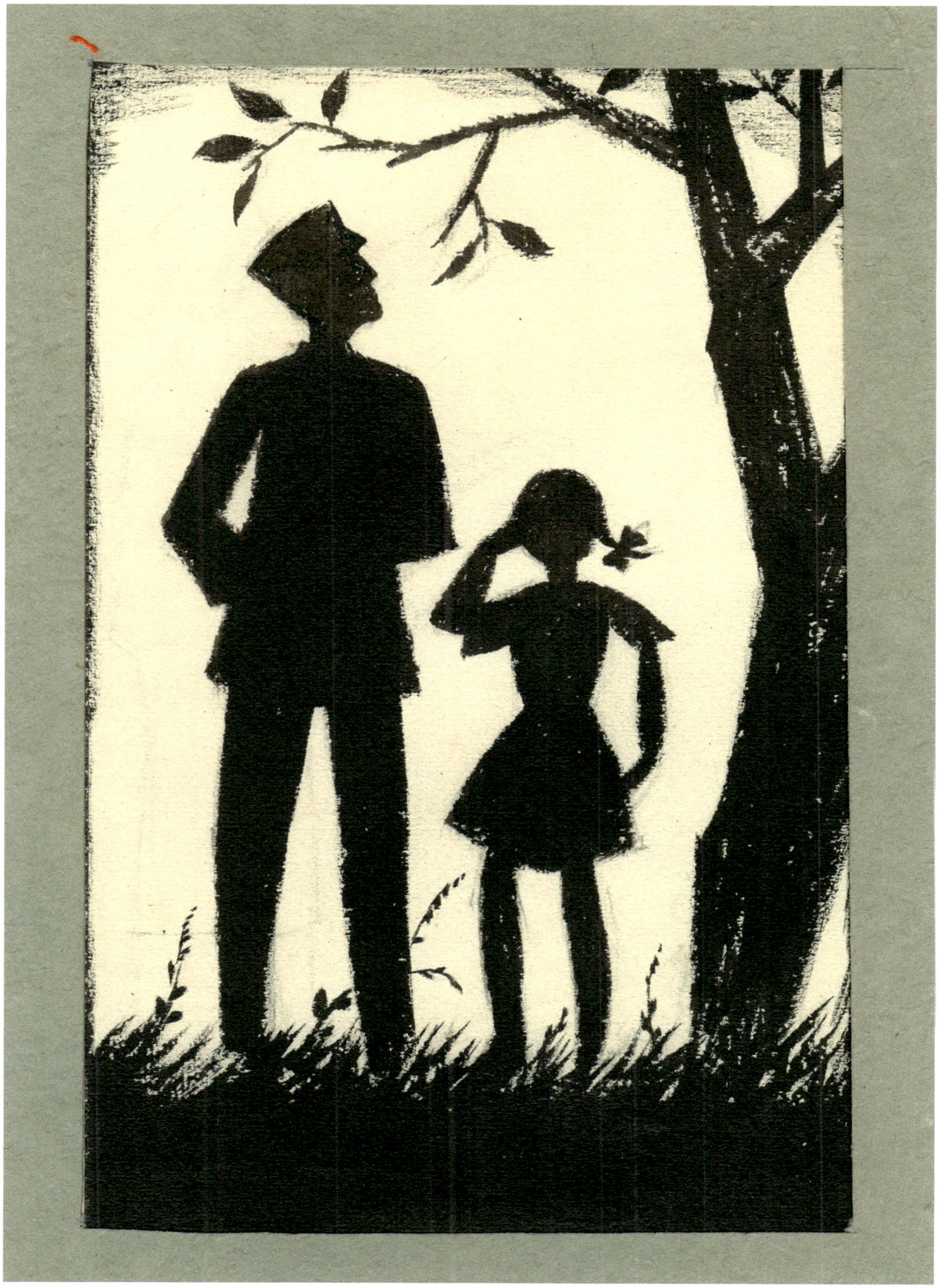

## Early prints
cat. 10–15

Yumeji produced relatively few individual prints during his lifetime. He published and sold his own prints through his shop Minatoya, which he opened with his ex-wife Kishi Tamaki (1882–1945) in 1914 (see figs. 2.4 & 3.2). The shop closed after just two years; thereafter the Osaka-based Yanagiya acquired the woodblocks and merchandise initially made for the Minatoya (see figs. 3.1, 3.3, 3.4, 3.7).

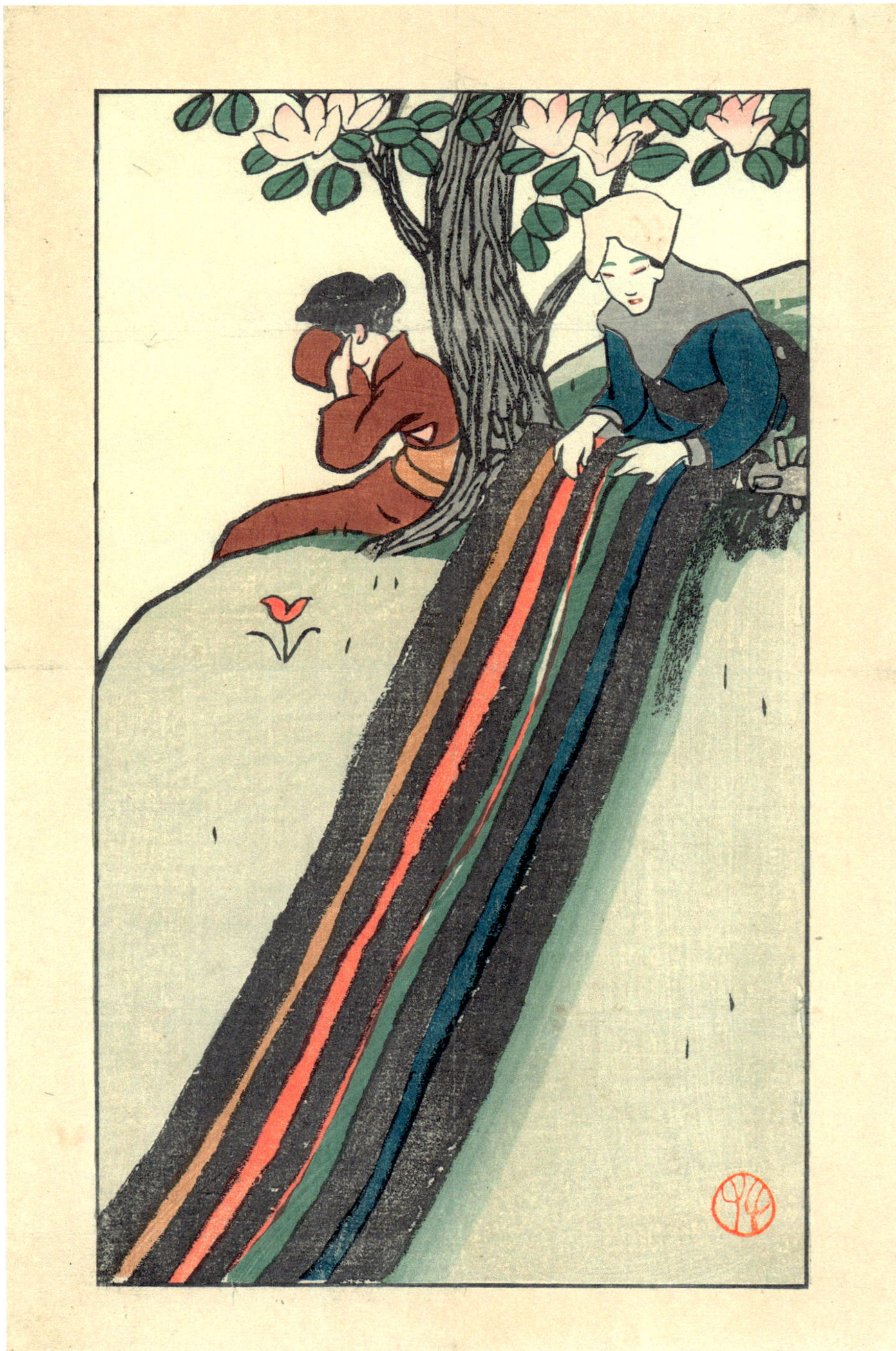

10. *Entering the priesthood* (*Tokudo no hi,* 得度の日)
From *Red peach* (*Komomo no maki,* 紅桃の巻)
Vol. 2 of *Land of blossoming cherries* (*Sakura saku kuni,* 桜さく国)
37.3 x 23.7 cm
Date: 1912
Seal: artist's 'grass' (*kusa*) seal
Publisher: Horupu Shuppan

A woman lays out fabric on a hillside, while a young woman leaning against a tree beside her weeps. The title *Tokudo no hi* (literally 'day of entering the priesthood') has Buddhist connotations, but here the figure of a sobbing woman might suggest that she is about to leave her present life behind to begin anew elsewhere. This image was a frontispiece illustration (*kuchi-e*), which was printed separately, folded and bound into the volume; the horizontal fold line is still visible.

[MdV]

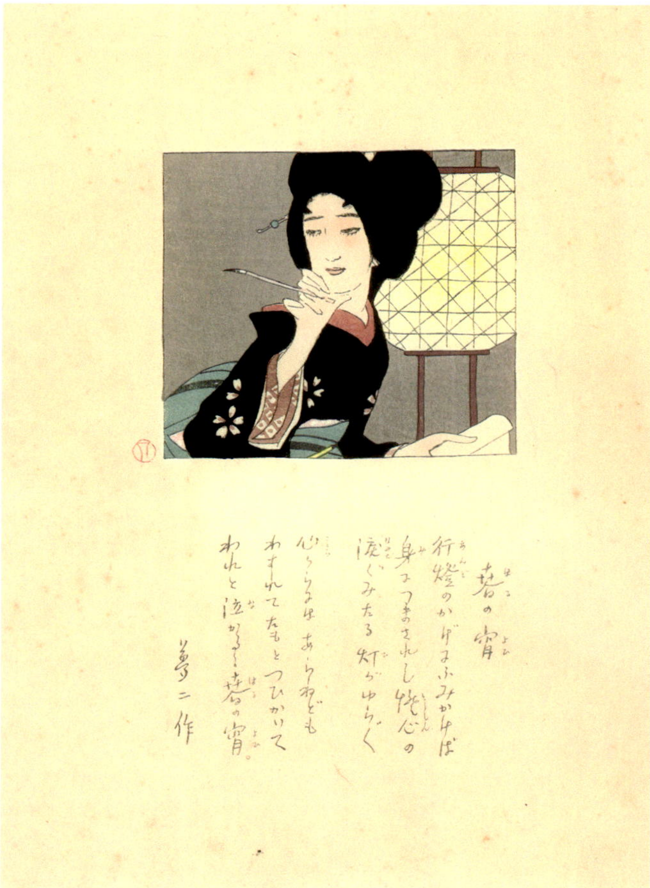

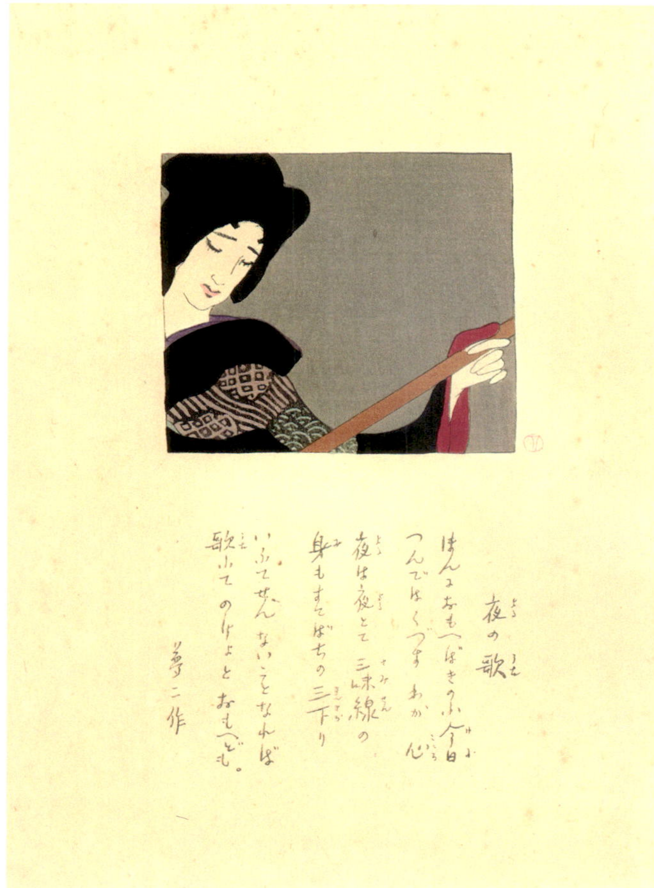

11. *Spring evening*
(*Haru no yoi*, 春の宵)
*Evening song* (*Yoru no uta*, 夜の歌)
From an untitled portfolio of two prints
24.5 x 17.5 cm (*Spring evening*);
24.5 x 17.6 cm (*Evening song*)
Date: 1913
Seal: artist's 'grass' (*kusa*) seal
Publisher: Hakuyōsha Shoten

These two prints are accompanied by Yumeji's own poems. The verse on *Spring evening* reads:

*andon no kage ni / fumikakeba/mi ni tsumasarete / tōshino / namidagumitaru / hiyuragu/kokoro kara ni waaranedo mo / wasureteta mo / to tsui kaite / ware to nakaruru / haru no yoi*

*Composing a letter under the light of the lantern my heart feels deep sorrow,*
*moved to tears by the lamp wick and flickering flame;*
*though insincere,*
*I could only bring myself to write that I had forgotten [the relationship]—I cry alone this spring evening.*[1]

The meanings behind many of Yumeji's poems are often difficult to decipher, but perhaps here the woman writing the verse could not bear to tell her lover directly that she has had to end their relationship.

1. Thanks to Nozomi Naoi for providing this translation.

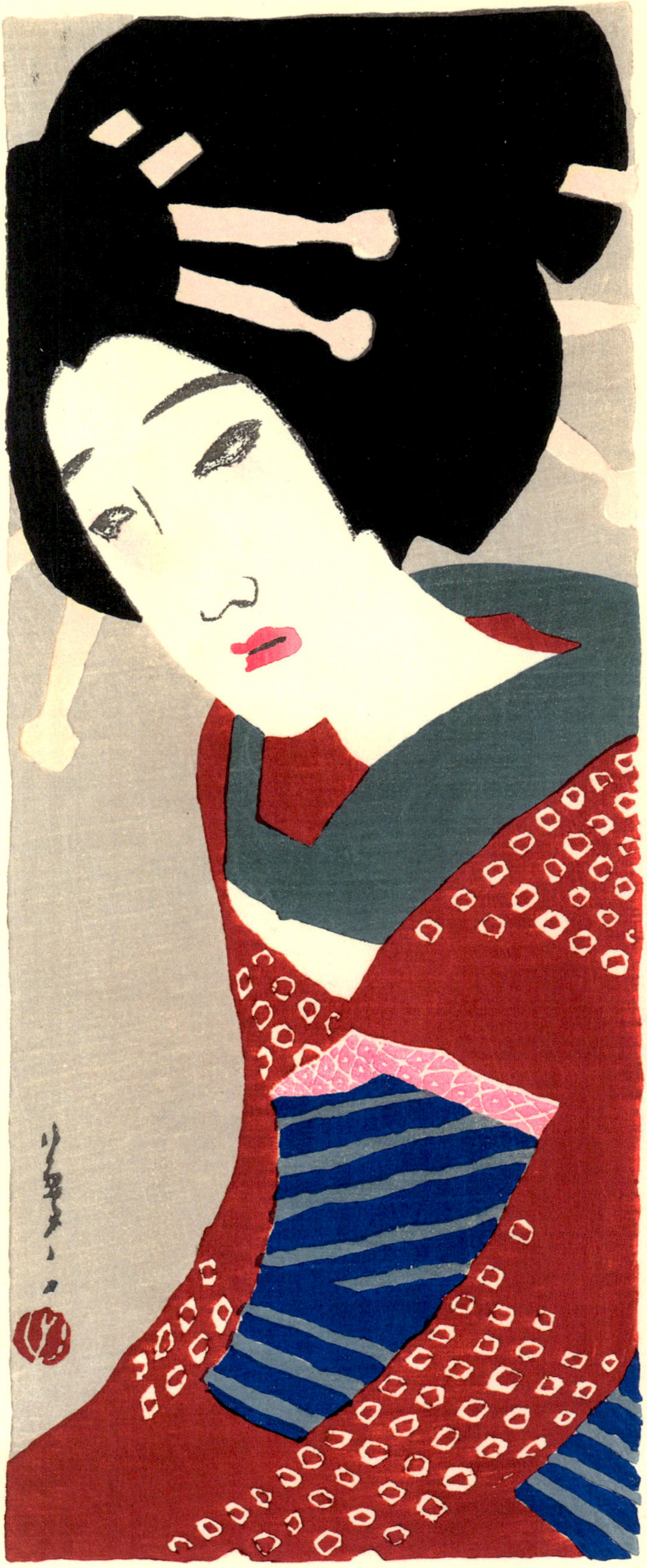

*Previous page*
12. *Koharu* (こはる)
42.8 x 28.0 cm
Date: 1914–1916
Signature/seals: *Yumeji* with a variant of the artist's 'grass' (*kusa*) seal; Yanagiya publisher's trademark
Publisher: Yanagiya

This is a variant edition; see also fig. 3.1.

13. *Bunraku dolls* (*Bunraku ningyō*, 文楽人形)
42.5 x 27.7 cm
Date: 1914
Seals: artist's comma-shaped (*tomoe*) seal, Yanagiya publisher's trademark
Publisher: Yanagiya

This work depicts the puppets used in *bunraku*, a theatre form that Yumeji especially enjoyed. He made numerous prints portraying characters from *bunraku* plays, in particular those by the celebrated playwright Chikamatsu Monzaemon (1653–1725). Yumeji's interest in *bunraku* was part of a greater fascination during the Taishō era for Edo culture, which for many represented a romanticised historical past. Yumeji was also a fan of kabuki and contemporary performance traditions, even dabbling in the production of stage backdrops for contemporary theatre.[1]

[NN]

1. Okabe, ed., *Seitan 130nen Takehisa Yumeji ten*, 102.

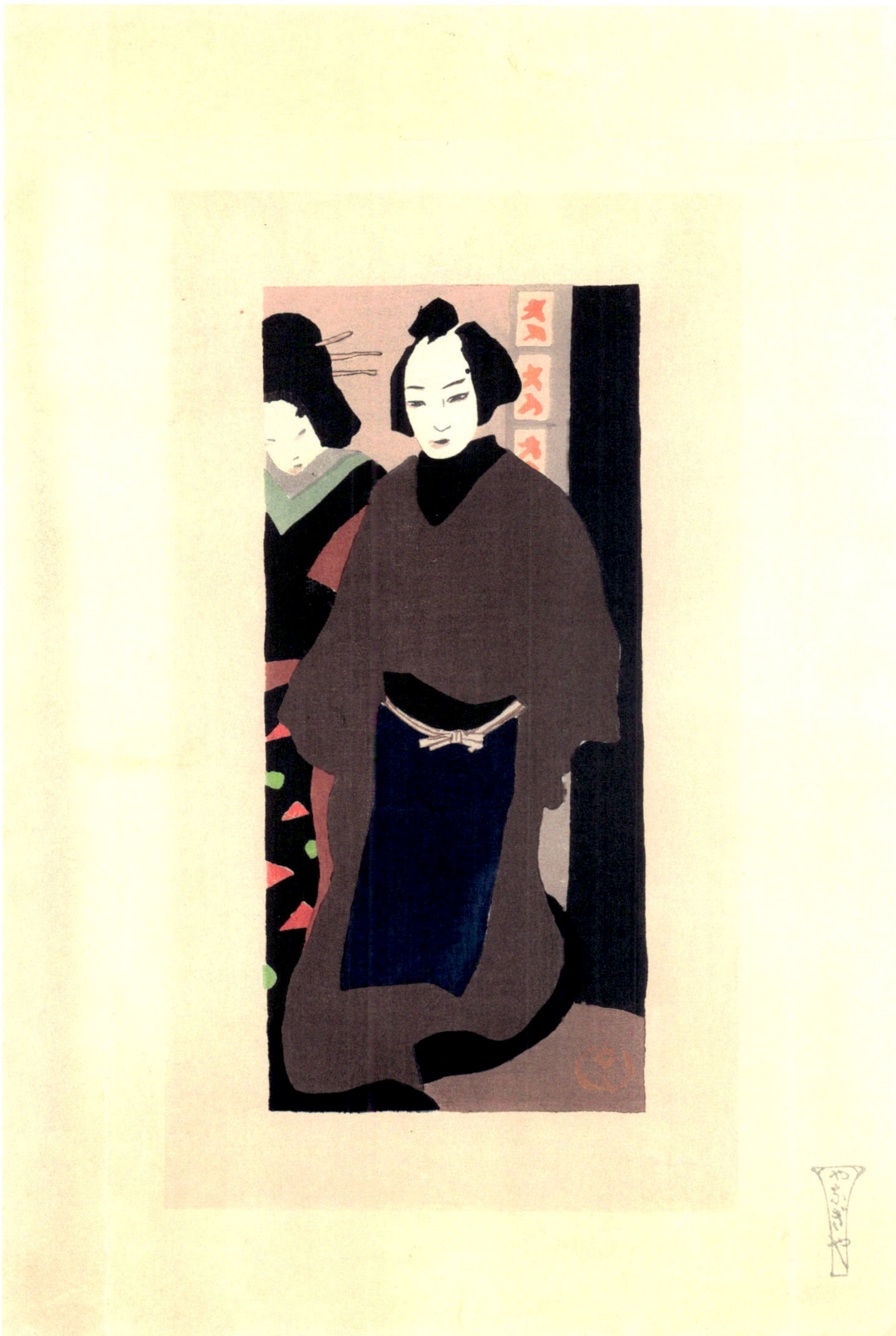

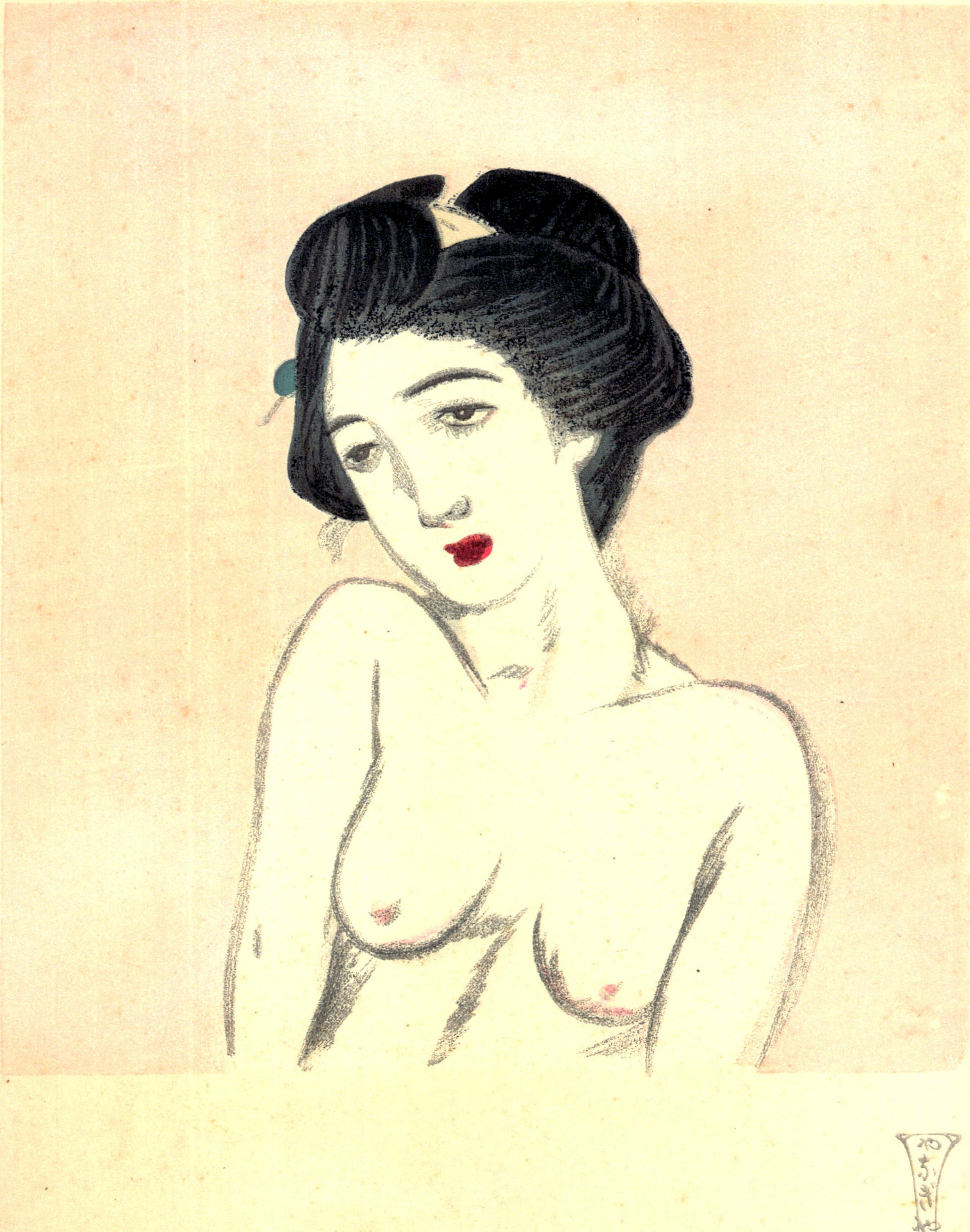

*Previous page*
14. *Nude* (*Rafu*, 裸婦)
42.9 x 28.3 cm
Date: 1914–1915
Seal: Yanagiya publisher's trademark
Publisher: Yanagiya

This intimate, delicate bust portrait conveys a sense of immediacy, as though Yumeji had just finished sketching his subject. Different versions of this image exist, including an example housed in the Kanazawa Yuwaku Yumeji Museum. It is in the shape of a circular fan with the woman's bust portrait filling the compositional plane and positioned such that the top of the handle falls between her breasts.

[NN]

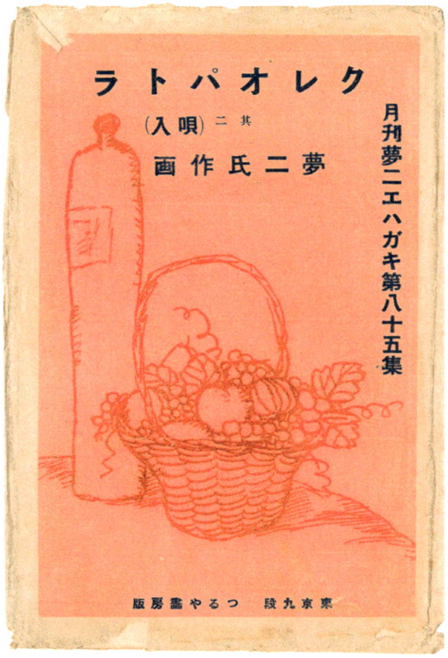


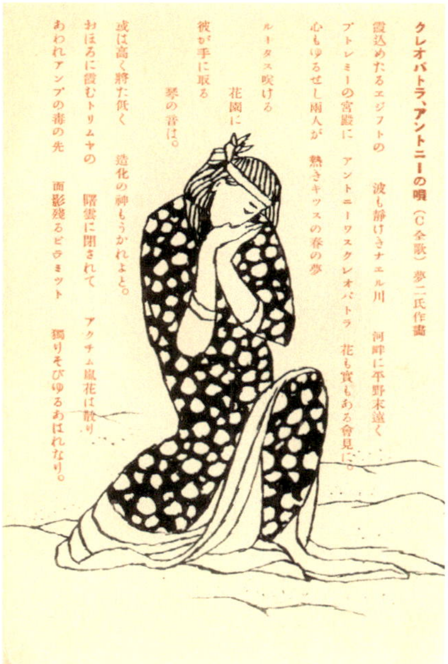


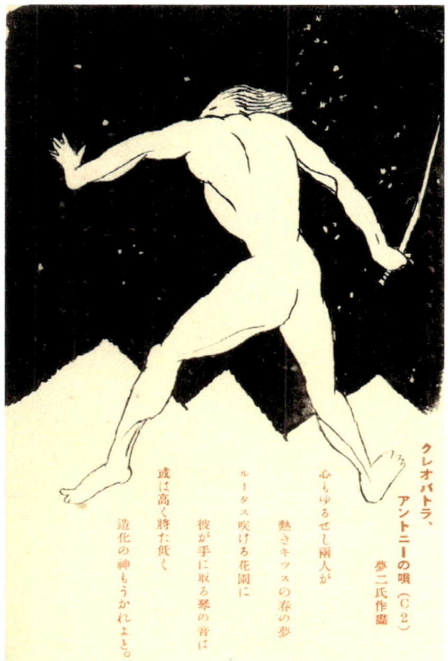


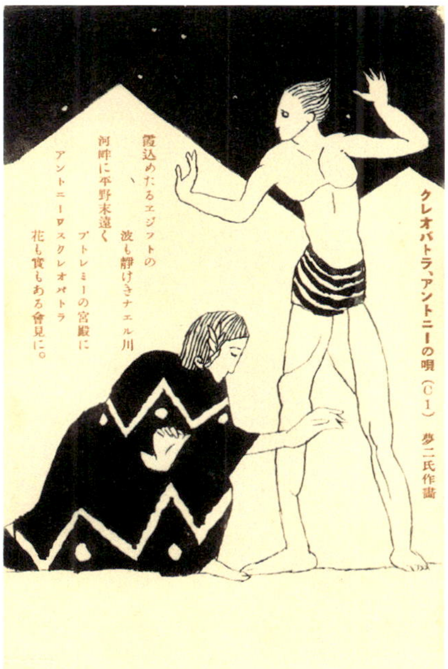


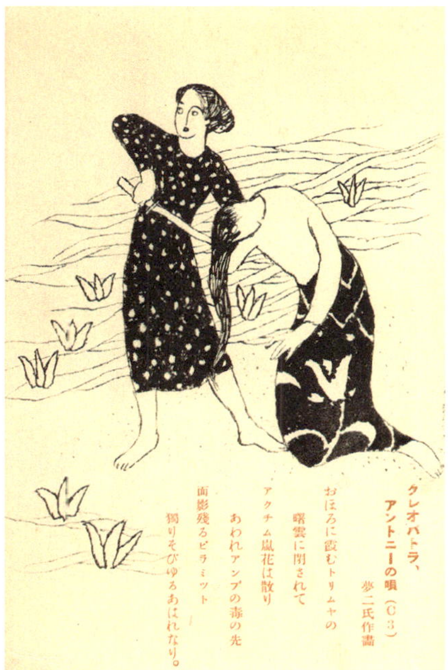


15. *Cleopatra, second song* (*Kureopatora, uta ni*, クレオパトラ　歌二)
From the series *Monthly Yumeji postcards* (*Gekkan Yumeji ehagaki*, 月刊夢二エハガキ), no. 85
14.8 x 9.8 cm (wrapper); 14.1 x 9.1 cm (cards)
Date: 1918
Publisher: Tsuruya Gabō

*Monthly postcards by Yumeji* began in September 1911 and finished in 1920 after 102 sets. Each set varied in theme and was sold with an illustrated wrapper for 15 *sen* (1 *sen* = 100th of a *yen*). The designs were generally simple, appearing in black and white and accompanied by a song or poem. The theme here is the *Song for Cleopatra and Antonius* (*Kureopatora to Antonii no uta*, クレオパトラとアントニーの唄).

[MdV]

## Senow music scores (*Senow gakufu*, セノオ楽譜) cat. 16–32

Senō (Senow) Kōyō (1891–1961) commenced publication of the series *Senow music scores* in 1915, and between 1916 and 1927 Yumeji designed more than 270 sheet-music covers for the Senow Music Publishing Company (Senow Ongaku Shuppansha).[1]

Despite their eleven-year collaboration Yumeji does not mention Senō in his diary, nevertheless, a hint at their working relationship surfaces in Senō's writings following the artist's death:

> *I think that Yumeji made most of his drawings for me when he was living in Shibuya's Udagawa- chō. In other words, after the Great [Kantō] Earthquake [of 1 September 1923]. At that time, Yumeji, his son Fujihiko and a woman named Oyō were living together. And Yumeji had requests from many [people] for various pictures, but [he] always gave preferential treatment to my orders. He said he liked designing for my firm because it was a source of enjoyment. Once he even visited me at three in the morning when he had just completed a piece.*

The scores issued by the Senow company were extremely popular during the Taishō, however, the fortunes of the firm declined in the following Shōwa era. Before this time, both amateurs and musicians bought sheet music, but with the Shōwa other large sheet-music publishers focused on the more demanding aspects of performance techniques. As a result, the Senow scores became out of step with the times. The company went into liquidation after the Second World War, later restarting under the name Sun Music Publishing Company (Taiyō Ongaku Shuppansha). Sun Music reprised some of Yumeji's designs, although without the decorative typography that the artist created for the covers. Instead, Senō opted for a simple template for all score covers and these never equalled the popularity of Yumeji's work during the Taishō era. All of the pieces illustrated here have the easily identifiable Senow publisher's trademark of a rabbit within a circular cartouche, the name '*Senow*' with the 'S' written as a reversed clef note and the sheet-music number. The majority of Yumeji's covers for this series were lithographs, as seen in all of the examples here. Woodblock-printed images were also produced but these tend to be smaller, measuring roughly 18.0 x 11.0 cm.

[MdV]

1. This number does not include the two supplemental series *Senow Yamada music scores* (*Senow Yamada gakufu*) and *Senow music scores: Fujiwara Yoshie* (*Senow gakufu: Fujiwara Yoshie*). Information for this text is based on Ishikawa, '"Senō gakufu" ni tsuite'.

*Next page*
16. *The sea* (*Wadatsumi*, わだつみ), no. 115
Lithograph, 31.2 x 23.2 cm
Date: 1919
Seal: artist's comma-shaped (*tomoe*) seal
Composer: Edward A. McDowell (1860–1908)
Translator: Futami Kōhei (dates unknown)

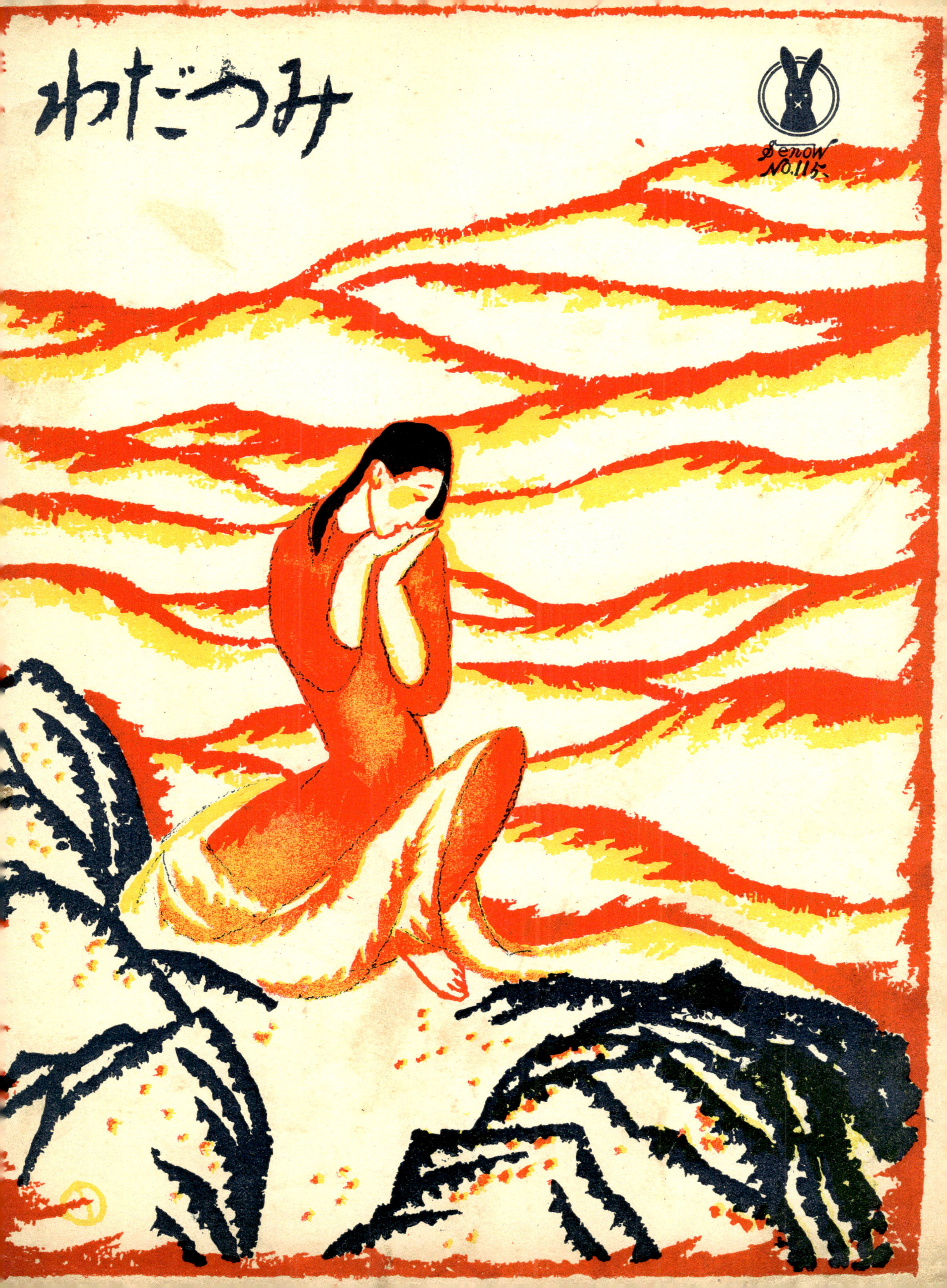

わだつみ
Senow
NO.115

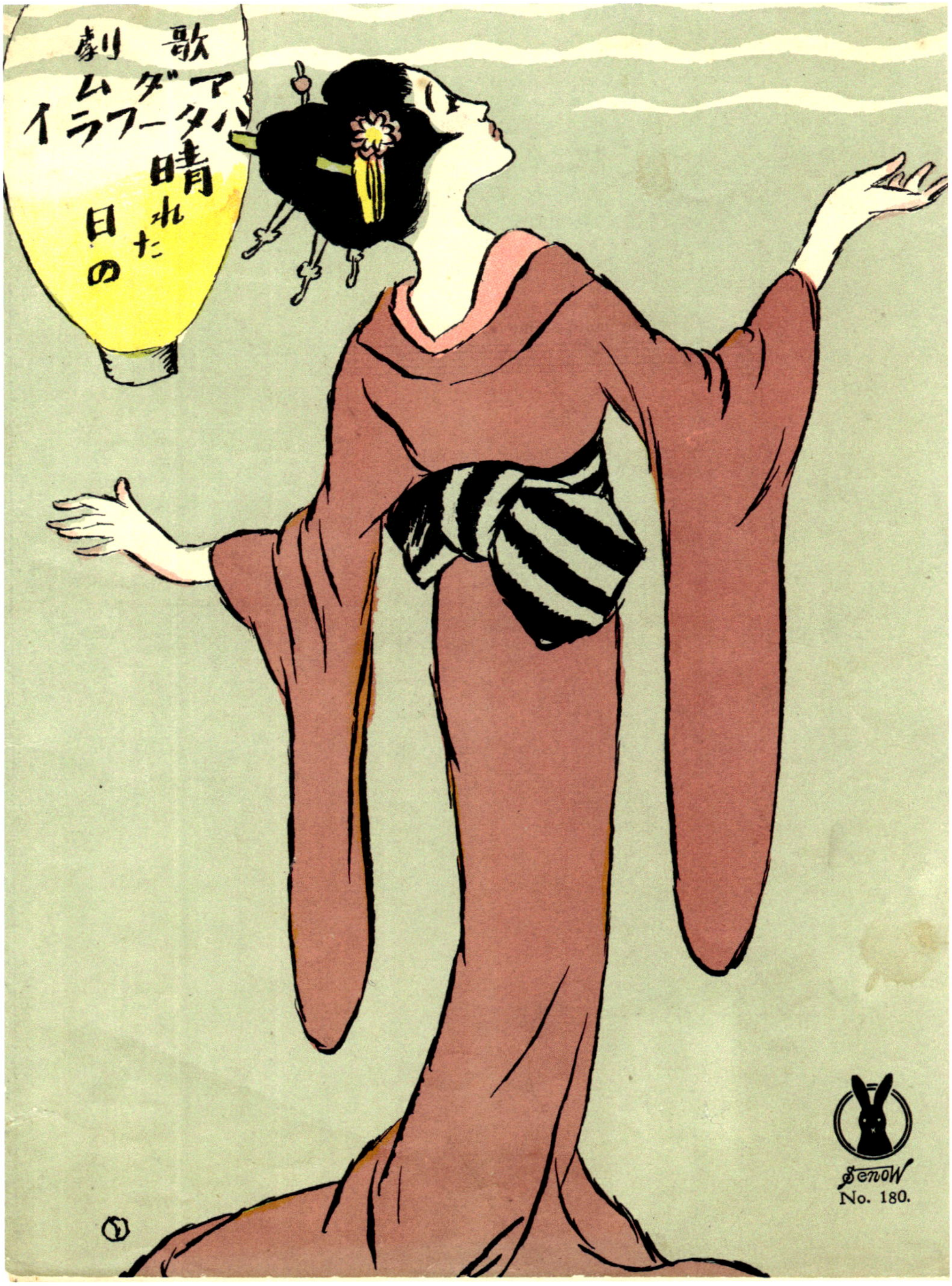


17. *'Un bel di, vedremo' Madame Butterfly* (*Hareta hi no kageki Madamu Batafurai* 晴れた日の 歌劇 マダム バターフライ ), no. 180
Lithograph, 31.2 x 22.7 cm
Date: 1920
Seal: artist's comma-shaped (*tomoe*) seal
Publisher: Senow Music Publishing Company
Composer: Giacomo Puccini (1858–1924)
Translator: Senō Kōyō (1891–1961)

This design for *Madame Butterfly* must have been a great success, since Yumeji used a similar composition for a dinner menu in 1936 (see fig. 1.7).

[MdV]

18. *Twilight song* (*Tasogare no uta*, たそがれの歌), no. 238
Lithograph, 31.1 x 22.9 cm
Date: 1921
Seal: artist's comma-shaped (*tomoe*) seal
Verse: Oyama Tokutarō (dates unknown)
Score: Fujii Kiyomi (1889–1944)

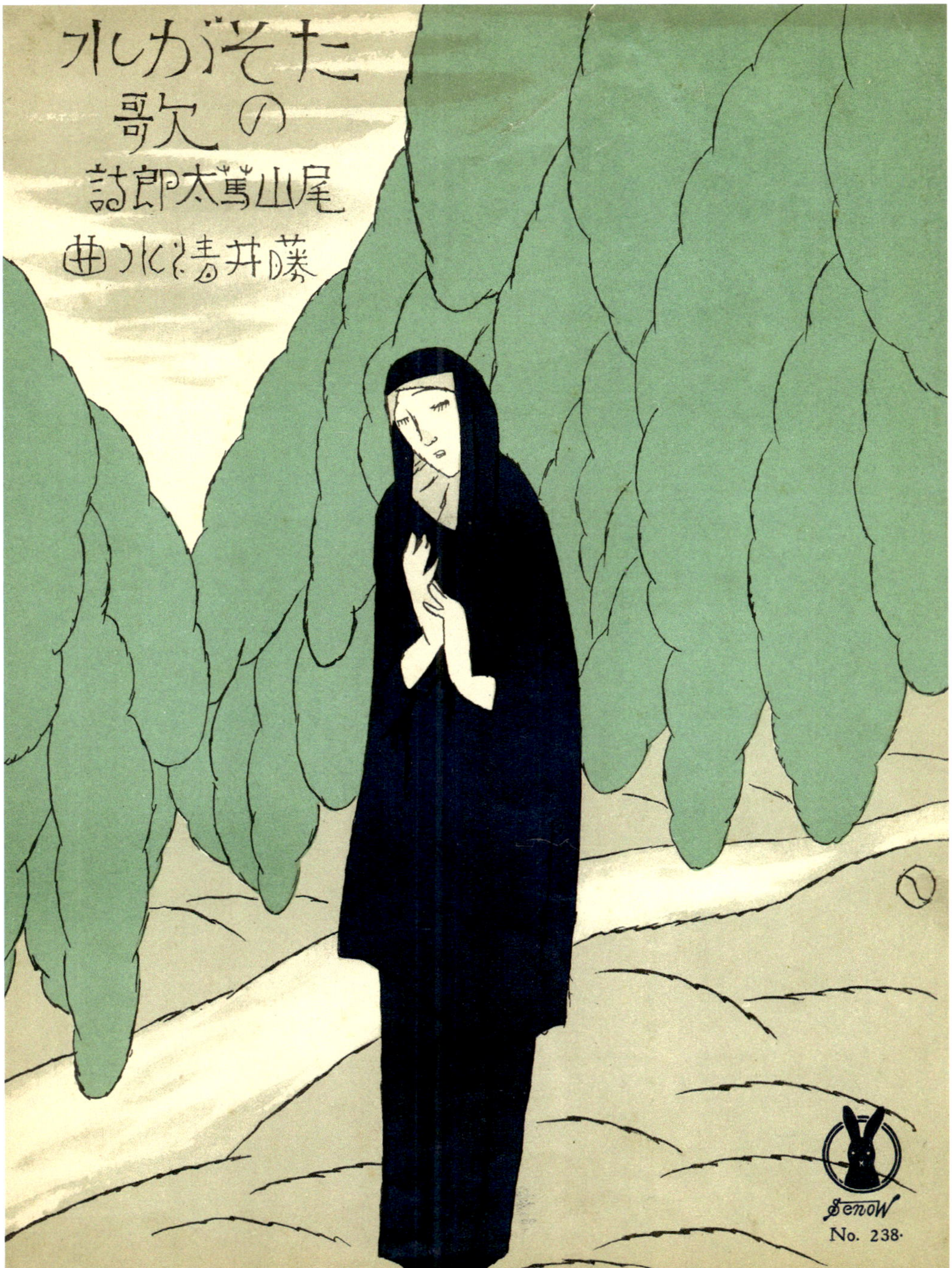

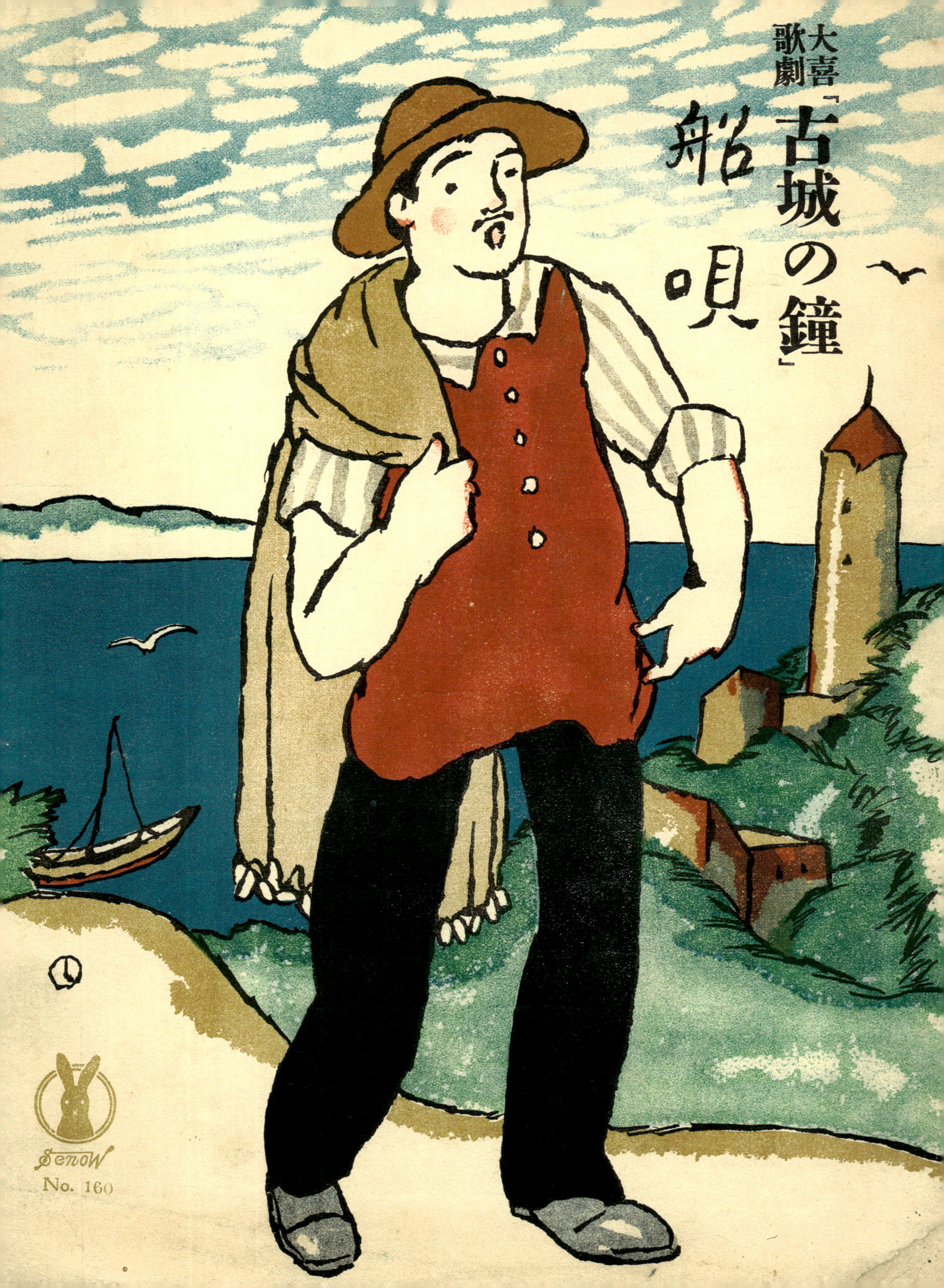
大喜歌劇「古城の鐘」
船唄
Senow
No. 160

*Previous page*
19. *On billow rocking* (*Barcarolle*): '*Les cloches de Corneville*' (*Funa uta kikageki Kojo no kane*, 船唄 大喜歌劇 古城の鐘), no. 160
Lithograph, 31.0 x 22.7 cm
Date: 1922
(originally published 1919)
Seal: artist's comma-shaped (*tomoe*) seal
Composer: (Jean-)Robert Planquette (1848–1903)
Translator: Kobayashi Aiyū (1881–1945)
See also cat. 68.

20. *Beauty spot* (*Nakibokuro*, 泣き黒子), no. 247
Lithograph, 31.2 x 22.5 cm
Date: 1922
Signature: *by Yumezi*
Composer: Tsuchiya Heizaburō (dates unknown)
Verse: Satake Someikyū (1888–1970?)
See also cat. 67.

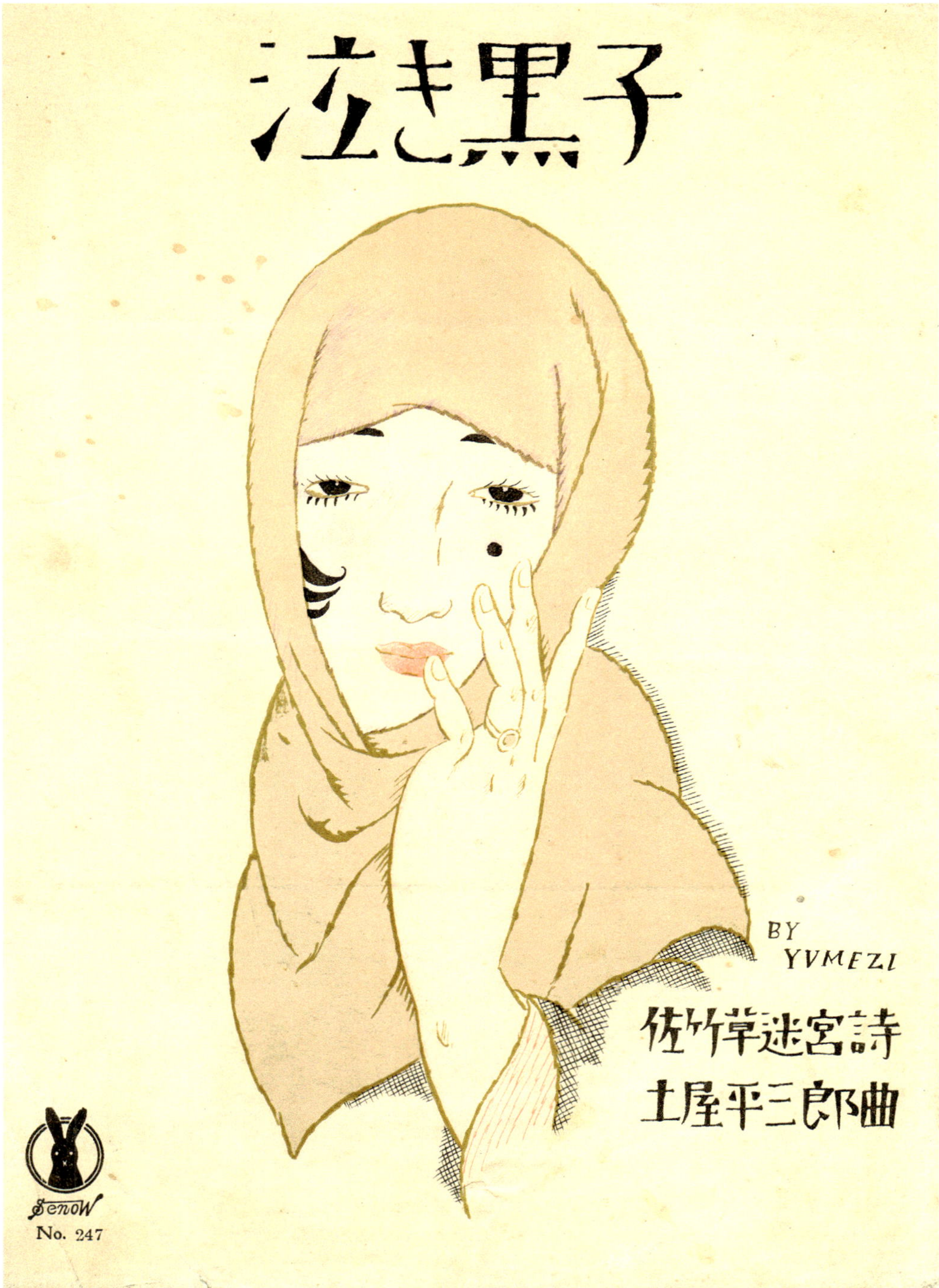

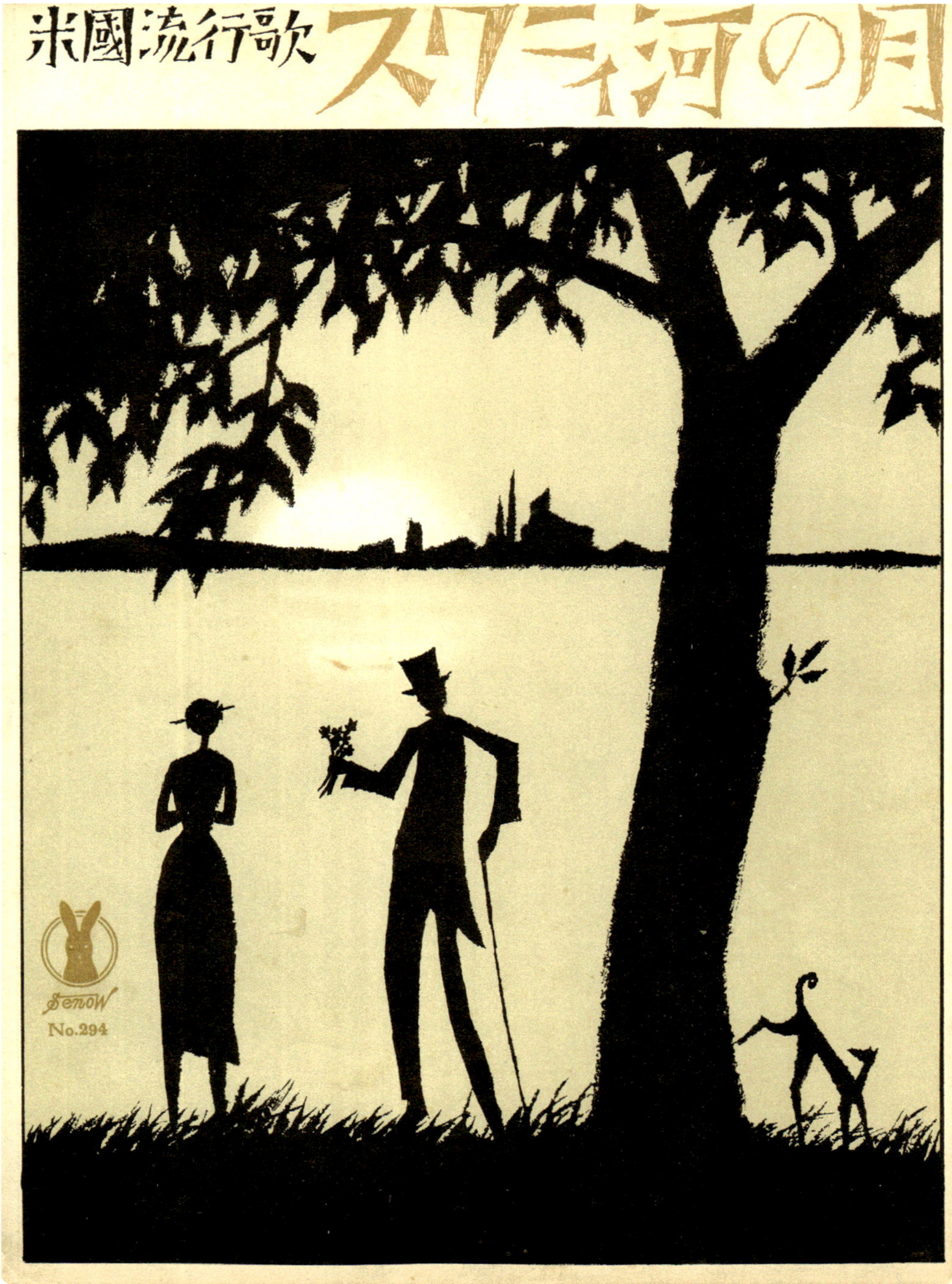


21. *'Swanee river moon', popular American songs (Swaniikawa no tsuki, Beikoku ryūkō uta,* スワニィ河の月 米国流行歌), no. 294
Lithograph, 31.3 x 22.7 cm
Date: 1923
Composer: H. Pitman Clarke (dates unknown)
Translator: Shibata Saian (1888–1971)

*Next page*
22. *Opera La traviata* (*Kageki Tsubakihime*, 歌劇椿姫), no. 53
Lithograph, 31.0 x 22.6 cm
Date: 1924 (originally published 1917)
Composer: Giuseppe Verdi (1813–1901)
Translator: Horiuchi Keizō (1897–1983)

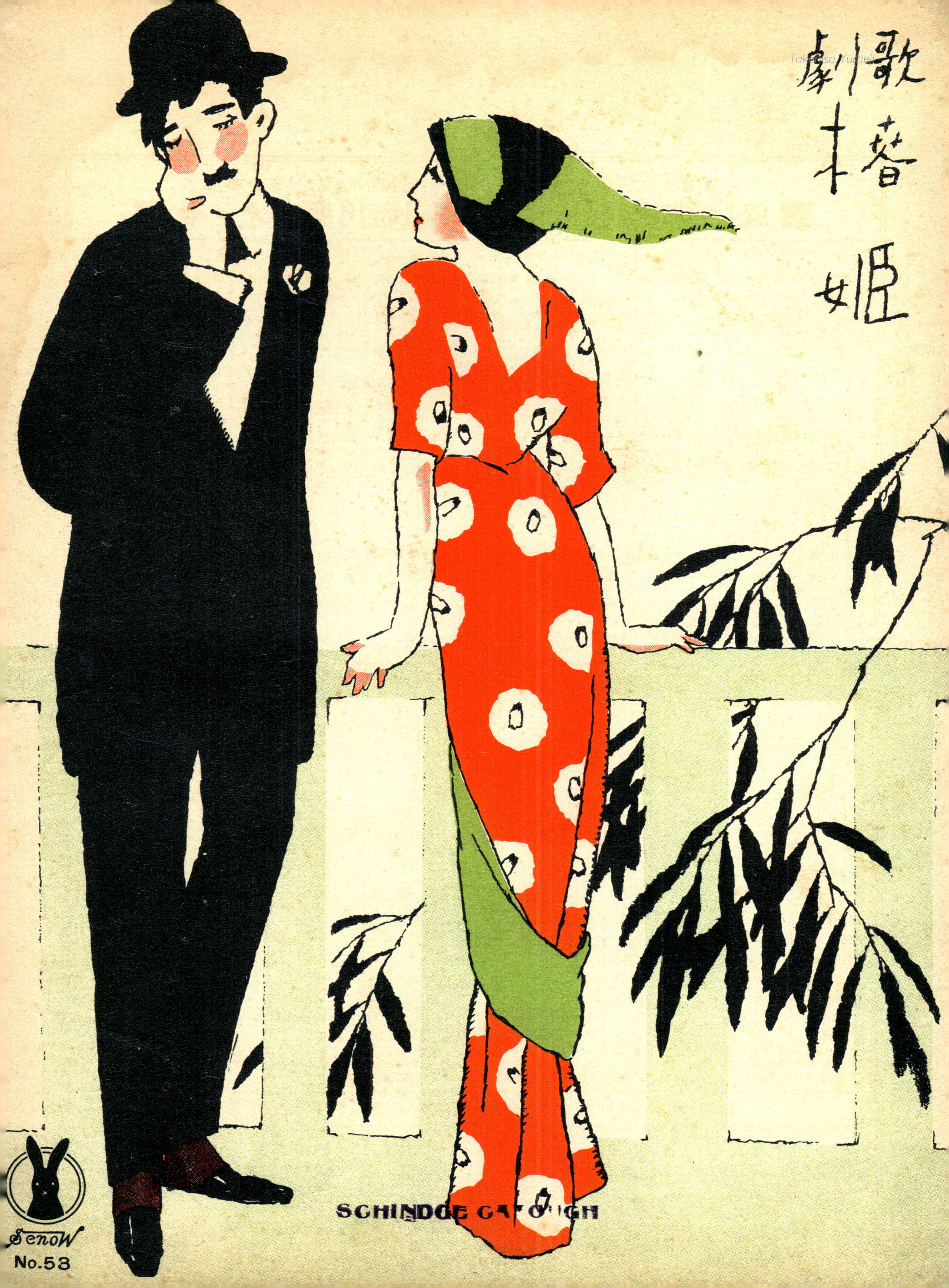
歌劇椿姫
Senow
No.58

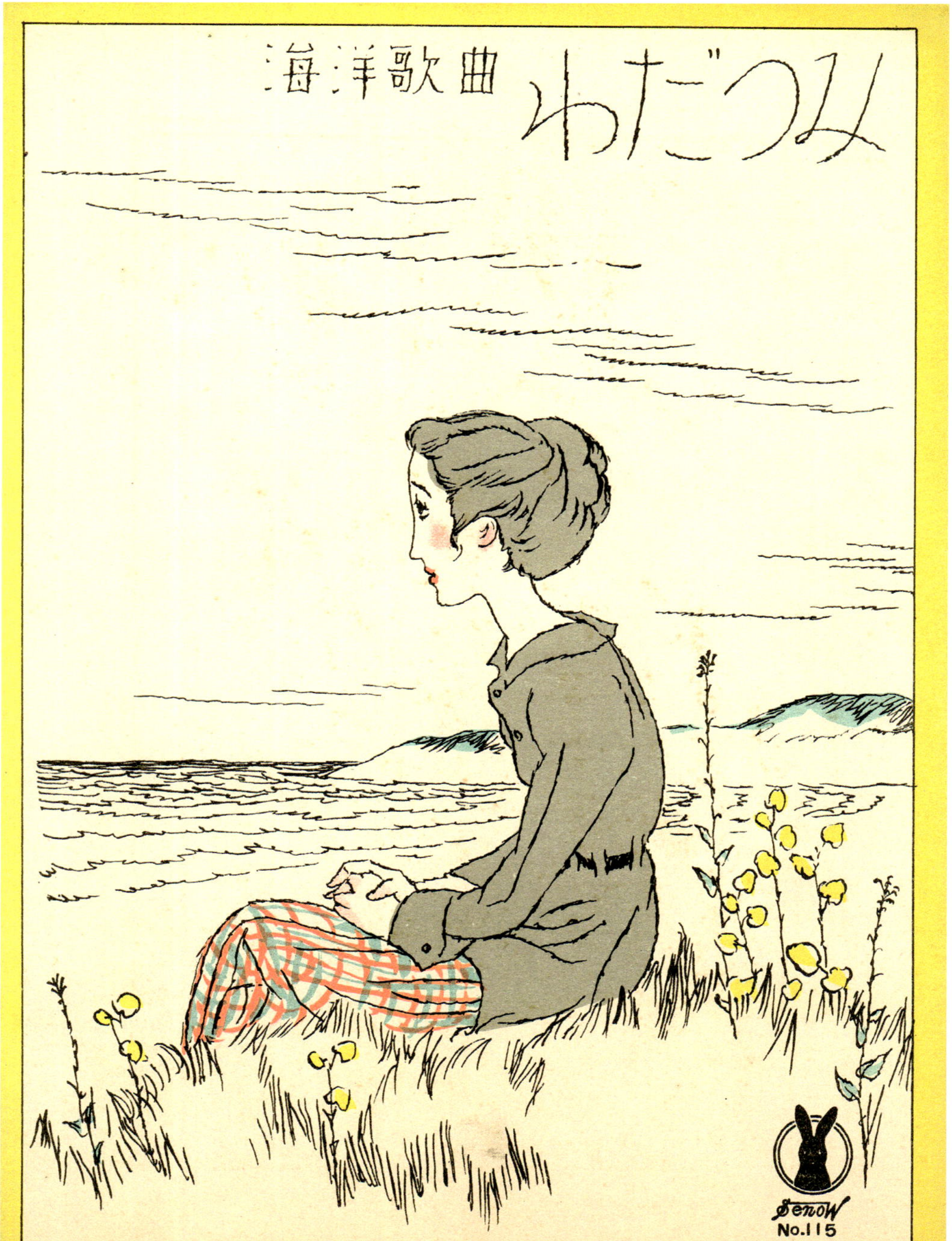


23. *The sea, songs of the sea (Wadatsumi, kayō kakyoku, わだつみ* 海洋歌曲), no. 115
Lithograph, 31.0 x 22.3 cm
Date: 1924 (originally published 1919)
Composer: Edward A. McDowell (1860–1908)
Translator: Futami Kōhei (dates unknown)

24. *Tomorrow's spring* (*Haru no ashita*, 春のあした), no. 215
Lithograph, 31.0 x 22 cm
Date: 1924
Seal: artist's comma-shaped (*tomoe*) seal
Composer: Fujii Kiyomi (1889–1944)
Verse: Takehisa Yumeji

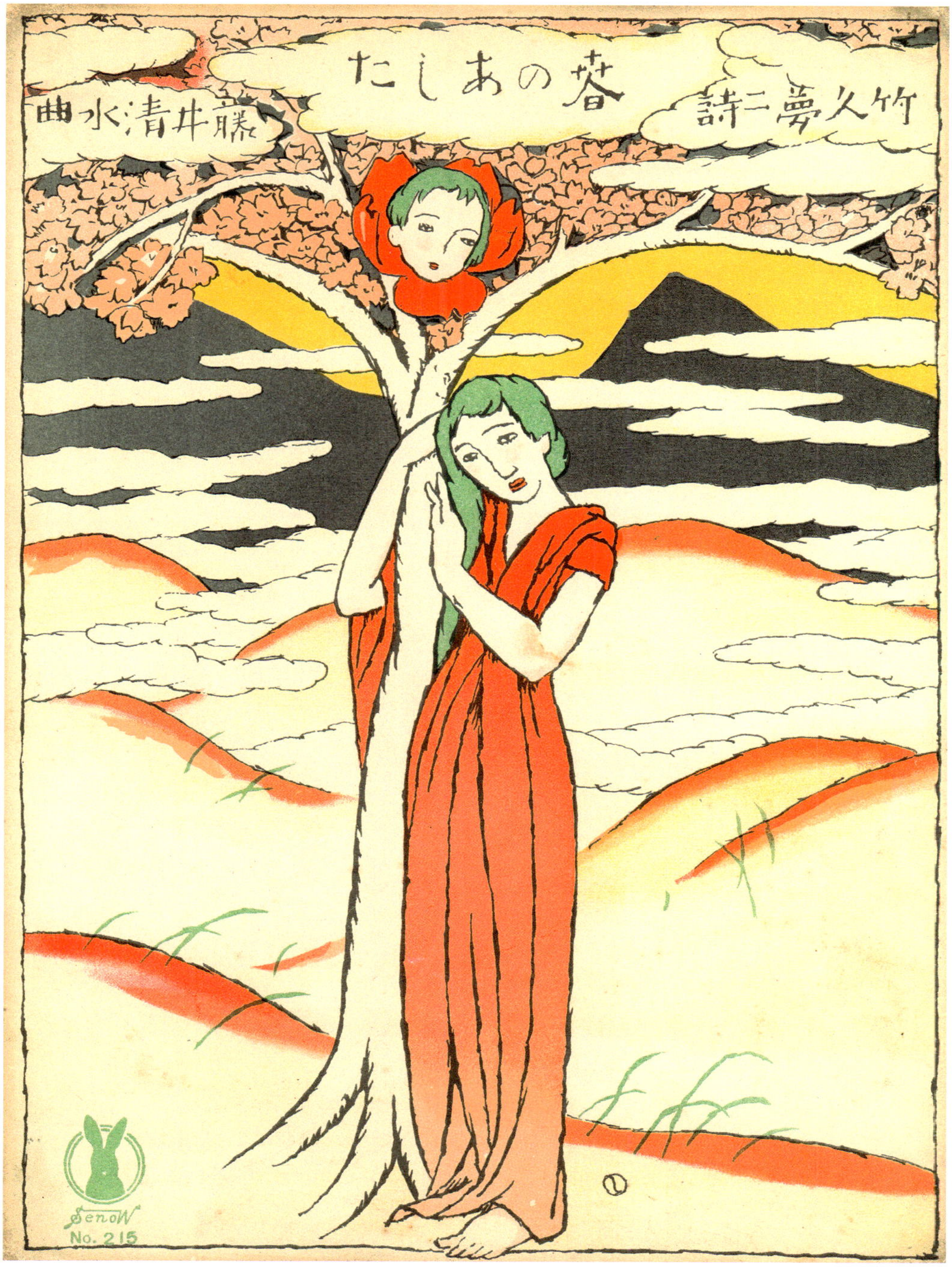

# 鍛はるる若人の歌

炬口東一詩・山田耕筰作曲

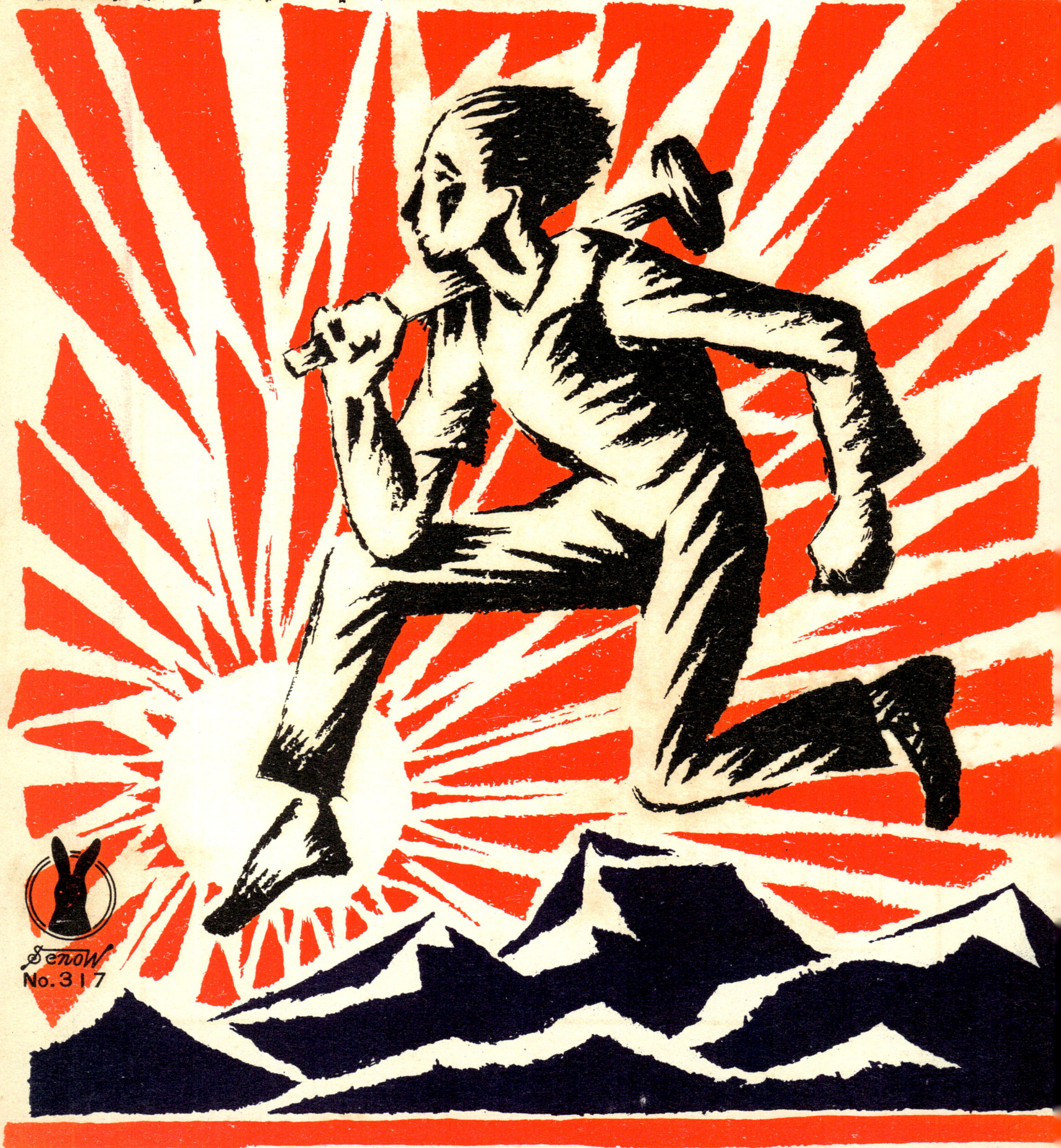

*Previous page*
25. *The young forger's song* (*Kita haruru wakoudo no uta,* 鍛はるる若人の歌), no. 317
Lithograph, 31.2 x 22.8 cm
Date: 1924
Composer: Yamada Kōsaku (1886–1965)
Verse: Hata Kōichi (1896–1957)

27. *Idyl: 'Forge in the forest'* (*Mori no kajiya,* 森の鍛冶屋), no. 379
Lithograph, 31.2 x 22.7 cm
Date: 1924
Composer: Theodore Michaelis (1831–1887)
Arrangement: Yamada Kōsaku (1886–1965)

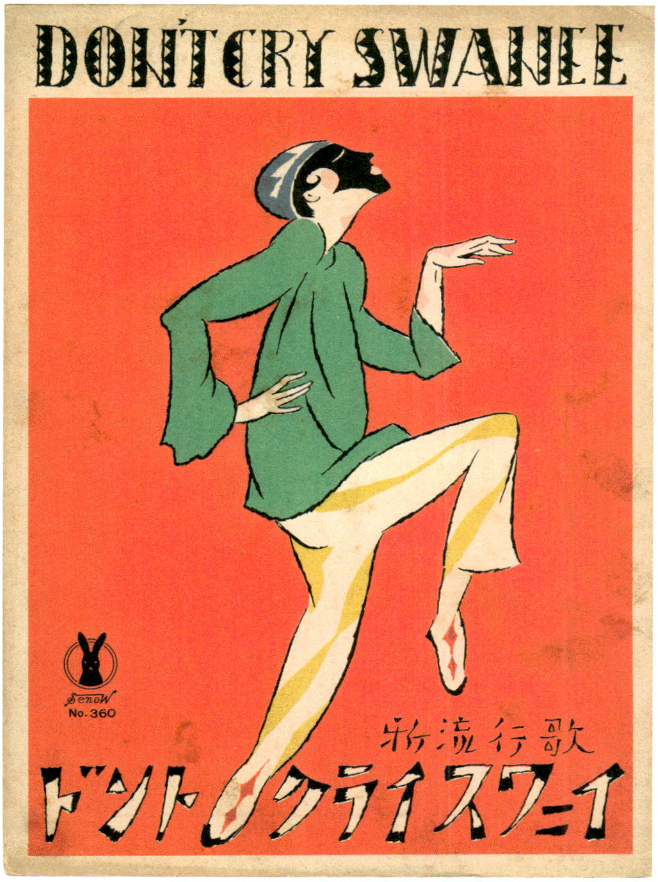


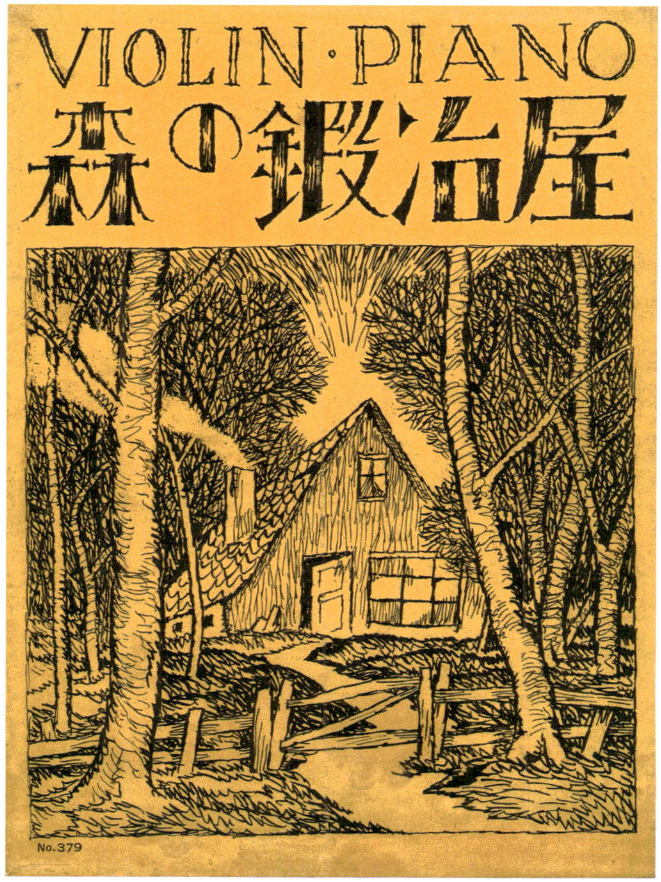


26. *Don't cry Swanee, new fashionable songs* (*Donto kurai Suwanii, shinryūkō uta,* ドントクライスワニイ　新流行歌), no. 360
Lithograph, 31.2 x 27.7 cm
Date: 1924
Composer: Al Jolson (1868–1950)
Annotation: Horiuchi Keizō (1897–1983)

The depiction of ballet-related imagery was not uncommon in the Taishō era: the Ballets Russes and its costumes by Léon Bakst (1866–1924) were known in Japan through journals and were extremely popular. Yumeji collected reproductions and newspaper clippings of things that intrigued him and assembled them into scrapbooks that are today housed in the Yumeji Art Museum in Okayama. This particular design demonstrates Yumeji's own interest in ballet and is almost identical to a photograph of the dancer Michel Fokine (1880–1942) in the role of Pierrot in *Carnaval,* a piece in the Ballets Russes repertory from 1910 (see left). [MdV]

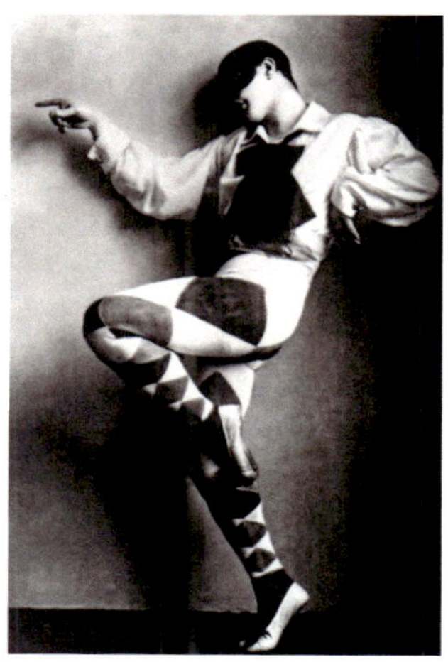

# 巷の雪

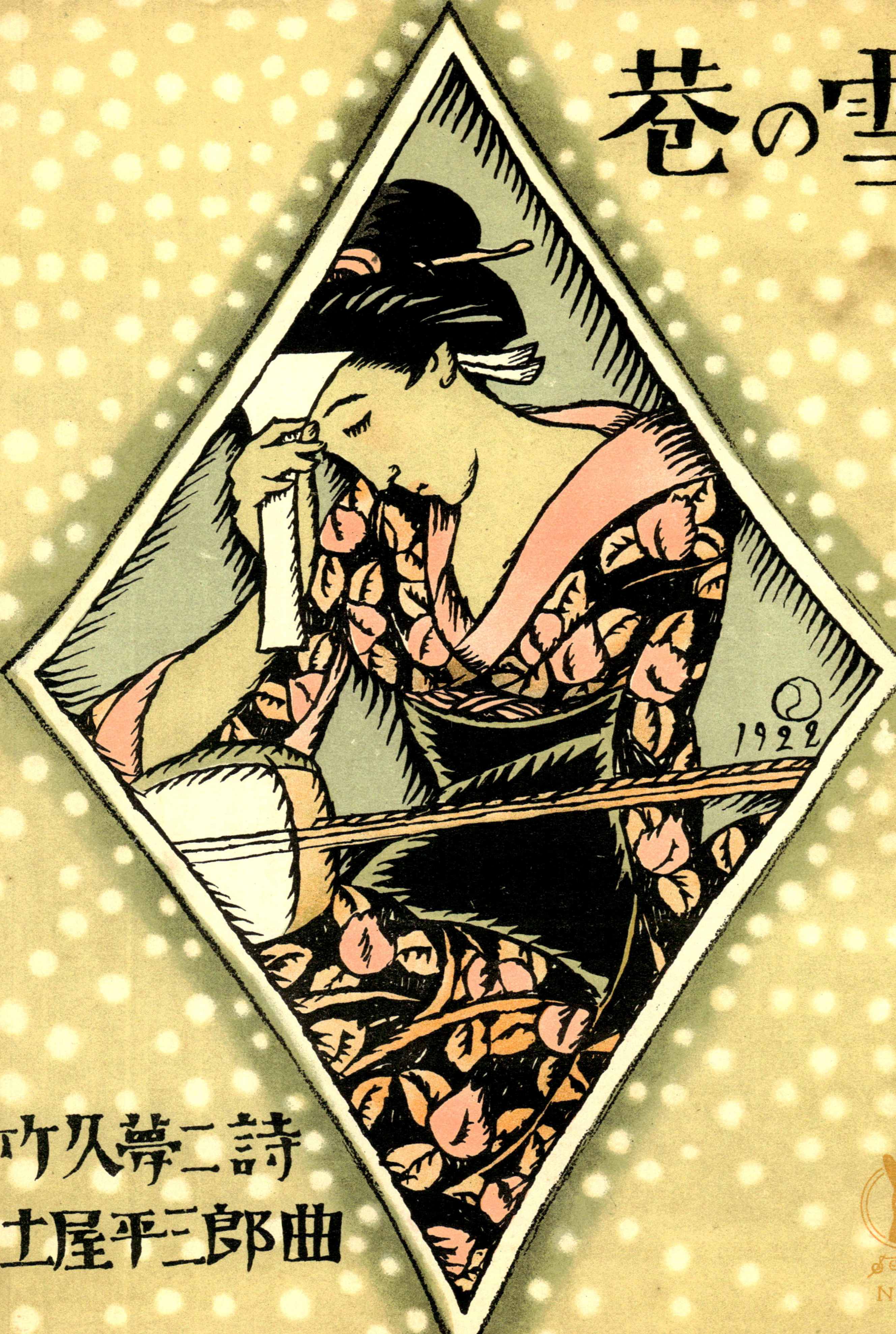


竹久夢二詩

土屋平三郎曲

Senow

No. 245

*Previous page*
28. *Snow in the streets* (*Chimata no yuki*, 巷の雪), no. 245
Lithograph, 30.8 x 22.3 cm
Date: 1925 (originally published 1922)
Seal: artist's comma-shaped (*tomoe*) seal with date '1922'
Composer: Tsuchiya Heizaburō (dates unknown)
Verse: Takehisa Yumeji

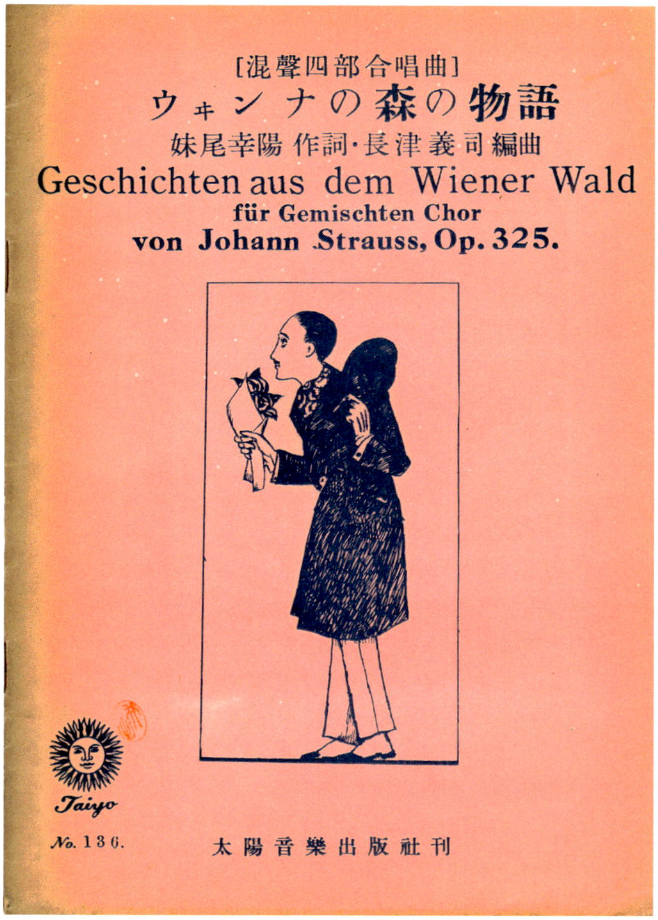


29. *Geschichten aus dem Wiener Wald* (*Uwinna no mori no monogatari*, ウォンナの森の物語)
From *Four-part harmony for mixed voices* (*Konsei shibugasshū kyoku*, 混聲四部合唱曲), no. 136
25.7 x 18.0 cm
Date: 1949
Seal (stamp): collector's stamp
Publisher: Sun Music Publishing Company
Composer: Johann Strauss II (1825–1899)

This work was originally designed for the cover of 'Beautiful nature' (*Uruwashiki tennen*, 麗しき天然), *Senow music scores*, no. 368, 1924.

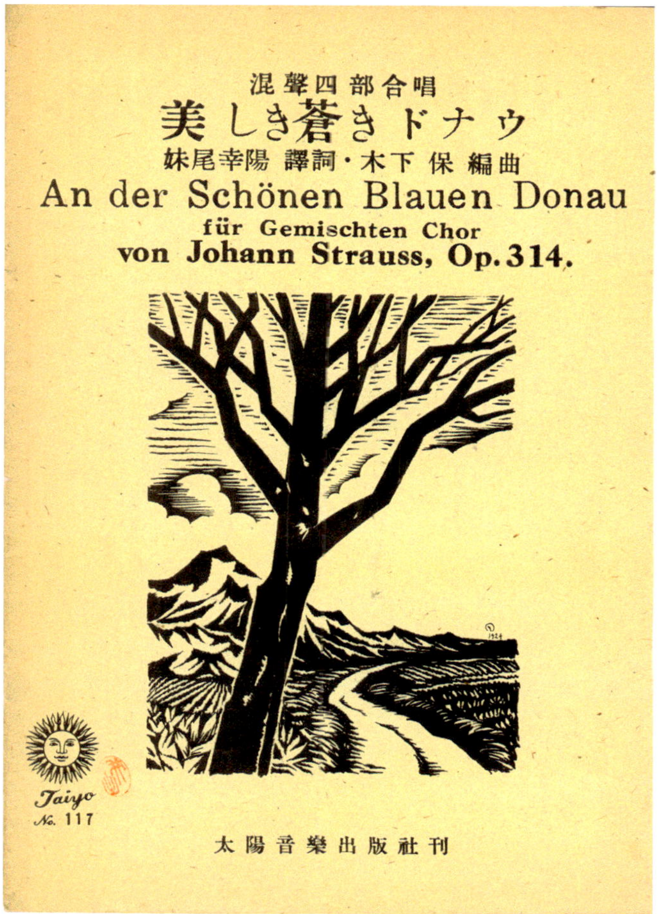


30. *An der schönen blauen Donau* (*Utsukushiki aoki Donau*, 美しき蒼きドナウ)
From *Four-part harmony for mixed voices* (*Konsei shibugasshū kyoku*, 混聲四部合唱曲), no. 117
25.7 x 18.0 cm
Date: 1949
Seals (stamp): artist's comma-shaped (*tomoe*) seal, collector's stamp
Publisher: Sun Music Publishing Company
Composer: Johann Strauss II (1825–1899)

This work was originally designed for the cover of 'O maiden dear' (*Koishi no otomo yo*, 恋しの乙女よ), *Senow music scores*, no. 446, 1926.

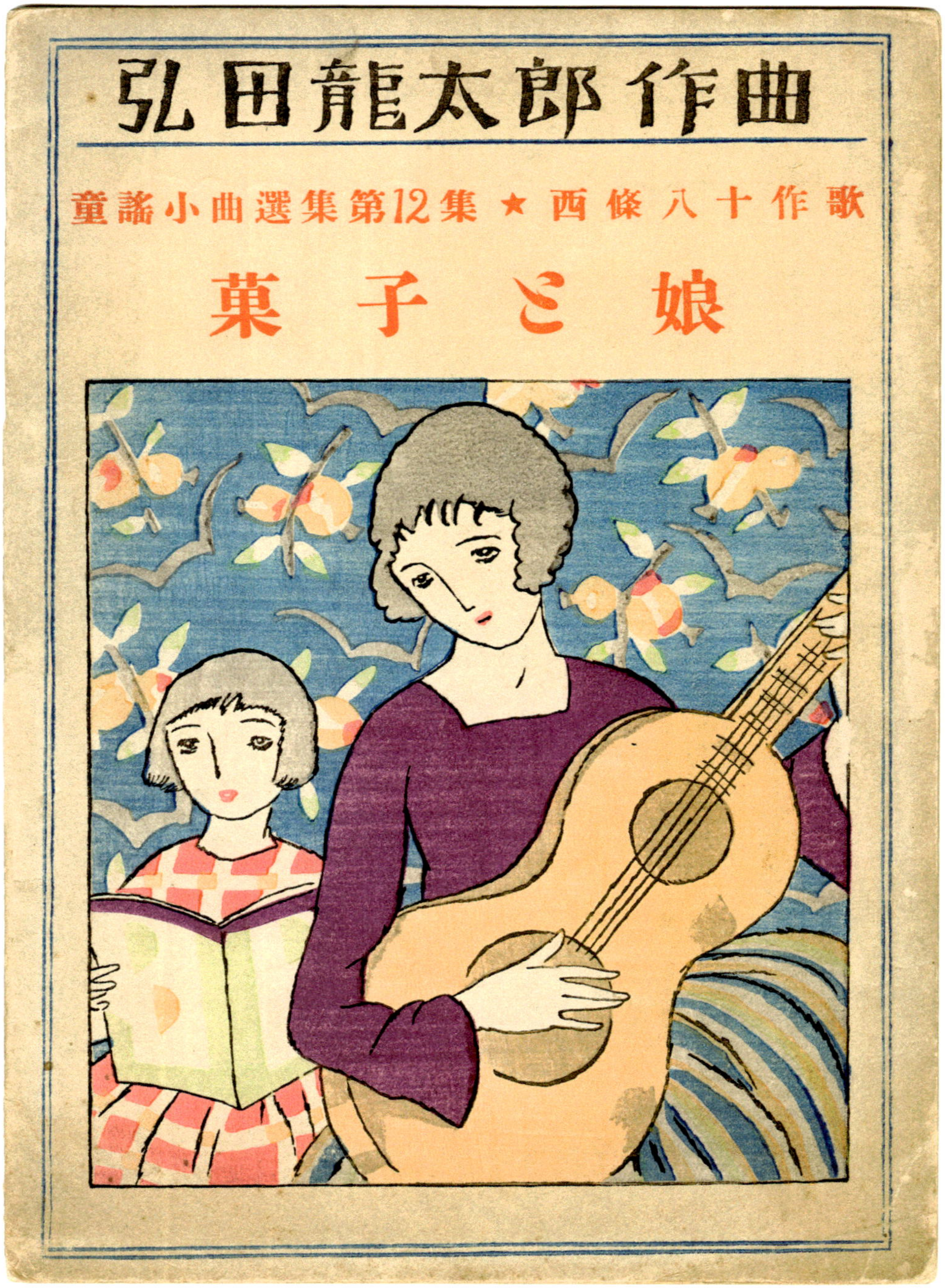


31. *Sweets and girls* (*Kuwashi to musume*, 菓子と娘)
From *Compositions by Hirota Ryūtarō: a compilation of children's songs* (*Hirota Ryūtarō sakkyoku: dōyōshōkyoku senshū*, 弘田龍太郎作曲 童謡小曲選集), no. 12
26.4 x 18.9 x cm
Date: 1930
Publisher: Kyōbunsha
Composer: Saijō Yaso (1892–1970)

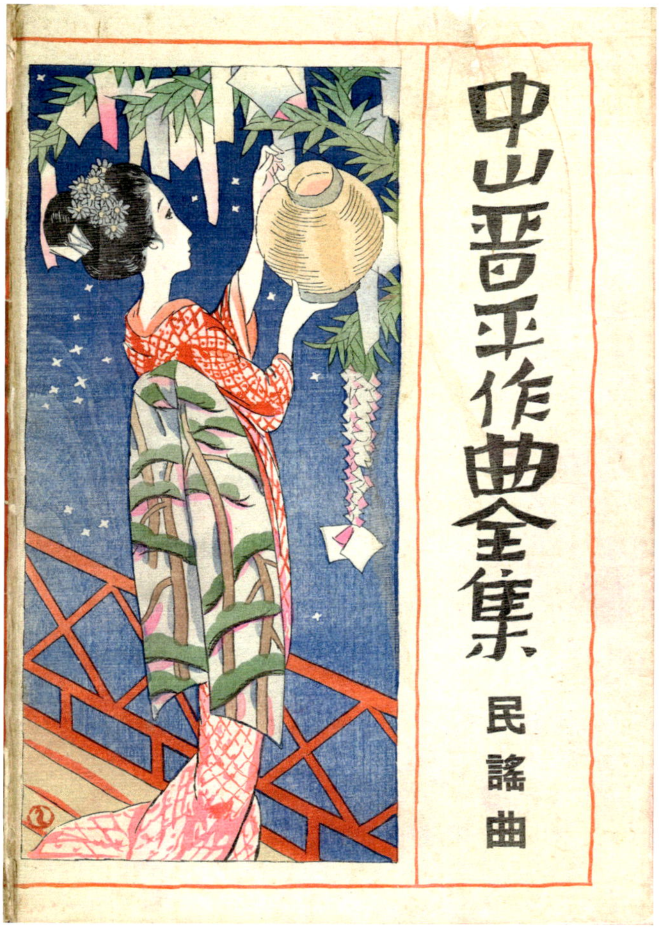


32. *Complete collection of works by Nakayama Shinpei: folk songs* (*Nakayama Shinpei sakkyoku zenshū: minyōkyoku*, 中山晋平作曲全集 民謡曲)
35.6 x 24.5 cm (cover)
Date: 1930
Seal: artist's comma-shaped (*tomoe*) seal
Publisher: Yamano Gakkiten
Composer: Nakayama Shinpei (1887–1925)

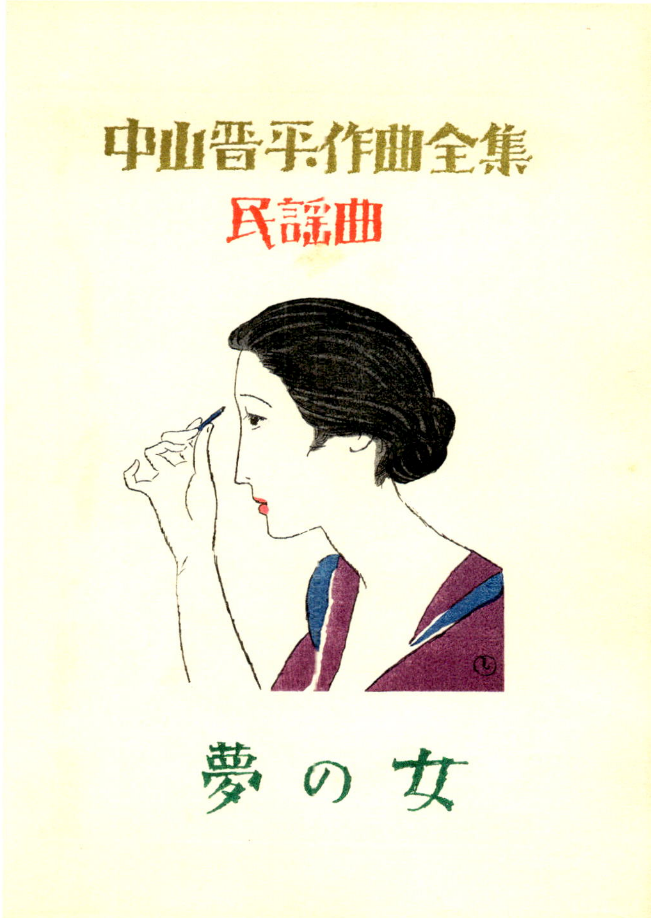


32a. *Dream woman* (*Yume no onna*, 夢の女)
34.4 x 23.5 cm
Seal: artist's comma-shaped (*tomoe*) seal

The main branch of the music store Yamano Gakkiten was located in Tokyo's fashionable Ginza district. It commissioned the composer Nakayama Shinpei to create a collection of popular music scores that were sold separately, and this set is a compilation of those scores. Shinpei selected twenty-eight well-known designs by Yumeji, most of which were reprised (and modified) from *The ladies' graphic* (*Fujin gurafu*).

The cover of the complete set mirrors a print entitled *Meeting stars* (*Hoshiai*), which was a segment within the serialised short story 'The woman's calendar prints of the twelve months' (*Fujin egoyomi jūnikagetsu*, 婦人絵暦十二ヶ月) that appeared in the first issue of *The ladies' graphic* in May 1924 (vol. 1 no 7) (see cat. 38).

There many different versions of this design of a woman applying make-up. The composition was first used in *The ladies' graphic* in October 1926 (cat. 61) and in the early 1930s it was adapted for this music cover. Slight differences between this and the original image include the omission of the 'frozen leaves' and the use of purple for the kimono. This purple version was also employed in the series *A collection of prints by* (*Yumeji hangashū*).

[MdV]

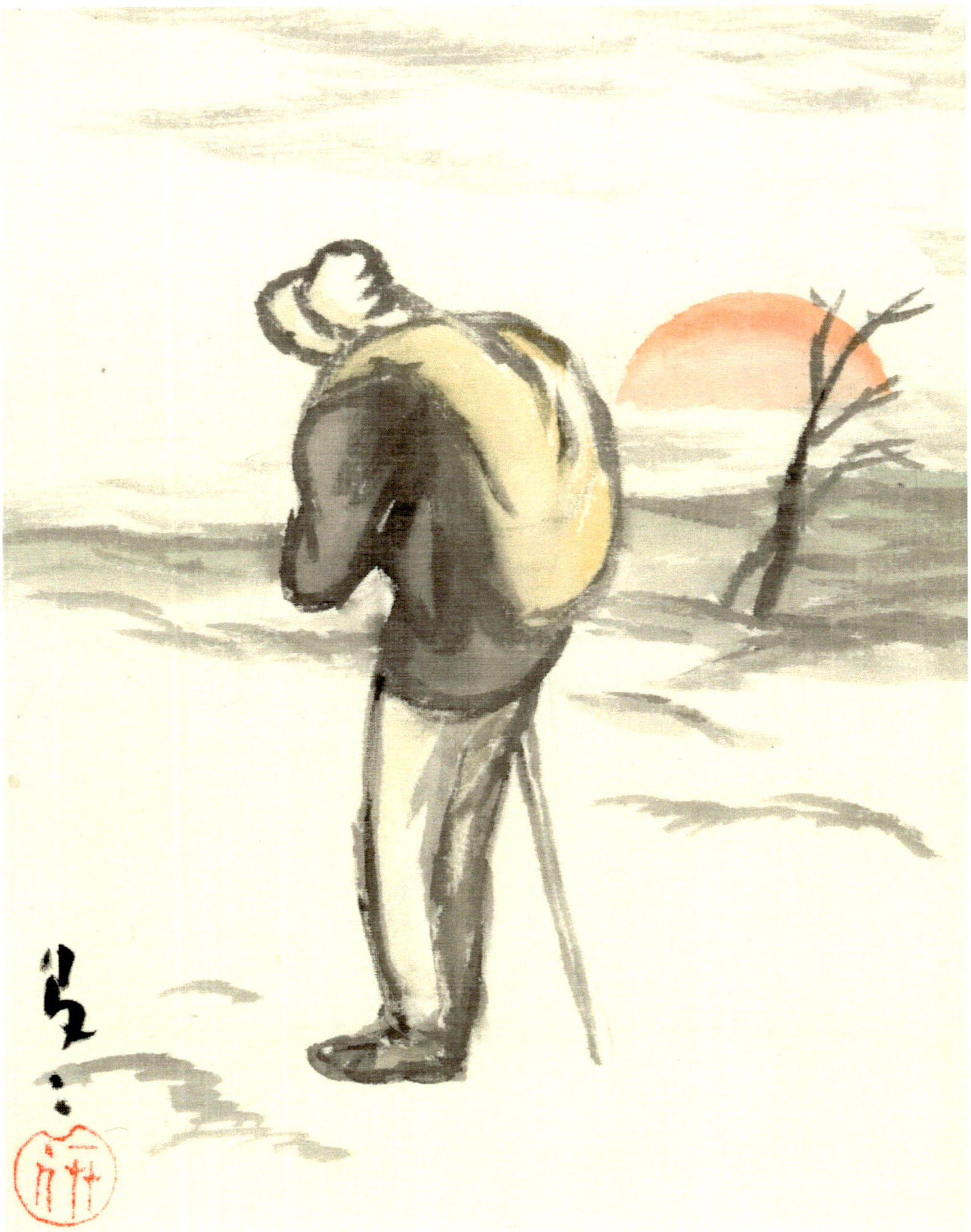

## Watercolours and paintings
cat. 33–36

As a self-taught artist not affiliated with any established school or artistic coterie, Yumeji was free to experiment with many different painting styles, including *nihonga* ('Japanese painting'), *yōga* ('Western painting') and watercolours. Throughout his career Yumeji created numerous watercolours on paper, hanging scroll paintings on paper and silk as well as 'square' format (*shikishiban*) paintings on silk, then mounted on cardboard (see also cat. 37 & 69a).

33. *Traveller with backpack and walking stick*
Painting on silk, 23.5 x 18 cm
Date: c. 1912
Signature/seal: *Yumeji* with artist's *Issōjin* seal

A similar composition of a boy holding an accordion with a setting sun and solitary tree on the right is seen in a painting on silk made by Yumeji in the early Taishō era (1910s).[1] The artist's seal, Issōjin (一艸人), appears on both Yumeji's paintings and graphic work.

[MdV]

1. Kawano, ed., *Yumeji 1884–1934*, 153, pls. 214 & 215.

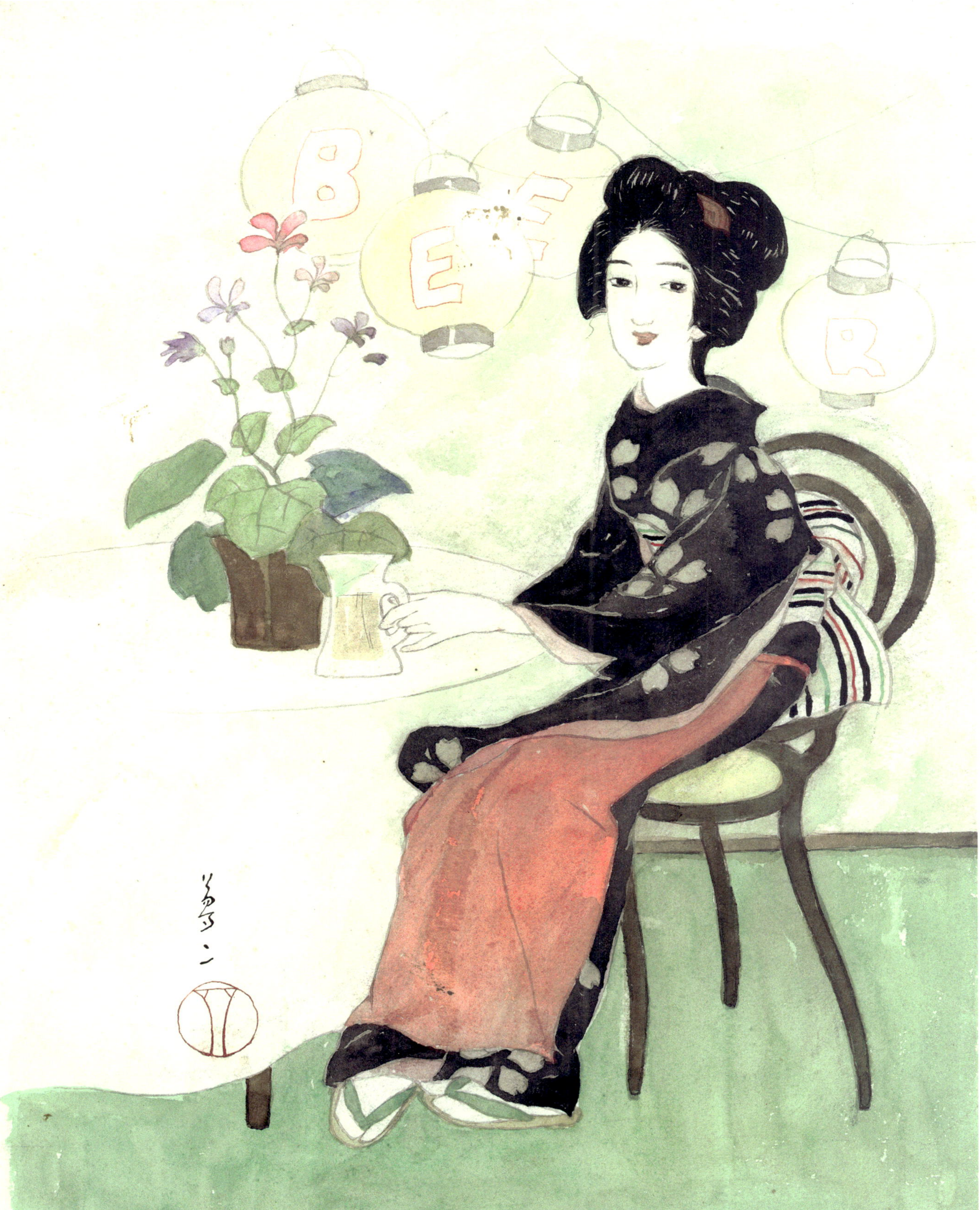
BEER

*Previous page*
34. *Woman in a beer hall*
Watercolour, 27.6 x 21.6 cm
Signature/seal: *Yumeji* with artist's 'grass' (*kusa*) seal

This image illustrates a woman dressed in a kimono decorated with a floral design and a red apron; she sits at a table with a mug of beer. The lanterns in the background are inscribed with the word 'BEER' in Roman letters, which hints that the venue is possibly a beer hall.

[MdV]

35. *Maiko with fan*
Painting on silk, 27.0 x 24.0 cm
Date: c. 1930
Signature/seal: *Yumeji* with the artist's *Shūjin sankō* seal

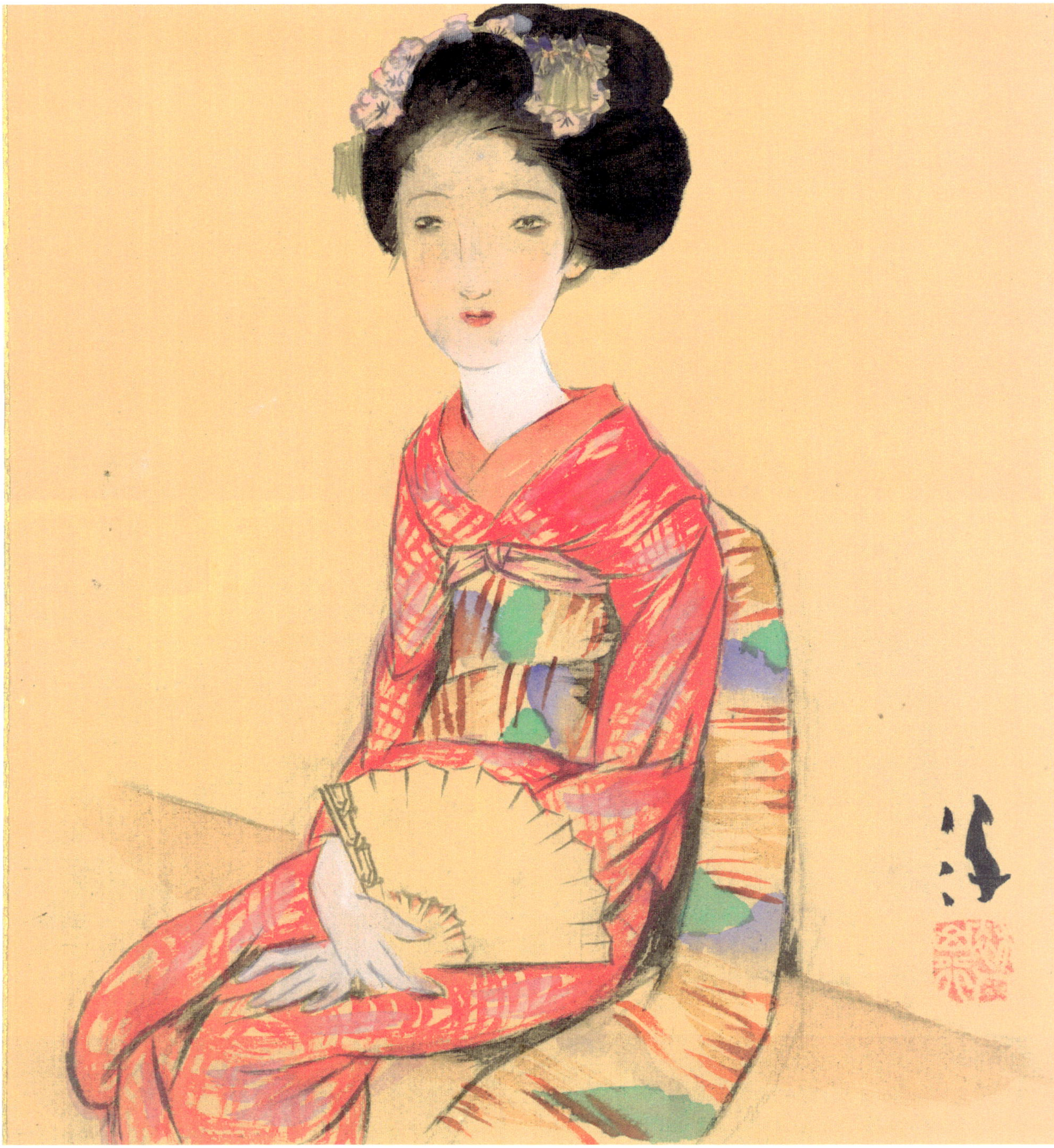

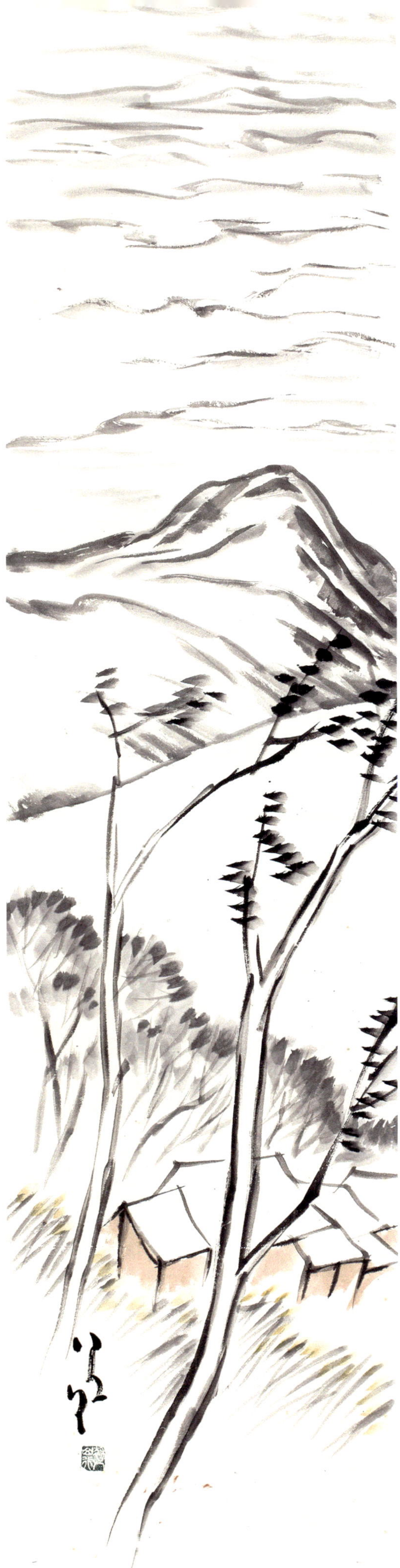

36. *Landscape*
Painting on paper mounted as a scroll, 129.0 x 31.0 cm
Date: c. 1930
Signature/seal: *Mushō* with the artist's *Shūjin sankō* seal

This scroll painting of a mountain scene with small cottages is similar to the sketches and paintings that Yumeji made in the 1920s. The mounting is decorated with white cherry blossoms and calligraphy.

[MdV]

## *The ladies' graphic* (*Fujin gurafu*, 婦人グラフ) cat. 37–65

The Tokyo-based Kokusai Jōhōsha launched *The ladies' graphic* (*Fujin gurafu*) in May 1924 and it ran until November 1928. The magazine targeted a female readership and included international news, matters relating to the lifestyle of the 'contemporary' woman as well as information about cuisine and current styles in clothing, hair and make-up.

In content and form, *The ladies' graphic* drew inspiration from Western fashion magazines. The cover and layout—along with a decorative frontispiece—was copied from the French journal *Art, goût, beauté, feuillets de l'élégance feminin.*[1] Publications like *Art, goût, beauté* employed the *pochoir* stencil-based technique, which produced crisp, vibrant images, but *The ladies' graphic* often opted for the more conventional medium of woodblock prints in combination with hand-coloured photographs, and on occasion lithographs. Yumeji's woodblock-printed cover designs were made separately and then pasted onto the cover or tipped into the inside pages as illustrations. This practice has unfortunately resulted in the dismemberment of many issues of *The ladies' graphic* as a way to capitalise on the sale of Yumeji's work.

Following the Great Kantō Earthquake of 1 September 1923, Yumeji worked increasingly as a commercial illustrator. This period coincided with his production of frontispieces, essays and articles for *The ladies' graphic*. Other artists, including Onchi Kōshirō (1891–1955), Itō Shinsui (1898–1972) and Fujiya Kōji (1898–1979), also contributed to the magazine. Yumeji's contribution to the *The ladies' graphic* can be seen as another point of contact with the then contemporary world of printmaking.

Yumeji's prints for the magazine showcase his repertory of female imagery, from the more conventional 'Yumeji-style beauty' (*Yumeji-shiki bijin*) to 'modern girls' (*modan gaaru* or *moga*). Unless otherwise specified, Yumeji's illustrations here are unsigned and unsealed (see figs. 4.15, 4.16, 4.17).

[MdV/SS]

1. Unno, 'Yumeji to gurafikku dezain' ('Yumeji and graphic design'), in Unno, ed., *Tokushū Takehisa Yumeji*, 112–15, and Ishikawa, '*Aru gu bote* to *Fujin gurafu*', 98–99.

*Next page*

**37. *Women at the beach***

**Preparatory watercolour for *Suitable bright clothing for a stroll at a summer resort (Hishochi ni tekihashii akarui sanpofuku*, 避暑地に適はしい明るい散歩服*)***

**27.0 x 19.1 cm**

**Date: c. 1926**

**Seal: variant artist's comma-shaped (*tomoe*) seal**

While Western fashions became increasingly popular after the Great Kantō Earthquake, not all Japanese women immediately adopted them. It is quite possible that the garments worn by these two women were not based on Yumeji's first-hand observations, rather on images from French fashion magazines such as *Gazette du bon ton: arts, modes & frivolités* or *Art, goût, beauté, feuillets de l' élégance féminine* that were in circulation from the 1910s to the 1930s and available in Japan (see cat. 37a). The composition of this particular watercolour is similar to images of women sporting the latest trends in *Art, goût, beauté*, suggesting that Yumeji may well has seen the magazine and copied from it. The finished woodblock print based on Yumeji's watercolour appeared in *The ladies' graphic* (vol. 3 no. 7, July 1926; see cover cat. 59).

[MdV]

*Next page (at right)*

**37a. Anonymous**

**Cover of *Art, goût, beauté, feuillets de l'élégance féminine***

**Date: vol. 5 no. 56, April 1925**

**Publisher: Charles Goy**

Rijksmuseum, Amsterdam

Two women, dressed in ensembles by the French fashion designer Jane Régny (active 1920s–1930s), carry parasols; the given title is '*Spécialiste costumes sport*'.

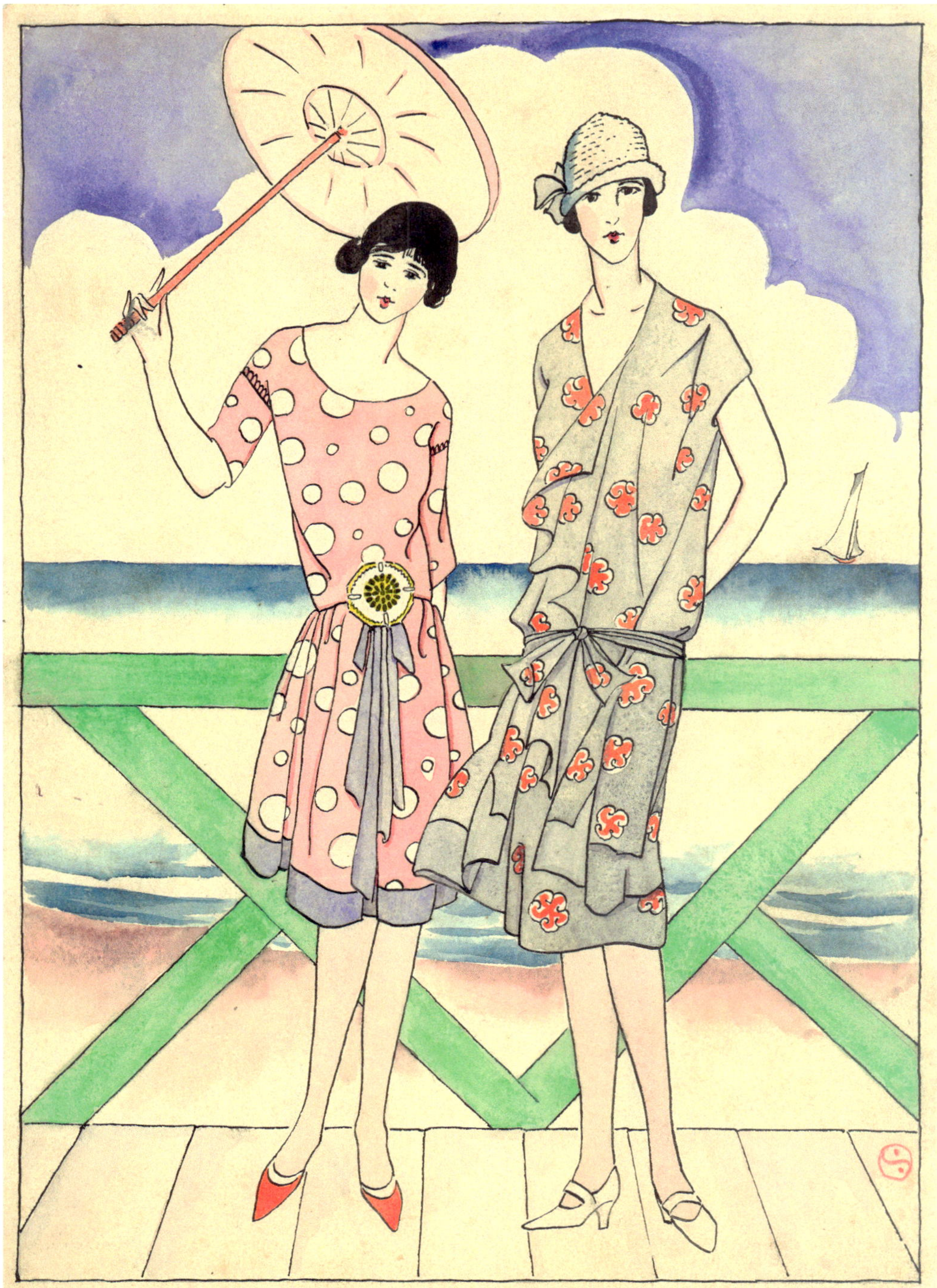

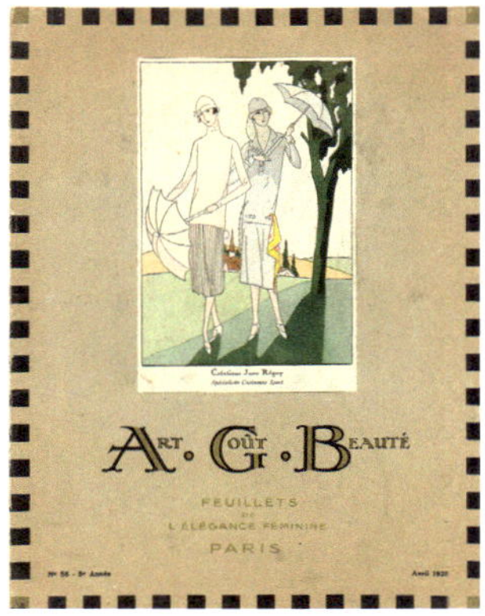
ART · GOÛT · BEAUTÉ
FEUILLETS
DE
L'ÉLÉGANCE FÉMININE
PARIS

婦人絵暦十二ケ月

七月

## 星合

竹久夢二

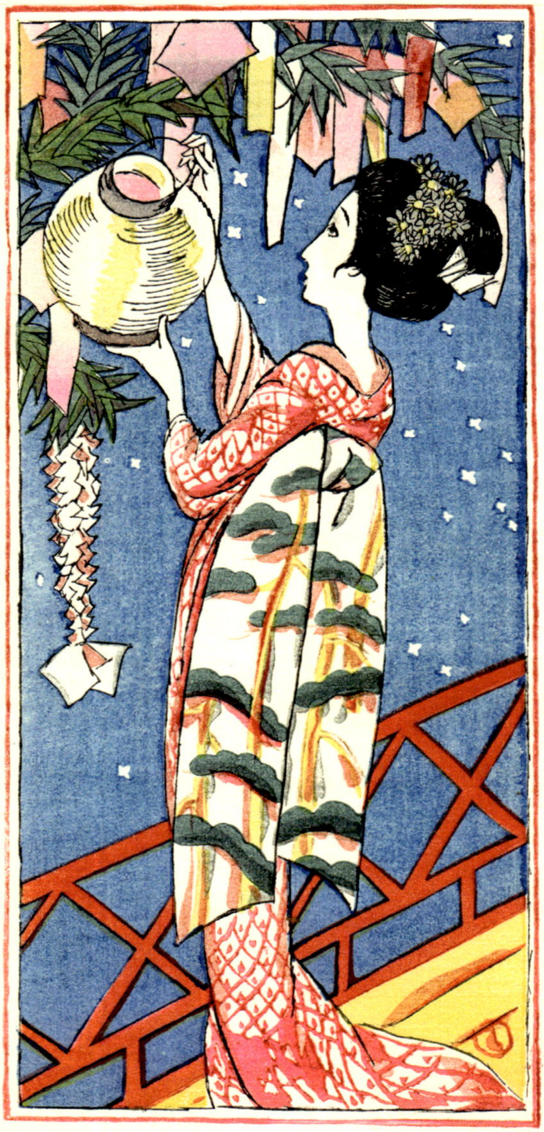

「郵便」

彼女は、その手紙があの人からであることをすぐ知つた。あけて見ると、白紙のまん中に黄ろい線が引いてあるきり何も書いてなかつた。それはVといふ字に似て垂直ですこし長く、左の線はやや傾いて短かつた。彼女は戀するもの、直感で「午前十時」とよんだ。Vの字は時計の針だ、黄は晝を意味してゐた。日附は書いてないが、戀人達にとつて約束はつねに明日であつた。

そこで彼女はお化粧にとりかかつた。およそ戀人に待たれてゐるといふことほど眞實な戀の瞬間はない。彼女のあらゆる自信と幸福は、實にこの化粧室の瞬間にあつた。それは彼女がずつと後になつて知つたことではあるが——。

逢つて彼を喜ばせることが出來るかどうかは、神様だけが御存じだ。彼女はとにかく彼を待たせることが出來るだけは、たしかであつた。彼女は牡丹刷毛を動かしながら、この貴重な瞬間を樂んだ。

◇

彼は運命の十字路に立つて待つた。辻の大時計はまさにVの字を描いたが、彼女は來なかつた。女つてものは代議士のやうなもので、きちんと時間に來たことがない。ゆつくり來るのが優越を示す所以だとでも思つてゐるのかしら。時計のVが直線になつても、左へ向いた〈の字になつても彼女は來なかつた。いろんな人間が往來を歩いてゆく。誰を見ても、みんな自由で健康で幸福さうだ。彼だけが何か世間から除物にされたやうで、しきりに忙しい。これはきつと街角に悄然と立つてゐる姿勢から來る感じだな、と彼は思つて、敷石の上を大股に歩いて見た。それは好い思付であつた。彼はすぐ快活になれた。

彼の所へはいま、白いパラソルで顔をかくして、呼吸をきらしながら、しかし、ゆつくりした足どりで、彼のベターハーフが歩いて來るはづである。

— 1 —

38. *Meeting stars* (*Hoshiai*, 星合)
(inside page)
26 x 12.3 cm (image); 32.5 x 24.5 cm (page)
Date: vol. 1 no 3, July 1924
Seal: artist's comma-shaped (*tomoe*) seal

A young woman is hanging a lantern for the Tanabata (Star) festival, which traditionally takes place on the seventh day of the seventh month. It accompanies the serialised story, 'The woman's calendar prints of the twelve months', written and illustrated by Yumeji. This design was also used for the cover of the *Complete collection of works by Nakayama Shinpei: folk songs* (see cat. 32).

[MdV]

*Next page*
39. *Fireworks* (*Hanabi*, 花火)
20.4 x 18.6 cm (image); 32.7 x 24.5 cm (cover)
Date: vol. 1 no. 4, August 1924

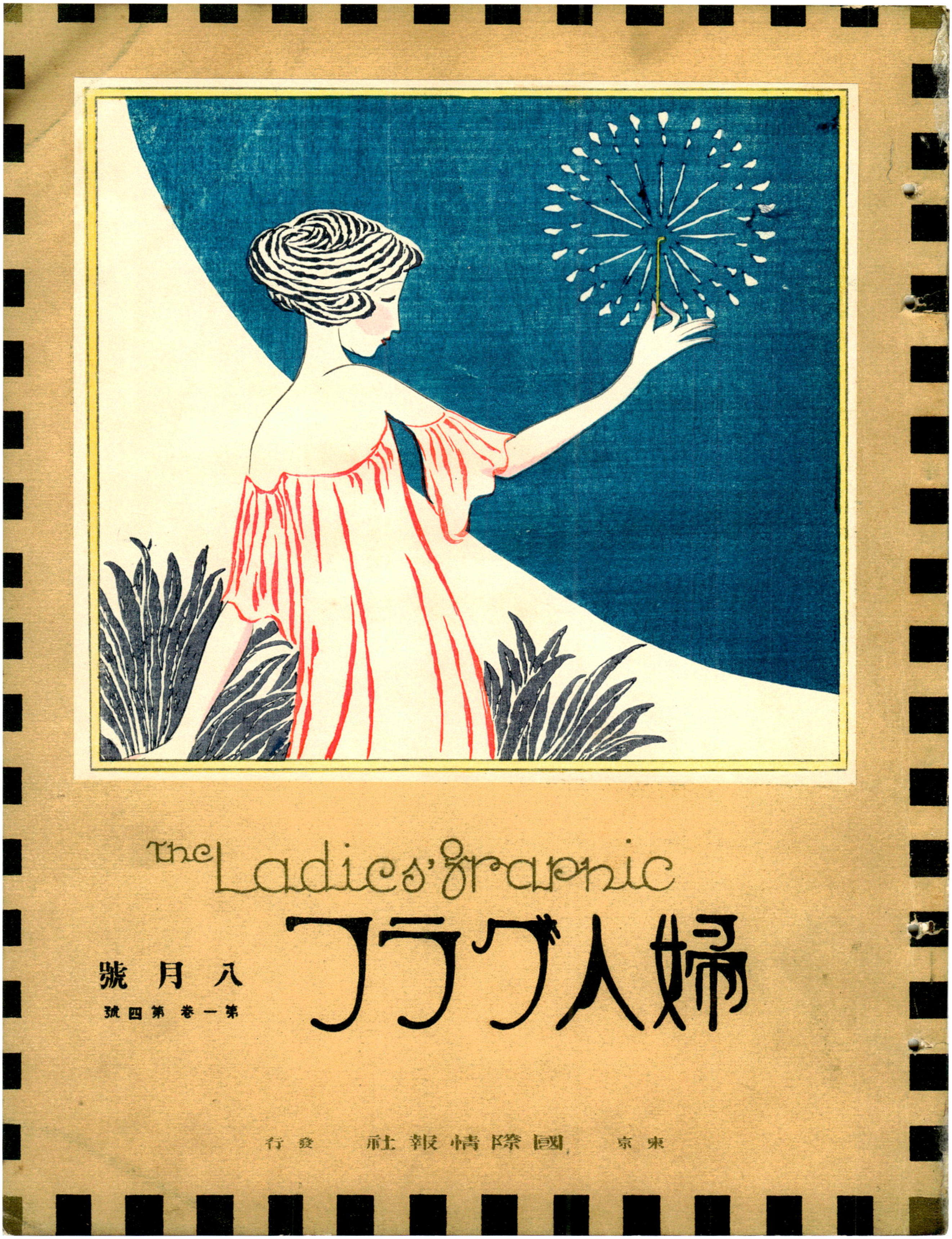
The Ladies' Graphic
婦人グラフ
八月號
第一巻第四號
東京 國際情報社 發行

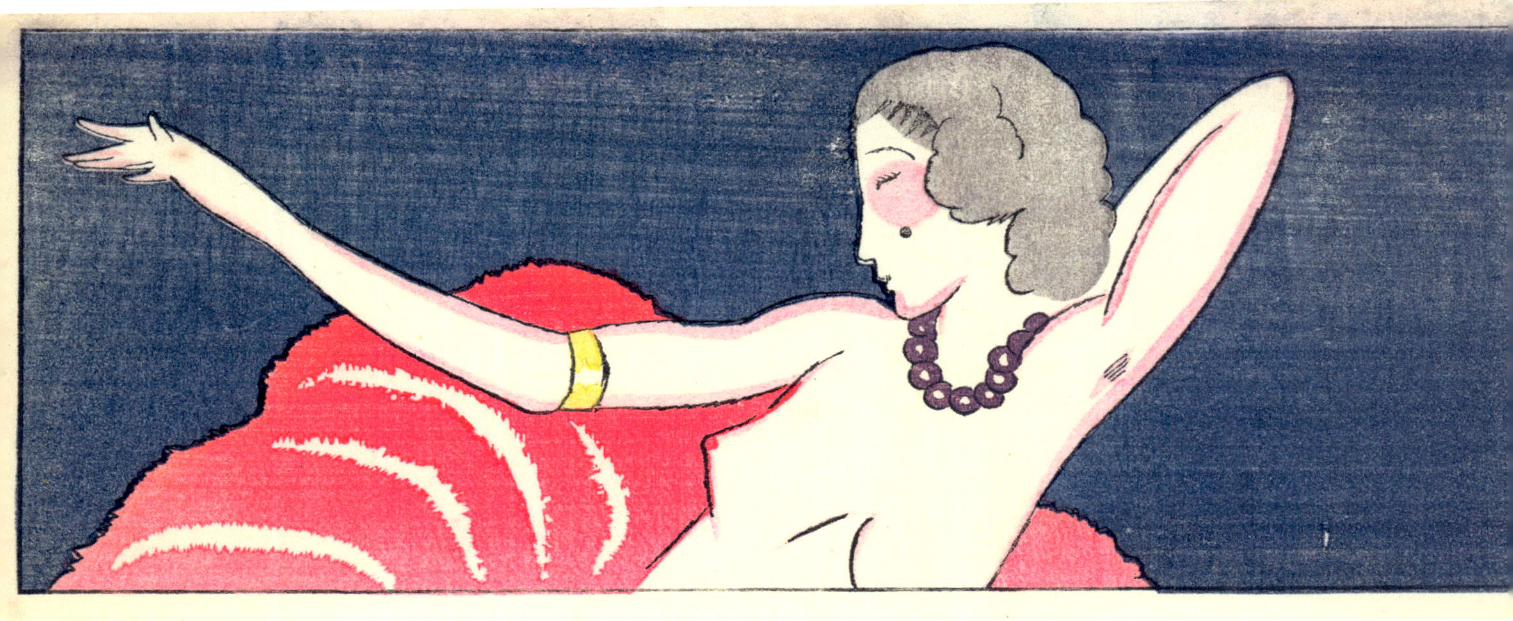

40. *Three questions of love*
(*Koisandai*, 恋三題)
8.0 x 19.5 cm
Date: vol. 1 no. 4, August 1924

Next page
41. *Autumn* (*Aki*, 秋)
19.2 x 20.3 cm (image);
32.6 x 24.7 cm (cover)
Date: vol. 1 no. 5, September 1924

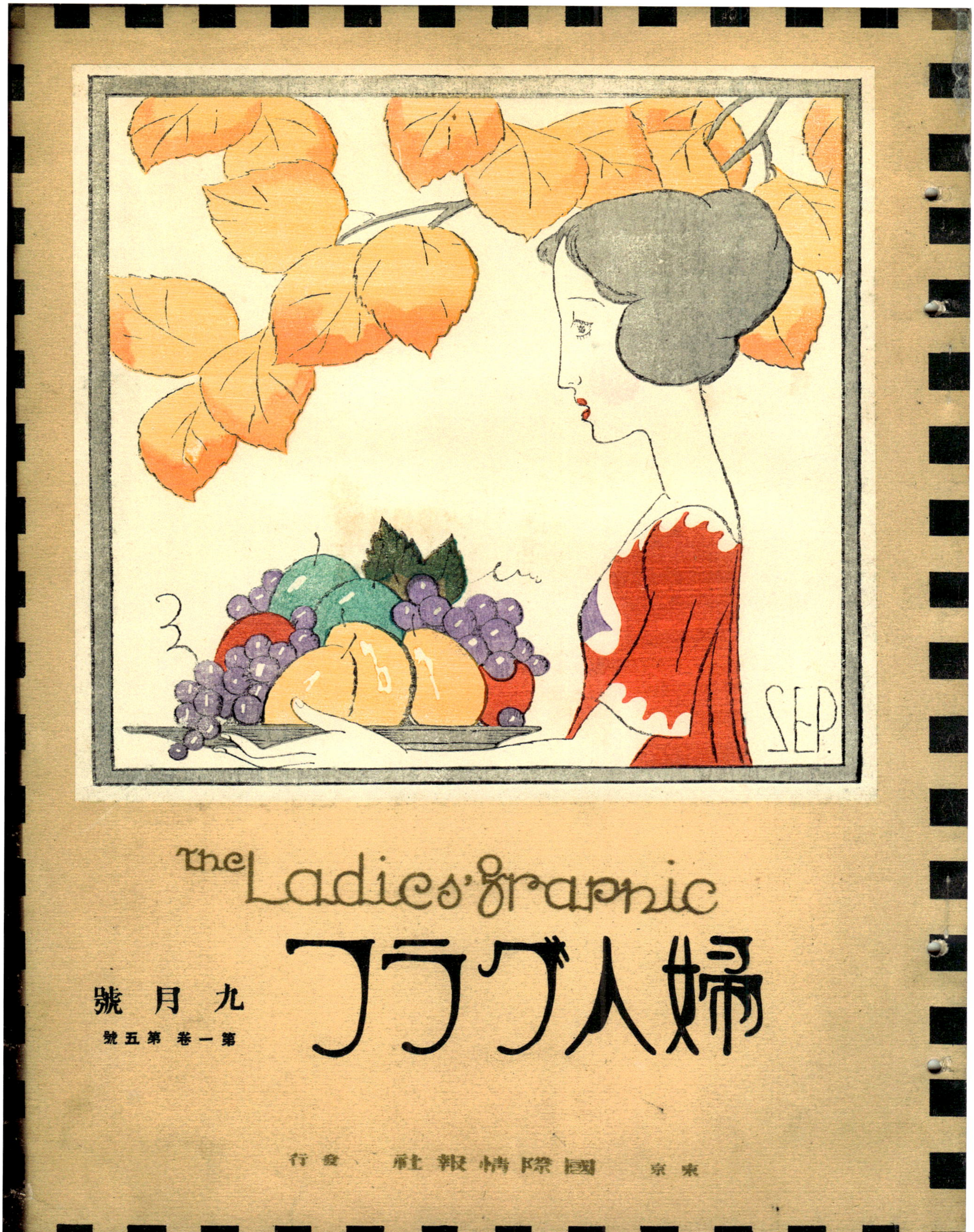
SEP.
The Ladies' Graphic
婦人グラフ
九月號
第一巻第五號
東京　國際情報社　發行

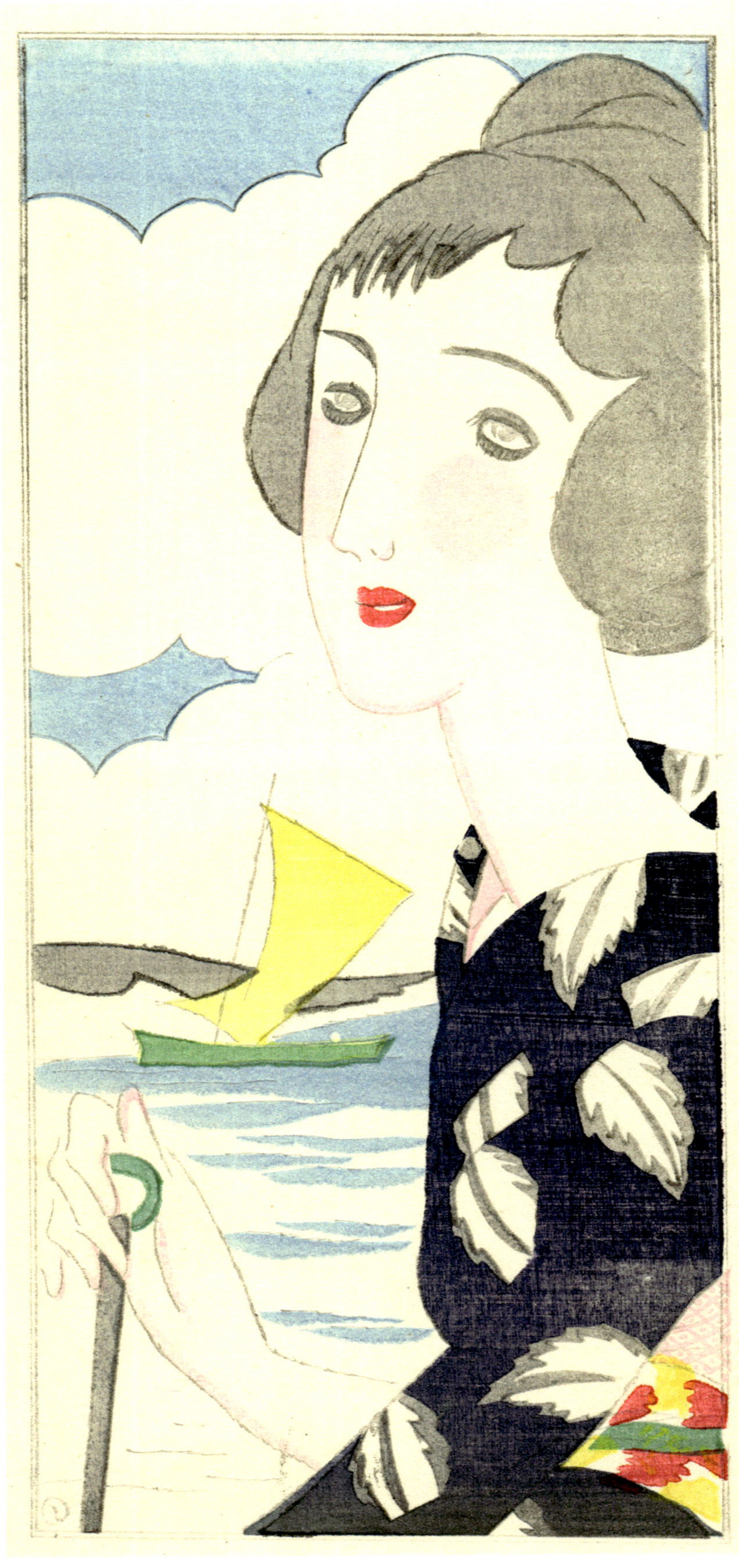

**42.** ***Brave lover***
**(*Yūkan na koibito* 勇敢な恋人)**
**23.3 x 10.9 cm**
**Date: vol. 1 no. 4, August 1924**
**Seal: artist's comma-shaped (*tomoe*) seal**

In the inaugural issue (May 1924) of *The ladies' graphic* featured the first instalment of the serialised short story 'The woman's calendar prints of the twelve months' (see also cat. 32a & 38). Yumeji contributed the text and illustrations to these. The prints in the first two instalments were in black and white, thereafter they appeared in colour. These were printed separately and tipped into the page. Following the magazine's fourth number in August 1924, Yumeji also contributed cover designs.

[MdV]

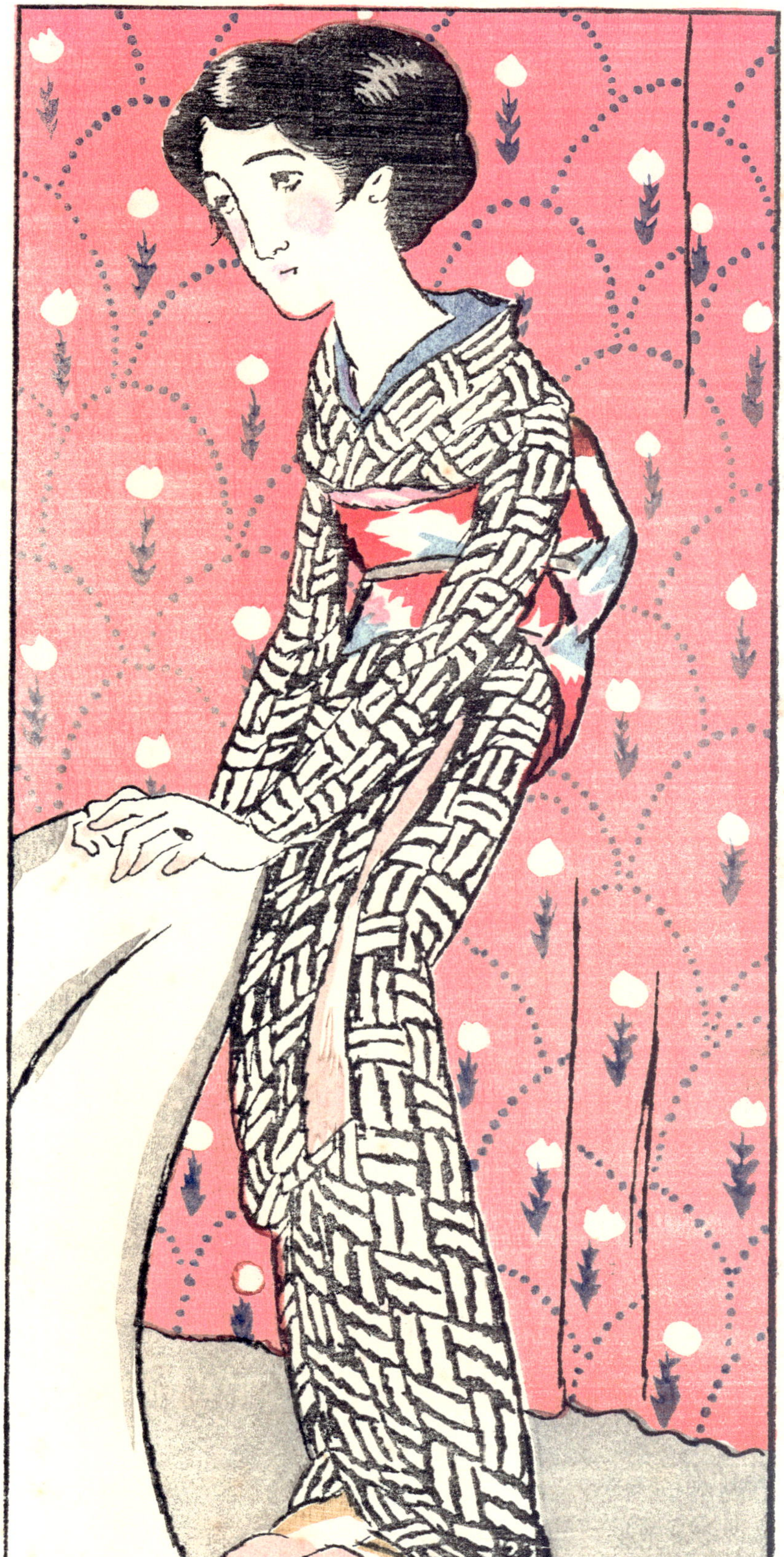

43. *Sofa* (*Neisu*, 寝椅子)
25.2 x 12.1 cm
Date: vol. 1 no. 7, November 1924

44. *Spring glance* (*Haru no me*, 春の眼)
23.1 x 11.2 cm
Date: vol. 1 no. 6, October 1924
Seal: artist's comma-shaped (*tomoe*) seal

45. *Final settlement of love* (*Ai no sōkanjō*, 愛の総勘定)
23.1 x 11.9 cm
Date: vol. 1 no. 8, December 1924

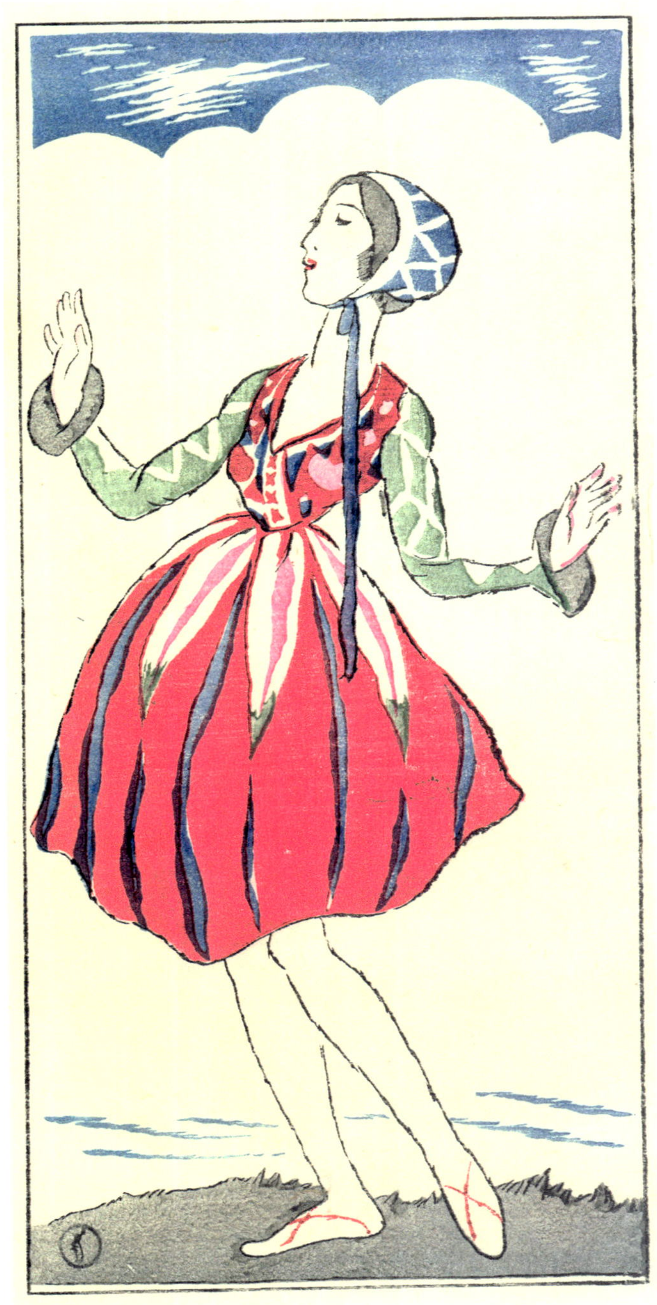

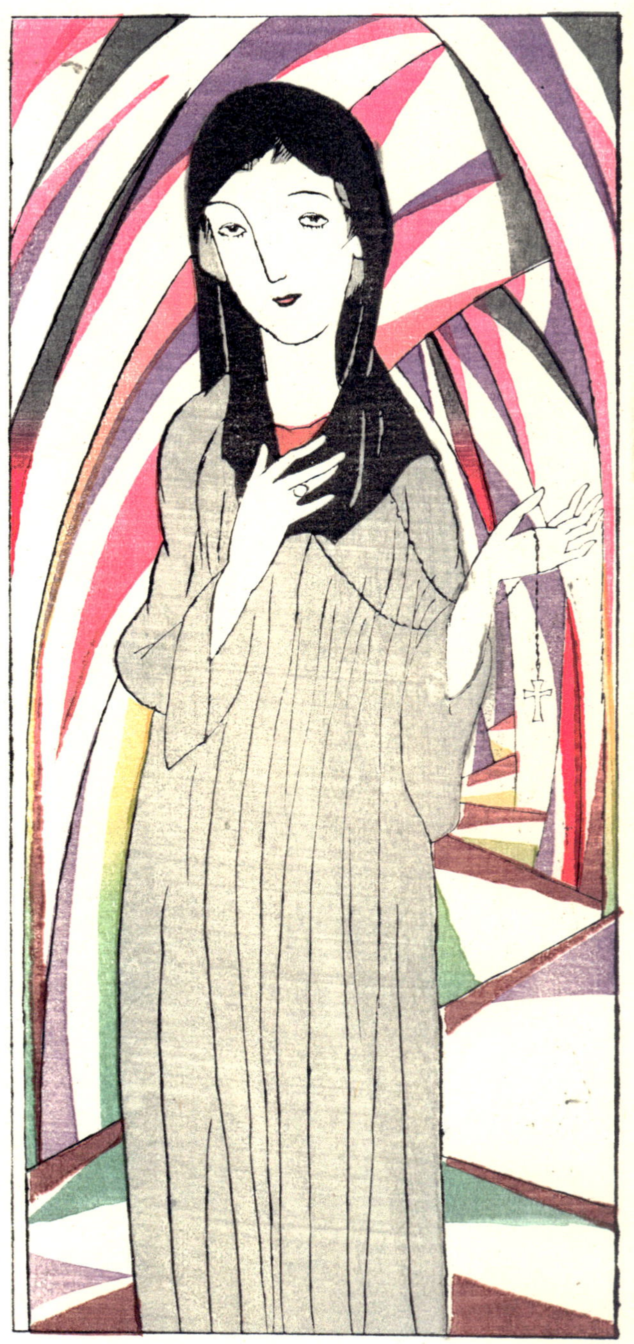

46. *Autumn tune* (*Aki no shirabe*, 秋のしらべ)
18.5 x 21.1 cm (image);
32.6 x 24.5 cm (cover)
Date: vol. 1 no. 7, November 1924

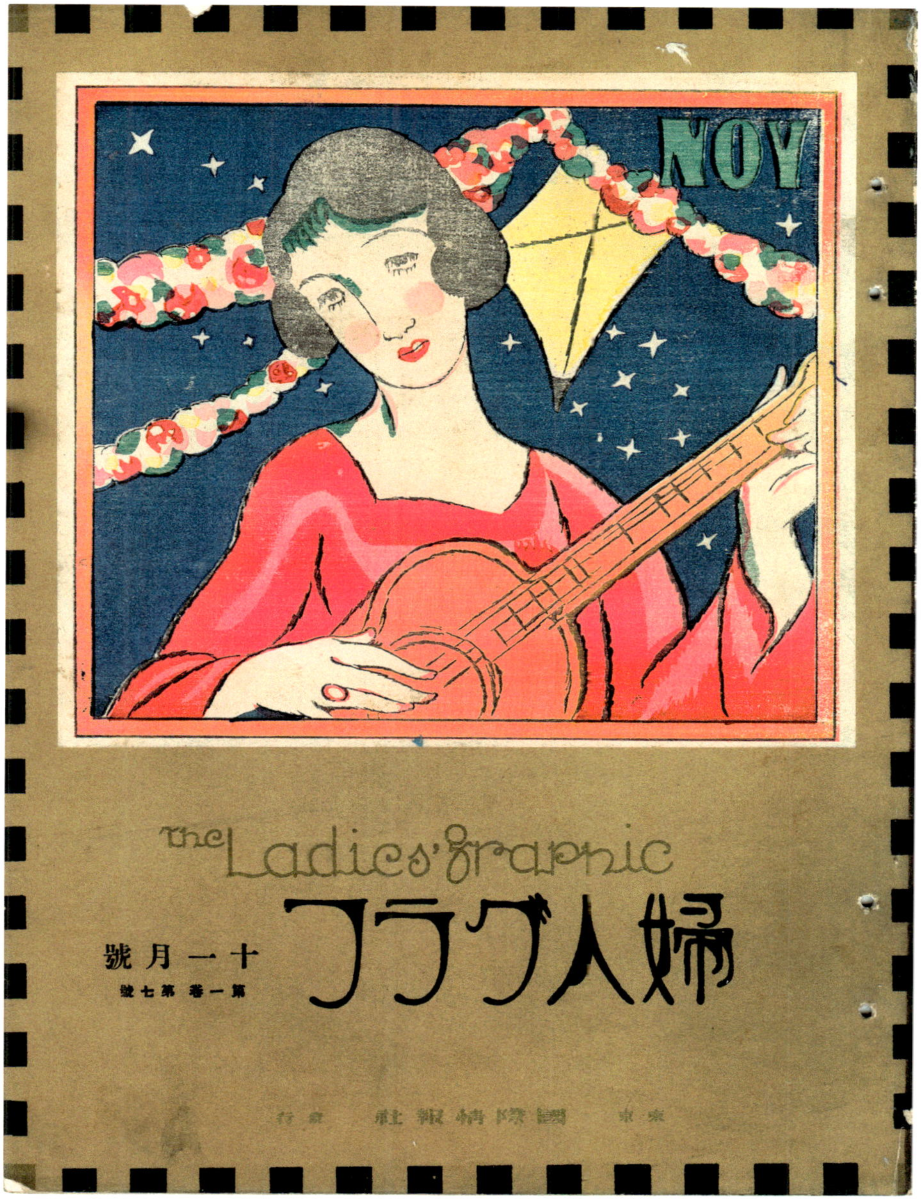


46a. Two pages showing the story 'Saint Mary' (*Maria Kannon*, 麻利亜観音)
10.6 x 10.9 cm (image right);
27.3 x 12.4 cm (image left);
32.6 x 47.4 cm (magazine open)
Date: vol. 1 no. 7, November 1924

The serialised story 'Women missionaries' (*Nyonin bateren*) is by Kanbara Haruo (1900–1960), who was interested in the history of early Christianity in Japan (see also fig. 4.16 & cat. 48). He was a pupil of the celebrated author of short stories, Akutagawa Ryūnosuke (1892–1927).

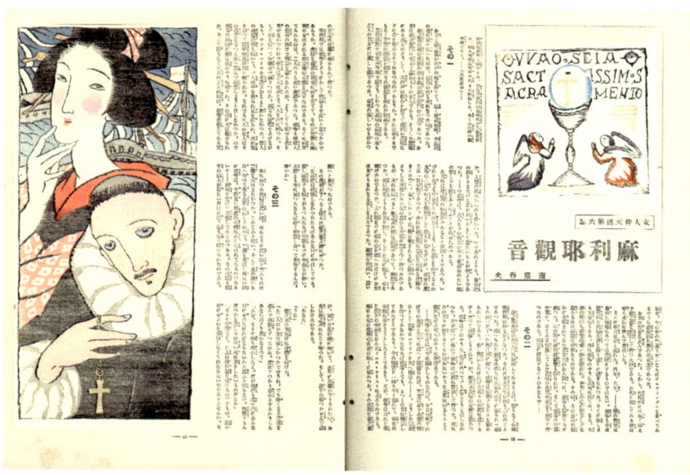

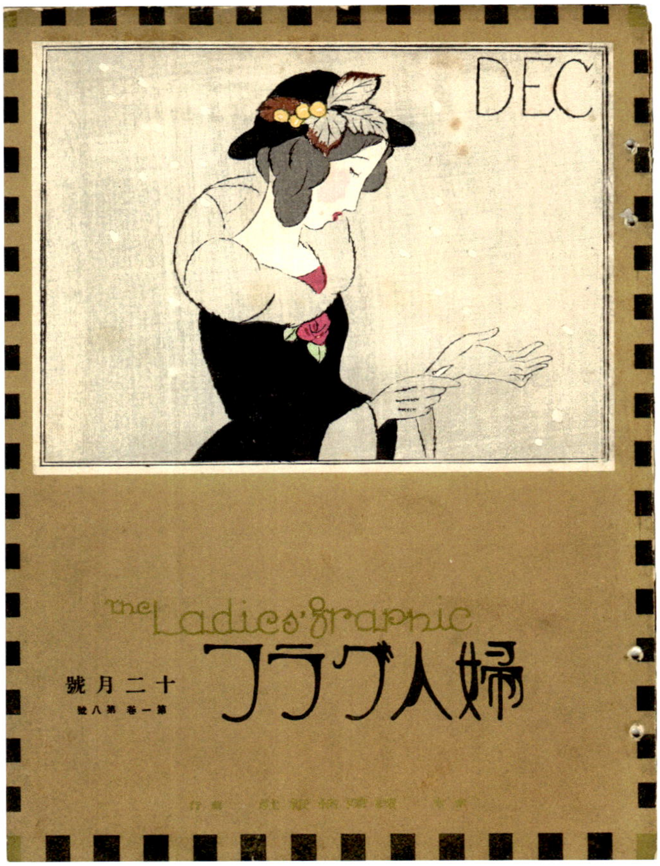


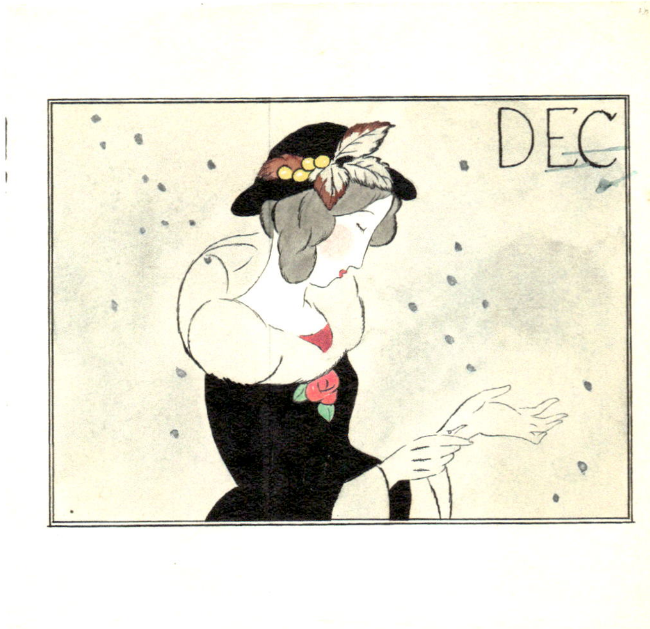


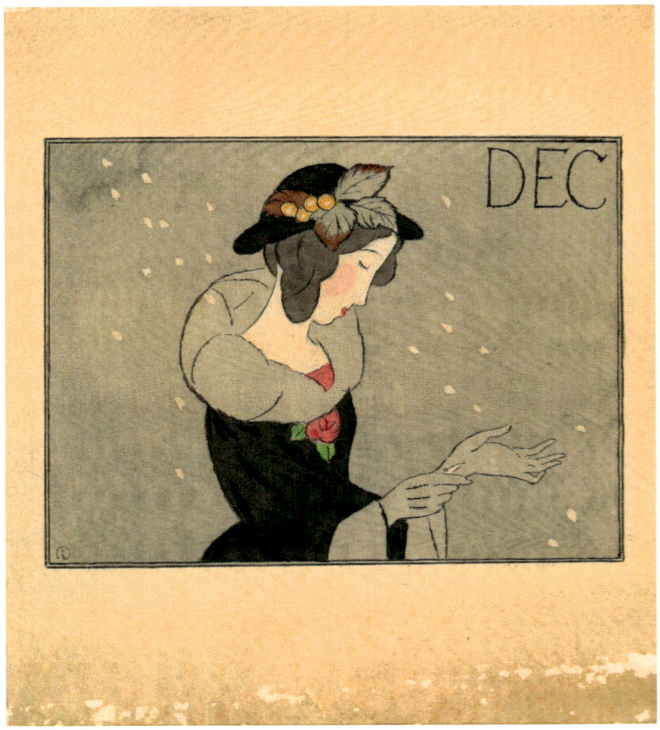


47. *Snowy wind* (*Yuki no kaze*, 雪の風)
16.5 x 21.7 cm (image); 32.9 x 24.4 cm (cover)
Date: vol. 1 no. 8, December 1924

47a. *Snowy wind*
Painting on paper, 23.4 x 24.6 cm
Date: c. 1924

47b. *Snowy wind*
Painting on silk mounted on cardboard, 27.1 x 24.1 cm
Date: c. 1924
Seal: artist's comma-shaped (*tomoe*) seal

Yumeji's designs for the covers and illustrations of *The ladies' graphic* were highly acclaimed. His contributions to the journal would have been a clever marketing ploy on the part of the publisher to entice buyers and increase sales. These two paintings—one on paper, the other on silk—were most likely made after the publication of *The ladies' graphic* issue and therefore testify to the popularity of this composition of a woman putting on gloves during a blizzard.

[MdV]

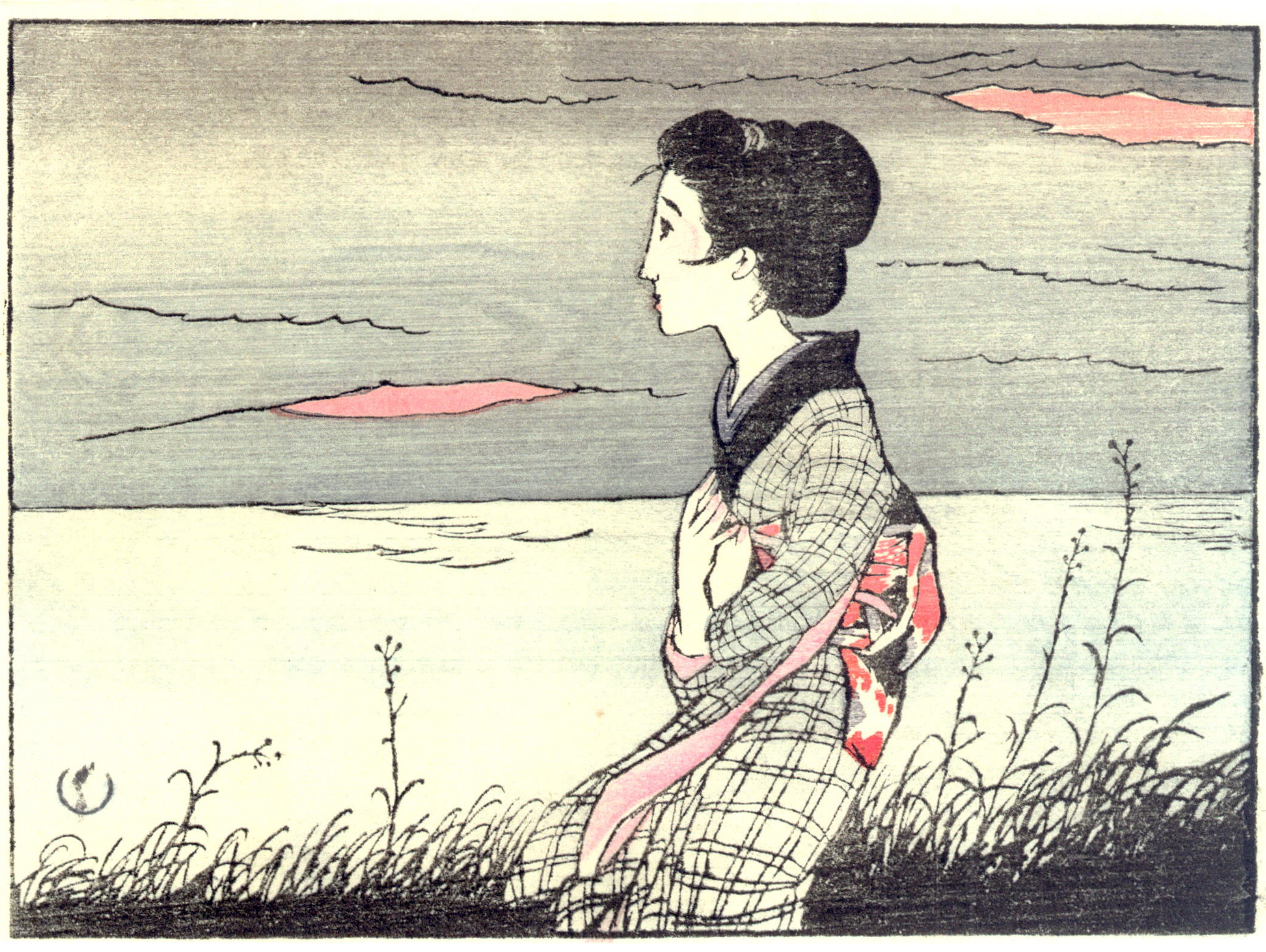

48. *Flower of Holland*
(*Oranda no hana,* 和蘭の花)
13.5 x 17.6 cm
Date: vol. 1 no. 6, October 1924
Seal: artist's comma-shaped (*tomoe*) seal

This illustration accompanied the fifth instalment of the serialised story 'Women missionaries' (see also fig. 4.16 & cat. 46).

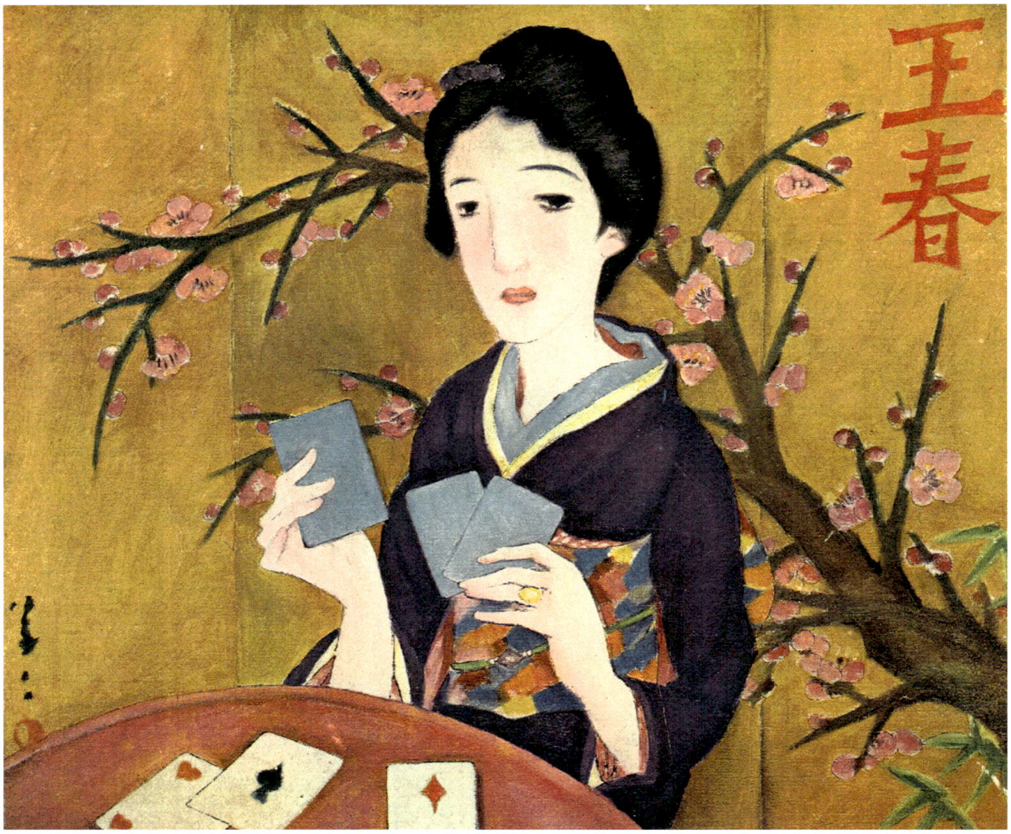


49. *New year* (*Ōshun*, 王春)
17.5 x 20.7 cm
Date: vol. 2 no. 1, January 1925
Signature/seal: *Yumeji* with artist's comma-shaped (*tomoe*) seal

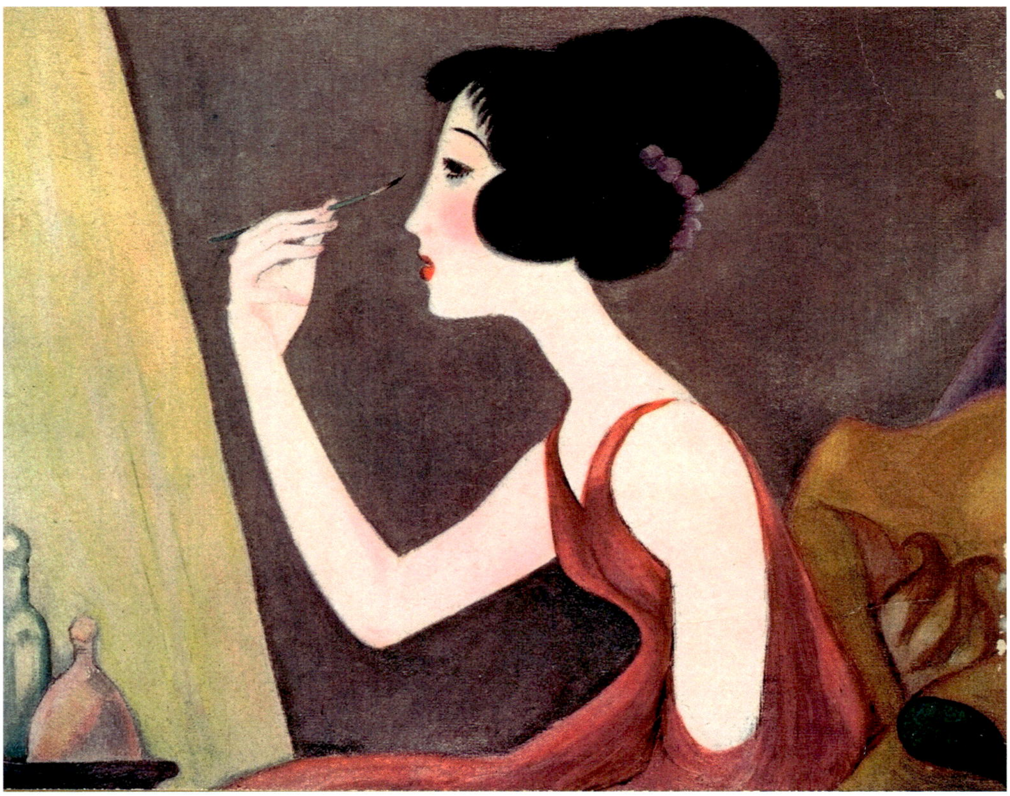

50. *Applying make-up*
15.8 x 20.0 cm
Date: vol. 2 no. 2, February 1925

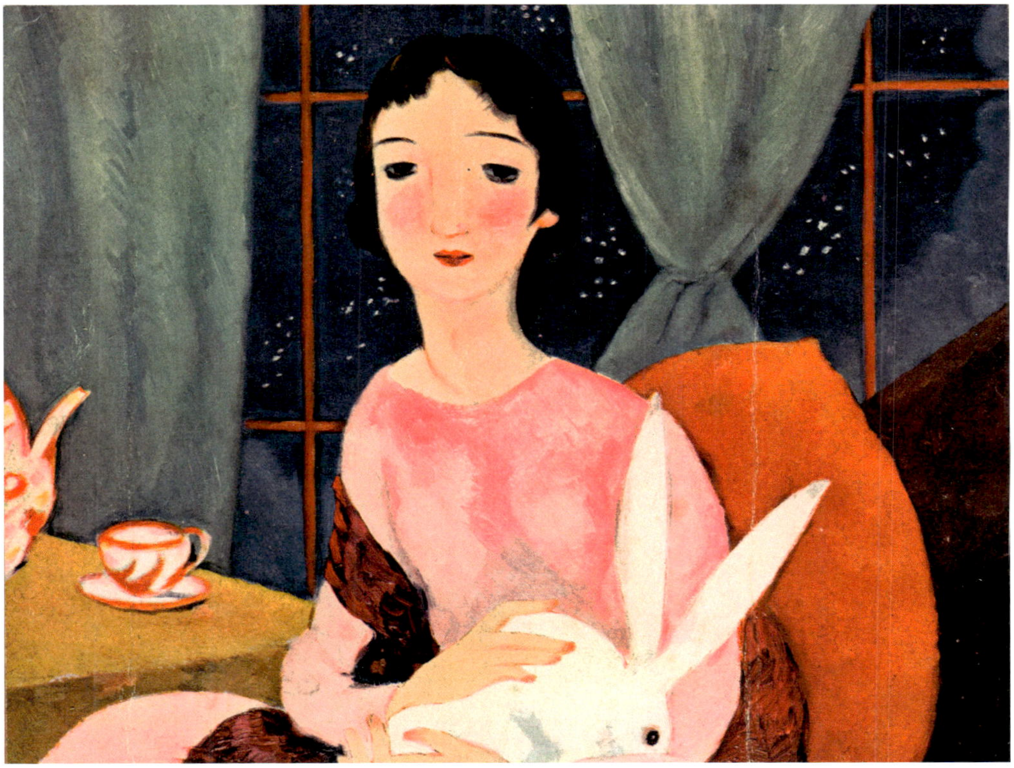

51. *Girl and hare*
19.9 x 32.7 cm
Date: vol. 2 no. 3, March 1925

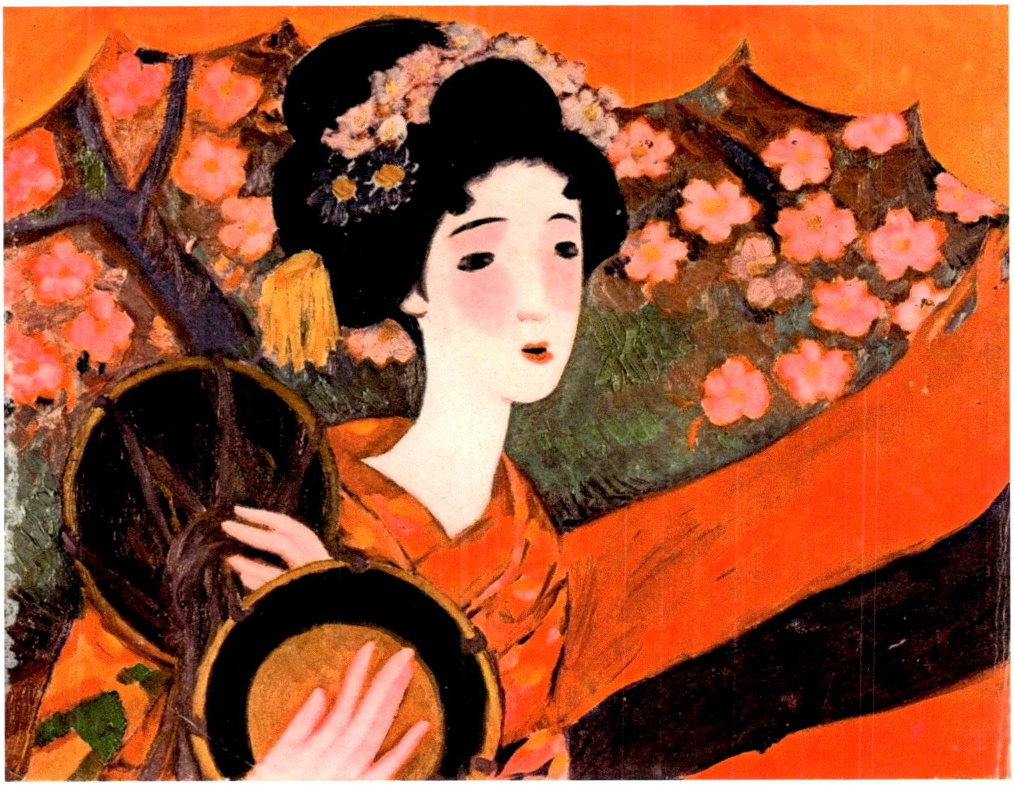

52. *Drum*
15.9 x 19.9 cm
Date: vol. 2 no. 4, April 1925

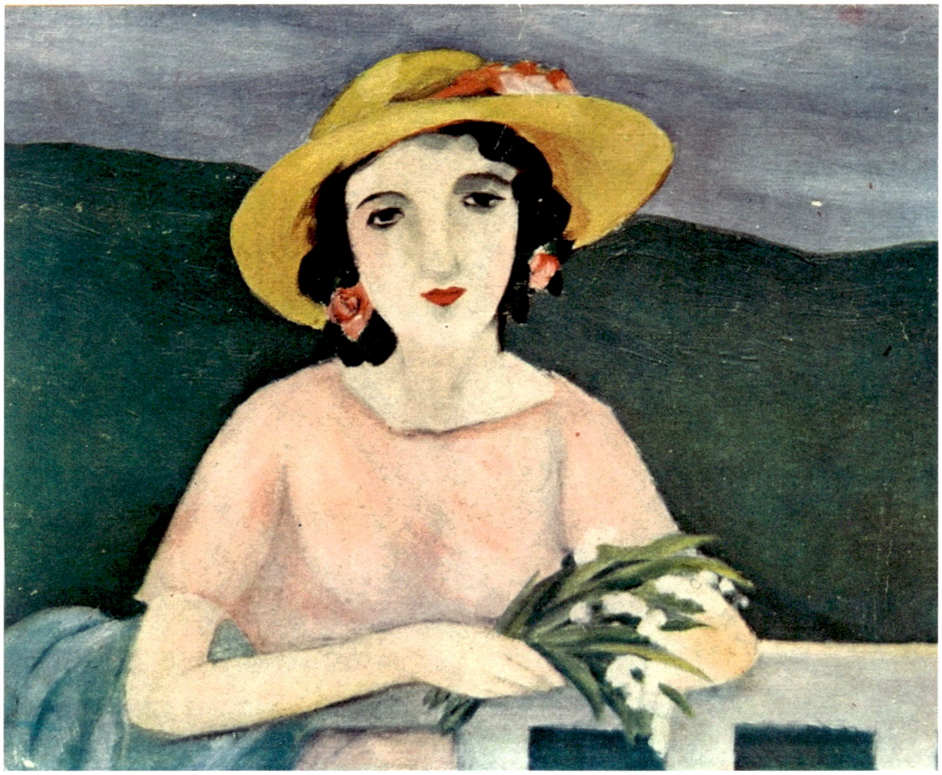

53. *Lily of the valley*
16.2 x 19.1 cm
Date: vol. 2 no. 5, May 1925

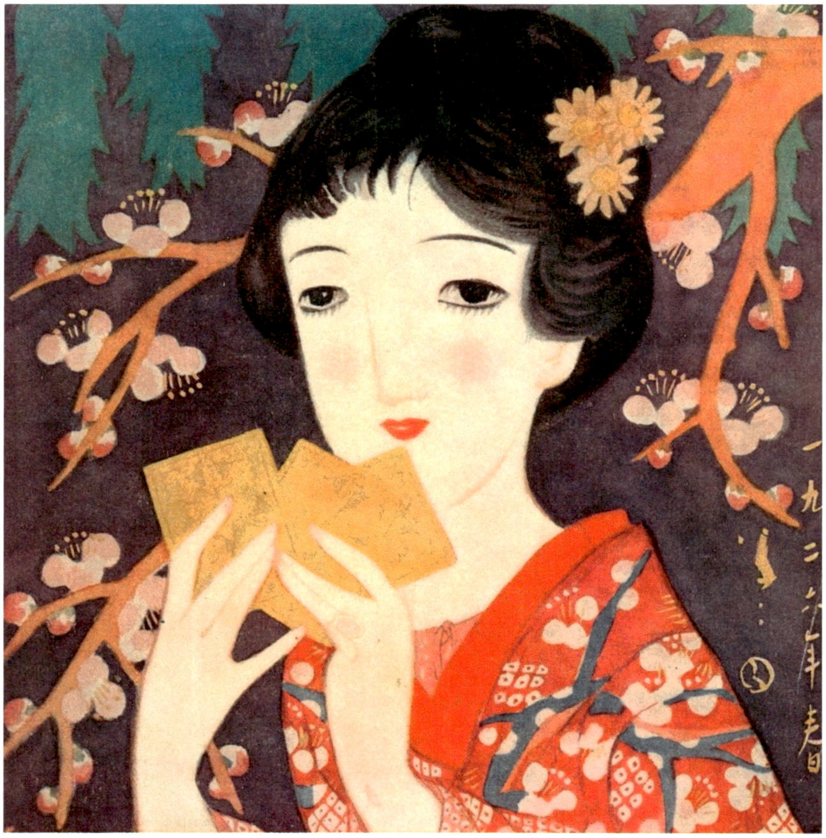


54. *Spring* (*Haru*, 春)
19.5 x 19.0 cm
Date: vol. 3 no. 1, January 1926
Signature/seal: *Yumeji* with artist's comma-shaped (*tomoe*) seal

55. *Legend of the second month* (*Jogetsu no densetsu*, 如月の伝説)
17.2 x 17.8 cm
Date: vol. 3 no. 2, February 1926
Signature/seal: *Yumeji* with artist's comma-shaped (*tomoe*) seal

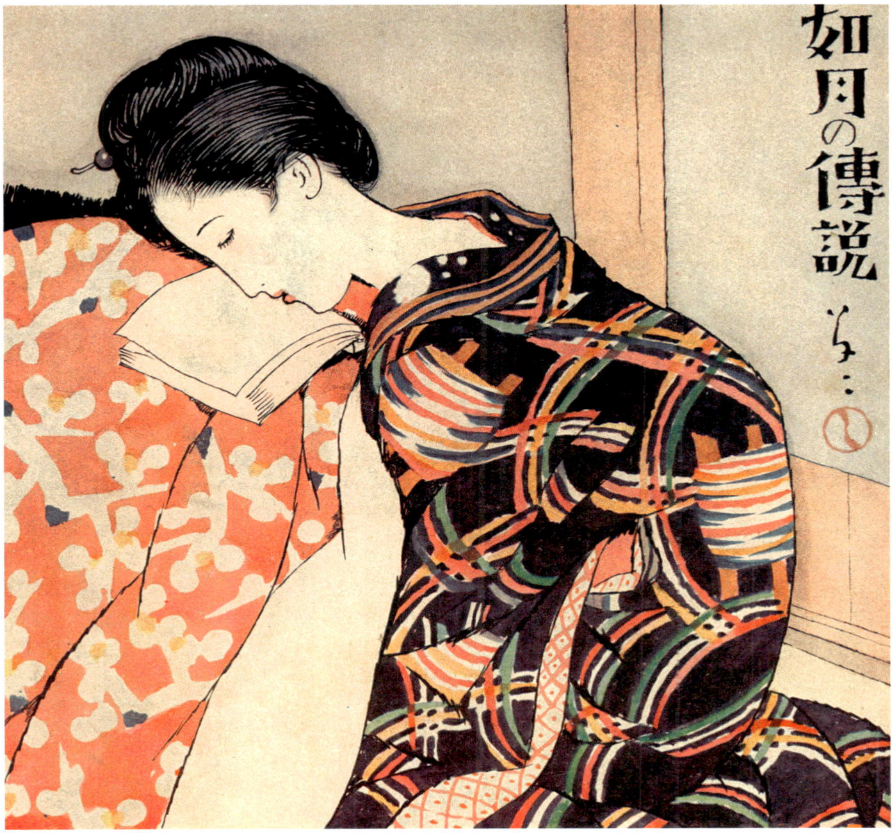


56. *Apl fool* [*April fools*] (*Eipuriru furu*, エイプリル・フール)
16.3 x 18.6 cm
Date: vol. 3 no. 4, April 1926
Signature/seal: *Yumeji* with artist's comma-shaped (*tomoe*) seal

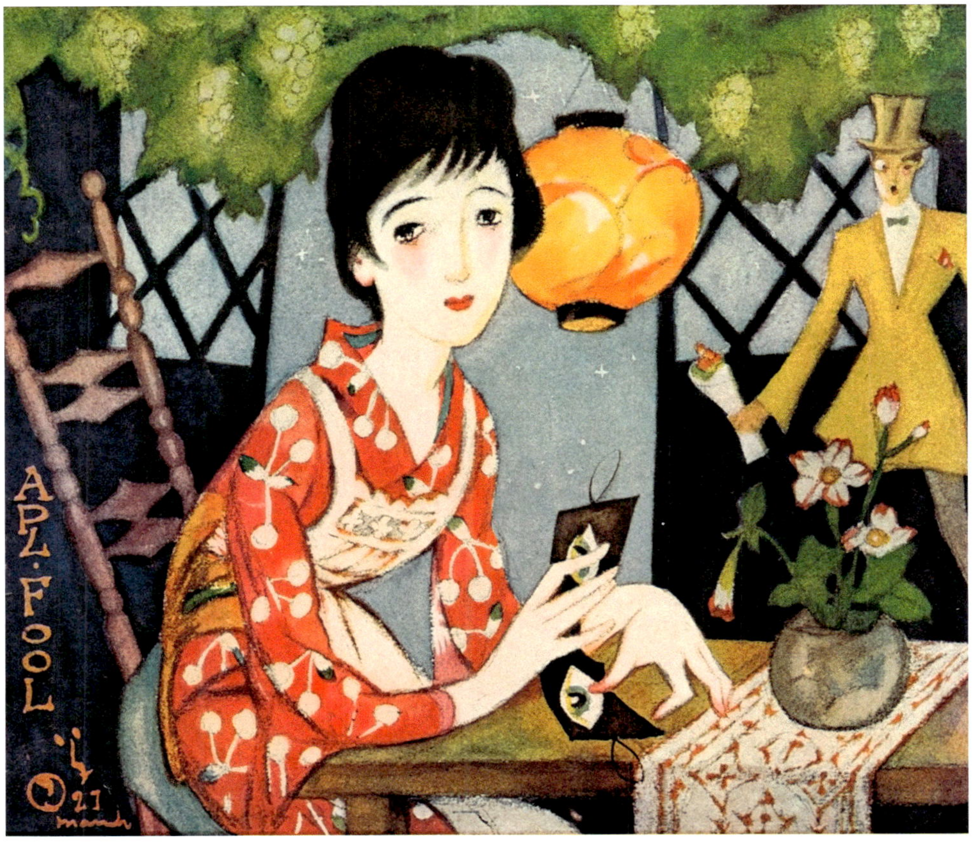

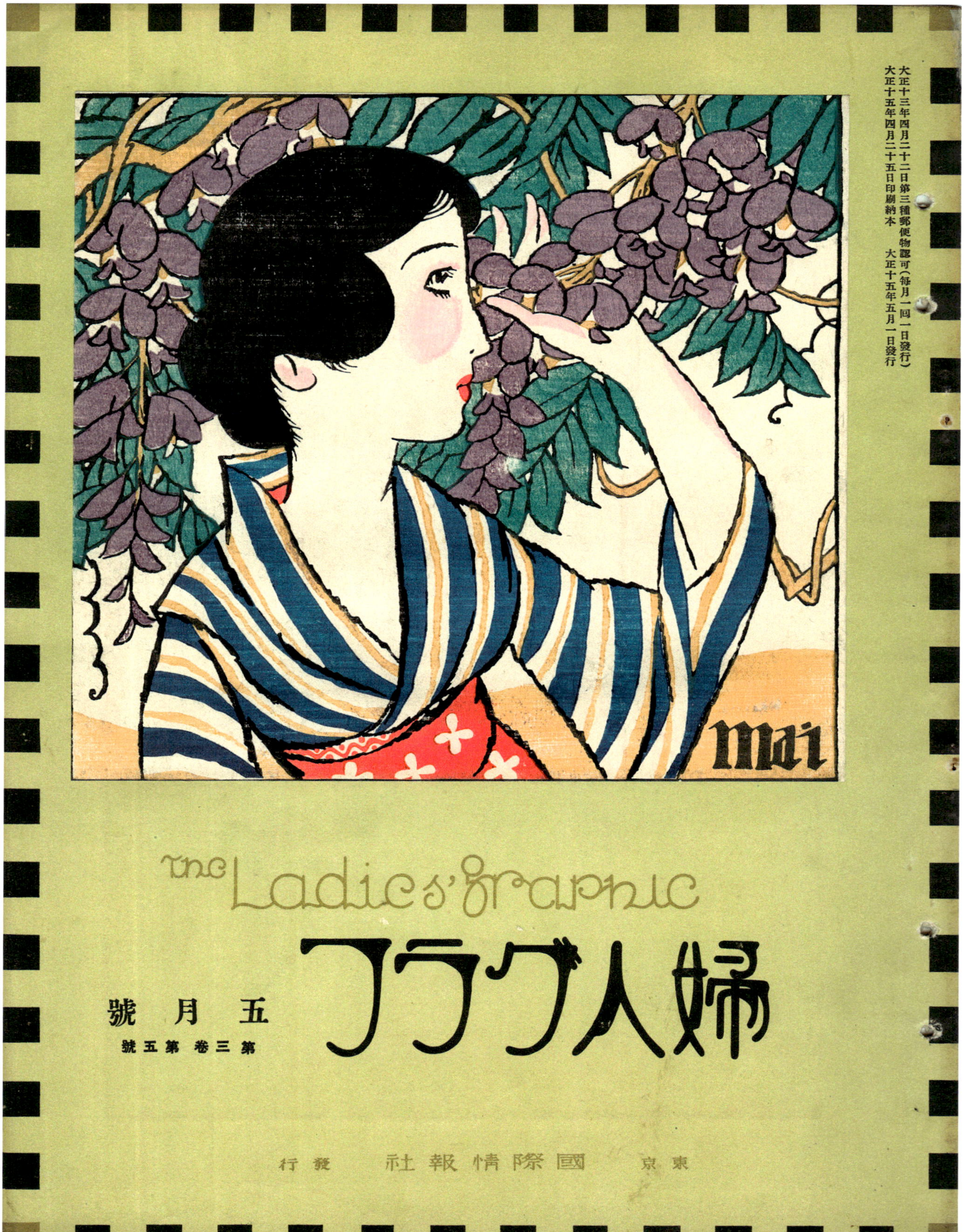

大正十三年四月二十二日第三種郵便物認可（毎月一回一日發行）
大正十五年四月二十五日印刷納本　大正十五年五月一日發行
mai
The Ladies' graphic
婦人グラフ
五月號
第三巻第五號
東京　國際情報社　發行

*Previous page*
57. *Mai* [*May*]
18.2 x 19.9 x cm (image);
32.8 x 24.7 x cm (cover)
Date: vol. 3 no. 5, May 1926

58. *Wicker chair*
18.1 x 19.7 x cm (image);
32.9 x 24.6 cm (cover)
Date: vol. 3 no. 6, June 1926

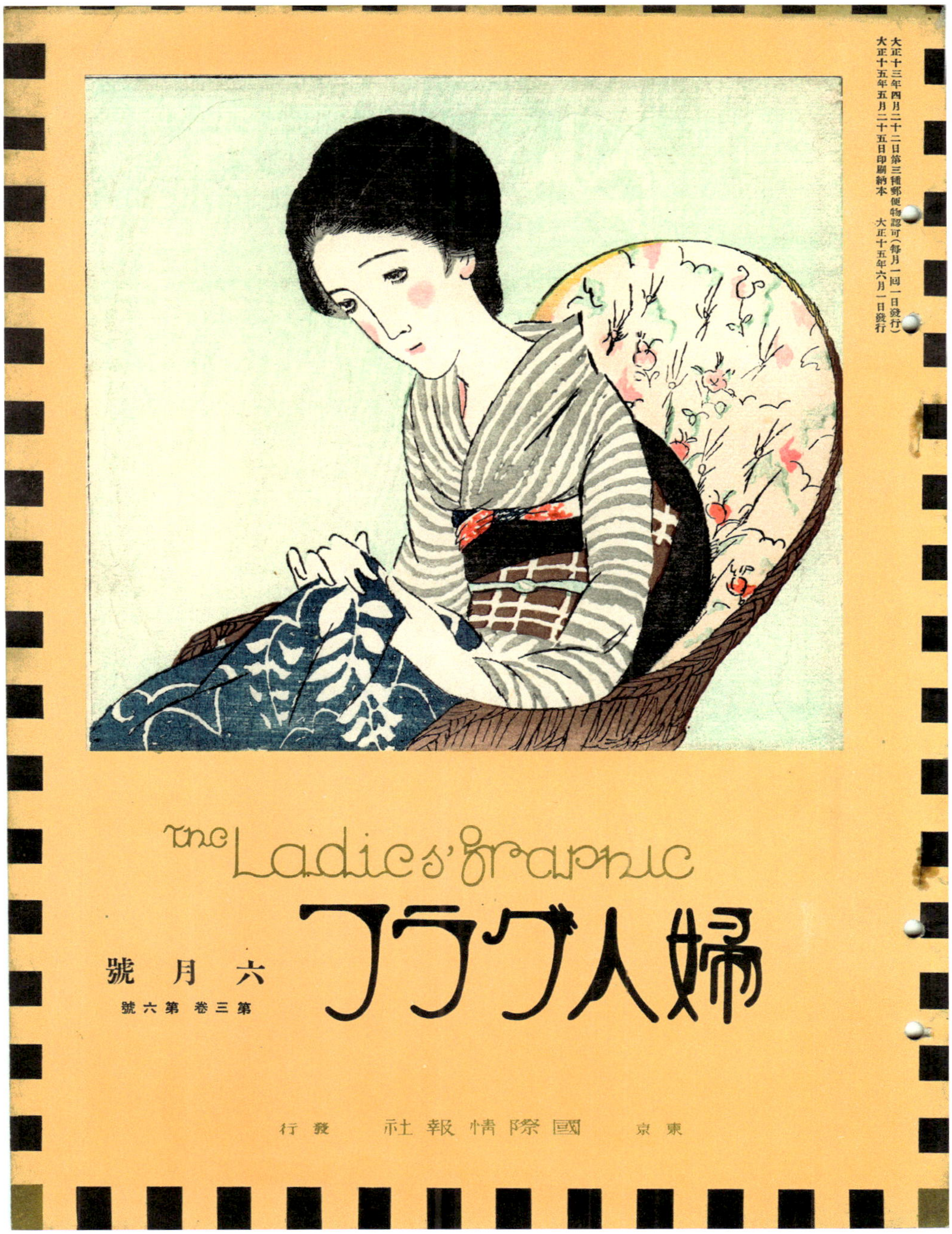

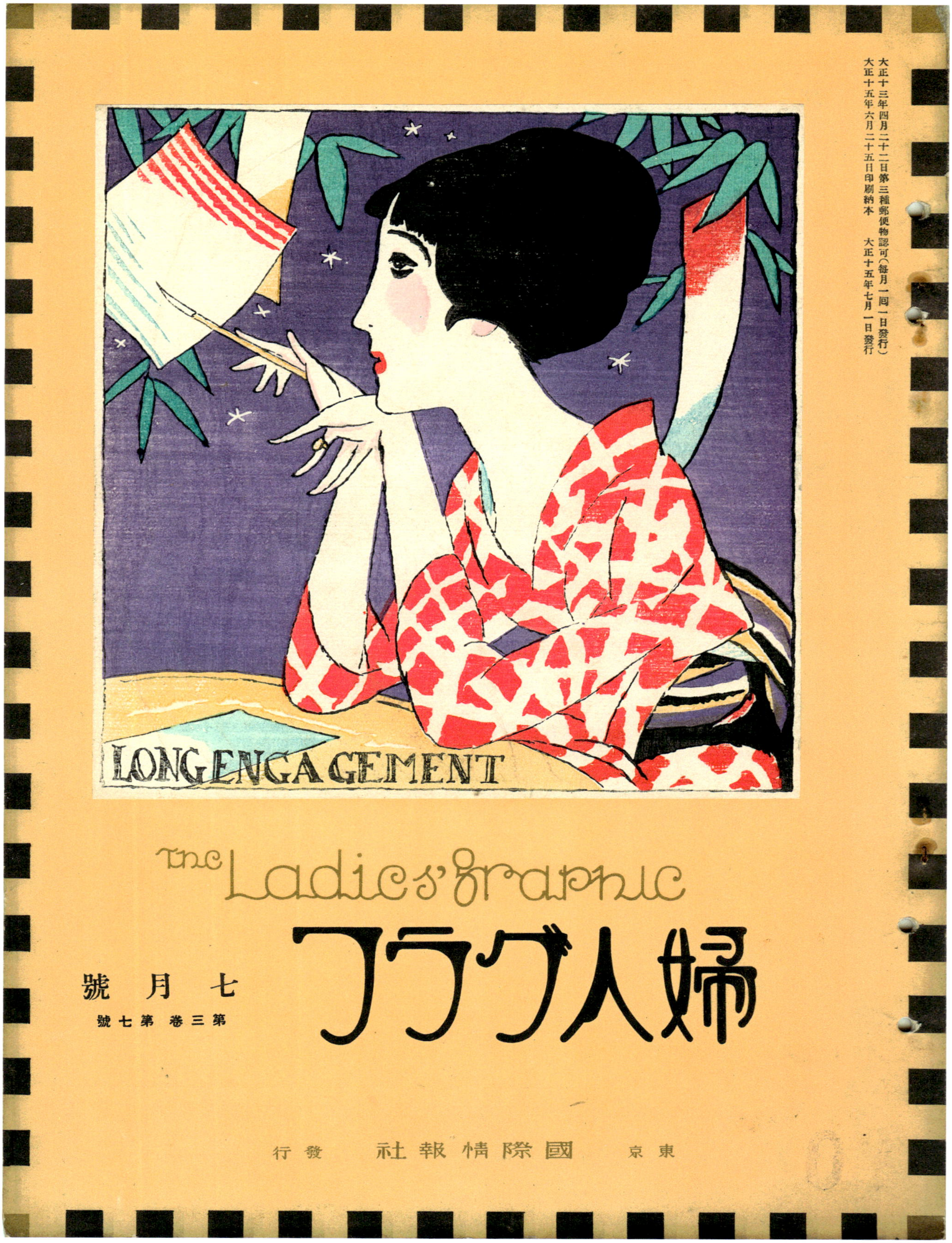
大正十三年四月二十二日第三種郵便物認可（毎月一回一日發行）
大正十五年六月二十五日印刷納本　大正十五年七月一日發行
LONG ENGAGEMENT
The Ladies' Graphic
婦人グラフ
七月號
第三巻第七號
東京　國際情報社　發行

Previous page
59. *Long engagement*
18.7 x 18.4 cm (image);
32.9 x 24.6 cm (cover)
Date: vol. 3 no. 7, July 1926

60. *By the window*
18.2 x 19.7 cm
Date: vol. 3 no. 8, August 1926

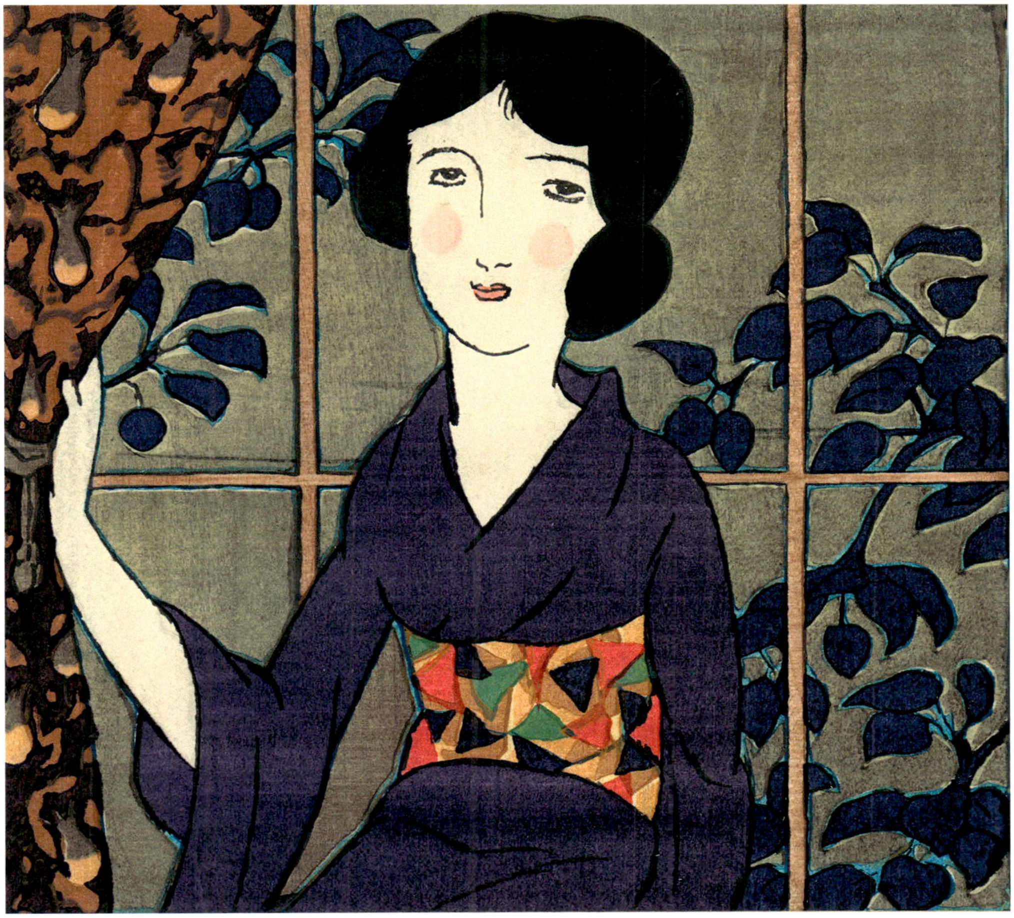

61. *Scattered frozen leaves*
(*Sōyō chiru*, 霜葉散る)
18.8 x 18.7 cm
Date: vol. 3 no. 10, October 1926
Seal: artist's comma-shaped (*tomoe*) seal

This design of a woman applying make-up was reprised repeatedly. It first appeared as an illustration (*sashi-e*) in *The ladies' graphic* from October 1926. It was later reused as a cover design for the 1930 series of music scores, *Complete collection of works by Nakayama Shinpei: folk songs* (cat. 32) and around the same time in *A collection of prints by Yumeji* (*Yumeji hangashū*) (fig. 1.13).
[MdV]

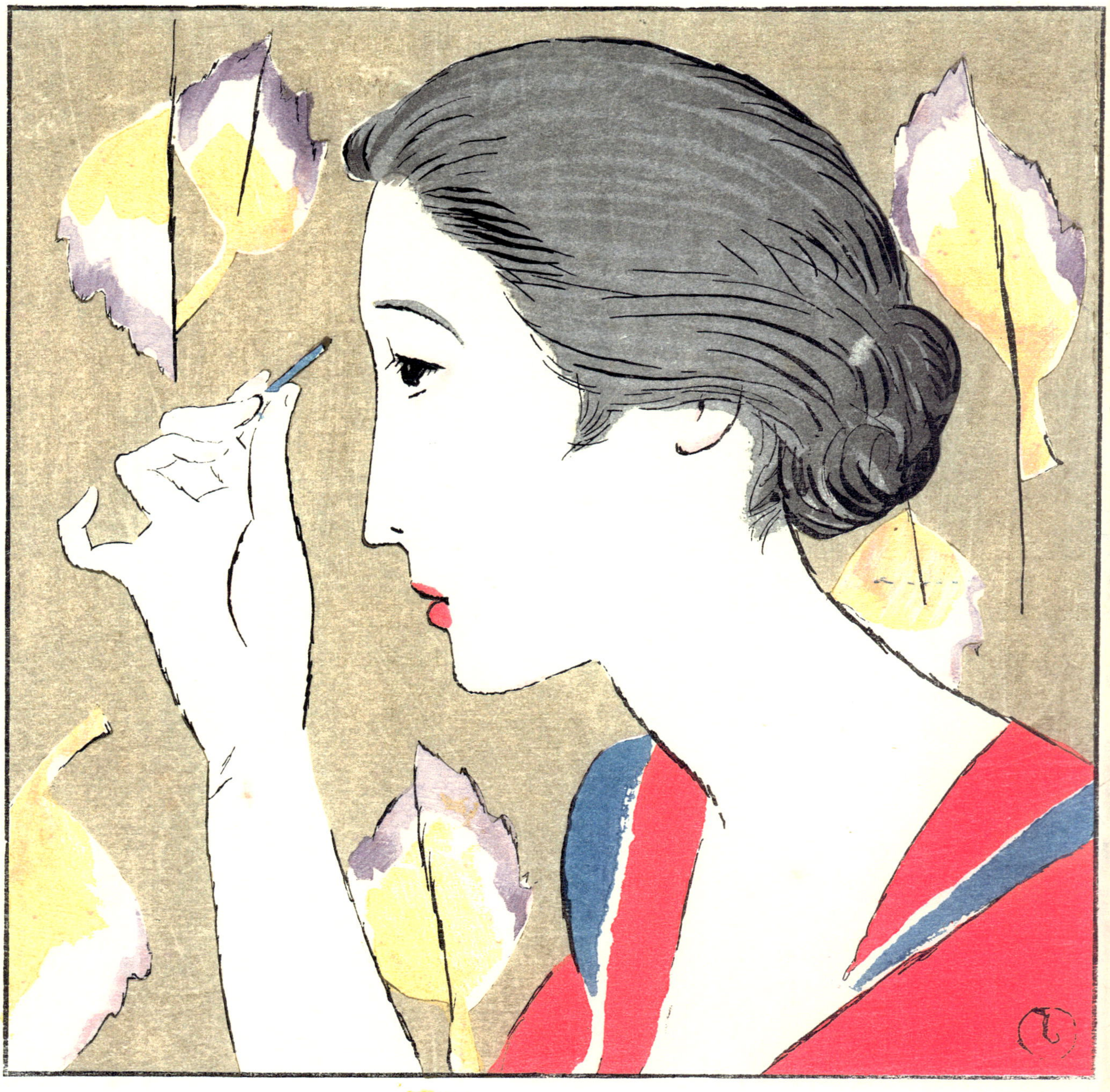

62. *Picnicking*
(*Pikunikku nite*, ピクニックにて)
20.4 x 17.2 cm
Date: vol. 3 no. 11, November 1926

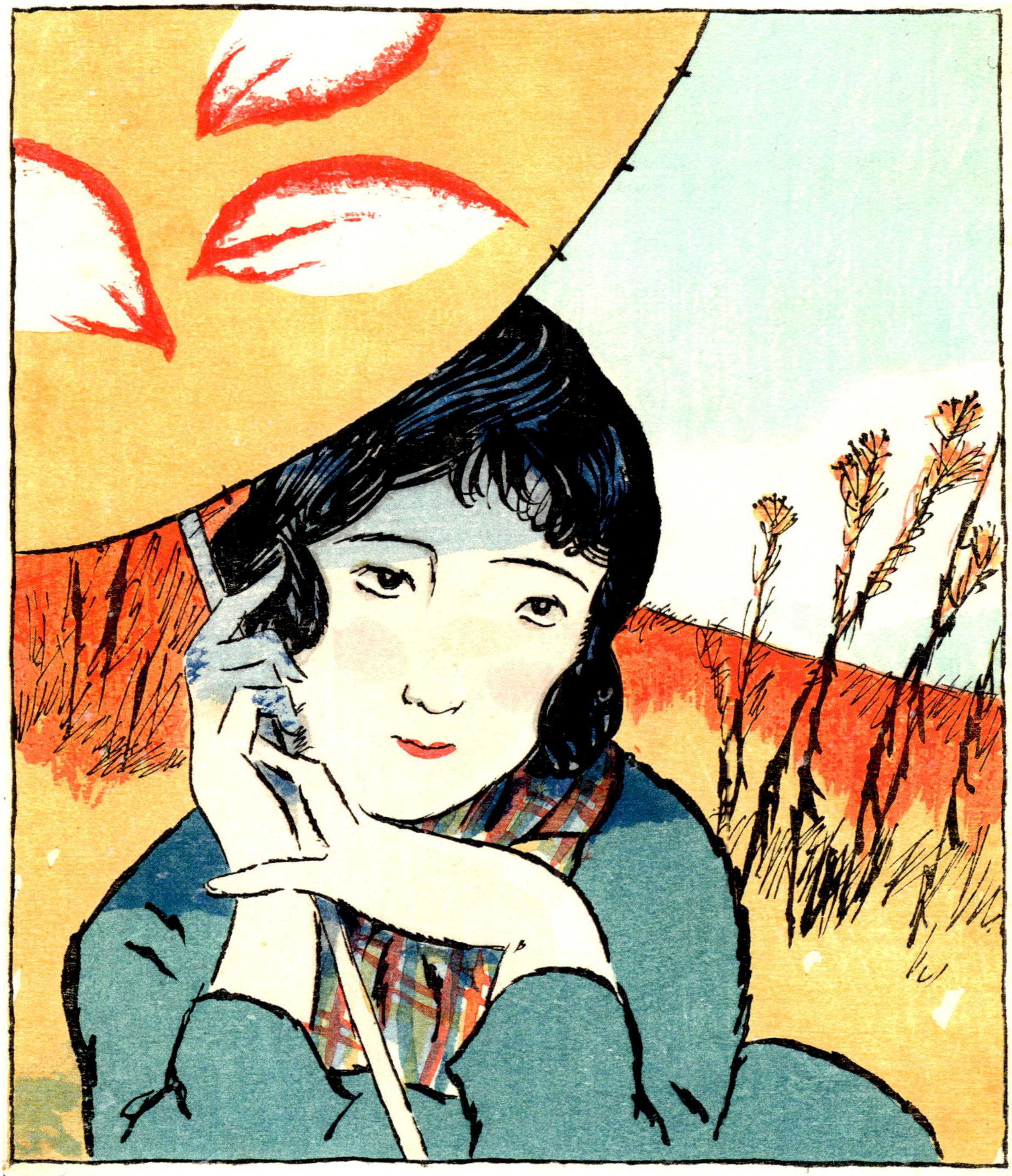

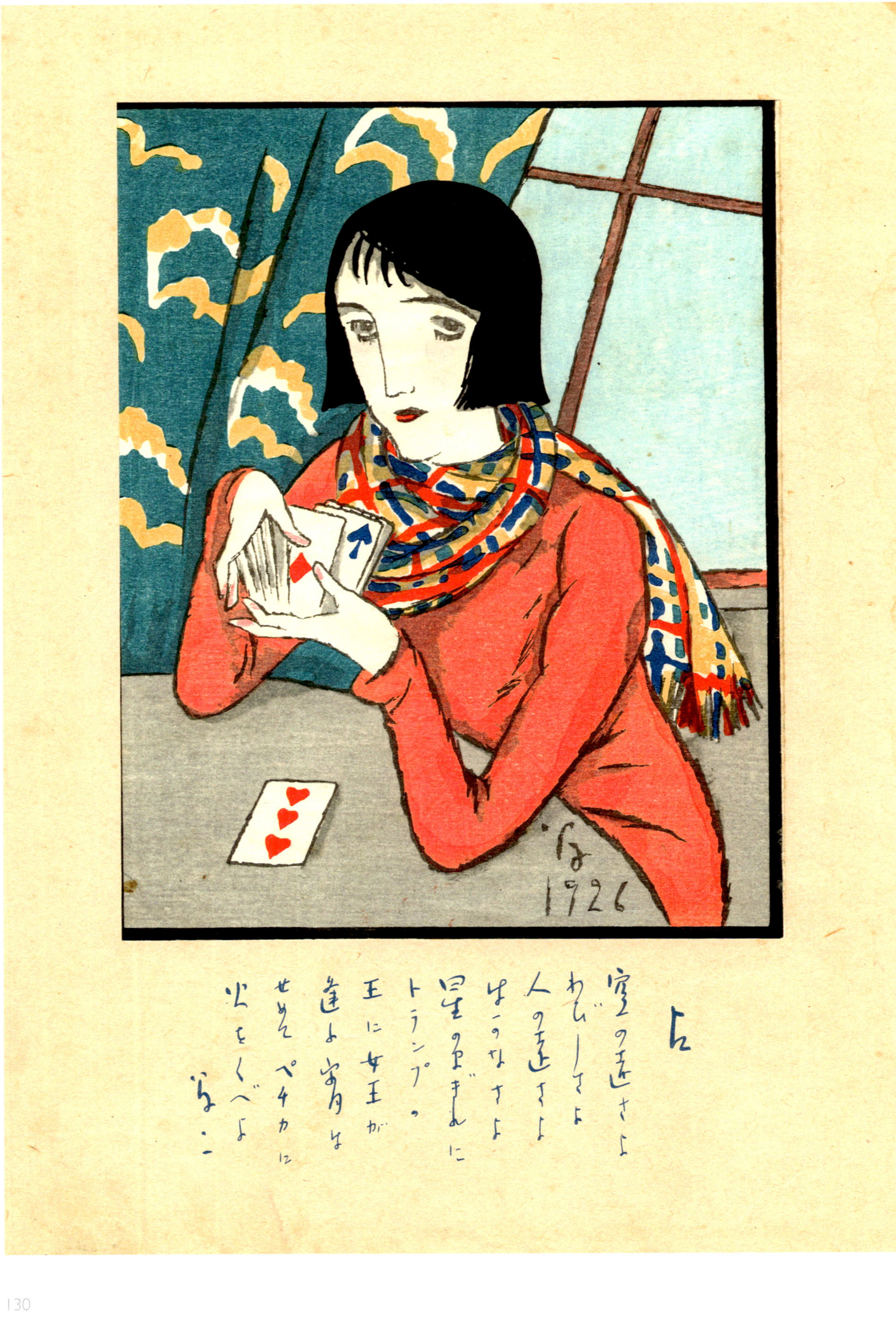
夢
1926
占
空の遠さよ
わびしさよ
人の遠さよ
はかなさよ
星のまぎれに
トランプの
王に女王が
逢ふ宵は
せめてペチカに
火をくべよ
夢二

*Previous page*
63. *Fortune telling* (*Uranai*, 占い)
33.0 x 22.8 cm
Date: vol. 4 no. 1, January 1927
Signature: *Yumeji*

64. *Legend of a snowy night*
(*Yuki no yoru no densetsu*,
雪の夜の伝説)
22.5 x 16.9 cm
Date: vol. 3 no. 12, December 1926
Signature: *Yumeji ga*

From the October 1926 issue of *The ladies' graphic* onwards, Yumeji's work took pride of place after the contents page in the form of frontispieces (*kuchi-e*). This work, *Fortune telling* (cat. 63) and *Mountain, mountain, mountain* (cat. 65) were each accompanied by one of Yumeji's poems.
[MdV]

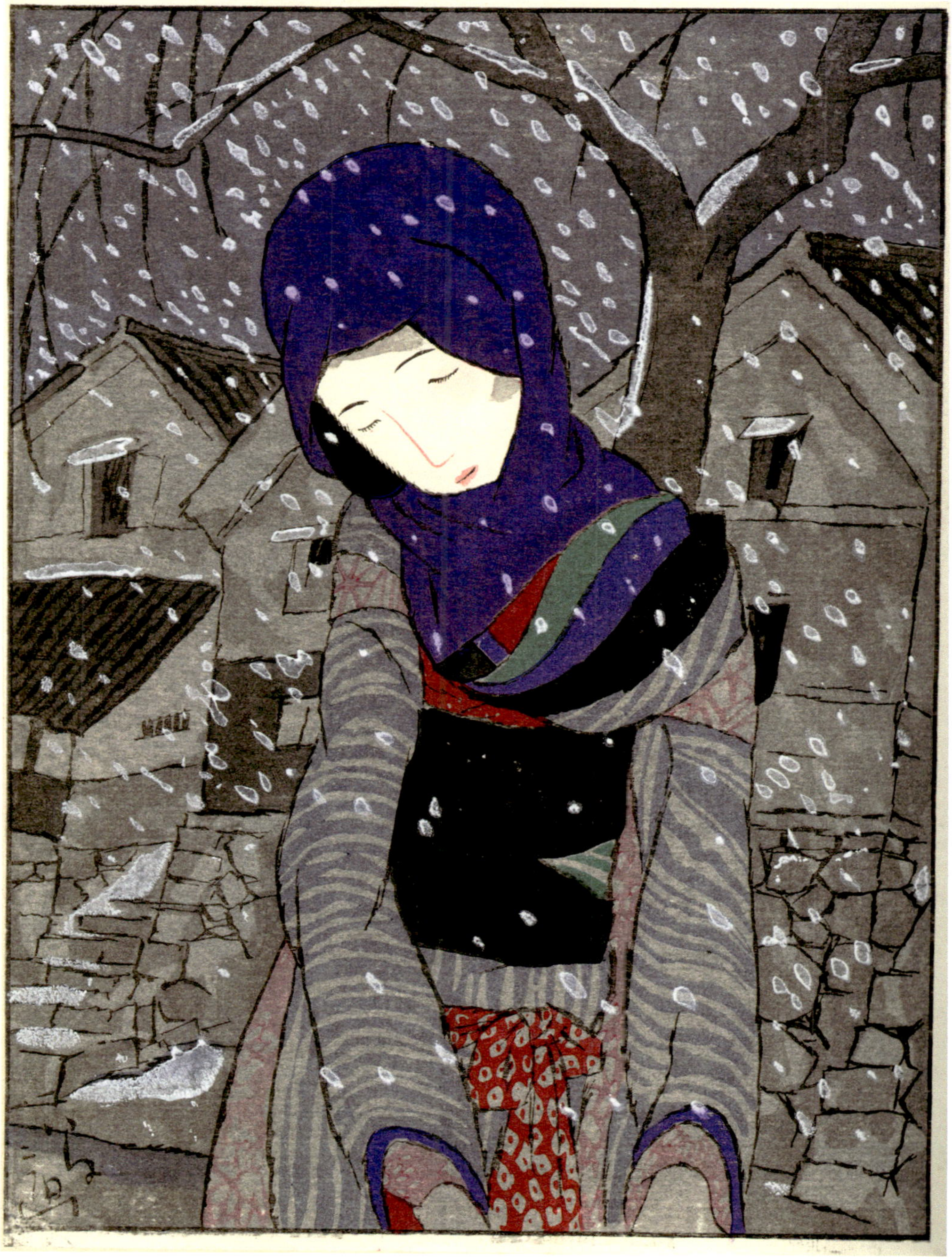

65. *Mountain, mountain, mountain*
(*Yama yama yama,* 山・山・山)
18.8 x 19.1 cm
Date: vol. 4 no. 2, February 1927
Seal: artist's comma-shaped (*tomoe*) seal

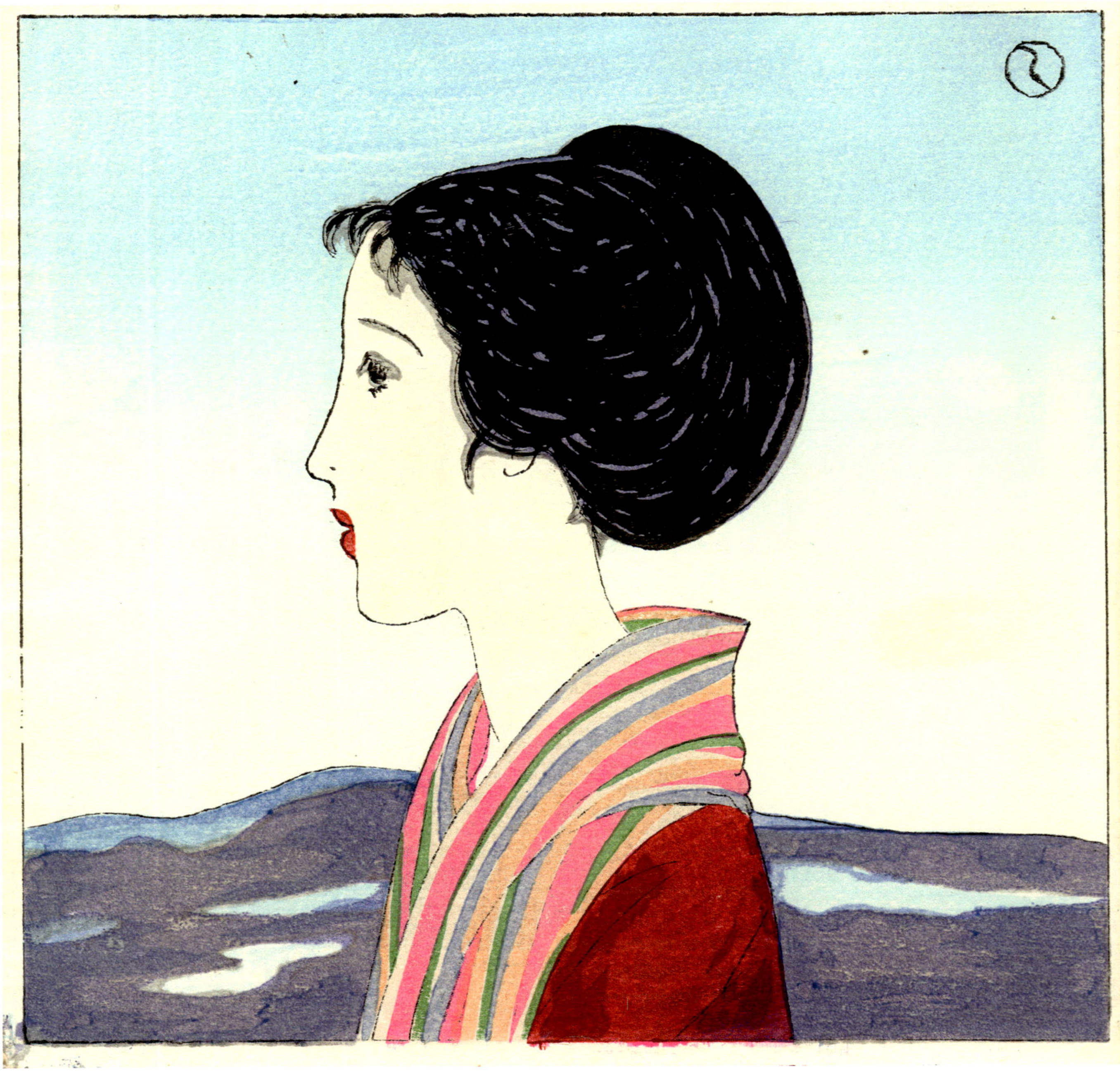

## Posthumous prints
cat. 66–83

The majority of Yumeji's woodblock-printed designs were released after his death in 1934. The publisher who was instrumental in having Yumeji's work recognised was the Tokyo-based Katō Junji (1885–1961). During the late 1930s and early 1940s, Katō and his team of artisan block-cutters and printers at the Katō Print Workshop (Katō Hanga Kenkyūjo) reused and rescaled numerous famous paintings, music scores and watercolours for series of prints and postcards.

*Ten subjects of women*
*(Onna jūdai,* 女十題*)*
Date: 1937–1938
Publisher: Katō Hanga Kenkyūjo
cat. 66–67

This set of ten bust portraits shows women in differing forms—most figures wear kimono with modern fashionable accessories and only one sports Western-style dress. *Ten subjects of women* was based on a group of watercolours created by Yumeji in 1921 for the Nagasaki collector Nagami Tokutarō. It remained faithful to the Yumeji's original works in terms of design and style, seen, for example, in the rough contour lines in this piece that convey the feel of watercolour brushwork. For another image from this set, see fig. 3.6.

[NN]

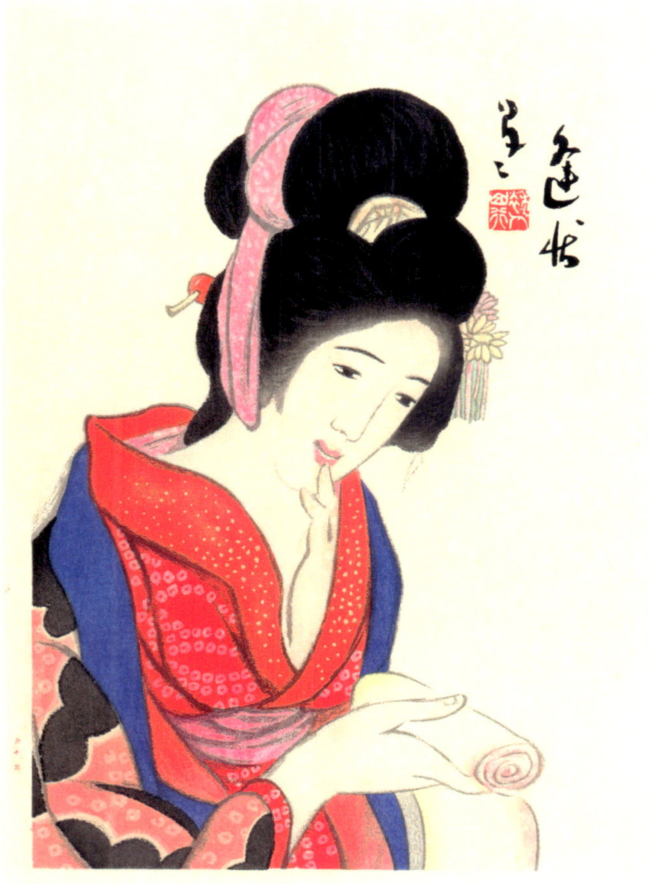

66. *Rendezvous letter* (*Aijō*, 逢状)
44 x 30.7 cm
Date: 1938
Signature/seal: *Yumeji* with square seal
Publisher: Katō Hanga Kenkyūjo

This bust portrait illustrates a woman engrossed in reading a letter, a common compositional trope in the genre of beautiful women (*bijinga*). The term *aijō*, or 'rendezvous letter', is a reference to the letters written by courtesans to regular clients in an effort to encourage their continued patronage. Perhaps the woman here, her left hand poised on her lips, is contemplating how to compose her letter. Her elaborately patterned kimono and over-kimono adds a sense of the decadent. While other prints from this set impart a more modern image of Taishō era women, this print conjures up what may have been a nostalgic perception of the Edo-period courtesan. The square seal on this print is seen on the artist's work from the middle to late Taishō era, the reading of its characters (愁人山行) remains unconfirmed.

[NN]

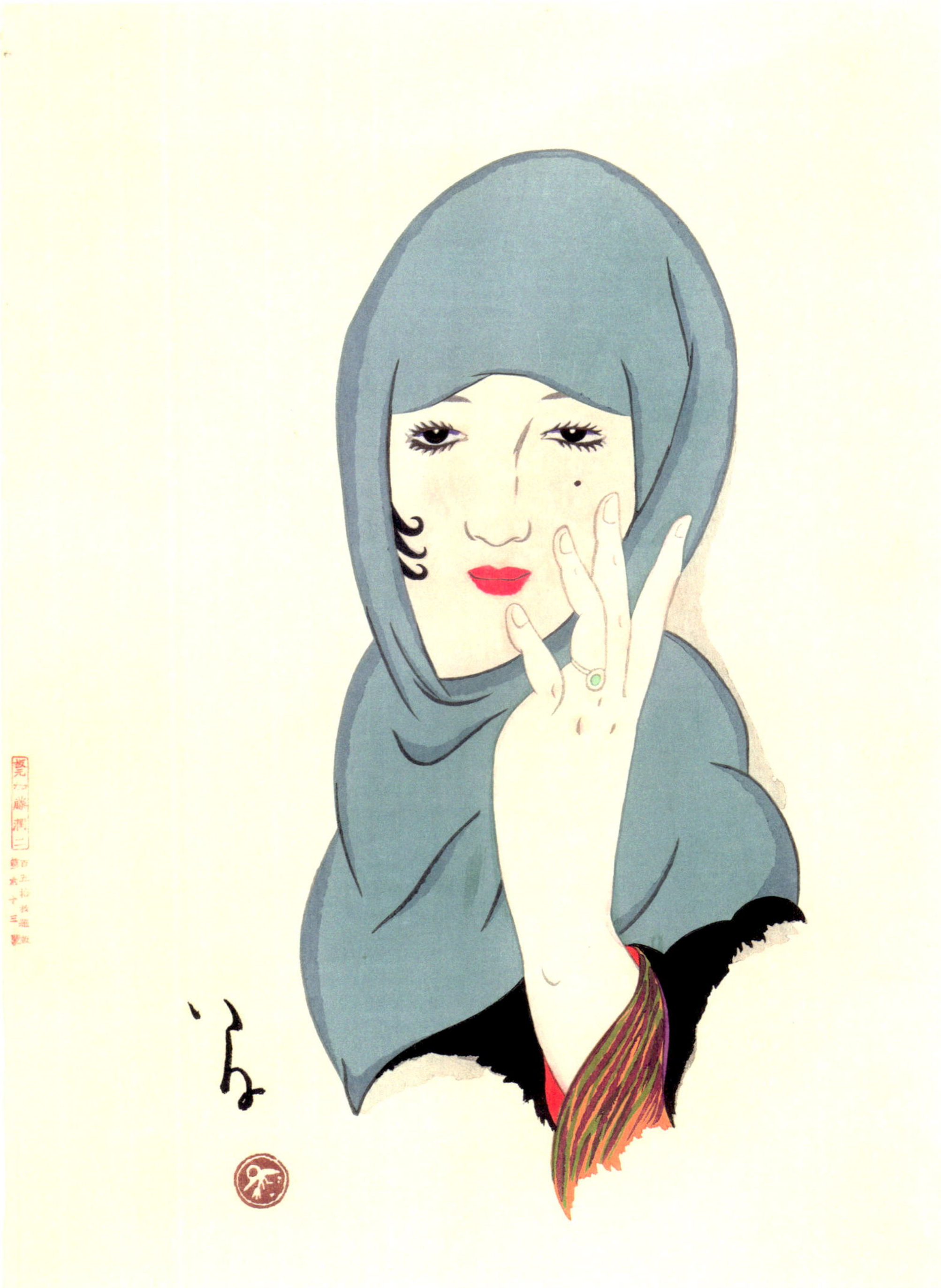

67. *Headscarf*
(*Okosozukin*, お高祖頭巾)
43.6 x 30.7 cm
Date: 1938
Signature/seal: *Yumeji* with unidentified artist's seal

Japanese women in the country's colder regions once wore this traditional style of headscarf; it would often cover much of the face. The publisher Katō Junji released the set *Ten subjects of women* in response to the demand for the artist's work following his death (see also cat. 20).

[MdV]

*Yumeji's masterpieces* (*Yumeji meisakushū*, 夢二名作集)
Date 1938–1939
Publisher: Katō Hanga Kenkyūjo
cat. 68–72

The thirty woodblock prints in this set are a selection of the most popular cover designs from the over 270 that the artist produced for *Senow music scores* (see figs. 2.7, 4.5, 4.7, 4.8, 4.10, 4.11, 4.13; also cat. 16–32). Katō Junji personally compiled the set and it reflects what he believed was representative of Yumeji's artistic diversity, ranging from the portrayal of beautiful women and landscapes to his fascination with Western artistic styles. For other images from this set, see figs. 1.2, 1.5, 1.12, 3.11, 4.6, 4.14.

[NN]

68. *Sailor's song* (*Funa-uta*, 舟歌)
33.8 x 25.5 cm
Date: 1938–1939
Seal: artist's comma-shaped (*tomoe*) seal

This composition was adapted from 'On billow rocking (Barcarolle): Les cloches de Corneville', no. 160 from the *Senow music scores* (cat. 19). This is one of the few pieces by Yumeji to feature a man, in this case a sailor singing as he strolls along a cliff. Yumeji's most celebrated male image is of the star-crossed lover Jihei (figs. 3.1 & p. 71).

[MdV]

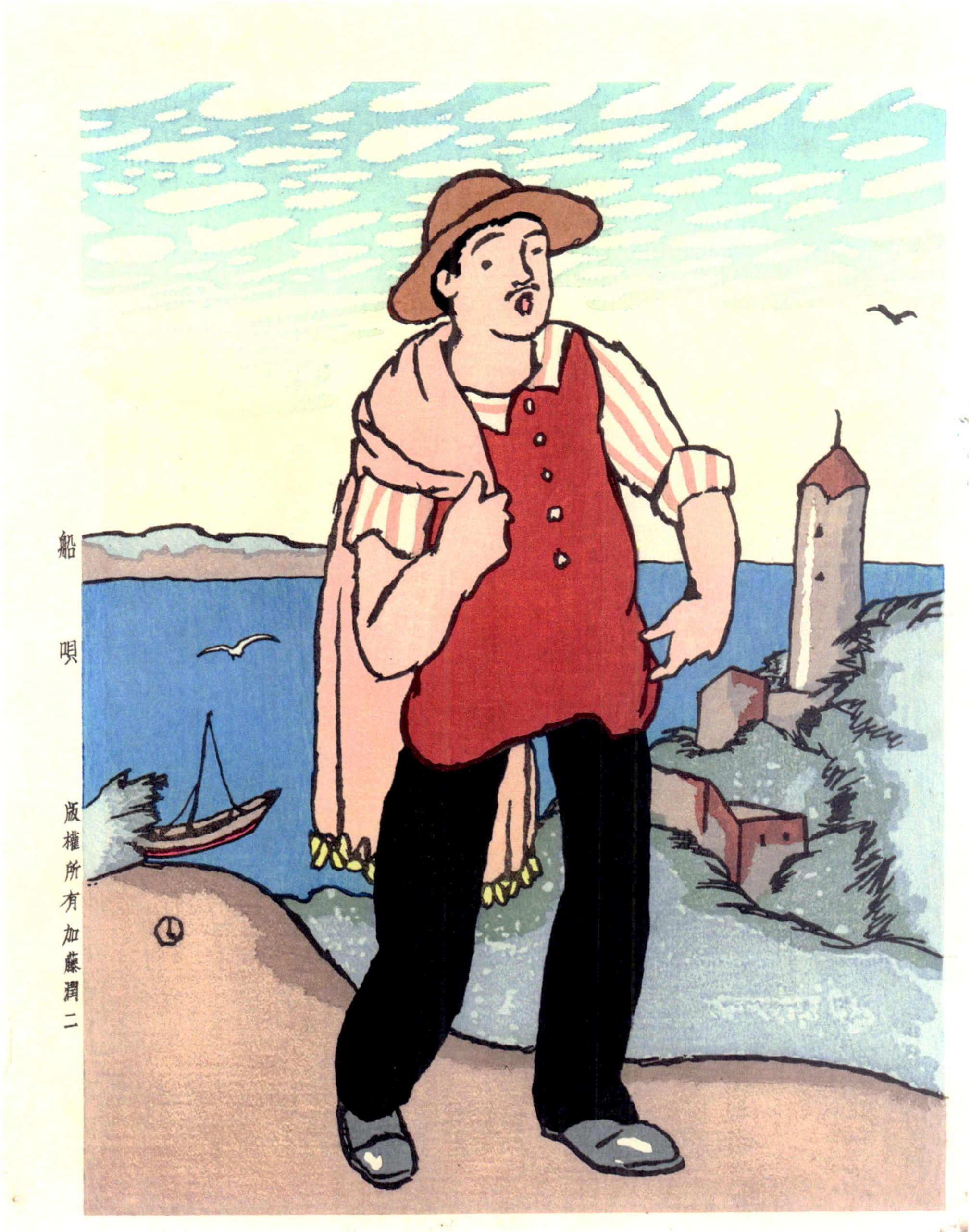

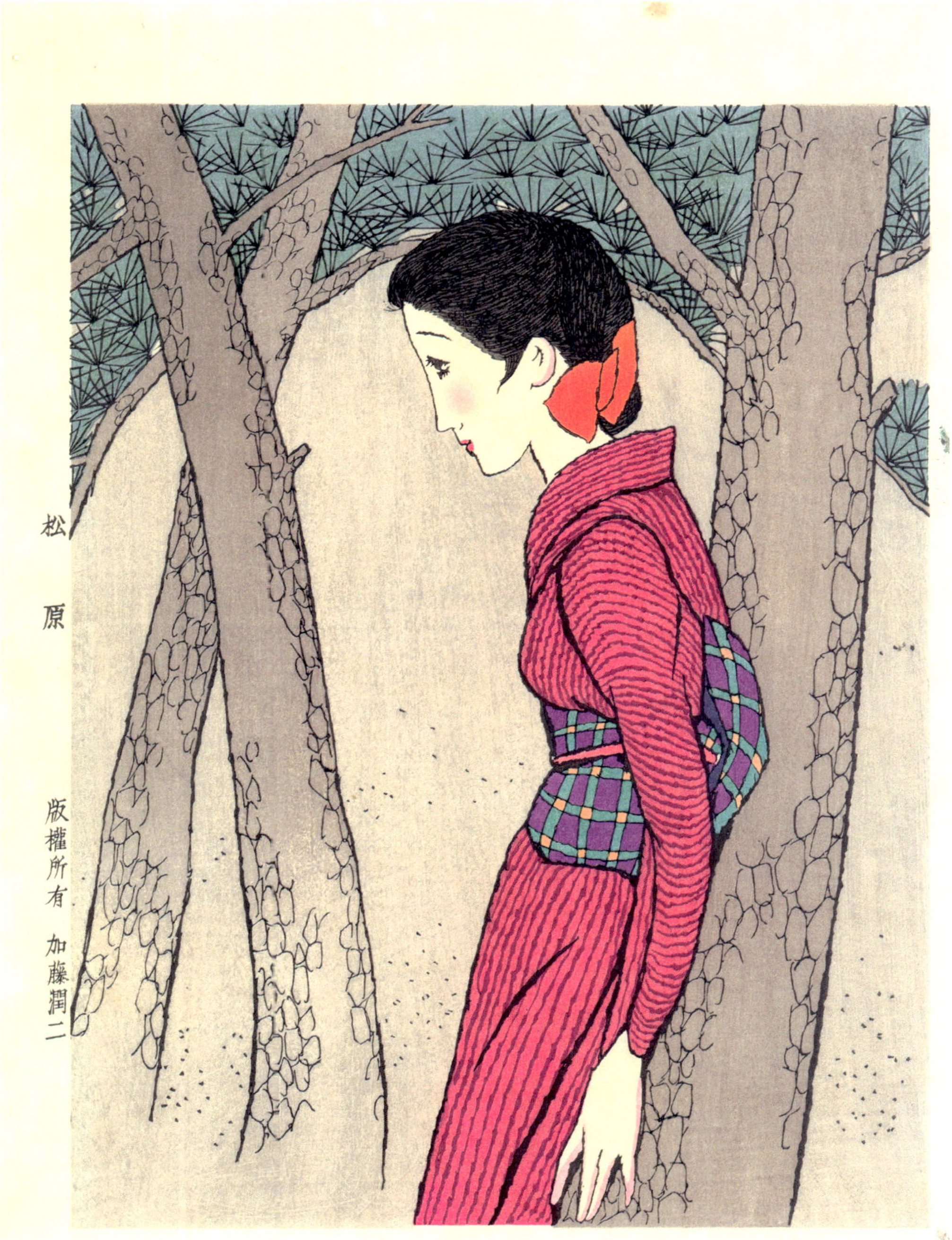


69. *Pine grove* (*Matsubara*, 松原)
34.2 x 25.5 cm
Date: 1938–1939

This reinterpretation of the design for *Pine grove* lacks the title cartouche at the top (see cat. 69a). Here, branches have been added and the colour of the kimono has been changed from grey to purple.

[MdV]

*Next page*

69a. Preparatory watercolour for the sheet-music cover *Pine grove* (*Matsubara*, 松原)
38.0 x 28.3 cm
Date: c. 1924
Score: Senō Kōyō (1891–1961)
Verse: Takehisa Yumeji

This preparatory watercolour was created for a cover design for the *Senow music scores*. Yumeji wrote the lyrics and the publisher Senō Kōyō composed the score, demonstrating that the artist-publisher collaboration sometimes involved more than just commissioning and production. Visible in the margin in this example are the colour swatches trialled for the image.

[MdV]

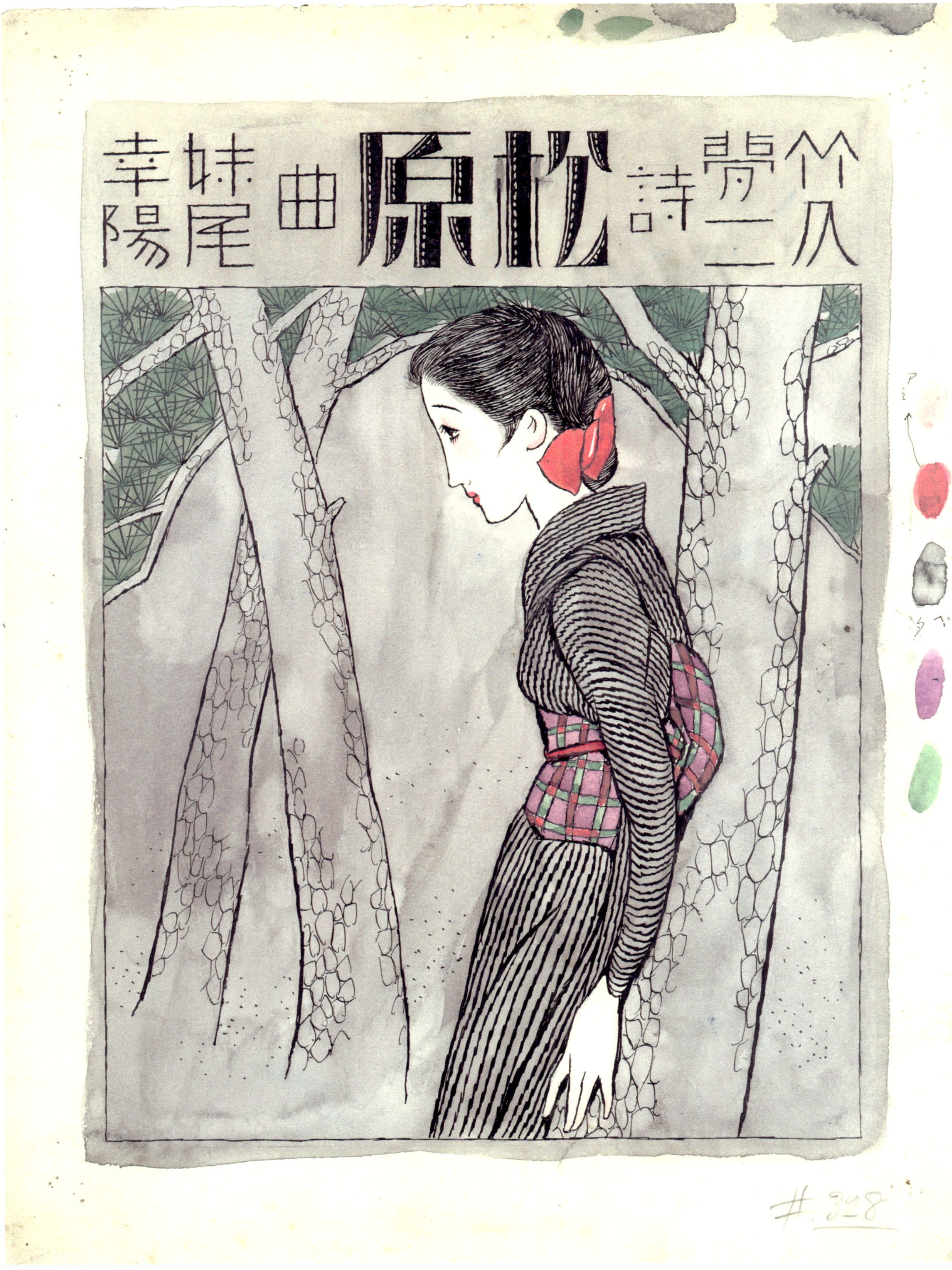
竹久夢二詩
松原
曲
妹尾幸陽
#.328

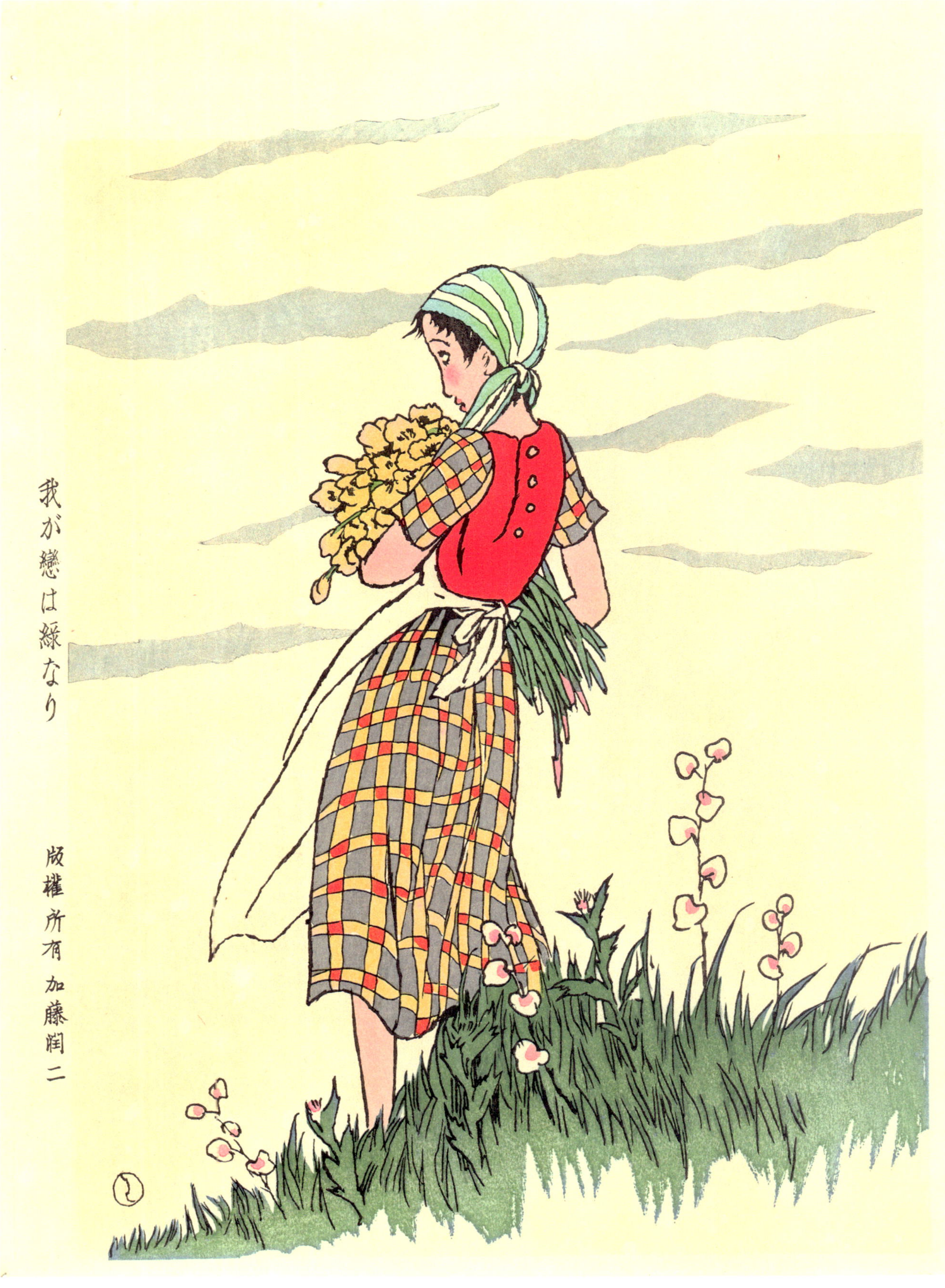
我が戀は綠なり
版權所有 加藤潤二

*Previous page*

70. *Our love is green* (*Waga koi wa midori nari*, 我が戀は緑なり)
38.0 x 24.8 cm
Date: 1938–1939
Seal: artist's comma-shaped (*tomoe*) seal

This print is representative of Yumeji's stock repertory of beautiful women in fashionable Western-style dress. Here, the subject stands on a hill, clutching a bunch of yellow flowers. The sleeves and skirt of her dress sport a bold pattern of yellow, red and blue cheques; her white apron flutters in the breeze.

[NN]

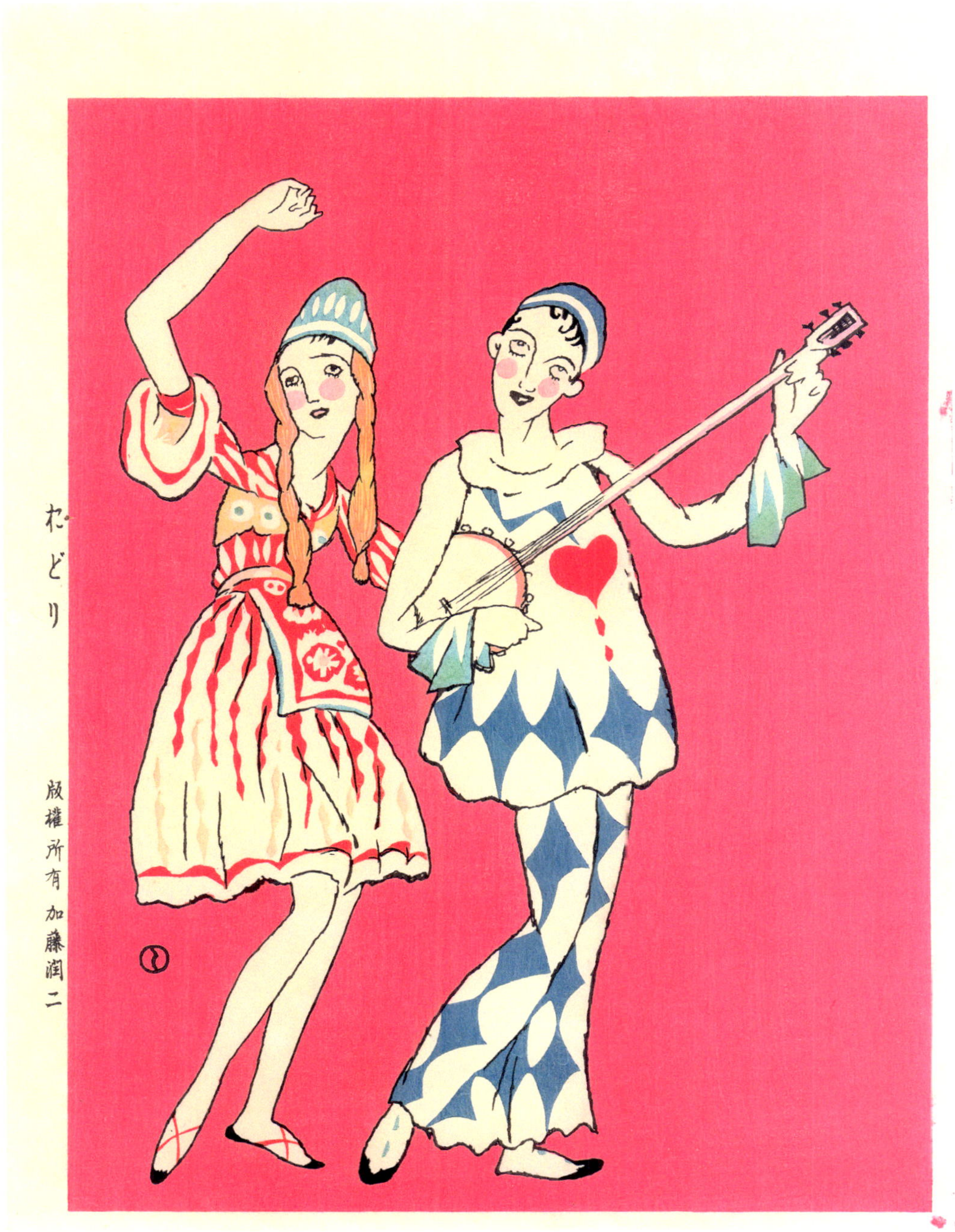


71. *Dancing* (*Odori*, おどり)
33.8 x 25.4 cm
Date: 1938–1939
Seal: artist's comma-shaped (*tomoe*) seal

Yumeji's interest in costume design for modern dance and ballet is clearly evident in this example. Here, two figures in Western costumes are set against an arresting pink ground in what appears to be a choreographed stance. Yumeji made many sketches of the dancers and the circus that performed in Tokyo's Asakusa district. This work reaffirms his diverse sources of artistic inspiration, including the French painter and printmaker Henri de Toulouse-Lautrec (1864–1904). The reproduction of Lautrec's lithograph of a female jester is seen in one of Yumeji's numerous scrapbooks, which are today housed in the Yumeji Art Museum in Okayama.[1]

[NN]

1. Okabe, ed., *Seitan 130nen Takehisa Yumeji ten*, 62–63.

72. *Recollections of old songs*
(*Koka no omoide*, 古歌の思出)
33.8 x 25.4 cm
Date: 1938–1939

Seal: artist's comma-shaped (*tomoe*) seal

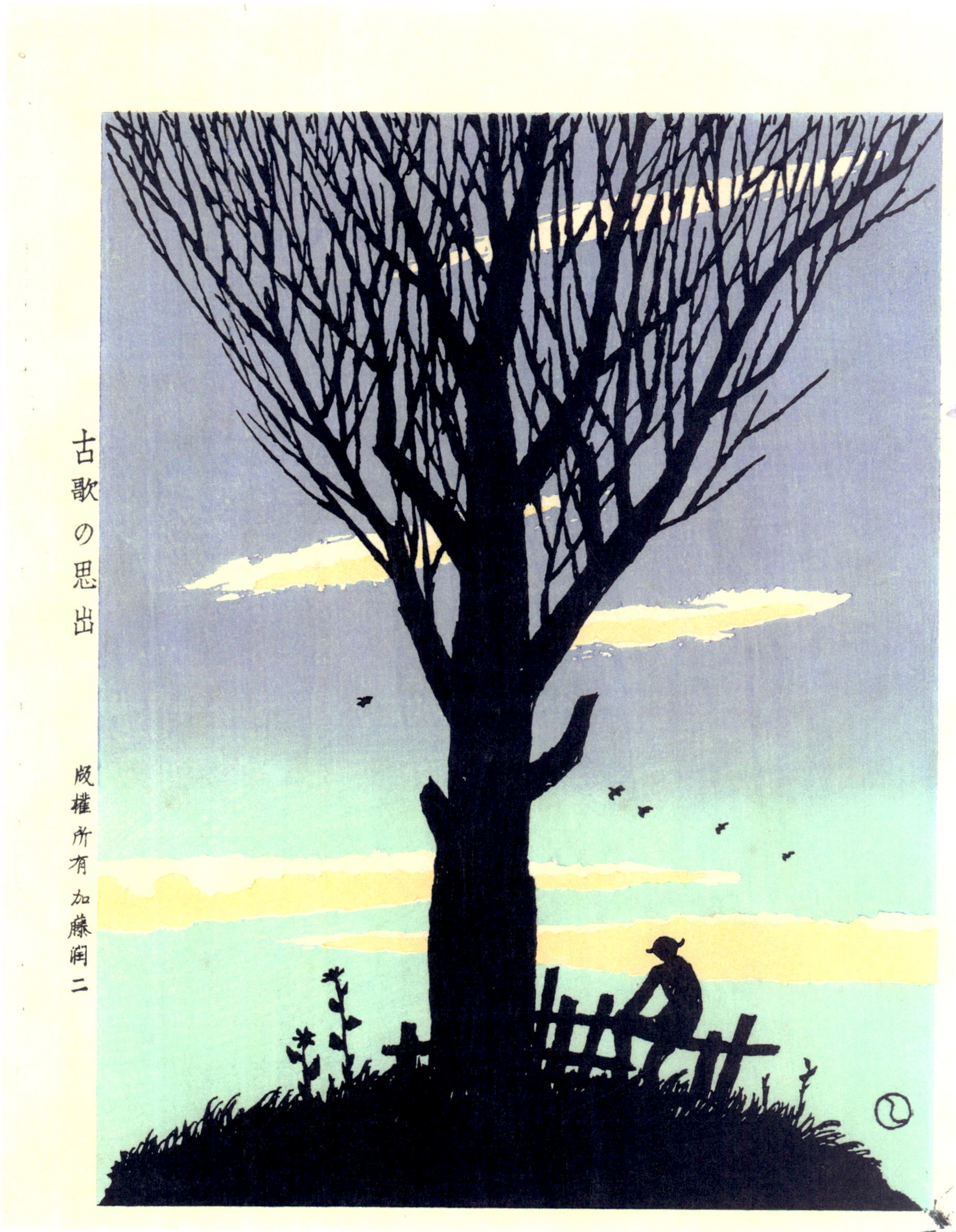

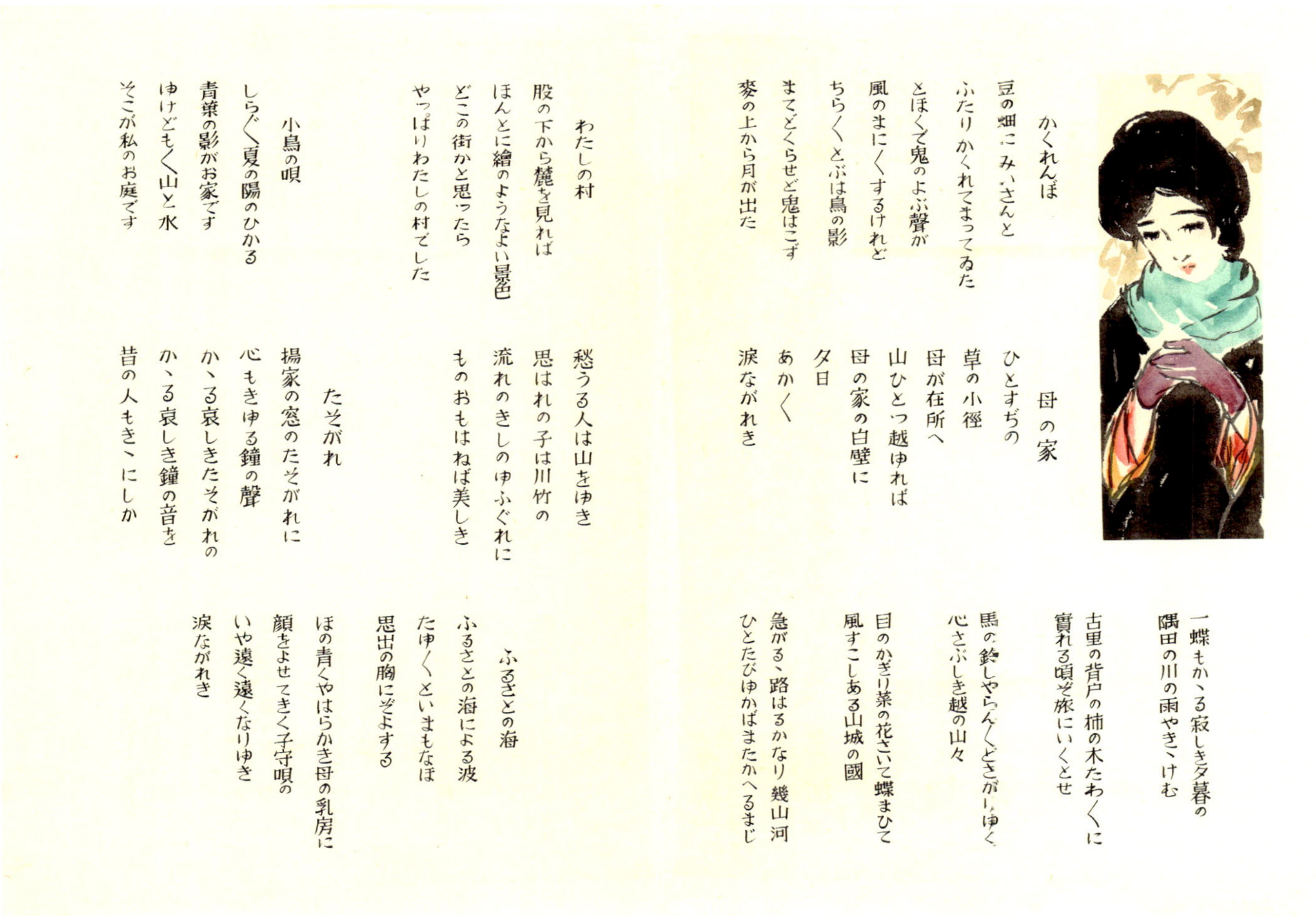

かくれんぼ

豆の畑にみいさんと
ふたりかくれてまってゐた
とほくで鬼のよぶ聲が
風のまにくするけれど
ちらくとぶは鳥の影
まてどくらせど鬼はこず
麥の上から月が出た

母の家

ひとすぢの
草の小徑
母が在所へ
山ひとつ越ゆれば
母の家の白壁に
夕日
あかく
涙ながれき

一蝶もかゝる寂しき夕暮の
隅田の川の雨やきゝけむ

古里の背戸の柿の木たわくに
實れる頃ぞ旅にいくとせ

馬の鈴しやらんくどさがりゆく
心さぶしき越の山々

目のかぎり菜の花さいて蝶まひて
風すこしある山城の國

急がるゝ路はるかなり幾山河
ひとたびゆかばまたかへるまじ

わたしの村

股の下から麓を見れば
ほんとに繪のようなよい景色
どこの街かと思ったら
やっぱりわたしの村でした

小鳥の唄

しらぐく夏の陽のひかる
青葉の影がお家です
ゆけどもく山と水
そこが私のお庭です

愁うる人は山をゆき
思はれの子は川竹の
流れのきしのゆふぐれに
ものおもはねば美しき

たそがれ

揚家の窓のたそがれに
心もきゆる鐘の聲
かゝる哀しきたそがれの
かゝる哀しき鐘の音を
昔の人もきゝにしか

ふるさとの海

ふるさとの海による波
たゆくといまもなほ
思出の胸にぞよする
ほの青くやはらかき母の乳房に
顔をよせてきく子守唄の
いや遠く遠くなりゆき
涙ながれき

*A collection of poetry and prints by Yumeji*
(*Yumeji shigashū*, 夢二詩画集)
Date: 1941
Publisher: Katō Hanga Kenkyūjo
cat. 73–79

The publisher Katō Junji drew from Yumeji's book illustrations, paintings and magazine cover designs to produce this set, which contains ten woodblock prints accompanied by poetry originally composed by Yumeji. The contents page, illustrated here (cat. 73), lists the prints and the verse.

[SS]

73. *Content page*, 42.8 x 59.7 cm

This page lists the texts and images in *A collection of poetry and prints by Yumeji*; for example, the poem for cat. 78, *My village*, appears on the upper right of the left-hand page.

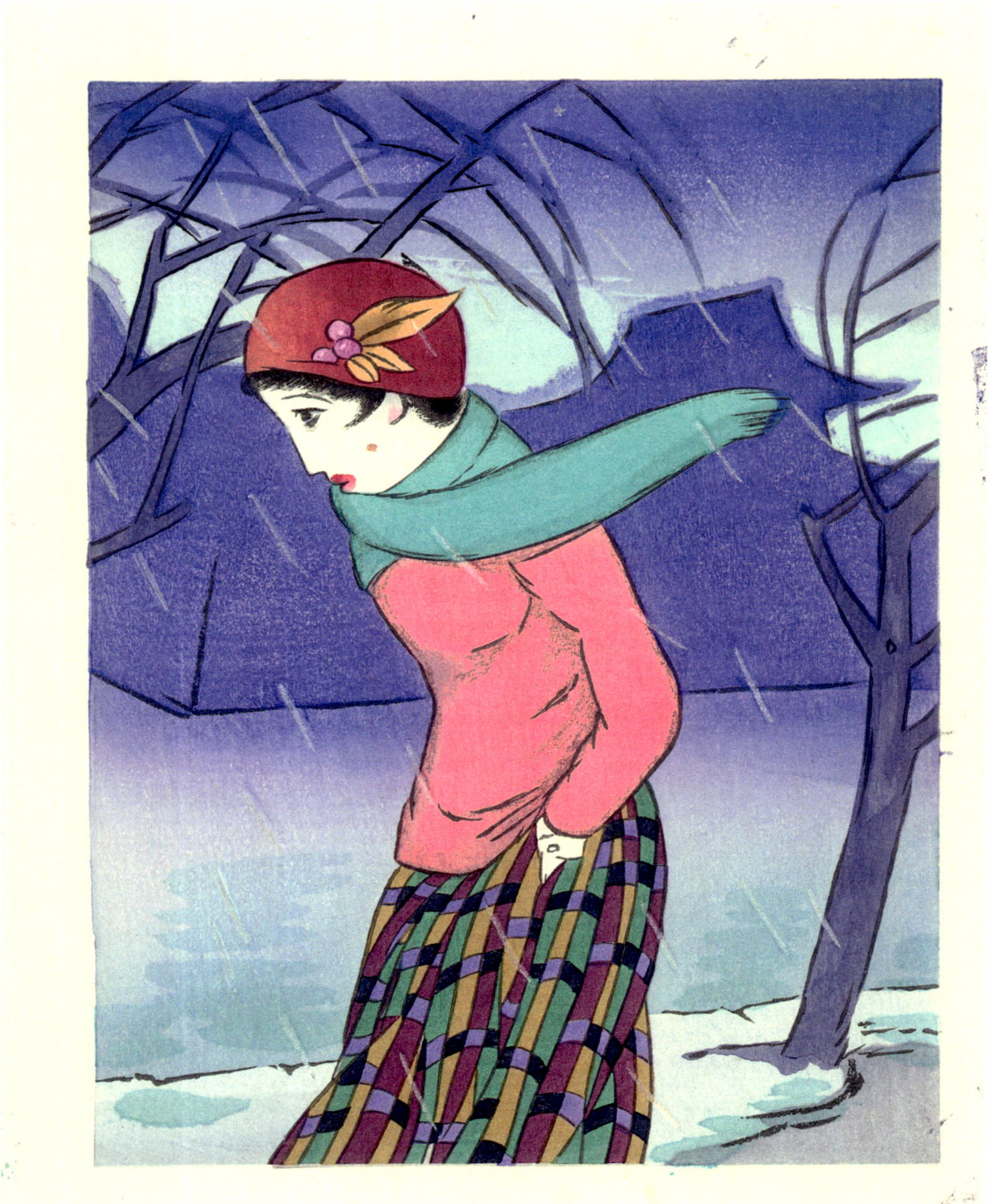

74. *Near the moat* (*Horibata*, 堀端)
21.0 x 16.6 cm
Date: 1941

The print shows a fashionably attired young woman sporting an elaborately patterned skirt, turquoise scarf, crimson hat and hat pin. Her figure is set against a rainy landscape rendered in shades of blue and purple.

[NN]

*Next page*
75. *Playing cards* (*Karuta*, かるた)
23.6 x 15.7 cm
Date: 1941
Publisher: Katō Hanga Kenkyūjo

This light-hearted scene shows four girls in brightly coloured kimono enjoying the new year's card game (*karuta*), in which one person reads a passage while the other players attempt to grab the corresponding card from those laid out before them. The plum blossoms in the vase in the upper right corner and the *mochi* (sticky rice cake) carried by the standing girl also add to the association of this composition with the new year.

[NN]

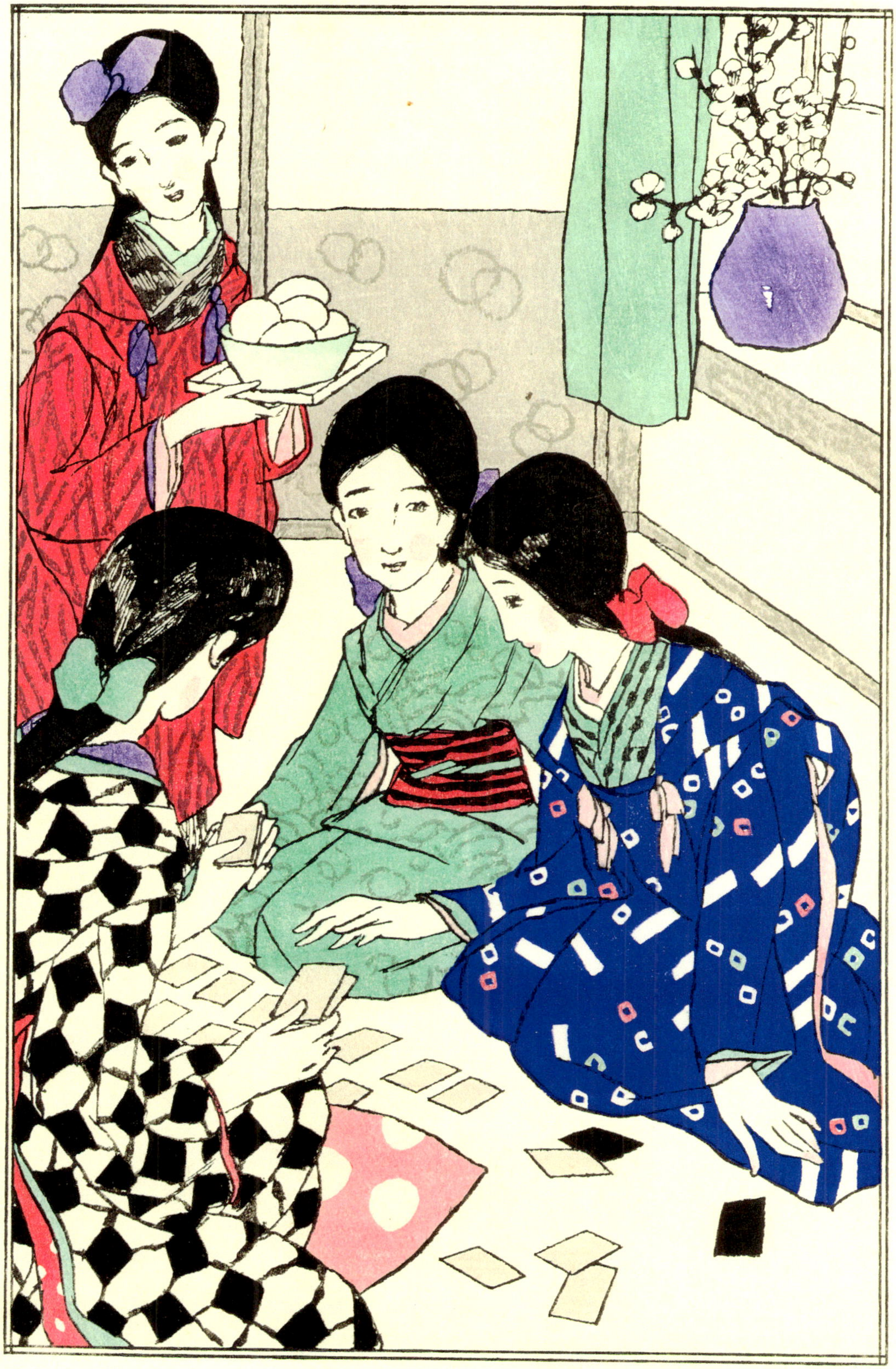

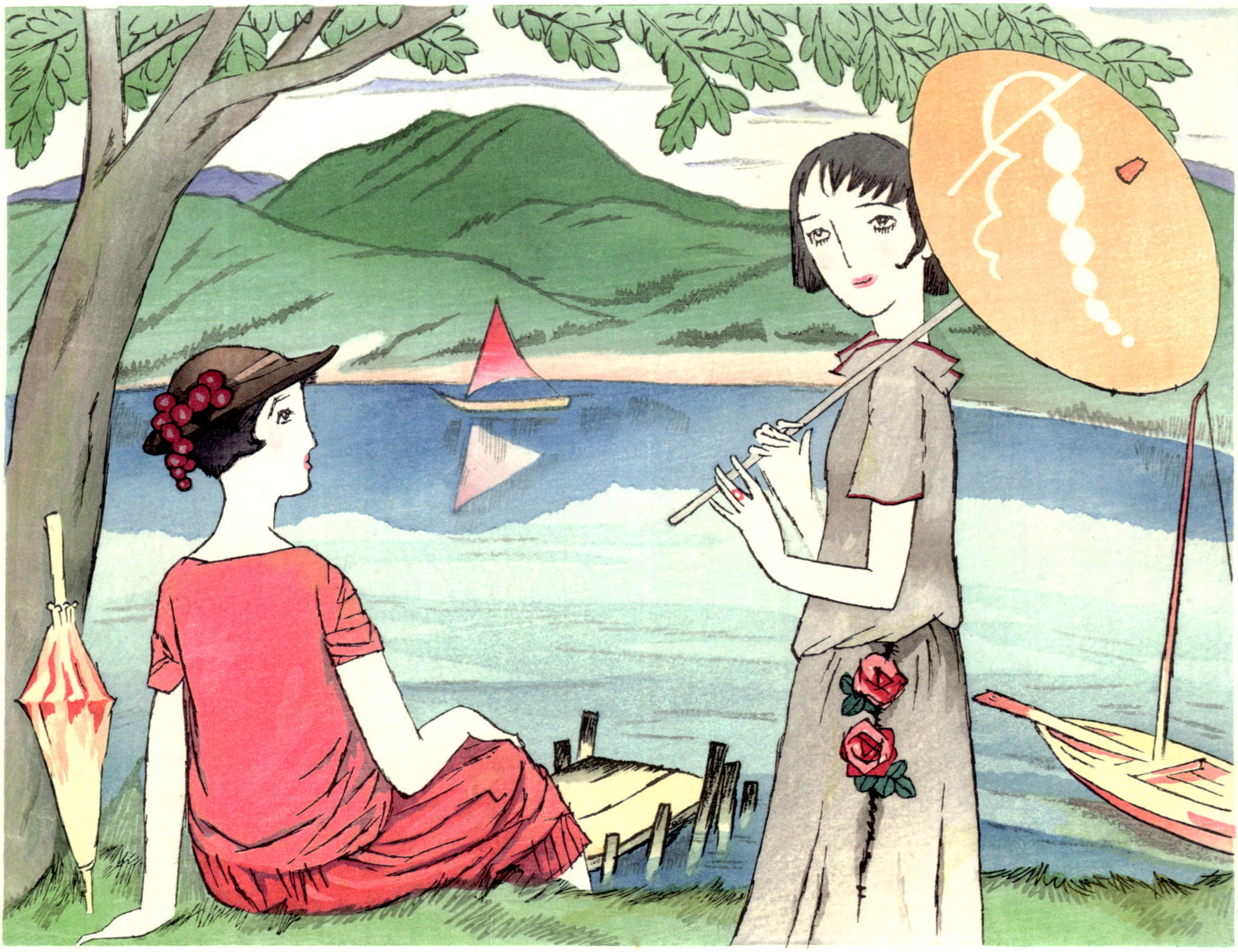

76. *Lake shore* (*Kohan* 湖畔)
22.0 x 29.5 x cm
Date: 1941

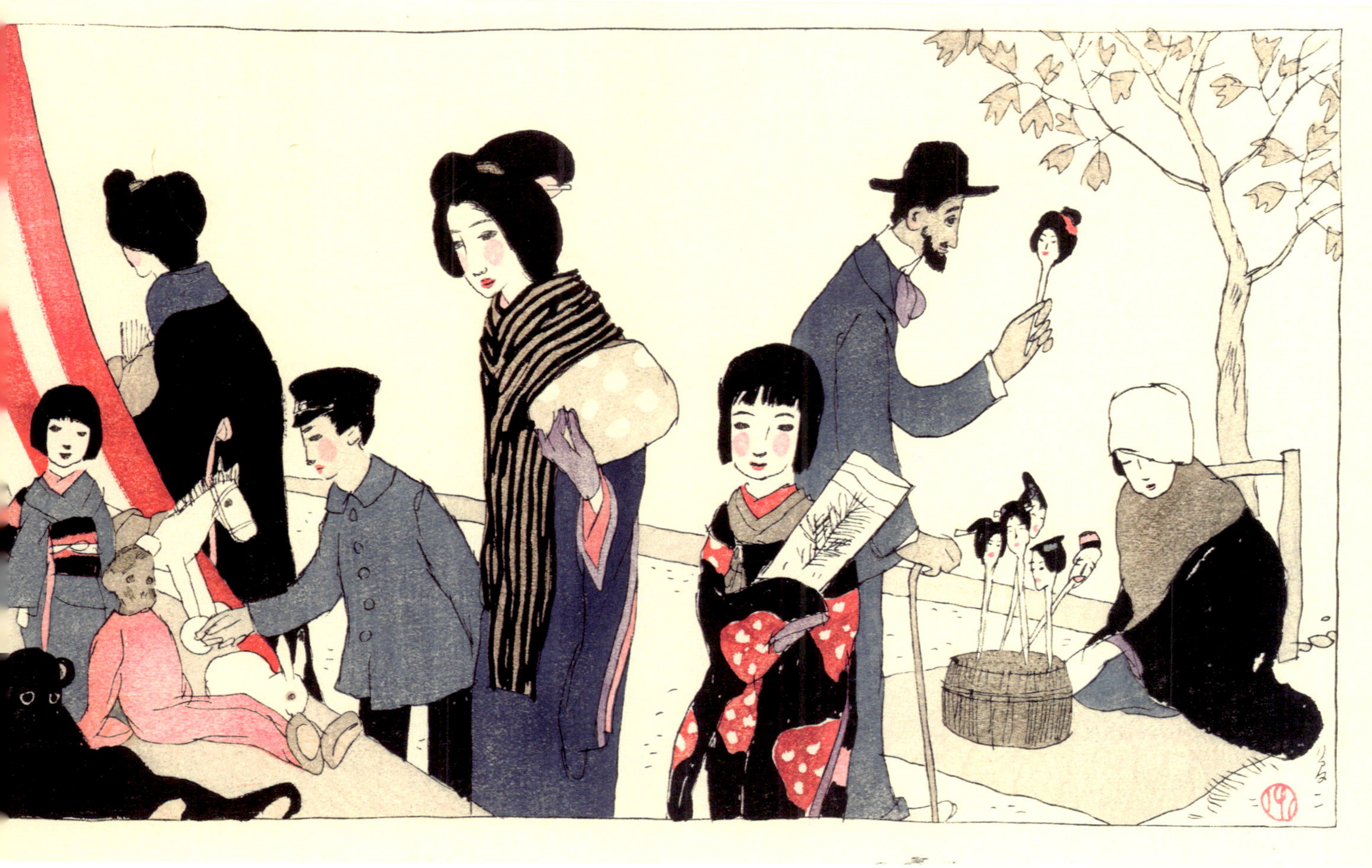

77. *Year-end market*
(*Toshi no ichi*, 歳の市)
17.8 x 30.1 cm
Date: 1941
Seal: artist's 'grass' (*kusa*) seal

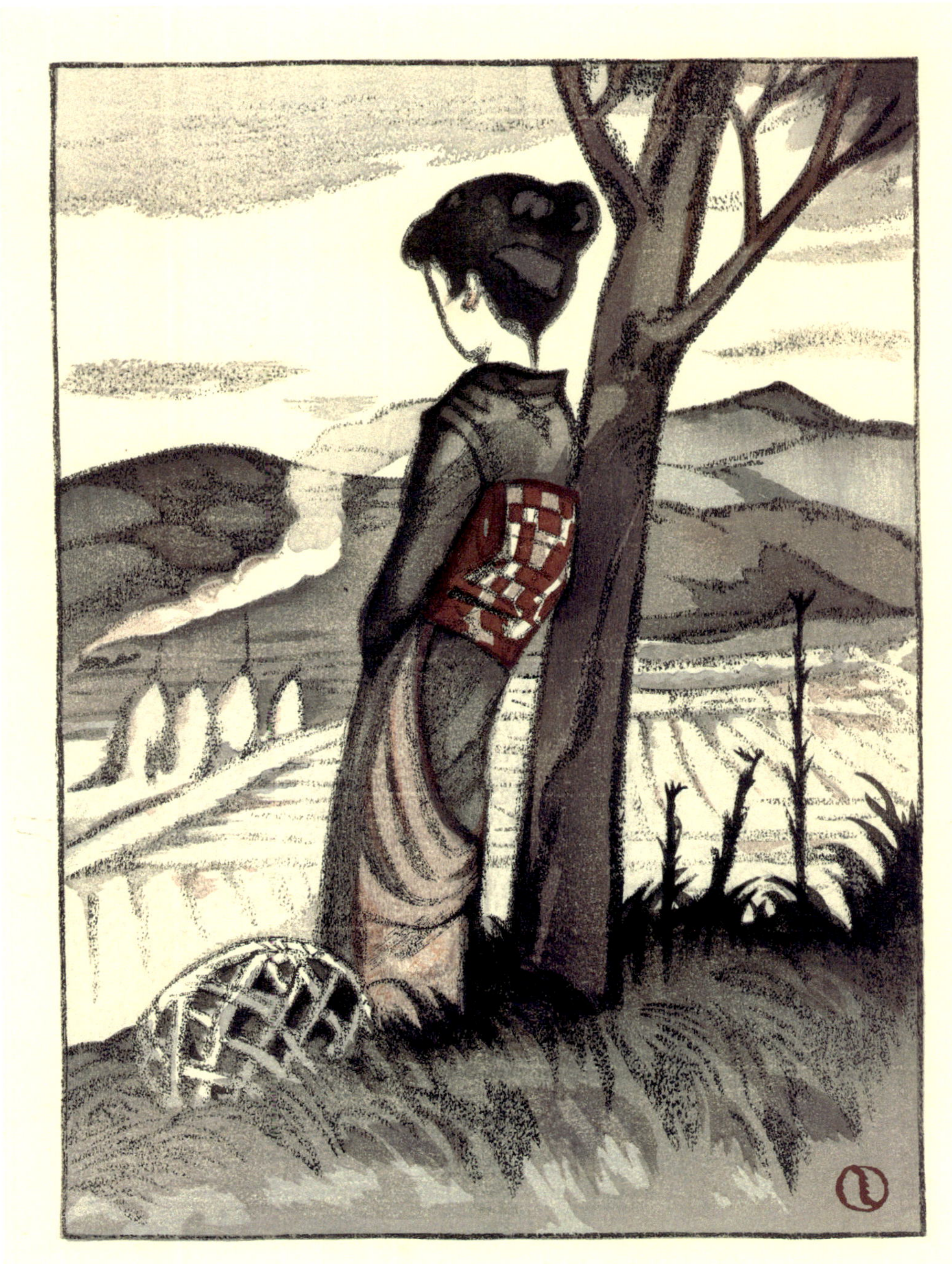

78. *My village* (*Watashi no mura*, わたしの村)
28.9 x 21 cm
Seal: artist's comma-shaped (*tomoe*) seal

*Watashi no mura*
*Mata no shita kara fumoto o mireba / honto ni e no yō na yoi keshiki / doko no machi ka to omottara / yappari watashi no mura deshita*

*My village*
*When you look at the foot of the mountain [bent over and] from between your legs,*
*the beautiful view is like a real painting;*
*just as I am thinking 'What town is that?', I realise that it is my own village.*

*Next page*
79. *Nostalgia* (*Kyōshū*, 郷愁)
17.7 x 16.3 cm
Seal: artist's comma-shaped (*tomoe*) seal

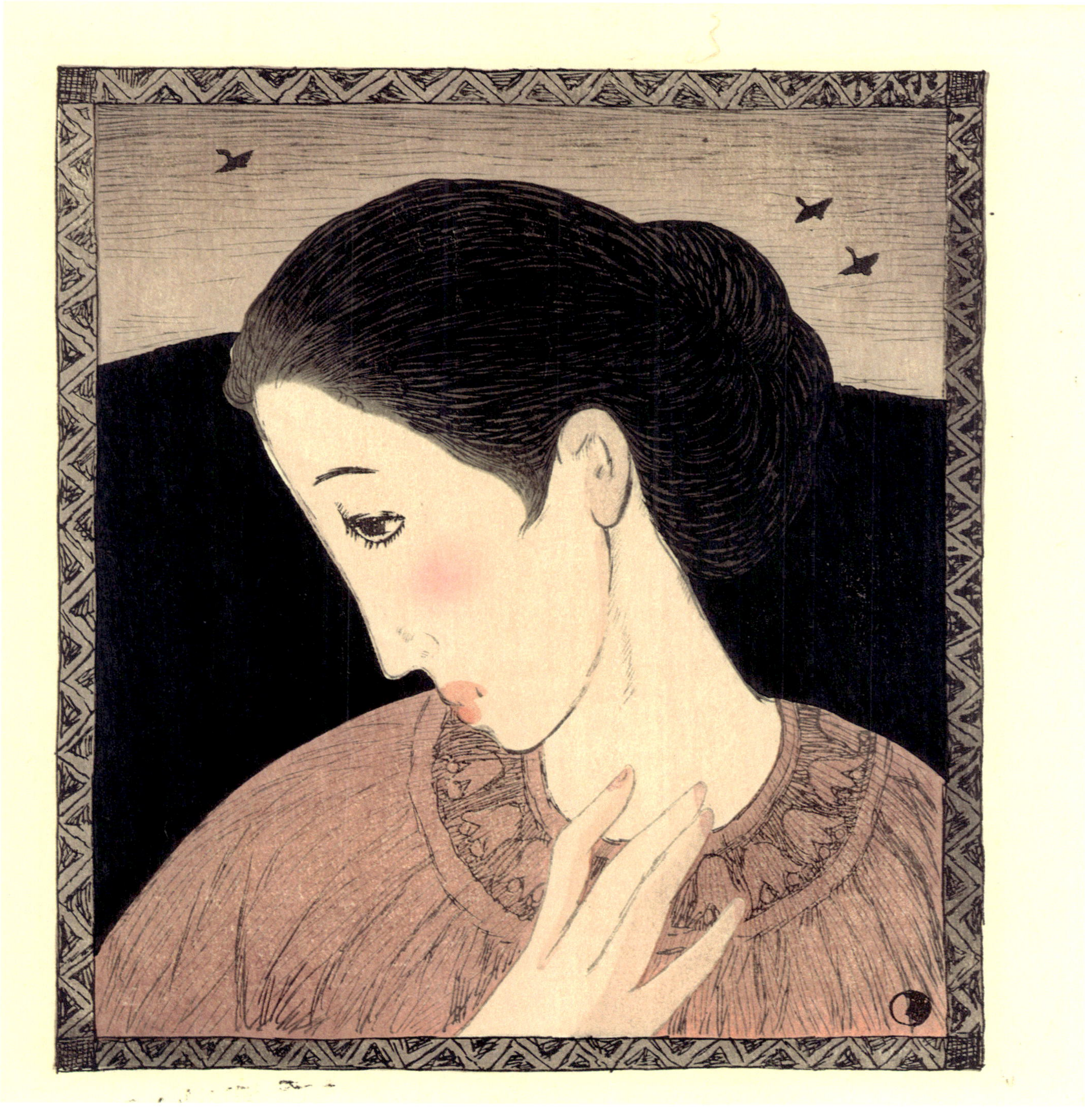

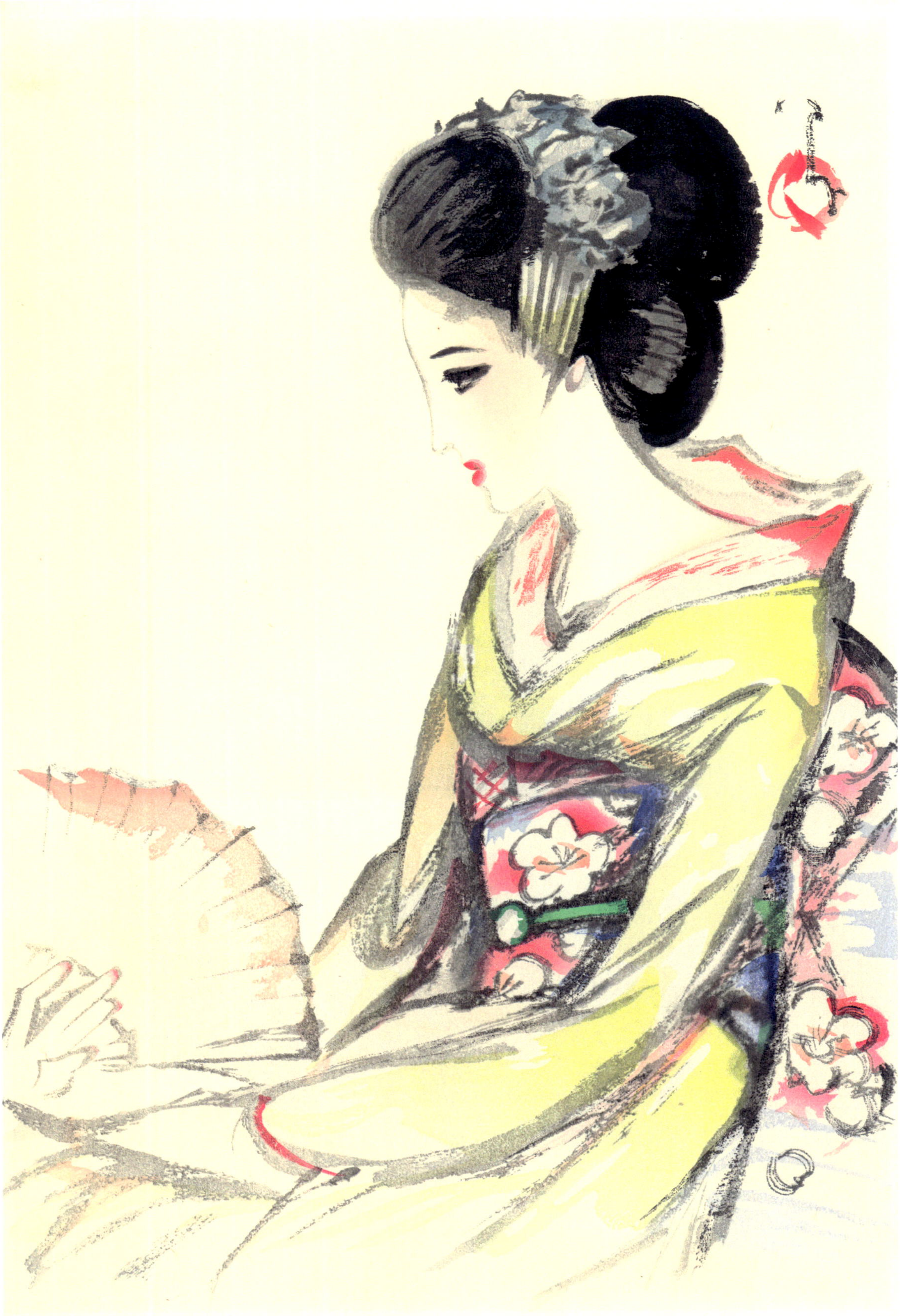

80. *Maiko*
(*Maiko*, 舞妓)
45.0 x 31.2 cm
Date: c. 1942
Signature/seal:
*Yumeji* with
artist's comma-
shaped (*tomoe*)
seal

*Twelve views of Nagasaki*
**(*Nagasaki jūnikei*, 長崎十二景)**
**Date: 1941**
**Publisher: Katō Hanga Kenkyūjo**
**cat. 81**

This series was based on a set of watercolour paintings Yumeji began in 1918 during his stay in Nagasaki with the art collector Nagami Tokutarō. They were completed in 1920 and were intended as an expression of gratitude for Nagami's hospitality. In his series of paintings Yumeji drew inspiration from *nanban* ('southern barbarian') art of the seventeenth and eighteenth centuries as well as more modern sources. For another image from this set, see fig. 2.5.
[SS]

**81. *Urakami Roman Cathedral***
**(*Urakami Tenshudō*, 浦上天主堂)**
**40.0 x 31.2 cm**
**Seal: artist's comma-shaped (*tomoe*) seal**

This image shows a young woman wearing a rosary and a cross with the Urakami Cathedral in the distance. The building was also known as St. Mary's and the original structure was destroyed on 9 August 1945.
[MdV]

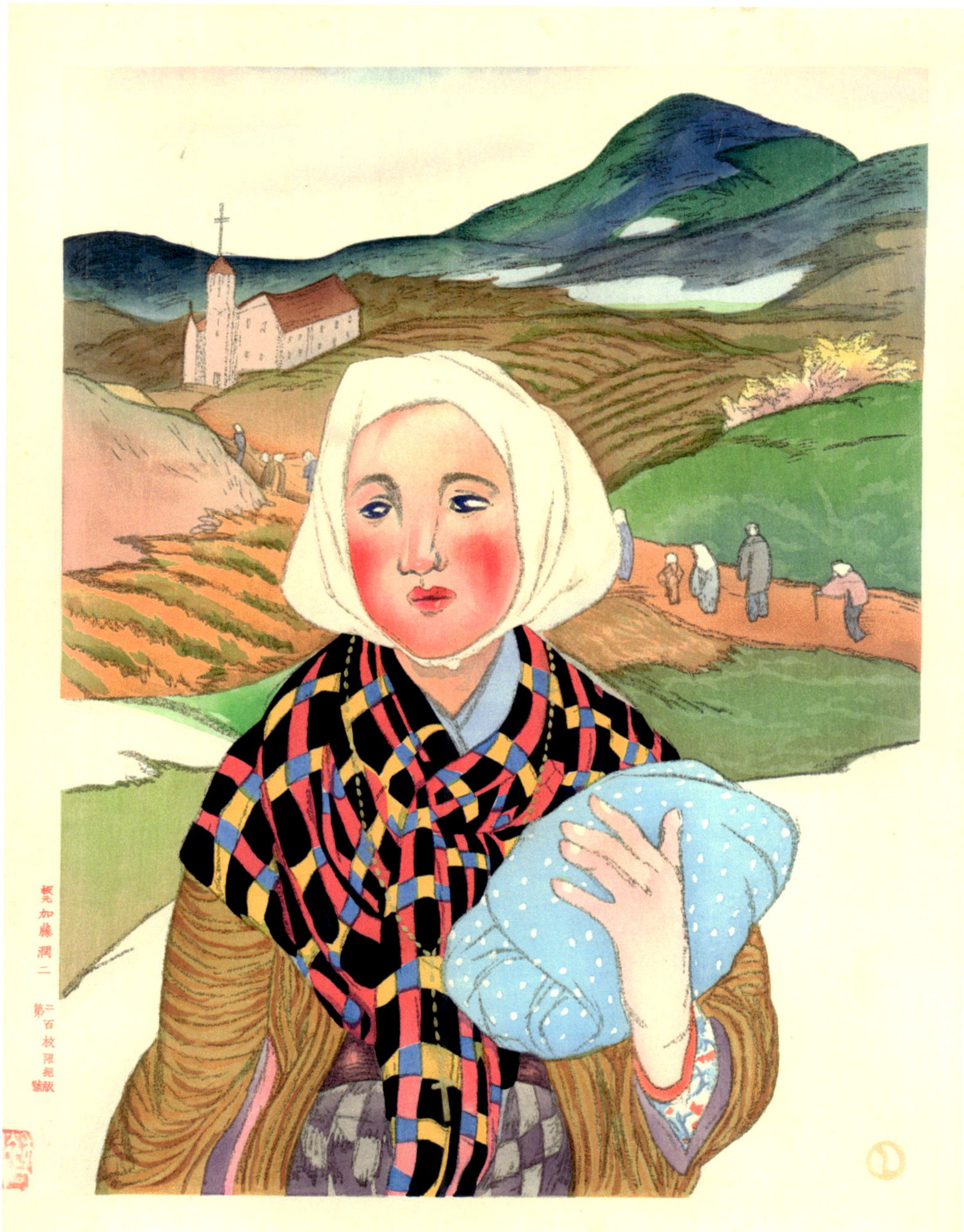

*Six views of Nagasaki by Takehisa Yumeji* (*Nagasaki rokkei Takehisa Yumeji*, 長崎六景 竹久夢二)
Date: 1938–1941
Publisher: Katō Hanga Kenkyū o
cat. 82

This set comprises six of the or ginal twelve watercolour paintings that the artist produced for the wealthy Nagasaki patron Nagami Tokutarō in 1920. The Katō workshop was faithful to Yumeji's designs, creating new woodblocks based on the original watercolours. For other images from this set, see figs. 1.6 & 1.7.

[MdV/NN]

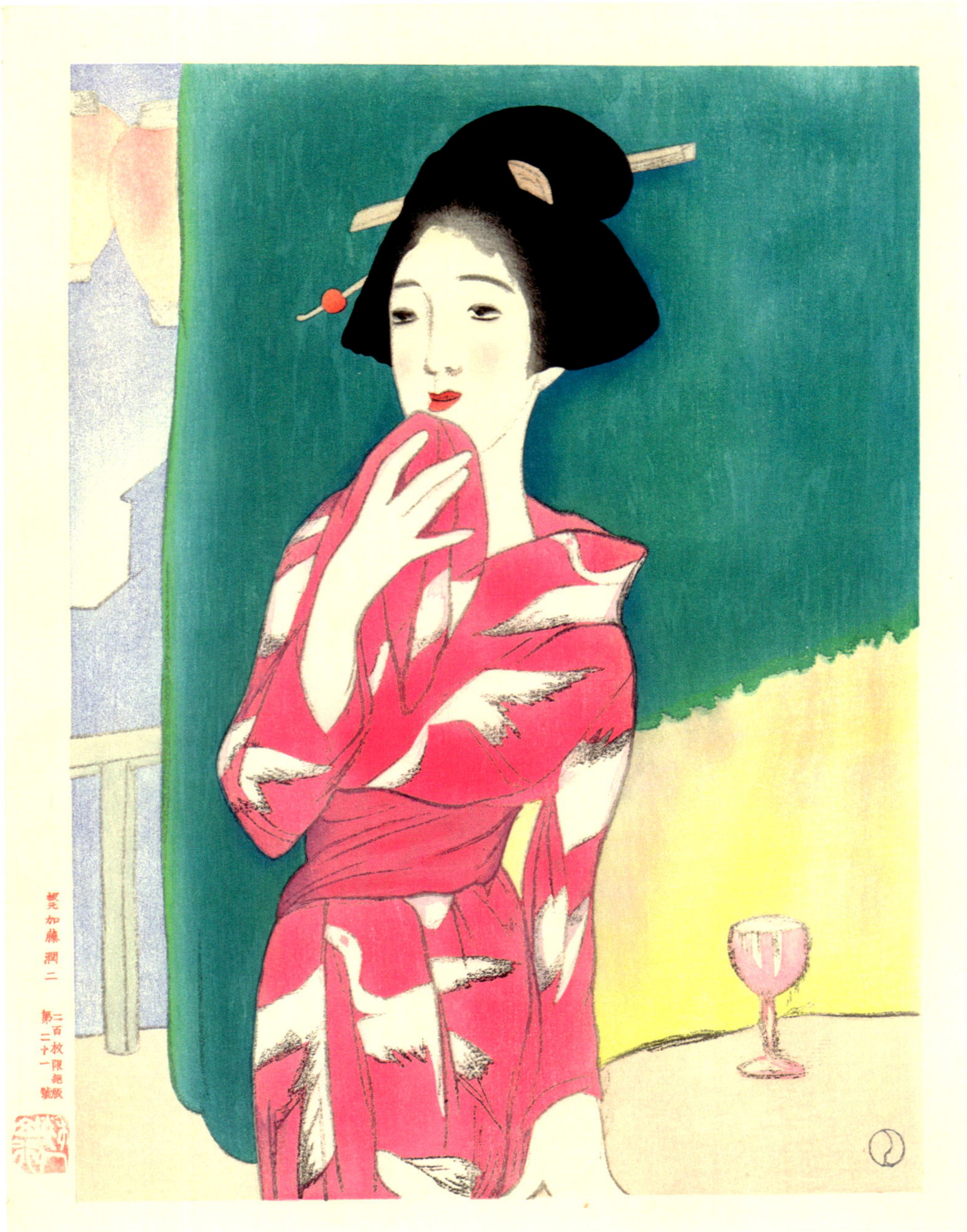


82. *A hillside house of pleasure* (*Oka no seirō*, 丘の青楼)
40.3 x 31.0 cm
Date: 1938
Seal: artist's comma-shaped (*tomoe*) seal

A woman, most likely a prostitute, wears a magenta kimono decorated with motifs of white herons. A glass of wine is set on the table to her left and a balcony ornamented with hanging lanterns is visible on the left.

[MdV/NN]

*Next page*
83. *Red kimono*
43.0 x 31.2 cm
Date: c. 1940
Signature/seal: *Yumeji* with the artist's *Shūjin sankō* seal
Publisher: Katō Hanga Kenkyūjo

This typical 'Yumeji-style beauty' wears a red kimono with a purple undergarment and is based on a painting from around 1930. The publisher Katō Junji copied the seal from Yumeji's works of the period.

[MdV]

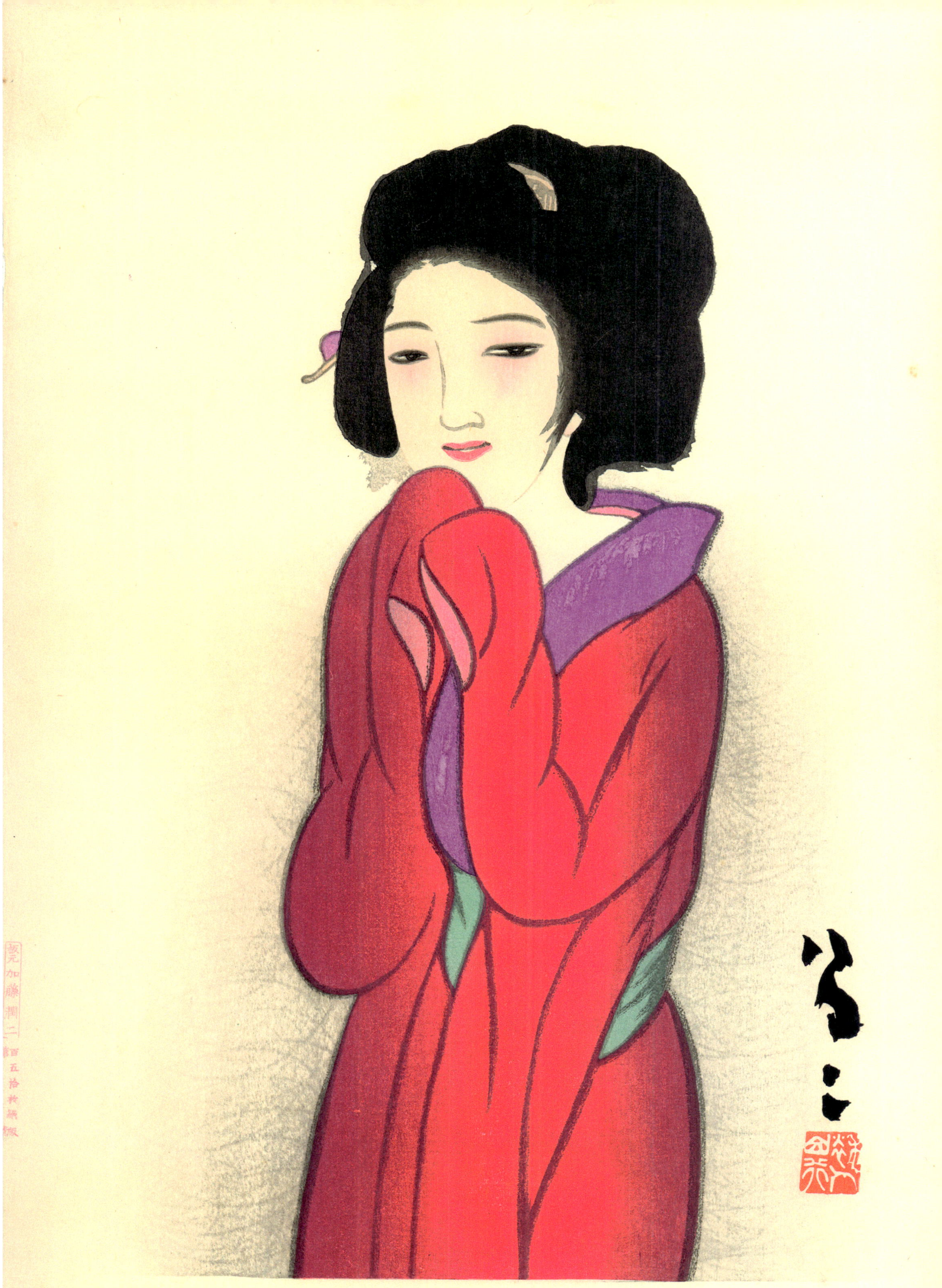
版元加藤潤二

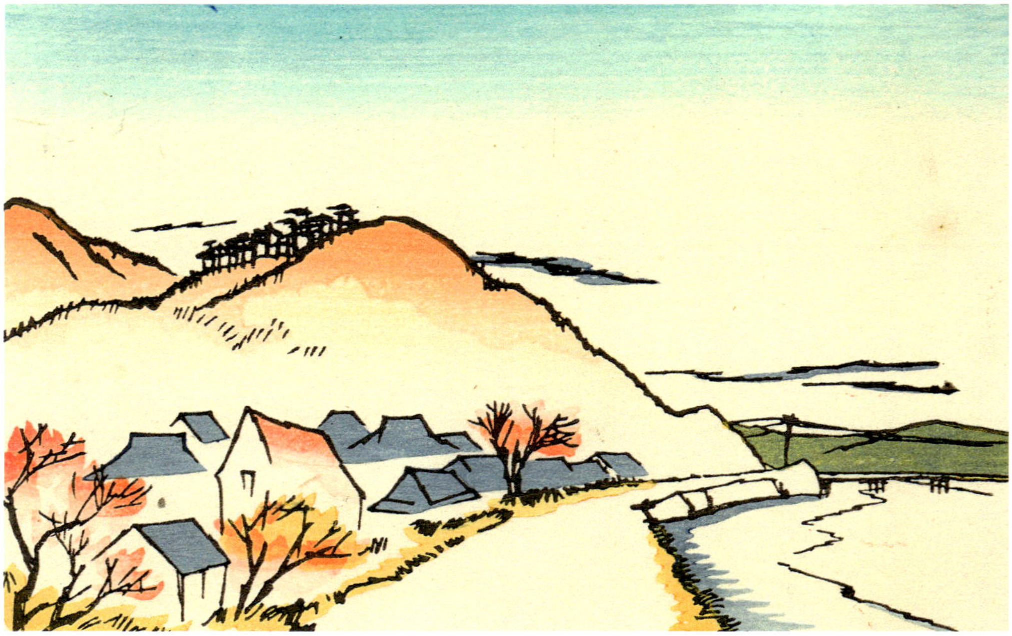

*Illustrated postcards by Yumeji (Yumeji ehagaki,* 夢二絵葉書)
Publisher: Katō Hanga Kenkyūjo
cat. 84–89

The Japanese government introduced flat-rate postage in 1900 and thereafter private companies were permitted to sell originally designed postcards This led to a boom in postcard production and Yumeji capitalised on this by issuing numerous sets of postcards; it is recorded that he made a new postcard design every month from 1910 to 1919.[1] This posthumously compiled collection by the Katō Print Institute (Katō Hanga Kenkyūjo) sought to recreate such works by Yumeji. The images themselves are taken from numerous sources, including from book illustrations like *Samisen (shamisen) leaves* (fig. 3.8a–b) and from magazines. The Katō Hanga Kenkyūjo issued three similar sets: one of fifty-six from 1937 to 1940, another of twenty-five in 1964 and the set in this publication of fifty, the publication date of which is unknown. For other images from this set, see figs. 3.13, 3.14, 4.2, 4.4.

[NN]

1. Yumeji Art Museum and Tenshin Memorial Museum of Art, eds., *Takehisa Yumeji no sekai*, 126.

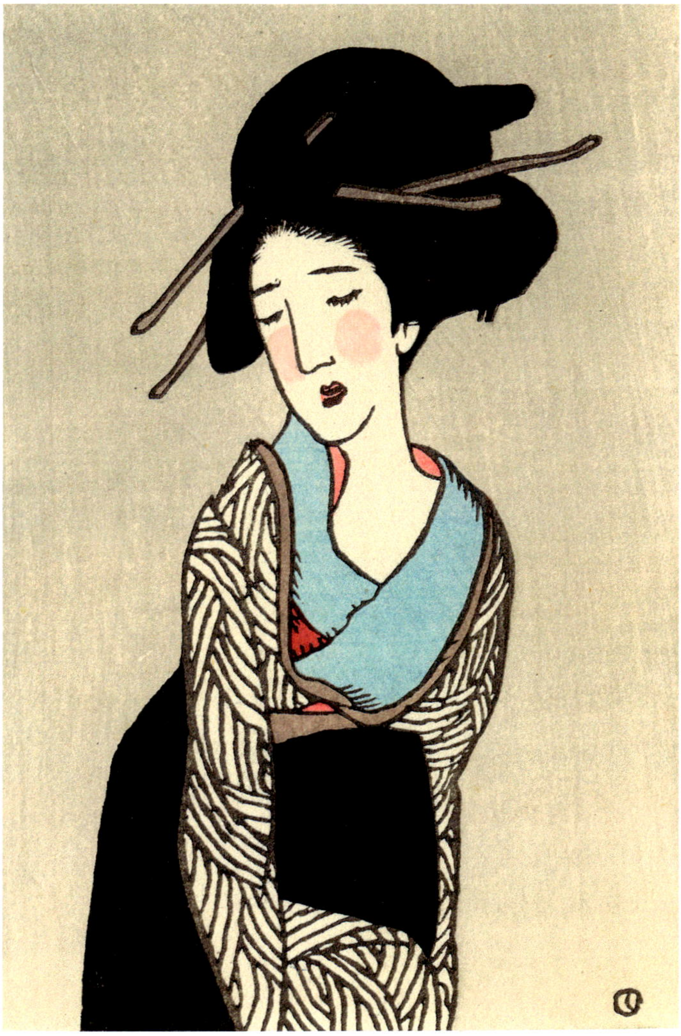

84. *Small town*
9.1 x 13.9 cm

85. *Melancholy beauty*
13.9 x 9.1 cm
Seal: artist's comma-shaped (*tomoe*) seal

*Next page top left*
86. *Two lovers*
13.9 x 9.1 cm

*Next page bottom left*
87. *Laughing beauty*
13.9 x 9.1 cm
Seal: artist's comma-shaped (*tomoe*) seal

*Next page top right*
88. *Beauty and yellow flowers*
13.9 x 9.1 cm

*Next page bottom right*
89. *Beauty holding a fan*
13.9 x 9.1 cm
Signature: *Yume*

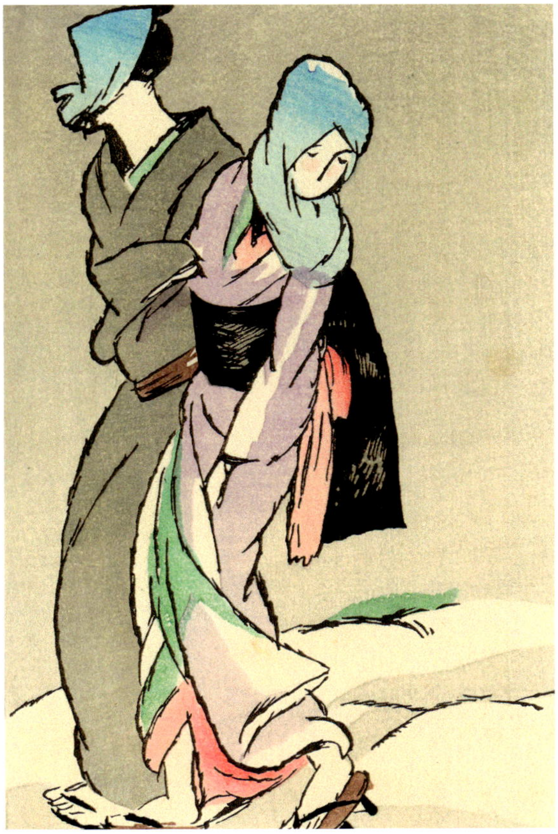

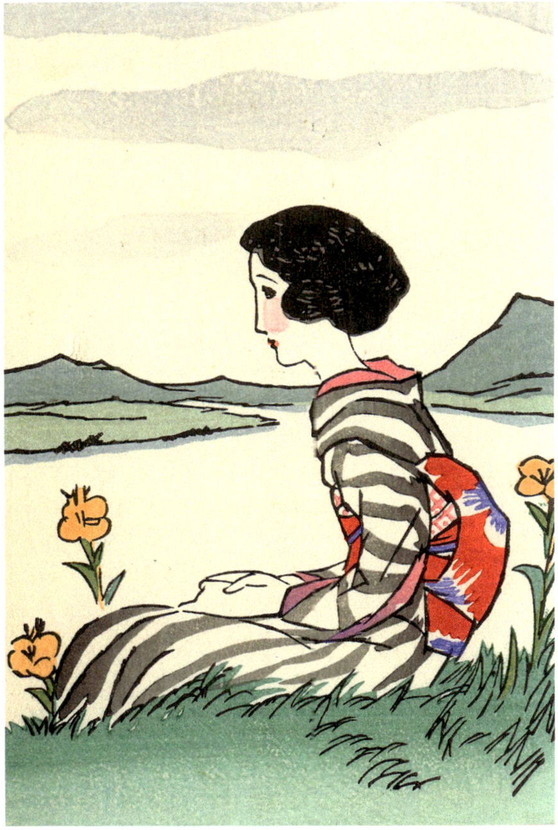

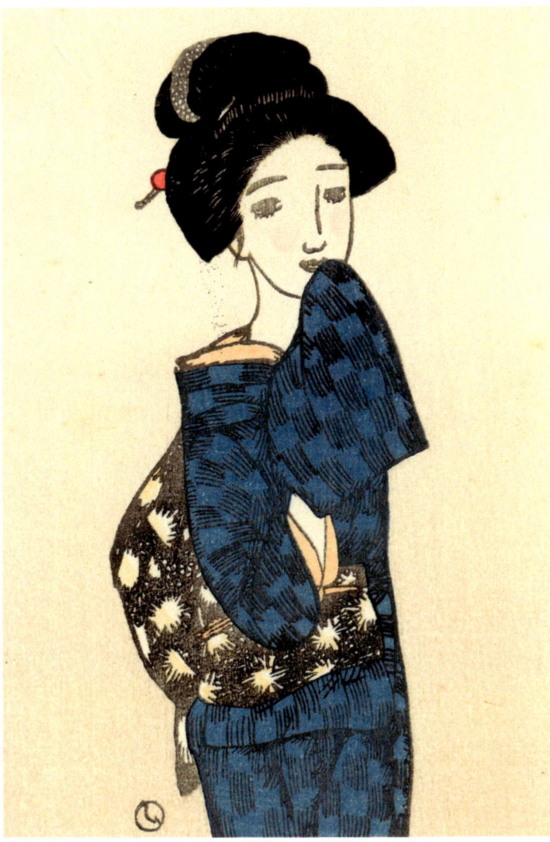

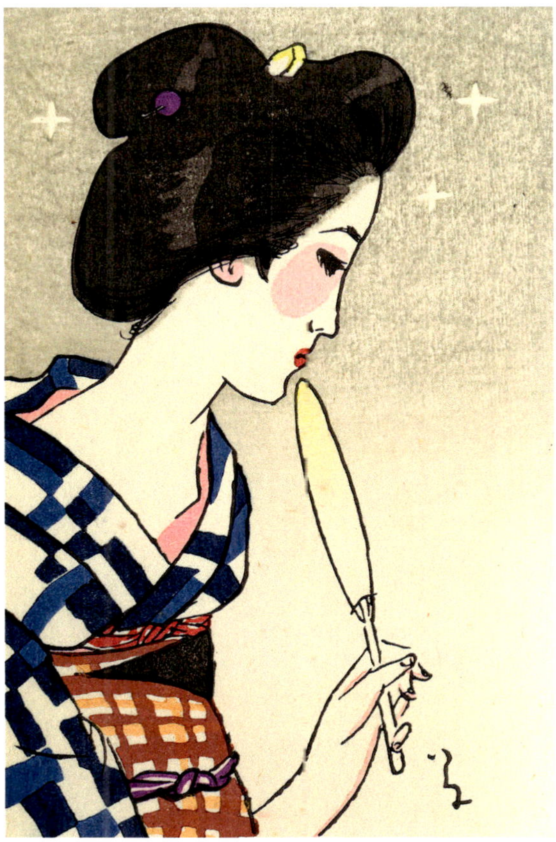

# Bibliography


**Aiga, Tetsuo, ed.** *Hanga* (*Prints*). Vol. 11 of *Genshoku gendai Nihon no bijutsu* (*Modern Japanese art illustrated*). Tokyo: Shōgakkan, 1978.

**Ajioka, Chiaki.** 'The lure of the city'. In *Modern boy, modern girl: modernity in Japanese art 1910–1935*, edited by Jackie Menzies, 28–53. Sydney: Art Gallery of New South Wales.

**Aoe, Shunjirō.** *Takehisa Yumeji*. Tokyo: Chūō Kōronsha, 1985.

**Arahata, Kanson.** *Kanson jiden* (*Kanson's autobiography*). Tokyo: Iwanami Bunko, 1975.

**Araki, Mizuko.** *Yumeji no ikokushumi* (*Yumeji's exoticism*). (Self-published): Okayama, 1995.

**Barmé, Geremie R.** *An artistic exile. A life of Feng Zikai (1898–1975)*. Berkeley and Los Angeles: University of California Press, 2002.

**Brown, Kendall H. and Sharon A. Minichiello et al., eds.** *Taishō chic. Japanese modernity, nostalgia, and deco*. Honolulu: Honolulu Academy of Arts; distributed by Seattle: University of Washington Press, 2001.

**___ and Hollis Goodall-Cristante, eds.** *Shin-hanga. New prints in modern Japan*. Los Angeles: Los Angeles County Museum of Art and Seattle: University of Washington Press, 1996.

**Chiba City Museum of Art (Chiba-shi Bijutsukan), Yumeji Art Museum (Yumeji Kyōdo Bijutsukan) and Wakayama Prefectural Museum of Modern Art (Wakayama Kenritsu Kindai Bijutsukan), eds.** *Takehisa Yumeji ten: egaku koto ga ikiru koto* (*Takehisa Yumeji exhibition—to paint is to live*). Chiba: Chiba-shi Bijutsukan, Okayama: Yumeji Kyōdo Bijutsukan and Wakayama: Wakayama Kenritsu Kindai Bijutsukan, 2007.

**Clark, John.** *Modern Asian art*. Honolulu: University of Hawai'i Press, 1998.

**Duus, Peter, ed.** *The twentieth century*. Vol. 6 of *The Cambridge history of Japan*. Cambridge: Cambridge University Press, 1988.

**Gluck, Carol.** *Japan's modern myths: ideology in the late Meiji period*. Princeton: Princeton University Press, 1985.

**Hamanaka, Shinji and Amy Reigle Newland.** *Onna-e. Kindai bijin hanga zenshū / The female image: 20th-century prints of Japanese beauties*. Tokyo: Abe Publishing Ltd. and Leiden: Hotei Publishing, 2000.

**Hartley, Barbara.** 'Text and image in pre-war Japan: viewing Takehisa Yumeji through Sata Ineko's "From the caramel factory"'. *Literature & aesthetics* 22, no. 2 (December 2012): 153–73.

**Hillier, Jack Ronald.** *The art of the Japanese book*. Vol. 2, 1000–3. London: Sotheby's Publications, 1987.

**Hosono, Masanobu.** *Takehisa Yumeji to jojō gakatachi* (*Takehisa Yumeji and the painters of lyricism*). Tokyo: Kōdansha, 1987.

**Ishikawa, Keiko, ed.** *Takehisa Yumeji 'zasshi no tanoshimi ten': mijika na geijutsu ni miru Taishō roman* (*Takehisa Yumeji 'enjoyment of magazines' exhibition: Taisho Romanticism seen through familiar art*). Tokyo: Takehisa Yumeji Bijutsukan, 1997.

___. '"Senō gakufu" ni tsuite. Gakufu shuppan shūhen jijō to Yumeji no shigoto' ('"*Senō* [*Senow*] *music scores*": the setting of the publishing environment of sheet music and Yumeji's work'). In *Yumeji 1884–1934. Avāngyarudo no jojō* (*Yumeji 1884–1934: lyricism as avant-garde*), edited by Kawano Minoru, 336–42. Machida: Ōtsuka Kōgeisha and Machida Shiritsu Kokusai Hanga Bijutsukan, 2001.

___. *Taishō roman techo: nosutarujikku ando modan no sekai* (*Notebook of the 'Taishō Romanticism': the world of nostalgia and the modern*). Tokyo: Kawade Shobo Shinsha, 2009.

___. '*Aru gu bote* to *Fujin gurafu*' (*Art, goût, beauté* and *The ladies' graphic*). In *Taiyō 221 bessatsu: Takehisa Yumeji no sekai: egaite tabishite koi o shite* (*Taiyō 221: special issue, the world of Yumeji: painting, travelling and loving*), edited by Takeuchi Kiyono (September 2014): 98–99.

**Iwakiri, Shin'ichirō.** *Meiji hangashi* (*History of Meiji prints*). Tokyo: Yoshikawa Kōbunkan, 2009.

**Jackson, Anna.** 'Fashioning the "Greater Taishō" era'. *Andon* 97 (2014): 110–16.

**Kaburagi, Kiyokata, ed.** *Gendai sakka bijinga zenshū* (*Complete works of pictures of beautiful women by modern artists*). 6 vols. Tokyo: Shinchōsha, 1931–1932.

**Kaizuka, Tsuyoshi, ed.** *Chinese-style dresses from Fujishima Takeji to Umehara Ryūzaburō*. Tokyo: Bridgestone Museum of Art, Ishibashi Foundation, 2014.

**Kanazawa Cultural Promotion Foundation (Kanazawa Bunka Shinkō Zaidan), ed.** *Takehisa Yumeji: Kanazawa Yuwaku Yumeji-kan shūzōhin sōgō zuroku* (*Takehisa Yumeji: comprehensive catalogue of the Kanazawa Yuwaku Yumeji Museum collection*). Kanazawa: Kanazawa Bunka Shinkō Zaidan, 2013.

**Kaneko, Yoshimasa.** 'Berurin ni okeru Yuhanesu Itten to Nihonjin to no kōryū' ('Relationship between Johannes Itten and the Japanese in Berlin'). *Dezaingaku kenkyū. Bulletin of JSSD* (Japanese Society for the Science of Design) 50, no. 6 (2004): 1–10.

**Kanzaki, Kiyoshi.** *Taigyaku jiken: Kōtoku Shūsui to Meiji tennō* (*The High Treason Incident: Kōtoku Shūsui and the Meiji emperor*). Tokyo: Ayumi Shuppan, 1977.

**Katō Print Workshop (Katō Hanga Kenkyūjo), ed.** *Katō Hanga Kenkyūjo annai* (*Guide to the Katō Print Workshop*). Tokyo: Katō Hanga Kenkyūjo, 1937.

**Kawakita, Michiaki.** *Modern currents in Japanese art*, translated and adapted by Charles S. Terry. Originally published as *Kindai bijutsu no nagare*. New York: Weatherhill and Tokyo: Heibonsha, 1974.

**Kawano, Minoru, ed.** *Yumeji 1884–1934.*

*Avāngyarudo no jojō* (*Yumeji 1884–1934: lyricism as avant-garde*). Machida: Ōtsuka Kōgeisha and Machida Shiritsu Kokusai Hanga Bijutsukan, 2001.

**Kawase, Chihiro.** 'Kurofune o daku onna' ('Woman holding a black cat'). *Kanazawa Yuwaku Yumeji-kan Museum* no. 13 (31 March 2013).

**Kimata, Satoshi.** 'Takehisa Yumeji *Dontaku* no ezō inyō ('Records of pictorial quotations in Takehisa Yumeji's *Dontaku*'). *Ritsumeikan bungaku* no. 2 (2006): 306–11.

**Kimura, Shigekazu.** *Takehisa Yumeji*. Vol. 8 of *Gendai Nihon bijinga zenshū* (*Complete collection of contemporary pictures of Japanese beautiful women*). Tokyo: Shūeisha, 1978.

**Kritter, Ulrich von, ed.** *Japanische Buchillustration. 1850–1985. Unbekannte Illustrationsgraphik seit Japans Öffnung zum Westen. Literarische Bildwelten des 20. Jahrhunderts. Teil V.* Göttingen: Goltze Verlag, 1996.

**Kudō, Eitarō.** *Takehisa Yumeji saikō* (*Rethinking Takehisa Yumeji*). Tokyo: Nishida Shoten, 1996.

**Kurita, Isamu, ed.** *Takehisa Yumeji—ai to shi no tabibito—* (*Takehisa Yumeji: traveller of love and poems*). Okayama: Sanyō Shuppansha, 1983.

**Merritt, Helen.** *Modern Japanese woodblock prints. The early years.* Honolulu: University of Hawai'i Press, 1990.

___ **and Nanako Yamada.** 'Yumeji's Twelve views of Nagasaki'. *Andon* 51 (1995): 5–11.

___ **and Nanako Yamada.** *Woodblock kuchi-e prints. Reflections of Meiji culture.* Honolulu: University of Hawai'i Press, 2000.

**Nagata, Mikio.** *Yumeji nikki* (*Yumeji diaries*). Tokyo: Chikuma Shobō, 1987.

**Nara, Hiroshi.** *Inexorable modernity: Japan's grappling with modernity in the arts.* Lanham: Lexington Books, 2007.

**Nosco, Peter.** *Confucianism and Tokugawa culture.* University of Hawai'i Press, 1997.

**Nozomi, Naoi.** 'Takehisa Yumeji and his modern beauty: the development of a new media environment in modern Japan'. Talk given at the University of Heidelberg Colloquy, 2011 (unpublished).

___. 'Beauties and beyond: situating Takehisa Yumeji and the Yumeji-shiki'. *Andon* 98 (2015): 29-39.

**Ogasawara, Yōko.** *Yumeji. Gyaman no fune* (*Yumeji. Diamond ship*). Tokyo: Ōmura Shoten, 2002.

**Ogawa, Akiko, ed.** *Takehisa Yumeji ten: Okayama, Ikaho futatsu no furusato kara* [seitan 120nen kinen] (*Takehisa Yumeji exhibition: from the two hometowns of Okayama and Ikaho* [120th anniversary]). Tokyo: Asahi Shinbunsha Bunka Jigyōbu, 2004.

___. *Motto shiritai Takehisa Yumeji: shōgai to sakuhin* (*Takehisa Yumeji: his life and work*). *Āto bigināzu korekushon* (*ABC* [Art beginners collection]) series. Tokyo: Tōkyō Bijutsu, 2009.

**Ogura, Tadao, ed.** *Takehisa Yumeji*. Vol. 3 of *Nihon suisaiga meisaku zenshū* (*Collection Japanese watercolour masterpieces*). Tokyo: Daiichi Hōkan Shuppan, 1984.

___ **and Hashitomi Hiroki, eds.** *Takehisa Yumeji, Aoki Shigeru*. Vol. 12 of *20seiki Nihon no bijutsu: āto gyararî Jyapan* (*Twentieth-century Japanese art: art gallery Japan*). Tokyo: Shūeisha, 1986.

**Okabe, Masayuki, ed.** *Seitan 130nen Takehisa Yumeji ten: Beru epokku o ikita Yumeji to Lotorekku* (*The 130th anniversary Takehisa Yumeji exhibition: Yumeji and Lautrec in the age of la belle époque*). Tokyo: The Asahi Shinbun, 2014.

**Okazaki, Makoto.** *Yumeji seiden* (*Yumeji's authentic biography*). Tokyo: Kyūryūdō, 1984.

**Omuka, Toshiharu.** 'David Burluik and the Japanese avant-garde'. *Canadian American Slavic Studies* 20, no.1/2 (Spring/Summer 1986): 111–25.

**Onchi, Kōshirō, ed.** *Shosō. Yumeji tsuioku tokushū* (*Yumeji special memorial edition*) 15, no. 3 (July 1936).

___, **ed.** *Shosō. Yumeji suketchi chōshō 1906–1929* (*Excerpts from Yumeji's sketch books 1906–1929*) 6, no. 6 (1938).

**Ōoka, Makoto, ed.** *Taiyaku. Oriori no uta / Poems for all seasons: an anthology of Japanese poetry from ancient times to the present*, translated by Janine Beichmann. Tokyo, New York and London: Kodansha International, 2002.

**Rimer, Thomas J., ed.** *Multiple meanings. The written word in Japan—past, present, and future.* Washington DC: Asian Division, Library of Congress, 1986.

___ **and Gessel, Van C. eds.** *The Columbia anthology of modern Japanese literature.* New York: Columbia University Press, 2013.

**Rin, Shukuki.** 'Gakufu no fūkei. Ongaku no Meiji, Taishō, Shōwa (Landscape of musical scores. Music of the Meiji, Taishō and Shōwa eras)'. *Kokuritsukokkai Toshokan geppō* no. 628 (2013).

**Schamoni, Wolfgang.** 'Die Shirakaba-Gruppe und die Entdeckung der nachimpressionistischen Malerei in Japan'. *NOAG Nachrichten der Gesellschaft für Natur- u. Völkerkunde Ostasiens* no. 127/128 (1980): 57–85.

**Schenk, Sabine.** 'Autorschaft und Inszenierung am Beispiel literarischer Werke Takehisa Yumejis' In *Neue Konzepte japanischer Literatur? Nationalliteratur, literarischer Kanon und die Literaturtheorie*, edited by Lisette Gebhardt and Evelyn Schulz. Referate des 15. Deutschsprachigen Japanologentags – Literatur II. Berlin, EB Verlag, 2014.

___. 'Takehisa Yumeji's designs for music score covers'. *Andon* 98 (2015): 40–48.

**Sezaki, Keiji.** 'Mitsukoshi kankō zasshi bungeisakuhin mokuroku' ('Catalogue of literary works in the magazine publications of Mitsukoshi'). *Doshisha Japanese Literature Journal* 51 (2000–2001): 62–91.

**Shirane, Haruo, ed.** *Early modern Japanese literature: an anthology, 1600–1900.* New York: Columbia University Press, 2002.

**Shizuoka City Art Museum (Shizuoka-shi Bijutsukan), ed.** *Takehisa Yumeji to Shizuoka yukari no bijutsu: Shizuoka ga hagukunda korekutâ, Shizuoka ga unda sakka, Shizuoka ni miserareta sakka* (*Takehisa Yumeji and art from Shizuoka: collectors nurtured in Shizuoka, authors from Shizuoka and inspired by Shizuoka*). Shizuoka: Shizuoka-shi Bijutsukan, 2012.

**Simon, Peter, ed.** *The Norton anthology of world literature. Vol. D.* New York: W.W. Norton & Company, Inc., 2012.

**Smith, Lawrence.** *Modern Japanese prints 1912–1989: woodblocks and stencils.* New York: Cross River Press and London: British Museum Press, 1994.

**Sodei, Rinjirō.** *Yumeji ikoku e no tabi* (*Yumeji's journey abroad*). Tokyo: Minerva Shobō, 2012.

**Stegewerns, Dick.** *Adjusting to the new world: Japanese opinion leaders of the Taishō generation and the outside world, 1918–1932.* Leiden, 2007.

**Stephens, Amy Reigle, ed.** *The new wave: twentieth-century Japanese prints from the Robert O. Muller collection.* London: Bamboo Publishing and Leiden: Hotei Japanese Prints, 1993.

**Strong McDonald, Susan.** 'Onchi Kōshirō: Taishō modernist'. PhD diss., University of Minnesota, 2002.

**Swinton, Elizabeth de Sabato.** *The graphic art of Onchi Kōshirō. Innovation and tradition.* London and New York: Garland Publishing, 1986.

**Takahashi, Ritsuko.** *Takehisa Yumeji: shakai genshō toshite no 'Yumeji-shiki'* (*Takehisa Yumeji: Yumeji-style as a social phenomenon*). Kunitachi: Buryukke/Seiunsha, 2010.
**Takehisa, Minami, ed.** *Takehisa Yumeji "Senō gakufu" hyōshiga zenshū* (*Takehisa Yumeji. Senō music scores: complete collection of cover illustrations*). Tokyo: Kokusho Kankōkai, 2009.
**Takehisa, Yumeji.** *Yumeji gashū* (*The Yumeji collection of work*): *Haru no maki* (*Spring*), 1909; *Natsu no maki* (*Summer*), 1910; *Hana no maki* (*Flower*), 1910; *Tabi no maki* (*Travel*), 1910; *Aki no maki* (*Autumn*), 1910; *Fuyu no maki* (*Winter*), 1910. Tokyo: Rakuyōdō.
___. *Sakura saku shima* (*Island of cherry blossoms*): *Haru no kawatare* (*Spring dawn*); *Mishiranu sekai* (*Unknown world*). Tokyo: Rakuyōdō, 1912.
___. *Sōga* (*Quick sketches*). Tokyo: Okamura Shoten, 1914.
___. 'Watashi no saisho no shakkin' ('My first debt'). *Gendai* (December 1930): n.p.
___. *Shuppan* (*Departure*), edited by Sawada Ishirō. Tokyo: Ryūseikaku, 1972.
___. *Sunagaki* (*Collection of works*), compiled by Yamamoto Kazuya. Tokyo: Nōberu Shobō, 1976.
___. *Takehisa Yumeji suketchi chōshō* (*Excerpts from the sketchbooks of Takehisa Yumeji*), edited by Onchi Kōshirō. Tokyo: Miraisha, 1984.
**___, Kawamura Karyō and Yamamura Kōka.** *Yumeji to Karyō. Kōka no Kantō shinsai rupo* (*A report on the Great Kantō earthquake by Yumeji, Karyō und Kōka*). Tokyo: Kuresu Shuppan, 2005.
**Takehisa Yumeji Art Museum (Takehisa Yumeji Bijutsukan), ed.** *Takehisa Yumeji Bijutsukan: sono bi to ai to kanashimi* (*Takehisa Yumeji Art Museum: beauty, love and sadness*). Tokyo: Takehisa Yumeji Bijutsukan, 2001.
**___, ed.** *Takehisa Yumeji: Taishō roman no gaka, shirarezaru sugao* (*Takehisa Yumeji: the hidden face of an artist of Taishō Romanticism*). Tokyo: Takehisa Yumeji Bijutsukan, 2014.
**Takeuchi, Kiyono, ed.** *Taiyō 221: bessatsu Takehisa Yumeji no sekai: egaite, tabishite, koi o shite* (*Taiyō 221: special issue, the world of Yumeji: painting, travelling and loving*) (September 2014).
**Tanaka, Seikō.** *Tsukuhae no gakatachi: Tanaka Kyōkichi, Onchi Kōshirō no seishun* (*Artists of the Tsukuhae: Tanaka Kyokichi's and Onchi Kōshirō's early period*). Tokyo: Chikuma Shobō, 1990.
**Tsurutani, Hisashi.** *Yumeji no mita Amerika* (*America as seen by Yumeji*). Tokyo: Shin Jinbutsu Ōraisha, 1997.
**Unno, Hiroshi.** *Toshi fūkei no hakken. Nihon no avāngyarudo geijutsu* (*Discovery of the cityscape. Japan's avant-garde art*). Tokyo: Yūbun Shoin, 2006.
**___, ed.** *Tokushū Takehisa Yumeji: modan dezain no tanjō* (*Special edition, Takehisa Yumeji: the creation of modern design*). *Hanga geijutsu* 71 (1991).

**Weisenfeld, Gennifer.** *Imaging disaster. Tokyo and the visual culture of Japan's great earthquake of 1923*. Berkeley: University of California Press, 2012.
**Winther-Tamaki, Bert.** *Maximum embodiment: yōga, the western painting of Japan, 1912–1955*. Honolulu: University of Hawai'i Press, 2012.

**Yamamoto, Kazuya.** *Takehisa Yumeji*. Tokyo: Nōberu Shobō, 1968.
___. *Oshiminaki seishun: Takehisa Yumeji no ai to kakumei to hyōhaku no shōgai* (*Unfettered youth: Takehisa Yumeji and his life of love, revolution and wandering*). Tokyo: Nōberu Shobō, 1969.
**Yamano, Hidetsugu, Ikezawa Mari and Nakao Yui, eds.** *Kawanishi Hide korekushon* (*Kyōto Kokuritsu Kindai Bijutsukan: shūzō sakuhin mokuroku IX*)/ *The Kawanishi Hide collection* (*The National Museum of Modern Art, Kyoto: collection catalogue IX*). Kyoto: The National Museum of Modern Art, Kyoto, 2011.
**Yūjōbō, Hideaki, ed.** *Taiyō 20 bessatsu: Takehisa Yumeji* (*Taiyō 20 special issue: Takehisa Yumeji*) (Autumn 1977).
**Yumeji Art Museum (Yumeji Kyōdo Bijutsukan), ed.** *Takehisa Yumeji ten. Yumeji Kyōdo Bijutsukan shozō* (*Takehisa Yumeji exhibition. Holdings of the Yumeji Art Museum*). Yokohama: Sogō Bijutsukan, 1988.
**___ and Tenshin Memorial Museum of Art, Ibaraki Prefecture (Ibaraki-ken Tenshin Kinen Izura Bijutsukan), eds.** *Takehisa Yumeji no sekai. Taishō roman no jojō gaka* (*The world of Takehisa Yumeji. Lyrical painter of Taishō Romanticism*). Kita-Ibaraki: Ibaraki-ken Tenshin Kinen Izura Bijutsukan, 2000.

**Websites for museums dedicated to Takehisa Yumeji**

**Kanazawa Yuwaku Yumeji-kan (Kanazawa Yuwaku Yumeji Museum), Kanazawa, Ishikawa prefecture:** http://www.kanazawa-museum.jp/yumeji/english/index.html
**Nikkō Takehisa Yumeji Bijutsukan (Nikko [Nikkō] Takehisa Yumeji Museum), Nikkō, Tochigi prefecture:** http://www.yumeji.co.jp/
**Sakata Takehisa Yumeji Bijutsukan (Sakata City Takehisa Yumeji Art Museum), (Sakata) Yamagata prefecture:** http://www.somaro.net/museum/
**Takehisa Yumeji Bijutsukan (Takehisa Yumeji Art Museum), Tokyo:** http://www.yayoi-yumeji-museum.jp/yumeji/outline.html
**Takehisa Yumeji Ikaho Kinenkan (Takehisa Yumeji Ikaho Memorial [Museum]), Ikaho, Gunma prefecture:** http://yumeji.or.jp/
**Yumeji Kyōdō Bijutsukan (Yumeji Art Museum), Okayama, Okayama prefecture:** http://yumeji-art-museum.com/07_index-e.html

# Index

*All references are to page numbers; those in bold indicate pages with illustrations*

# Contributors

**Nozomi Naoi** is Assistant Professor of Humanities (Art History) at Yale-NUS College, Singapore. She specialises in modern Japanese art and wrote on Takehisa Yumeji for her dissertation *Beyond the modern beauty: Takehisa Yumeji and the new media environment in early twentieth-century Japan* (Harvard University, 2014) and more recently 'Beauties and beyond: situating Takehisa Yumeji and the *Yumeji-shiki*', *Andon* 98. She has also published on the development of Japanese posters: 'The modern beauty in Taishō media', in *The women of shin hanga: the Joseph and Judy Barker collection of early twentieth-century Japanese prints* (2013).

**Sabine Schenk** is Academic Coordinator at the Kyoto office of Heidelberg University and Visiting Lecturer at Ludwig-Maximilians-Universität, Munich. She is currently working on her PhD, *Art Nouveau in Japan: romanticism, ornamentality und intermediality in early twentieth-century Japanese visual culture* (LMU, Munich). She organises international workshops, such as the annual *Forum of East Asian Art History*, presents and publishes on early twentieth-century art and design, with a particular focus on Takehisa Yumeji (e.g. 'Takehisa Yumeji's Music Score Covers', *Andon* 98).

**Chris Uhlenbeck** is Curator of the Nihon no Hanga museum, Amsterdam. He has been responsible for the creation of numerous exhibitions in the Netherlands and abroad, beginning with *The new wave, 20th-century prints from the Robert O. Muller collection* (1993) and others including *Japanese erotic fantasies: sexual imagery of the Edo period* (2005). More recently, he has collaborated with the Japan Museum SieboldHuis in Leiden, organising exhibitions on the print designers Utagawa Hiroshige (2011), Tsukioka Yoshitoshi (2012) and Utagawa Kuniyoshi (2013). He is most interested in the interplay between the commercial constraints of traditional printmaking and the creative freedom of artists.

**Maureen de Vries** is Assistant Curator of the Nihon no hanga museum, Amsterdam. She has co-authored numerous catalogues for the collection's exhibitions on 20th-century Japanese prints. She authored *Troubled times and beyond: Japanese prints 1931–1960* (2013) and contributed to the exhibition and catalogue *Yoshitoshi* (2011). She is active in the Japanese cultural scene in the Netherlands with her organisation of symposia, and is a board member of the Society for Japanese Arts and the Heinz M. Kaempfer Fund.